C0-AQG-778

ECSTASY OF MISERY

6000 Miles on the
Pacific Crest Trail

Wrong Way
From L.A.

Thanks Jim for all the
help through the years
Bab
1/14/15 Wrong Way
No9

Copyright ©
2014

DEDICATION

In my dedication of Ecstasy of Misery, I would like to thank Linda Robison, my longtime girlfriend. During this time, she continued to help me on my four major hikes along the Pacific Crest Trail. It really helps to have a back-up team at home so they can send food and different supplies that a thru-hiker might need. Thank you, Trail Perfect.

ECSTASY OF MISERY

TABLE OF CONTENTS

ECSTASY OF MISERY

Cast of Characters

Abominable Slowman

Apple Pie

Bandana

Batteries Included

Bear Bait (trail name given to a 4-yr old boy at the kick-off party)

Be There Now

Belcher

Billy Goat

Bloody Stick

Bobka

Buddha

Chance

Chipmunk

Cliff Hanger

Cloud Walker

Cry Baby

Detour

Dragon Fly

Free Radical

Frog

Goat Breath

Green Lantern

Grunt

Huff and Puff

Chaos Brothers

Kokopelli

Leprechaun

Let It Be

Long Haul

Lugnut

Madame Butterfly

Meadow Ed

Mercury

Mountain Goat

Navigator

Northerner

No Way Ray

Puck

Scooter and Toes

Shutter Bug

Snickers

Steady

T-Bone

Tea Tree

Trail Mix

Tripping Ant

Weather Carrot

Yogi

Yoyo Man

Wrong Ways High Carb Diet

Loose 65 lbs. in 5 months including

35 lbs. the first month! Eat all you want!

Pizza, Ice Cream, Cheeseburgers, Fries

Pies too! and Candy.

Diet is easy to follow

just read this book.

Wrong Way

Journey One: Hinkle Calls My Bluff!

Just before Thanksgiving of 2001, I was at Chuck Hinkle's house. I've known Chuck for a long time. He owns 'Hinkle's Tree Service and Palm Tree Sales'. We were discussing my favorite topic, backpacking in the High Sierras, and I told Chuck of my dream to walk the Pacific Crest Trail (PCT) from Mexico to Canada in one non-stop hike. I had walked the trail before but not all at one time. Chuck said something that blew me away: "I'll give you $4000 if you decide to make your dream come true."

I could not believe it, and although it was a dream of mine to walk the PCT from Mexico to Canada in one season, I just was not ready for it, mentally or physically. It was almost Thanksgiving and I thought I would wait on the offer for a while to see if Chuck was serious or not. As weeks went by and Christmas arrived, I realized that Chuck was very serious.

On New Year's Eve of 2001, I decided to take up the challenge. It was too late to do it in 2002 because I would need more time to prepare. I had a year and four months to get in shape and try to save money. I knew the trip would cost more than $4000. It's not just the cost of the actual trip, but the cold fact that while away, I would still be billed for things like health insurance and car insurance and other nasty things.

Linda Robison, my girlfriend, would have to wait on that new car I was going to help her buy. My parents would have to waive my rent and my dad would pay my bills with the money I left for him. I ended up getting a joint bank account with him so he could write my checks for me. The biggest loss of doing this type of trip is the loss of income from my tree-stump removal service.

Being single and not having kids to raise and not having payments to make on cars, stump grinders, tools, or other such things, was kind of a motivation. How many other 56-year-old men were in my situation? Not many....

During 2002, I worked pretty hard and I trained at the gym with weights.

ECSTASY OF MISERY

I did plenty of legwork with the weight machines, as well as upper body work. I was more interested at that time in keeping muscles hard and strong, especially my legs. Starting in January 2003, I would put my weights away and just walk first without a pack and then later on with a pack.

The number one thing I had to do however was to lose weight. I knew I would lose a lot of weight very quickly on the trail, probably a pound a day, but it was still better to start off light. At 217, light for me was to get below 190.

Getting in shape was very important. Walking the PCT was brutal. I know because this would actually be my second time walking this magnificent trail. In 1978, I trekked from Ashland, Oregon, to Campo, California, walking all of California from north to south. In 1998 I walked the state of Oregon from Seiad Valley, California, to Cascade Locks on the Columbia River, which is the border or Oregon and Washington State. Then in the year 2000, I hiked the state of Washington and finished that section of the PCT in Manning Park, British Columbia, Canada.

These three major hikes gave me the right to say that I had walked the complete PCT as a section hiker. This trip, however, would give me the chance to walk the complete PCT in one season. This is a major accomplishment that every hiker would cherish.

My training started January 1, 2003. It consisted of long walks on Sundays. I'm lucky to live in La Habra. It's a good place to train, due to Powder Canyon, located in La Habra Heights. You also pass a huge Chinese Buddhist Temple promoting views of the San Bernardino Mountains, the San Gabriel Mountains, and the Pacific Ocean.

Every Sunday was the biggest training day of the week. I would get up about 7am, get ready to leave my house by 8am. Then I would walk up the hill on Harbor Blvd, and catch the trail at the Rowland Heights Water District building.

The rest of the day I would hike around these Southern California foothills, doing anywhere from 12 to 15 miles with a pack on my back. The other days of the week I would walk only two or three miles around my neighborhood.

It was during this time that I decided I should go to the dentist, and to Lens Crafters to have my eyes tested and get two new pairs of glasses. I also had to go to my HMO-Kaiser Permanente to have some basal cells burned off my back. I knew I would be spending a lot of money, but I knew I should take care of things before I left.

What set me back the worst of all was that Kaiser wouldn't be able to see me for five weeks. I needed to get the skin cancer taken care of and it would take a couple of weeks to heal.

This development was a bummer for me, because I would miss the kick-off party that was held every year. The party is put on by Trail Angels on the last weekend of April, with a free barbecue and breakfast.

When I heard the weather reports of late snowfall in the Sierras and some snow in the local mountains, I didn't feel too bad about missing the kick-off party any more. This would give me more time for the snow to melt and I felt that leaving after the main group, which might consist of about 300 hikers, would alleviate the problem of crowded campsites and lodging opportunities in certain small towns, like Idyllwild, Big Bear, and Wrightwood.

By March, my legs were in pretty good shape. I was doing more miles and adding more weight to my pack. The weight was added by bottles of water and rocks that could add or subtract from my pack. I normally carried a lunch and cell phone along the Powder Canyon Trails since I was out there for seven or eight hours.

My problem was the same as it had been for my other three hikes, and that problem was losing weight. I have never been able to do so and it looked as though I wouldn't be very successful this time either.

The last two weeks of April arrived and I felt it was time to get some publicity on my giant hike. My mother always tries to get me in the local news-papers. She and Linda called the Orange County Register, the Whittier Daily News, and the Fullerton Observer. The Whittier Daily News and the Orange County Register both sent reporters to my house to interview me.

The Register sent out a reporter named Eric Carpenter and photographer Bruce Chambers, who took a lot of pictures of me. I showed both of them the equipment I would be using on the trip. They seemed to be very interested in my trip, staying three hours and asking a lot of questions.

ECSTASY OF MISERY

Eric Carpenter told Linda he wanted me to call him at different points throughout my trip so he could write update stories on how I was doing. He had received several phone calls and emails from people who had read the story in the Register and were interested in follow-up stories of my trip. I did call him several times and Eric wrote six or seven articles from the start to finish of my trip, as well as a couple of articles after I returned home.

It was now April 15th, about when I wanted to leave, but due to the skin cancer treatment on my back and the healing process, I would have to wait until May 1. I had never had an HMO and didn't expect that I would have to wait five weeks to have basal cells removed. I called Kaiser many times, hoping to get in sooner, hoping someone would cancel and I could get their appointment, but it didn't happen.

The last couple of weeks of April were spent getting my equipment together. I bought an ultra-light backpack that weighed only 35 ounces called the Go-Lite Trekker. It was 4500 cubic inches and I figured it would be big enough to hold all my stuff. My old backpack that I had probably carried for 3000 miles had sentimental value to me and was very comfortable, but it weighed five and a half pounds. I would save about three pounds of weight with the new backpack.

I decided to take two pairs of shoes, a pair of running shoes, and light-weight boots. I'd take a pair of thin socks to wear with the running shoes and two pairs of socks for the boots. I also would take a pair called 'cobbler socks' and a pair of thick wool socks.

I was afraid of getting blisters. I felt that if I started to get a blister or a hot spot, I would change my footwear. The hassle with this is I would always be carrying an extra pair of shoes or boots in my pack, causing more weight and bulk. I would like to go just in running shoes, but I had little confidence in them after I'd gotten so many blisters in 1998 on my Oregon trek.

My stove would be powered by a propane and butane combination cylinder, with a pocket rocket burner that was made of titanium. The stove weighed about two and a half ounces.

My shelter would be a tarp that I would string between two trees. A tarp has the advantage of being lighter than a tent and having more ventilation. I had confidence just taking a tarp because of my Washington hike in the year 2000.

I bought plenty of dehydrated meals, which were expensive. I received a few dehydrated meals for Christmas 2002 from friends who knew I was going to do the PCT. Power bars, instant rice, mashed potatoes, instant breakfast, milk and instant oatmeal were the basic foods that I would be starting out with. I would be taking candy, beef jerky, and some trail mix.

I love having coffee every morning at home, but it's a beverage I usually don't drink on the trail. It seems to be easier for me to just break camp in the morning and go. This also saves some time and fuel. Anyway, the cold, lonely trail in the morning would always wake me up.

A back-up team at home is also very important for a Pacific Crest thru-hiker. Someone has to send you supplies, equipment, any information you may need to know about the trail, and what's going on at home. They also provide encouragement. I had about the best you can ask for in Linda, my long time girlfriend. She had experience being part of my back-up team from my previous hikes. She was mobile and always home when I needed her.

Even though Linda never thru-hiked the PCT, she knew quite a bit about the trail and would remind me of things to take or do along the vast distances that the trail traversed. My parents were also part of my back-up team, but the main burden lay with Linda.

The last days came and went. My first departure date had been changed to May 4th, due to the fact that my mom wanted my sister to baby-sit my mom's dog, Emma, a totally spoiled golden retriever. I didn't like the delay but stayed cool with it. Maybe leaving a little later would give more time for the late snows to melt in the Sierras and local mountains.

Finally Saturday, May 3rd arrived and it was time to head to Mexico. It had rained quite a bit on Friday and it was somewhat of a rainy day on Saturday. I was concerned about new snow that may have fallen in the local mountains, especially in the Mt Jacinto and Baden-Powell areas.

I did my last minute errands and at about 1pm, Sue, my sister, took a couple of quick pictures of me, my parents, and Linda. Soon after, we all climbed into the Oldsmobile, and set off on this momentous adventure. The first part of my journey had begun.

We decided that night to stay in El Cajon, which was about 40 miles from Campo, California, the southern terminus of the mighty Pacific Crest Trail.

After dinner that night, I loaded and unloaded my pack, taking out things I just wouldn't need. My strategy was to go as light as possible at first until I got in better shape and lost some weight.

My legs were in decent shape, but as for my body weight, well, I had totally failed to lose any weight at all. I knew that I would pay a price for not losing weight, especially the first month of the trip. During my other three hikes in '78, '98, and 2000, I had lost about 30 pounds or more in the first month! I knew this would be the case again.

The drive from El Cajon to Campo seemed to take forever. The road was very slow because of the constant curves and wet pavement. The sky was still cloudy but it looked like this last rainstorm was on its way out. The desert mountains started to flatten out a bit and then a small settlement appeared. The sign read Campo. I was here at last!

We drove past the town, which looked about the same as it did back in 1978. About a mile south of the town lay the Mexican border and the southern monument of the PCT. We drove over the last few hills on a wet dirt road that took you right up to the monument. My heart was jumping. I was in a daze. It was hard to believe that I was finally here and about to begin my journey.

When I got out of the car I was jolted by a 40 mile per hour wind and a temperature of about 45 degrees. This was my first reality check. I thought I would be leaving on a bright, sunny morning with birds singing and just everything totally righteous. I was going to leave my down vest with my parents, but my mom said that I better take it, and I agreed.

At the monument, we took a lot of pictures of me with my parents, of me with Linda, also a picture of the great wall of Campo that supposedly guarded us from Mexico. In 1978 there was only a barbed wire fence instead of this brown 15 foot high wall. In those days you could easily put your foot under the barbed wire and touch Mexican Earth, a symbolic act that you would be walking from Mexico to Canada.

Examining the bottom of the brown monster, you could see small tunnels under which immigrants had crawled. I put my foot under one of these dug out places and touched Mexico. I then went back about 50 yards to the monument and wrote my name in the register. "On this day, May 4th, 2003, I Robert T. Raley II, also known as Wrong-Way, will attempt to hike to Canada, 2650 miles." We took one last picture of me at the monument holding up a large sign I made that said "Thank You, Chuck". Without Chuck Hinkle's financial help, I probably wouldn't have been doing this trip.

It was time to leave, an emotional time for everybody who walks the trail. I was looking forward to taking off, for the last few days had been emotional. After hugging and kissing my loved ones, I took the first steps towards Canada. I couldn't believe it. This day I had thought of many times was here. I was starting out. I actually walked about 20 feet and then walked back to the start of the trail and started out again to savor the moment. I was waving as I went. I walked down the dirt road about 75 yards to the actual beginning of the trail and with one last wave, I headed down the trail as I watched my girl and my parents drive off, heading back home. I was alone with the cold wind and wet weeds. I was very excited.

I felt free on the PCT. But it's not the type of freedom where one can just casually loaf around and have fun. A thru-hiker becomes a slave in a lot of ways to the PCT. The vast distance that has to be traveled is almost insurmountable. It's like having a job. One must rise early and walk late almost every day.

A hiker must try to keep himself and his clothes relatively clean. He has to keep his belly well fed. A 175-pound hiker can burn up to 6000 calories per day. He must keep on the right trail and make sure he is going in the right direction.

People walking the trail must keep warm and dry and deal with all kinds of weather conditions. Hypothermia is the number one danger on the trail. Bears, rattlesnakes, and mountain lions are what most people think are the biggest dangers. But the statistics will tell you they're not. Drowning and falling are greater things to worry about.

Somewhere on the list of dangers are other people. There are some yahoos and bums that you will undoubtedly run into sometimes near towns and roads. In some ways, it seems to me that the PCT might be safer than the cities where you have to deal with speeding traffic and other negative elements.

While I walked along I thought of these things. I also thought about the overwhelming adventures that I would have, the people I would meet, and other hikers. I could be on this trail for five months. Man alive, that was a long time!

As my mind floated around thinking about all of this stuff, a cold jolt of reality hit me. I looked down and from my waist to my toes I was soaking wet. I had hiked only about a half-mile and the wet weeds along the trail had been constantly rubbing against me, saturated my boots, socks, pants, and underwear. The trail was already starting to fight back.

I kept a steady march, which was the best way to keep warm. I figured that with the sun starting to appear between the racing clouds, the weeds would dry out and so would I.

I soon passed Campo, which had a large parking lot for the Border Patrol's trucks and jeeps that were parked all over the place. There was a small store nearby, but I wasn't interested in buying anything. I was running on emotion, excitement, and the wonder of it all.

Soon the trail came down to Highway 94, the same highway I drove on to get to Campo, which was east to west. I crossed the highway and found my first water cache. Water caches are one-gallon plastic bottles placed by trail angels and association members of the PCT along certain stretches of the PCT, especially the southern desert. They are placed about 50 to 100 yards from these small highway and jeep roads.

I didn't need any water at this point. I still had about a pint of water that I took out of the car. It was a good thing that I took that water with me, because upon further examination, every bottle was empty, which was no surprise. I knew that I was walking behind a herd of people that were here last week, on their way to the kick-off party at Lake Morena.

I was steadily climbing uphill on a real good trail. The weeds were dry and my nylon running pants were almost completely dried. My boots and socks, however, were like lead and still soaked. I thought about changing into my running shoes but didn't want to stop.

For the next few hours as I hiked on the trail, my boots were filled with water. My goal that night would be to get to Howser Canyon. Lake Morena would have to wait until tomorrow. It looked like Howser Canyon would have water.

As I walked along the trail, about eight miles from Campo, I noticed some rocks that looked kind of familiar. Could these be the rocks I slumped against back in 1978? On my last night on the trail when I walked California, it had rained like crazy and all I had was a bivy bag which leaked like a sieve and completely soaked my sleeping bag! The new material called Goretex had failed to keep me dry and I spent one hell of a miserable night doing isometrics and eating the last of my candy to keep warm. I didn't think daylight would ever come. But I still was wondering if these could be the same rocks that I saw 25 years ago. Who knows?

After a short break I headed back to a continual climb for about a half hour and then rounded a corner to find another hiker sitting on a rock.

This dude was large and had a good size pack that sat on the ground beside him. "Hey man", I said, "what's happening?" He told me his name was Mario and he was heading to Mt Laguna. He didn't know how far he was going, maybe as far as Warner Springs, and he only had two weeks to do it.

I told Mario that two weeks is a long time just to walk to Warner Springs. He said, "Not for me. I go heavy. I'm not impressed at all with these people with little sissy packs. I go luxury. My pack weighs about 60 pounds." Then he began to tell me about the stuff he carried, like a far out radio and a stereo system that fit around his head that played CDs. He also had a seven pound tent, a huge flashlight, a knife, and a full length extra thick Thermarest to sleep on. This stuff cost him more than a thousand dollars!

This was the first time Mario had gone backpacking and he wanted it to be as comfortable as possible. I told him that's cool, whatever makes you happy, man. I tried to explain to him the difference between a backpacker and a thru-hiker was that thru-hikers have to go as light as possible because of the vast distances they must travel. That's when Mario asked me how far I was going. When I told him Canada, he flipped out and told me I was crazy.

We decided to head out together, at least to Howser Canyon, where he also wanted to camp for the night. I took this time to take my soaking, heavy boots off and put on my nylon socks and running shoes. I tied my wet boots to the outside of my pack.

Mario took off first and I followed him up the trail, he talked about his chopper and how he already missed it. I couldn't believe how my feet felt. It felt like I had wings on my feet! My pack was a little heavier. My boots rocked back and forth, which started to annoy me, but my feet felt good and I had renewed energy. Mario flipped out and said, "You can't walk in those, man, you'll hurt your feet and sprain an ankle". He told me about his Vasque boots that had cost him $200.

I explained to Mario that one pound on your feet is like six pounds in your backpack. Mario said, "No way, man, how could that be?" I told him to just think how many times in a 12-hour hiking day you pick up and put down your feet. Mario stood fast with his heavy boots and said "No, man, I care too much about my feet to treat them like that."

Both of us hiked up a small ridge and then began to drop down to Howser Canyon. I went ahead of Mario, who started to slow down considerably, probably because of his weight and his 60-pound pack. I came down to a dirt road that didn't have a trail sign on the other side of it.

I went up the road about 100 yards and came back to where I had started. I was just about to get my topo strip map out when another hiker came down the trail. I introduced myself, using my trail name, Wrong Way. He told me he was "Cruisin' Carson". He asked me where the trail was and I told him I didn't know and was about to check the map.

Cruisin' Carson looked irritated and mumbled that he had trained a year for this walk. We both walked about 150 yards, but found no trail. Carson said he was sorry, but that he was in a hurry and started bushwhacking down the side of the hill towards the bottom of Howser Canyon.

I could see the trail on the side of the canyon, but it was too risky to do what Carson, the old boy who was 62, was doing. It was a good way to get hurt. The fact that he was dressed just in shorts and a t-shirt in combination with his age made it twice as stupid. I could see those mean weeds rubbing and snapping into his bare legs. Ouch! Man, no way was I going to try that.

A few minutes later, Mario came down the hill. I told him what had just happened and told him that I felt the trail was a couple hundred yards down the road, according to the maps.

Mario, however, wasn't satisfied and pulled out his global positioning system and said that I was sort of right, but it looked like we had to go further than that, it looked like you just had to follow the dirt road down there. It didn't look that way to me, based on the way it looked on the road map. We were heading in the right direction. About 200 yards down the dirt road, we found the PCT and well-maintained trail, heading down the canyon to Howser Creek below.

My first night on the trail was spent at the bottom of Howser Canyon Creek, with my new buddy Mario. Two other guys, Jim and Mike, came down the trail. Upon rapping with them a bit, I found out that Jim was going all the way to Canada, and his buddy was going as far as Big Bear.

I had only walked about 15 miles on my first day. It was a beginning. Tomorrow I would have more of a full day and perhaps I could do at least 20 miles. Lake Morena was only five miles away. This was usually the destination of most PCT hikers on their first day walking the trail. It was considered safer, because it was further from the border and illegal immigration. It was also where the kick-off party was held near the lake.

I pitched my tarp between two trees and a bunch of poison oak, which seemed to be all over the place, talked with Mario awhile through his elaborate seven-pound tent, and soon went to sleep.

The next morning, May 5th, I woke up at about 6:30am and broke camp at about 7am. I surprised Mario and the other two guys with my early start. I told Mario I was heading out and would see him at Lake Morena. I usually break camp quickly by organizing my stuff the night before. I also feel hitting the trail as early as possible is important, so that's why I never have breakfast or even coffee. I don't eat until I have walked five or six miles.

So I headed out and started climbing out of Howser Canyon, switch-backing up the trail to the top of the ridge. After walking across a couple of small ridges, I saw Lake Morena down below, and it wasn't long before I reached the County Park.

I was kind of surprised that this was a big park in such a small place.

ECSTASY OF MISERY

There were picnic tables, bathrooms, and piped in water. The water I went to first, because I was plenty thirsty since I ran out of water the night before. I washed my hands and face and waited for Mario to come down the trail.

There was a good greasy spoon in town, which I was looking forward to. About an hour later, Jim and Mike went by and they seemed not to notice me, as I waved at them. Whatever, I said to myself. Then Mario appeared, bounding down the trail, all 280 pounds of him, with a 60-pound pack!

We walked down Lake Morena Road to a small grocery store and the café, where we had a great breakfast. After breakfast, we went back to the park. Mario had to take care of some business with his girlfriend on the telephone. He wanted her to activate his other credit card!

I didn't know how much longer I could walk with Mario. He was a funny guy, good company, and very interesting – but too slow of a hiker. I sat in the park and waited for the guy, as I guarded his pack, for what seemed a couple of hours. It was probably only an hour, but I was anxious to hit the trail. I wanted to use the public showers, but I had promised to watch Mario's backpack and I was afraid to take my eyes off of it.

Finally, Mario appeared, walking across the park. "Everything is cool," he said, "I told my girlfriend about you, man, and when we get close to Julian, she's going to pick us up and take us to town to buy some of that famous apple pie they have there." I was kind of pissed off because he had been gone a long time, but I kept cool and tried to explain to him I didn't have time for detours, that Canada was a long distance away.

I said good-bye to Mario and told him maybe I would see him later along the trail, maybe at Mt Laguna, which was about 27 miles away. He didn't look very happy, but I couldn't wait until it was cooler at the end of the day to walk.

It was now around 2pm. More than half the day shot and I only had covered five miles. I headed down Lakeshore Drive, looking for that elusive PCT. A few school kids came down the street and I asked them where the trail was. They told me it was about 100 yards down the road. I walked down the road and found the trailhead with the beautiful PCT emblem mounted on a post. Then, once again, I headed north walking into the great wide open.

I was hiking at a pretty good pace, probably about 3 miles per hour. I wanted to cover more miles, so I could get as close to Mt Laguna as possible. That way I would be able to get to the Mt Laguna post office by 4pm Tuesday, to pick up my first supply box of the trip.

The hiking was rather easy as I descended down to Boulder Creek campground. There I found Mike and Jim arguing about something. "We're having technical problems", Mike said. I told them that's part of just starting out. Trying to get it completely together is normal. I said this trying to be as polite as possible.

I passed these strange guys up and headed out of the closed campground. I crossed Boulder Creek Road and headed north. I walked until about 8:30 that night, until almost dark. I came to Long Canyon Creek, which had water, and made camp. I didn't use my tarp because the weather was nice.

I woke the next morning at about 6:30am and by 7am I was marching to Mt Laguna. During the morning hours, I saw plenty of birds and tons of lizards scurrying about doing their morning chores. I was constantly looking ahead in case a rattlesnake was on the trail. One must always be aware of those guys. Getting bit out here would be a bummer.

To me, rattlesnakes seemed pretty cool for a poisonous snake. They usually try and get out of your way and they always give you that famous rattling warning. Very few thru-hikers ever get bit on the trail. Their bite probably wouldn't penetrate a fast moving hiker.

In rattlesnake country, it wasn't too smart to wear headsets that would prevent hearing the warning sounds. I could just see some dude walking along listening to Sympathy for the Devil by the Rolling Stones and not hearing the rattle and getting bit. If he wasn't rocking out, he would have avoided the bite!

I started to ascend back into more mountains. To my delight, I entered pine tree country for the first time. I had shade at last. I was so excited about this that I took out my single-use camera and took a picture. The PCT looked great as it curled its way through the alpine forest towards Mt Laguna.

About an hour later the wind picked up and the clouds appeared. The weather was changing. It was cooler now, which had me concerned, as a fast moving fog blew by me.

ECSTASY OF MISERY

The store, post office, and lodge in Mt Laguna were located together. Across Highway 1, the campgrounds spread out among the pine trees. I only had a few minutes to get my package before the post office closed.

I couldn't believe how grumpy the lady at the post office was. She made the comment how she wasn't on vacation like I was. I told her that I really didn't consider this a vacation, as I was trying to achieve my quest to walk the PCT in one season. I told her there was a lot of work involved, how you had to get up early every day and walk late in the day.

The lady said that she knew all of that, that she's heard it all before. She said she was going to do a section of the trail in a few weeks, but on horseback. She said that she would never walk the trail, that her mother didn't raise her to be stupid and told me "to each his own" and to have fun on the trail.

As I was about to leave, the lady said to me how I must be a Democrat, which was an odd thing to say. I told her that I was, which I knew would bug her and it did, because she slammed the door of the post office behind her as she walked to her car.

Man, how uptight can you be? I tried to be friendly, but it was to no avail. I thought how lucky she was to spend her days up here in the mountains. I was thinking that maybe I might love to have her job and maybe even trade jobs with her, let her hand grind some stumps in 95-degree weather with no shade, tossing a 500-pound stump grinder back and forth with dirt, dust, and wood chips flying in your face.

That's work, man, and to tell you the truth, it helps to keep me on the trail. I would be grinding stumps in the summer and I always would consider this when the going gets rough out on the trail. My work also keeps me in reasonably good condition. I believe it is one of my keys to success in my three major hiking adventures.

I had my package and headed for the store that was right next door to the post office. The weather was getting worse. The wind was blowing about 50 miles per hour and it started to rain. The trees of the campgrounds were leaning over from the wind.

I decided to get a cabin and to my relief, there were plenty of cabins available. The price was great, too. They had a PCT hiker special, only $38 a

14

night. They wanted cash or personal checks, but no credit card. Since it was early in my walk, I had the cash.

My cabin was really cool. It had two single beds, a good shower, micro-wave, a small black and white TV, and a good heating system! Man, I was in paradise, with running water and a toilet, yea, righteous!

I went back to the store and bought some burritos, chicken dinners, and of course ice cream. While I was in the store, I met three people who were walking the complete trail. One was a tall and skinny guy named Ronnie. He was probably in his 20's and had hiked the Appalachian Trail the previous year.

I had a little trouble understanding Ronnie because of his accent, but from what I could gather, he had walked from Mt Laguna to Anza and back to Mt Laguna again! I couldn't believe it. He told me it was because of the late snows in the Sierras and local mountains. It seemed crazy to me. He said his friend "Florida Bob" had done it twice! I was amazed at these two dudes that I felt were a bit strange. They had walked some 200 miles from Mt Laguna to An-za and back! They had to be in good shape.

There was another guy in the store named Anthony. He was about 22 years old and buff. He also had walked the Appalachian Trail the year before. Anthony told me he had trained for this hike by running 10 miles per day in Yo-semite Valley. He told me he didn't expect the PCT to be so difficult because the PCT is a contour trail.

I asked Anthony how he got the trail name "Tripping Ant". He said be-cause once he tripped over a log that had mass quantities of ants crawling on it. His friends laughed and after that started calling him "Tripping Ant". I left the store feeling a little intimidated, to say the least. I headed back to the cabin with a microwave dinner and a half-gallon of ice cream. The next morning I woke about 7am, used the bathroom, and opened the door. Holy-moly! The weather was as bad as it was the night before, maybe worse. The wind was blowing about 50 miles per hour. Rain and fog blew across the road that was in front of the cabin. The temperature outdoors was about 40 degrees and not that much warmer inside the cabin. It was damn miserable. It looked like I wasn't going anywhere today. This would be my first layover day of the trip. I hadn't intended it to be, but the unbelievable weather didn't give me much of a choice.

Mike and Jim were at the store. It looked like they were going to get a room too. They didn't seem interested in talking to me, but listened to Ronnie from Israel rap away. Ronnie said, "You know if you're willing to hike just 20 miles from here, you will be out of all of this bad weather. Once you get off the desert ridge, the sun comes out and it warms up."

We listened to Ronnie, trying to overcome his heavy accent. I then headed back to the room, not really doubting Ronnie's word about good weather. He should know, since he had walked to Anza and back to Mt Laguna, but why would you come back to weather like this? It seemed to me that it would be much nicer to hang around the desert town of Anza, perhaps, basking in the warm sun, than to hike back to Antarctica!

I spent the day watching TV and washing my clothes out in the sink. I guess my body and mind were still pretty much in shock. And I thought my legs could use the rest.

The next morning, about 7am, I opened the door, hoping for the best, but the weather still hadn't changed. It was now May 8th. What the hell? It's late spring, man, not early winter. What was going on? I got my gear ready and started to leave. I couldn't afford another day off. I had to go. So with just an inexpensive emergency poncho covering up my bundled up body, I left Mt Laguna, walking north along the desert rim as clouds blew by me.

Soon, I was back on the Pacific Crest Trail, heading north. The wind seemed to get stronger. The rain had stopped. The trees were soaked and drops of water would fall down, smacking against my poncho. I wore my wool hat, gloves, a long-sleeved shirt, a wool flannel shirt, and a down vest. I had on two pairs of long pants, one over the other. First was a pair of nylon running pants, and on top of those, a lighter pair of nylon pants. On top of the long pants, I wore my running shoes with a pair of nylon socks. I was reasonably warm with the poncho, though at this time it was serving more as a wind block than a raincoat.

The trees disappeared, replaced by desert shrubs, which soon started looking like sparse skeletons of burned beach wood. A fire had burned a huge area here a few years ago. This made the wind even worse because there wasn't any windbreak at all. With nothing to block the wind, my pace had really slowed down. For 12 hours I walked in this windstorm, maybe doing a mile and a half per hour. The wind blew from north to south. It felt like nature was telling me, "Buddy, you aren't going anywhere". There were times when I could lean into it with all my weight and not even begin to fall forward. If I put my arms out, I felt I could almost fly. It was miserable.

Towards the end of the day, I arrived at Pioneer Mail Campground that had water and picnic tables. It was too early to camp. The wind was still merciless, so I marched on.

I finally came to some cliffs that blocked the wind. What a relief. I decided to make an early dinner of beef stroganoff, and take advantage of this tranquility. For the first time I began to appreciate the view of the desert far below. Oriflamme Mountain looked great, as did Cameron Valley. It was beautiful up here, but the damn wind kept me from enjoying it.

After dinner I started walking along a cliff. As I rounded a bend on the trail, I came upon two head stones. There were fresh flowers on the head stones. I read the inscriptions and realized that these two guys died here while hang gliding, right after bailing off the cliff. I wondered if they had died at the same time, on the same flight, maybe on separate gliders. It was pretty sad.

One head stone read, "May They Soar Eternally to New and Greater Heights." I spent a few minutes here, astounded that anybody would jump off this cliff, especially with this wind. I wish I knew what happened for sure. I guess it will always remain a mystery to me.

It was starting to get dark. I was pretty tired. The wind kept pounding against me. I started looking for a place for a campsite, when I saw what looked like a flat place down below. Since it was about a couple of hundred yards below the ridge, I reasoned the wind would be blocked out and it should be relatively calm. The ground there was black from fires, but that was the way it was almost everywhere around this part of the trail.

Linda and myself at the Mexican border 1978

Linda and myself at the Mexican border 2003

My Mom and Dad say good-bye at the border

Journey Two:
Mexico to Idyllwild
Jumping Jack Flash I Got The Gas!

I headed down the slope, leaving the trail and arrived at the spot. What I thought was a flat area was still sloped quite a bit. The worse problem, however, was the wind. It was still unmerciful, blowing at about 50 miles per hour.

I put my tarp between two Manzanita bushes that were burned. The bushes were still strong enough to support my rope. The hellish part was trying to put up the tarp. The wind made it almost impossible. Finally after a long time, I managed to put it up. I was lucky there were big rocks around there to hold the sides of the tarp down to the ground. My titanium stakes just pulled out of the black, charred soil.

I was lucky there was another bush on the side of the tarp where I put a tie-out cord that helped keep the side with all the wind from coming in on me. Finally with the combination of rocks and stakes, I was able to secure the tarp. I climbed in. I was getting cold. I hastily put out my ground tarp and mat, then my sleeping bag. I climbed in quickly with my clothes on. It didn't take a long time to figure out that I had definitely picked the wrong place to camp.

The wind that night was horrible, blasting the side of my tarp, threatening to rip it apart at any time. Now and then the wind would subside, but within a couple of minutes, I would hear the sound like a runaway freight train roaring down from the ridge and then blasting me with all kinds of force.

Turbulent winds whipped inside the tarp from both of the open ends, blowing black, burned grit all over me. All night long this went on. It seemed to get colder too. I have to admit I was kind of scared. I wasn't prepared for this stuff. Christ, it was May 10th, not December 10th. I was east of San Diego, not Nome, Alaska, man.

The next morning I got the hell out of there, glad to be alive. Black grit was all over me, but at least my tarp held together all night. Soon I was back on the ridge, heading north, feeling very happy that I had survived. But then I noticed, which bummed me out, my glasses were scratched all to hell from the grit that had blown into my glasses case. I took them off and put on my shades, and to my horror, they were also scratched. I was depressed, again. Only six days into my trip and both of my new glasses were wrecked. Four hundred dollars down the drain. The trip of my life and I would have to look through scratched lenses!

I was so pissed off, I couldn't believe it! This trip was now starting to be a disaster. I walked along completely depressed. I would have to at least get one of them fixed. The blended bifocals were expensive. Somehow, I would have to get them fixed. I thought maybe I could get by with my regular glasses; my shades I would use as a back-up, especially when there were very bright situations, like white rocks or snow. I also could buy some clip-on sunglasses that would clip over my clear lenses.

One thing for sure, I had to get my regular glasses repaired. I would have to depend on my girl Linda Robison to do it. Linda had my glasses prescription. She would have to go to Lens Crafters in Whittier, California, and do this for me. The frames were undamaged, but somehow I would still have to get these frames to her. Since it had only been two months ago that I had bought the glasses, the lens replacement would be half-off. It might cost me around $150. I started to feel a little better now. The trail started to go eastward, down Chariot Canyon. At last I was getting off this nasty wind-blown ridge.

I started dropping into the desert, switch-backing towards the desert floor below. The wind started to subside, visibility improved and the temperature increased. Towards the bottom of the canyon I came to a trail junction. Here the PCT and the California Riding and Hiking trails split apart. I could tell that the old PCT was the California Riding and Hiking Trail. It headed right through San Felipe Valley and crossed the highway below. The new PCT trail headed in a more easterly direction. I was glad to see a small sign pointing me in the right direction. I followed a jeep road about a quarter of a mile and then found the trail.

For the next 10 miles or so, I followed a nice trail and made good time. The trail started out as a flat traverse across the desert toward a place called

Scissors Crossing. It was very hot. The thermometer on my compass read 95 degrees. My body was trying to adjust to the difference between the heat of the desert and the cold and wind on the ridge. The heat was stifling. I was getting low on water, and starting to get a little scared. I thought I might have to hitchhike when I arrived at Scissors Crossing, if the creek nearby was dry. About 7pm, I arrived at Scissors Crossing. I was thrilled to see a large water cache. I think this place was called Scissors Crossing because the two highways crossed there. Highway 2 and Highway 78 crossed each other and formed what looked like a pair of scissors, maybe, if you were looking down from an airplane or helicopter. That was my guess.

I decided to camp here for the night, because from here the trail started to climb into the San Felipe Desert Mountains. As I looked at the map, I was shocked to find that there wasn't any water until Barrel Springs, which was a scary 22 miles away. I pitched my tarp that night and slept on some soft sand.

I woke up in the morning feeling really rested. I was extremely tired from the horrid windy night on the desert ridge. I purposefully slept in and didn't break camp that morning until 8:30am. Right before leaving, I tanked up on water. I knew I would have to have about 12 pounds of water, since I'd have 22 miles to go before my next water supply at Barrel Springs. I knew I needed at least that much, because if I didn't make it to Barrel Springs I would have to cook dinner and camp with what I had. The 90 degree temperature at 8:30 in the morning reinforced the need for plenty of water!

Soon I was heading up a series of switchbacks, climbing out of the desert floor that was spread out before me. I probably climbed nearly 1000 feet before the trail leveled out and started heading north once more. The weight of my pack was killing me. My right shoulder ached, a lot. These ultra light packs weren't designed to carry much over 30 pounds. I began to drink water profusely. I had read where one shouldn't ration water like you always see in the movies. Use the water for only drinking to get it in you quickly. By rationing water, you can start to dehydrate sooner. Of course the faster you drink the water, your pack becomes lighter and you're able to be more efficient as you hike.

The Pacific Crest Trail now leveled out a bit; the big climb was over. The trail was in excellent condition and beautiful desert flowers abounded everywhere. What looked like a cactus had gorgeous red flowers that flowed in the sunlight. There were beautiful views of the desert down below. I could see Highway 78 below and the old PCT route, which rolled along a couple of hundred yards from the road. Now and then I would see a PCT post with the green emblem, which was always a welcoming sight. On one occasion, as I rounded a corner, I saw a blue belly lizard sitting on top of one of these wooden posts, doing push-ups! It cracked me up. This dude was definitely in shape, as he manipulated ultra-rapid push-ups with a perpetual smile on his face.

Three or four hours went by, and then suddenly there was a water cache! The cache was in a good area. But man, if I had only known that was there, I wouldn't have had to carry 12 pounds of water on my back.

I sat down there, under the shade of a large bush and had an early lunch. A few minutes later, after guzzling all the water I could handle, I headed out. The rest of the day I followed an unrelenting trail, up and down and around and around, wandering all over the place for no apparent reason,. That evening I crashed on a side of a hill, about two miles or so from Barrel Springs. I was pretty happy with myself, because I had traveled about 20 miles that day in the heat and carrying a load of water. Plus the fact I had slept in that morning.

The next morning I got up at 6:30am and started walking about 7am, my best start yet. A few miles later I reached Barrel Springs, which had water pouring out of a pipe. I sat down and had breakfast that mainly consisted of power bars and raisins. I also washed out one of my long-sleeved shirts, my face and under arms. Warner Springs was only 10 or 11 miles away and I didn't want to smell too bad when I arrived. My shirt only took 15 minutes to dry in the hot morning sun of the desert and I headed out.

The walking was relatively easy. It didn't seem to be as hot as the day before. Soon I was walking along San Ysidro Creek, which had large oak trees growing beside it.

I climbed out of that little valley and began walking across rolling desert meadows that were still green from the slight winter rains. Cows were grazing all about. They looked up at me and stared, then went back to munching on the grass. I passed a large group of rocks; one looked like an eagle, which was appropriately named Eagle Rock. A few hours later I was walking in the shade of sycamore and oak trees along Canada Verde Creek. It was quite lush with vegetation. The creek moved along pretty well. I was out of water, but decided to wait until I got to Warner Springs before getting a drink. In a few minutes I reached the highway and Warner Springs School. From there I headed up the road for a mile or so and reached Warner Springs Resort. Warner Springs Resort was once a place that had mineral baths, where people came to swim and soak in the hot tubs and a large swimming pool. I heard it had done really well at first, but then went broke in the late '70s. In fact, I stayed here in 1978 when I did my California stroll. I believe the resort was hurting then. There's a golf course that was just west of the resort; that probably kept the resort in business. I headed right into the restaurant that was on the golf course. I ordered a giant turkey sandwich and about three cokes. It was great. As I was eating, I watched the Lakers and the Spurs battle it out in a televised basketball playoff game. Shoot, Kobe, shoot!

The food was great and inexpensive. I tried to sit away from people as best I could, so they wouldn't smell me. These were the first humans I had seen in almost four days. I was lucky to get to the restaurant when I did, because the place closed a few minutes later. I felt really good now, as I ventured across the street to see if I could get a room for the night. I felt I had a good chance because it was Sunday, and the weekend was coming to an end. I was right. A couple of the smaller rooms were available. I grabbed one, and thought "a soft bed tonight!"

The next morning, after having an excellent breakfast at the golf course restaurant, I headed over to the post office and picked up my supply package. While doing so, I met two young guys who were hiking the trail.

"All the way to Canada. No problem," they said. I asked their names: Jason and Justin. As far as using trail names, they would use different names at each register. They thought that was real cute. They both thought that the trail wouldn't be a problem because they were cross-country runners at the University of Alaska. They were taking a semester and summer to do the PCT.

I said, "Good for you guys, but I don't think the PCT will be a piece of cake". I said, "Man, it's pretty grueling." They chuckled as they headed across the street to the store.

ECSTASY OF MISERY

I headed back to my room to put my new food supply in my pack. I thought of those dudes. Yeah, it must be nice to be young and in shape like they were, but that didn't mean that they would make it all the way. A lot of it has to do with determination, putting up with the aches and pains, being homesick, knowing hot showers are a rare thing, so one has to acclimate to being dirty. It's putting up with the mosquitoes, gnats, snakes, and bears. And the weather could make life pretty miserable.

There were times when it would be kind of lonely. Before I got to Warner Springs, I hadn't seen anyone in four days. These guys had each other for now, but that can get old really fast. Their chances of making it all the way were 50-50. I would find out, because I'm one that likes to write and read in the PCT registers, which is about the most official way to tell if someone has been there. I'd keep on these guys no matter what new trail names they came up with. I can spot them. I didn't leave Warner Springs until 10am. The post office didn't open until 9am, so I couldn't avoid a late start. I was soon hiking along Agua Caliente Creek and battling hordes of gnats. These little bastards would fly into my eyes, nose, and mouth. They would constantly flutter in front of my face, traveling with me. The closer I got to the water, the more numerous they were. I finally got my mosquito head-net out and put it over my head. This helped a lot.

I had entered a new section in the Pacific Trail guide, section B, Warner Springs to San Gorgonio Pass. This section was definitely a rugged section of Southern California.

I would have to climb out of this current area and into the San Jacinto wilderness and then down into the San Gorgonio Pass. These two mountains were both over 11,000 feet in elevation. The heat would probably be the worst problem. Water, and even snow, could be another problem. This is what the PCT is famous for, different ecological environments. Desert cactus to Ponderosa Pines, a whole gamut of different plants and trees.

As I climbed out of Warner Springs Valley, I was into another cluster of dead pine trees. Here the desert started to get into the higher elevations. Years of little rain fall had weakened the trees. Then the infamous Bark Beetles invaded and killed the tree. In 1978, there were very few dead trees; a definite change was taking place. Could it be global warming? Who knows, but the desert was invading the highlands.

Desert chaparral was a lot better than nothing. Some of these plants grew in high enough where you can just barely sit underneath them, giving a worn-out dude like myself a little shade. Greasewood plants are probably the most dominant of all the desert plants. They are called Greasewood because of their texture and that they can be flammable. There's also Sagebrush, Buck Brush, Sumac, Ocean Spray Ribbon Wood, Coffee Brush, Holly Leaf, Cherry and Mountain Lilacs.

Mountain Mahogany is the most interesting of the desert plants. If the conditions are just right, they can grow from a bush into a tree. I used to cut these trees down for firewood in the Big Bear area. You had to have a $10 permit and the tree had to be completely dead. The wood was incredibly dense and extremely heavy. We called it Red Iron Wood. It would burn for hours in a fireplace, putting out all kinds of heat. These days, with the ever increasing population and popularity of 4-wheel drive vehicles, the dead Iron Wood trees are hard to find.

I hiked along most of the day on a well-maintained trail. It was hot, about 95 degrees, and I soon began to get low on water. I was definitely becoming more concerned. Around 2pm, I ran out of water. According to the topo strip maps in the California portion of the hike guide, the next water supply was Chihuahua Valley Road. The temperature now, according to my compass thermometer, was nearly 100 degrees.

Finally I went over a ridge and looked down to a desert valley below. I could see a dirt road below me. This had to be Chihuahua Valley Road. I soon walked up to it and noticed a small sign. My heart sank. The sign said "No H2O. Tank is dry!" I was shocked. No water, Oh my God, what am I going to do?

Almost directly behind that sign was another small sign that read "H2O 50 yards ahead!"

Now my heart was jumping for joy as I walked across the road and down the trail towards this water cache. There still was the chance that the water might be gone, either used by hikers, or possibly some kids or motorcyclists could have dumped it out. I was soon relieved, because one gallon bottles of water were set all about the place, under a Greasewood bush to help keep them somewhat cooler. "Thank you, Frank!"

Frank was the trail angel who placed the water bottles under the bush. He paid for the water with his own money and hauled the water out there. What a great guy to take the time to do this.

I camped here that night. It was a flat area with soft sand that made it nice for sleeping. I ate dinner around 7:30pm and soon fell off to sleep. I had only covered about 17 miles that day because of my late start leaving Warner Springs. But at least I had plenty of water. Tomorrow would be a big mileage day for sure.

I got up easily the next morning, mainly because the sun was already pounding on me at 6:30 in the morning. After getting all my stuff together, I picked up the place and made it look a bit neater. Animals, probably coyotes, had toppled over the cooler box and had eaten some power bars. There was a PCT register which I signed and said, "Thank you Frank for you saved this 56 – year-old's ass". I put a few dollars in the PCT bank that helps buy more H20 for other hikers and then I left, getting a good start.

Soon I was walking alongside Buchmort Mountains and passing Combers Peak, with an elevation of about 6100 feet. I was glad to be hiking at elevations of four to five thousand feet. It was probably 10 degrees cooler than on the desert floor. Zillions of lizards ran about, big ones, small ones; once one cut across the trail and I almost stepped on him. The opuntia cactus was in bloom all over the place. Its beautiful red flowers glowed in the sun, as I took a couple of pictures.

In the early afternoon I arrived at Tule Springs. I filled my plastic water tanks. Tule Springs was just off the trail and had water pouring out of a pipe. It was strange there was water in these dry desert mountains. Where in the hell did it come from? I was sure glad it was there. A few miles further I crossed Coyote Canyon Road that headed down to Terwelliger Valley and Kamp Anza. In the old days the trail traveled down along Bailey Road and then went almost straight to the little town of Anza. The trail had also skirted around an Indian reservation. Who knows, there might be a gambling casino down there now.

I remembered when I was talking to Ronnie from Israel, he told me that there was a great place to stay down there for free, due to another great trail angel. I didn't have any reason to go down there. I was doing fine. My left knee was even feeling better. My next supply stop was a day and a half away and that was the beautiful little town of Idyllwild. A few hours later, I climbed up to and crossed Pines to Palms, Highway 74. I remember this highway, because just a few months ago I drove on it with Linda on our way to Laughlin, Nevada, where we would take three day vacations, relaxing at Harrah's Casino right on the blue Colorado River. Man, I have to admit, that sounds nice right now, but back to reality.

I crossed the road and then the dirt parking lot that Linda and I had parked at and where we had taken a short walk. Soon after the trailhead at the parking lot, I arrived at a big metal PCT sign and map. The map showed the route up to San Jacinto. There was also a water cache, a PCT register, and a coffee can with some tobacco and rolling papers in it. I had a late lunch here, of Top Ramen soup, and an after dinner smoke. Then off I went, heading north into the great wide open.

The landscape really started to change. Big white boulders appeared. It almost felt like I was in the High Sierra range. I can see why geologists say that this range of mountains, from around Warner Springs to Mt San Jacinto, are actually part of the Sierras range. Strangely enough the San Bernardino and San Gabriel ranges are separate mountain ranges. So when you are walking the mountains you are really walking the southern-most extremity of the mighty High Sierra range of fantastic California.

The weather began to change, as well as the scenery. Cold winds started blowing in gusts. Around Pyramid Peak the wind increased and so did the low flying clouds that at times hid the trail before me. I kept on hiking. It was now about 6pm. As I gained altitude on this ridge, it became colder and colder.

I had to get off of this ridge. Looking at the map, I decided to bail at Cedar Springs Camp Trail. It sounded like a good campsite with water and trees. So at the trail junction I began jamming down hill for about a half a mile and arrived at Cedar Springs campsite at 7pm. I quickly found a good campsite, put up my tarp and then got some water. Everything was mellow until about 8pm, that's when the wind began to hit the place. It sounded like a freight train roaring down the hill. But this time I had conifers to block some of the huge, cold wind gusts. My God, I was glad I was off the ridge. It must be hell up there.

The next morning I headed up the Cedar Springs Trail, to the mighty PCT. Despite the heavy winds, I had slept pretty well the night before. I was anxious to put in quite a few miles again today in order to get as close to Idyllwild as possible. It took about a half hour to climb back up to the PCT and I finally hit the trail heading north once more. The crazy winds had dissipated and it looked like a real nice day was in store for me.

I walked past Fobes Saddle, Spitler Park, and then Apache Peak, getting excellent views of Palm Springs on the one side of the crest and Lake Hemet on the other side. Antsell Rock and South Wall Peak were the next objects along the trail. Everything was great.

The canyons below were magnificent. This was probably one of the most picturesque vistas in Southern California. Soon after passing South Wall Peak, I ran into my first encounter with snow. Snow patches covered the trail here and there, always hiding themselves in the shade. That evening, I camped in Little Tahquitz Valley, only a few miles from the famous Devils Slide Trail that branches off the Pacific Crest Trail and heads down into the little mountain community of Idyllwild.

The next morning I headed back to the ridge to find the trail and pick up where I had left off the day before. After following it for a while, it disappeared into the snow. I walked around following other people's footsteps, but they didn't seem to know which direction to go either. After checking the map, I decided to go back to where I camped then continue towards Saddle Junction and Powder Springs. A trail headed right towards this area that began to get wider and wider. I finally reached Saddle Junction where I met the PCT coming off the ridge, where a good portion of it would likely be buried in snow. I soon passed Powder Springs and began heading down the Devils Slide Trail, towards Fern Valley where I would catch a road to Idyllwild.

While I was hauling butt down the trail, I passed a middle-aged woman coming up the trail. We both said hello as I headed down the hill. Wow, this was the first person I'd seen in about four days since I left Warner Springs! Soon I started to see more and more people. I believe they were locals, doing their workout routines. This was definitely a good way to work out. What a beautiful trail. Little waterfalls bounced around beside the trail every so often. The trees were really nice too, towering high in the sky. I reached the trail-head parking lot and the Fern Valley road. I used the bathroom, trying to spruce up a bit.

I knew I had at least two miles of road to walk, downhill to Idyllwild. I mentally prepared myself for the short walk on the road. There was very little traffic. Down the road I went, anxious to get to Idyllwild, hoping to find a room somewhere. Yeah, a shower sounded great. Real food too, perhaps a giant cheeseburger with a chocolate shake!

After walking about a mile and a half I heard a person call out, "Are you a thru-hiker?" I told her yes, that I was doing the PCT. She said her son was walking the trail in sections. This year he was going from Cabazon to Mt Whitney. "Great", I said, and asked what his name was. She said, "Molasses." "Cool, I'm Wrong Way." She then offered me a ride to the center of the town and to the Tahquitz Inn which was an expensive, but nice, motel. After getting her car out of the garage, we took off.

We talked about the horrible conditions of the trees in the community. So many were dying, due to years of below normal rain and snow fall. The trees get weak and then the Bark Beetles hit and it's curtains for the trees. Some people are actually selling their homes because they can't afford the cost of a tree service to remove the infected trees. Soon we were in town and she showed me the many restaurants, stores, and the post office. Molasses' mom dropped me off at the Tahquitz Inn, where I got a room for $50 a night.

It was Friday, May 16th. It had taken me 12 days to get here from Mexico. I was just a few days behind schedule. The new trail was different from the old 1978 trail. There was an addition of about 40 miles from the Mexican border to Warner Springs. This was 40 miles that a hiker had to carry water, as well as fry in the desert sun.

After taking a long shower, I decided to head to the center of town and get some food. I had a great lunch of fried chicken and mashed potatoes. After lunch, I went to the post office. I thought it was great that the restaurants, stores, and post office were all within walking distances of each other. The little town of Idyllwild was very nice and definitely was set up for tourists. There were specialty shops all over the place. I soon arrived at the post office. I asked for my supply box, showing my ID to the lady working inside. She took off to look for it. I began to get nervous when she was gone a long time. Then came the bad news. My supply box wasn't there. I couldn't believe it. It had been mailed on Monday and it was supposed to be sent by Priority Mail. It was now Friday; it should have been there. Hell, I only live 75 miles from here. The lady in the Post office told me it would most likely be there tomorrow, the last truck would come in at about 2pm and that I should be there about 2:30.

I left the post office bummed out. Man, I hope that damn package gets here tomorrow. I headed back to the Inn and watched some TV. Later I ate dinner at a Mexican restaurant, with a thru-hiker named Dave who was from Texas. Dave was doing the PCT in sections and only going as far as Big Bear City. After a great Mexican dinner, I went back to my room and washed my cooking gear and water bottle. This kind of stuff gets continually dirty on the trail. It's imperative that hot, soapy water be applied to these vessels at all pit stops along the way. Tomorrow would be a day of rest, a time to eat like a pig and do my laundry. But the big question mark is what will I do if my supply box doesn't arrive?

The next morning I slept in, making the most of the soft bed. This place was pretty big. It had a couple of small rooms that would sleep five to six people. The lady who owns the Inn had told me that the previous weekend, every room was filled with thru-hikers. That would make sense. There would be the hikers that left a week before I did. Probably a lot of them were at the 2003 kick-off party. There could be over 300 people ahead of me.

It was now May 16th. I needed my supply package. Although the post office was closed on Saturdays, I was told by an employee that if I came at 3pm and knocked on the door, a lady named Jean would give me my package. That's if it arrived! There was nothing else to do but wait.

PCT outside San Diego

Horny Toad thru hiker

Heading into the San Jacinto Mountains

Journey Three: Idyllwild to Big Bear

I went and had breakfast, did my laundry and took pictures of beautiful Idyllwild and Jonathan's wood sculptures.

Three o'clock rolled around, so I headed down to the post office. I knocked on the door and finally got a response. Jean opened the door. I told her my situation. She was really nice and understanding. She then went to look for my package. A few minutes later she returned with the bad news. No package!

Now it was time to make a decision. Should I wait until Monday when the post office opens again at 3? Man, that would be too late. No way could I waste two more days, then what if it didn't arrive Monday? I was going to have to buy some supplies out of the store and the fancy ski and backpacking shop. My package would be sent back to my girl Linda, and then she could use the supplies for other packages.

By 6pm that night, I had purchased all the food I needed to get to Big Bear, my next re-supply point that was about four days away. I headed back to the Tahquitz Inn. The manager asked me about my package. I told her my situation and to my surprise, she offered to give me a ride the next morning to the Devils Slide Trail. She was heading down to Hemet for some kind of meeting. She was in a motel ownership club. I would have to be ready to leave by 8am. This was a break for me. I headed to my room and started getting my stuff together. Tomorrow I would be back out into the great wide open.

I slept pretty well that night. I woke up the next morning around 7am, took a long hot shower, and then got my stuff together. By 8:15am Evelyn, the hotel owner, and I were off to Fern Valley and the Devils Slide Trail. At the Devils Slide Trail, I said good-bye to Evelyn and she wished me good luck. I was on my way again. I had lost one day of hiking, having to stay an extra day in Idyllwild. I also spent a lot more money that I wanted to. But like the Rolling Stones say, "You can't always get what you want. But if you try sometimes, you get what you need".

My legs were rested from the two day rest. My pack wasn't really too heavy, being I had no water. There was water at quite a few places along the next 15 miles. By not having a heavy pack, my progress was pretty fast. Before I knew it, I had joined the PCT once again, heading north. I felt great and excited.

The San Jacinto Mountains were beautiful. I have walked this area three times before, mostly to climb Mt San Jacinto which promoted a fantastic view of the desert, and its communities thousands of feet below. Patches of snow appeared here and there, especially in the shady areas of the trail.

About midday I hit Fuller Ridge and a whole lot of snow. To make it worse, Fuller Ridge was undulation, up and down. I tried to step in the other footprints in the snow, but couldn't always do that. I fell a few times. Running shoes are pretty bad in the snow. One can't kick flat places in the snow like you can do with boots.

It probably took me three hours to get off the ridge. There were great views all along the way. That evening I arrived at the Fuller Ridge remote campsite. There I met a couple, Granny and Pappy, who were trying to go all the way to Canada. After some deliberation, I decided to camp there for the night. Tomorrow would be a long hard day including a change of environment one could hardly believe. I would be dropping into the desert below and it could get really hot.

Granny and Pappy were having a difficult time. The cold winds and fog had demoralized them. Granny was especially having a rough time. They both were older than me. Pappy was 65 and Granny was 58. They had walked the ATP a few years ago. Granny and Pappy thought the PCT would be easier because it was a contour trail, but they had been shocked into reality by the environmental changes, the heat, the cold, and the vicious winds.

Since I was staying for the night, I hoped I had enough water for cooking and washing up, enough to get me to Snow Creek, which lay at the bottom of the San Gorgonio Pass.

I put up my tarp and set up camp. As I was setting up camp, a young woman zipped by, moving at a really good pace. I heard Granny and Pappy mention to her about camping here for the night since it was getting late. But she said no, that she wanted to do more miles and off she went, mumbling that it sure had been a long day. I cooked some chicken and noodles. As I was about to go to sleep, I heard a crashing sound of rocks, bouncing off of other rocks. There was definitely a rockslide somewhere. Man, these mountains were alive!

The next morning I broke camp about 7am. I told Granny and Pappy, who were also getting ready to leave, that I would see them later. I then headed out of Fuller Ridge remote campsite. This would be a really interesting day. I would be practically diving out of the mountains, dropping some 8000 feet or more, to the desert below. Down, down, and down I hiked on a rather sparse looking trail. What a view of Mt San Gorgonio! It was completely snow-capped and yet right down below me was the desert, which was probably 100 degrees.

An hour later I really started to feel the heat. The lower I got, the hotter it got. Soon my water was gone. I was starting to get a bit nervous. When you run out of water and it's hot, you start thinking the worst. I knew there was water somewhere near Snow Creek, but I still had three or four miles before I would arrive there.

The trail was really poor. It was most annoying. I thought of Granny and Pappy in back of me. I hope they had water. In 1978 the PCT was different. It was part of the Black Mountain Trail that followed the crest of the San Jacinto Mountains and came out of the mountains at Cabazon, California. This is one of the rare parts of the trail that had been shortened by the new trail. At least the old trail had water here and there.

Two miles from the bottom, I met a dude named Jack, who was hiking Agua Dulce to Mexico. He was hurting. It was so damn hot. I told him about Granny and Pappy who were just in back of me and how I was concerned about them. He told me that he had plenty of water and that he could probably give them some if they needed any. I told Jack according to the guidebook, if he got low on water, he could take the jeep road that ran in front of Fuller Ridge campsite. I told Jack to make a right and go down the jeep road for about a mile or so, that there was supposed to be a campground called Black Mountain which has piped in water! He said thanks for the tip and off we headed in our separate directions. The last couple of miles were horrible. I was thirsty. The trail was rough and it was getting worse with each step I took. I didn't even see any lizards. Man, you knew it must be bad.

Finally after one or two huge switchbacks, I had made it down. To my joy there was a drinking fountain, which was dedicated to a trail angel. I drank about two quarts of water before heading out, carrying a half-gallon with me. Soon I was on a paved road that led to the Snow Creek Trailer Park, where I didn't see a soul.

The trail across the desert looked like it was real straight on the guide-book map, it fooled me. I was soon on the trail heading in an amazingly straight trail towards the 10 freeway. My compass thermometer read 99 de-grees, but felt hotter. About an hour later, I started to approach the freeway. I would definitely take a long rest underneath the freeway. The shade would be a great relief.

I arrived at the 10 freeway, passing first under a bridge. I quickly got out my ground tarp, placed it on the ground and crashed on top of it with a plastic water bottle by my side. I was feeling sort of lightheaded and totally wasted. Suddenly I heard a voice near me, amazed to see a cute young girl standing there. At first I thought she might be Asian, until she got closer and I could see her face better. She seemed to be concerned if I was ok. I thought that she was probably the girl that flew by me at the Fuller Ridge remote campsite.

I found out her name was Jenny and she was walking the complete trail from Mexico to Canada. She was from St Paul, Minnesota, and was hiking the PCT alone. She told me that she had been training hard for this hike and it looked it. She looked about five foot and three inches tall and probably weighed about 115 pounds of muscle. I asked her how her parents felt about her hiking and being so far from home. She told me they were a little worried, but they knew she had to do this quest of hers. Her mom, who was in a wheelchair now, was quite a hiker in her day.

I drank some water and ate a power bar for the electrolyte benefit as I rapped to the girl. I told her since she was walking alone, maybe she should team up somewhere with a group or a nice guy. She kind of laughed and seemed a bit embarrassed. Jenny said that she didn't think so, that she had only seen a couple of thru-hikers. I told her that there should be plenty of peo-ple ahead because I heard that over 300 people left the kick-off party at Lake Morena. I also said to her that she would meet up with a guy before she reached Northern California and meet some nice couples and other girls. About 90% of the hikers were her age; the average age of the hiker walking this trail was 25 years old.

The hottest part of the day was over and I started to feel better. I left the shade of the 10 freeway before Jenny did, not wanting to impose myself on this young girl. I was old enough to be her grandfather. Hell she probably liked being alone. In a lot of ways I know I did. I told her that I might see her later as she passed me by. I laughed and then left.

On the other side of the freeway was a dilapidated community called White Water. There wasn't a store, gas station, restaurant or post office. There were just small wooden homes, most of which looked either unoccupied or unin-habitable. I guess I had walked about a mile when I came to a sign that read H2O with an arrow pointing to an old house up a small incline.

There were broken down cars, trucks, and tractors that filled the area. I reached a small pink structure that had broken down RVs parked beside it. In front of a bungalow was a stand with bottled water on top of it. Man, was the water cold. I started filling my platypus water container with the precious liq-uid, since it would be quite a ways before I reached White Water Creek.

Just then I hear a voice come from the first structure asking if I would like a hotdog. I was at first startled to hear someone, but then I said hell yes! Two people appeared, a guy and a girl. They asked me to come in and have a soda. I introduced myself, of course, as Wrong Way. The young couple were Scooter and Toes from Canada. Scooter and Toes told me that this place is the PCT famous Pink Hotel. There was a refrigerator with food and ice cream. There was also a stove and a hiker's box. What a place, I said, and out here in a junkyard between Mt San Gorgonio and Mt San Jacinto, looking over San Gor-gonio Pass, with the smog of L.A. rolling in. Could anybody ask for more? Hey it doesn't get any better than this! The two Canadians gave me a look, wonder-ing if I was being funny or was I crazy.

After downing a hotdog, I remembered Jenny at the freeway and told

ECSTASY OF MISERY

Scooter and Toes about her. We all went out to see if we could see her. Sure enough, she was coming up the dirt road. We all yelled to her to come in, that there was food and water here. Toes began telling me about the Pink Hotel and how people stop here for food and water and how most of them crashed here. I decided I would stay here tonight too. I had to hydrate myself or something. I was still having some problems ever since I had flopped under the 10 freeway. I'm too fat right now to push it. Thank God I'm only 56 and not 25 or I wouldn't know what to do.

For the next hour we sat around rapping. I talked about my favorite hiking hero Scott Williamson. I had a picture of me and Scott in Washington that I had brought from home. Jenny asked a few questions about the PCT. I told her what I could remember about my hike from north to south in 1978. It didn't really reassure her. I did tell her that today's trail, thanks to the Pacific Crest Trail Association, is much improved.

Jenny said that she had to leave. She had to be at Kennedy Meadows by June 12th, where she had some crampons sent to her. I asked if her next stop was Big Bear and she said no, Agua Dulce. I said to her that I meant her next stop for supplies and Jenny said that her next supply pick-up was Agua Dulce and her last stop was in Anza. Her pack must have weighed a ton. She said it was a bit heavy, but she had a lot of dehydrated stuff, that she had made herself and she didn't eat a lot.

Jenny took off, hauling ass across the rising desert terrain. The sun was going down and gave a softer view of the desert. It was cooling down fast. Jenny was smart to leave when she did. She would have a good hour or more of walking before it got dark. For me, however, it was back to the sanctuary of the old folks home, the Pink Hotel.

Scooter, Toes, and I sat around the table eating stuff and drinking cokes. I told them about Granny and Pappy and how I hoped they make it. Scooter and Toes seemed very concerned and decided to walk down towards the freeway to see if they could find them. They took some water and munchies. I thought that was nice of them. You could tell that they had been sitting around all day and needed to get out and do some walking. While they were gone, I took a splash bath and washed out a couple of shirts. I found a place to crash in one of the RVs parked next to the main structure. Scooter and Toes came back a few hours later, unable to find Granny and Pappy. "Hey man, don't think we'll be seeing them any more!" With that said, I said goodnight and crashed in the RV.

The next morning I awoke at 6am and ready to leave after having breakfast at the Pink Hotel Kitchen and after using the pit toilet. Scooter and Toes were still sleeping, which was a little problem, since I had to go in there and get some of my camping equipment, but I didn't want to disturb them.

A small truck suddenly appeared at the kitchen door and an older man got out. He was the trail angel that kept the Pink Hotel "alive". He asked me if I was heading out soon and I said yes, that I was just waiting for Scooter and Toes to get up. He then walked up to the door and pounded on it. He told them that it was time to rise and shine. He told them they would have to leave today since this would be their fourth day there. Toes said they were going to Big Bear today and that they were going to hitchhike because it was too hot for them.

I said good-bye to Scooter and Toes and headed down the trail to White Water Canyon Creek where the next water stop was. It was getting hot, very quickly. I got a lousy start. It was 8am before I started hiking. This was a real stupid thing to do. I wasted two hours of cooler temperatures by getting up late and waiting for my Canadian buddies to wake up. I crossed the desert heading for White Water Canyon and soon began heading for those giant wind propellers. Their spacey looking propellers were all over the place, catching any wind they could and spinning away on their giant stands.

The trail started to take a sharp turn and headed steeply uphill. It was too steep, in fact, to be a contour trail. I believe the trail may have been trying to leave the area of the giant propellers as quickly as possible. I had wondered if there might have been a problem in the past, with hikers messing around on those things. This almost looked like a temporary trail. Finally, after much agony, I got to the top of this sandy ridge. I was exhausted and burning up from the hot desert sun.

The trail started to level out a little bit. I was moving at a faster pace, but was really uncomfortable. An hour later I arrived at White Water Canyon. It was difficult to follow the trail across the white rocky terrain of the canyon.

ECSTASY OF MISERY

Rocks piled on top of each other, called ducks, helped out a lot. When I arrived at the rushing creek, I made lunch and took a little break. I thought about Scooter and Toes and how they made the right decision to hitchhike to Big Bear. They wouldn't have been able to negotiate this part of the trail and the British Columbians would have trouble dealing with the heat.

After a little break, I was soon heading out of White Water Canyon. I began to climb the saddle dividing these two desert canyons. The temperature had risen to over 100 degrees where I was standing, looking down on Mission Creek. There was water down there and since I was getting low on water, and my throat and feet were parched, I headed down the switchbacks to Mission Creek below. At first I didn't see any water and then sure enough, I did. For the next two hours, until dusk, I headed up the canyon.

The damn gnats were so bad that I had to put my head net on to get some relief. I camped at about 8pm that evening, on a sandy part of the creek that provided a level smooth ground. I had put in 12 miserable, and uninteresting, hours that day. Tomorrow would be another long day too. I was to climb as high as I could into these San Bernardino Mountains and get out of the miserable desert heat. I slept quite well that night; the soft sand made a good mattress, plus I was really tired.

The next morning I got up and broke camp in about 15 minutes. I was off climbing Mission Creek and it looked different since the last time I was here. In 1978, the trail was pretty much non-existent. You had to follow ducks and red tape, as you climbed over rock after rock. There seemed to be more vegetation now. In 1978, it had been a very snowy year. Even though I had traveled through here in the last few days of October, the creek was much fuller than it was now in May! The biggest difference was at Fork Springs, which was hardly recognizable. The water was rushing pretty swiftly back in 1978, but now it was just a couple of lazy flowing creeks.

The PCT ran along one side and then the other and finally it came to an end. The trail seemed to curve to the west a bit and then leveled out a little a few miles later. I reached Mission Creek Trail Camp. Here I found the springs. I tanked up on cold water. I had a late lunch of Top Ramen.

After lunch, I headed out once more, climbing out of the campgrounds and crossed a dirt road. After a bit more climbing, the trail leveled off and headed in a more easterly direction. The trees began to get bigger. I was in the mountains again. The sun was setting and everything looked golden. Now and then I had views of Mt Jacinto and the desert below. I was pretty proud of myself because the terrain was very rugged and the weather was frying. That evening I walked late, hoping to get over Onyx Summit. When I saw Coon Creek Jump Off, I knew I wasn't too far from the pass. It was now starting to get dark as I trudged along on a beautiful mountain trail. I wanted to get as far as I could possibly get to Big Bear tomorrow. I put my "strap-on" flashlight around my head at around 8:20 because it was getting too dark. I believe this coal miner flashlight was a real breakthrough for thru-hikers. The lead-burning bulb kept the three AAA batteries from getting too weak for quite a while, much better than regular flashlights. A hiker can walk at night, maybe at a slower pace, with the coal miner type flashlight, but can put in more miles per day.

So off I went, hoping to get over Onyx Summit. The trail was interrupted by dirt roads. A car drove down one of these roads. I doubt the driver saw me. Suddenly, I heard an incredible growl. It was very loud and sounded like a pissed off bear! A second growl sounded louder than the first. It freaked me out! The sounds were right in front of me, and up a small hill. No way was I going to follow the PCT up there! I was amazed and scared that the damn thing would come hauling ass down the trail and have me for a late supper.

I walked down the dirt road and saw a dimly lit cabin not too far away. I decided to head towards the light, because it was in the opposite direction of the loud roaring sound. Suddenly a guy came out and grabbed something from the wooden porch. I decided to speak out, which kind of startled him for a second. I said, "Hello there, sorry to bother you, but I'm walking the PCT from Mexico to Canada." I asked if he had ever heard of the PCT and he said that he hadn't. "Well I was marching down there a few yards where the trail crosses the road and I heard a huge ungodly roar."

By this time the guy's wife was looking out the window, wondering what the hell was going on. Then she came out and I repeated the story to her. They both started laughing like crazy. She said, "Don't worry, that's a 12 foot high grizzly you heard, but it's caged up." Then she continued to say that they were training it for the movies and they also have a lion. Wow, I laughed with them now. "Thanks for the info. I guess I'll get back to the trail and head to Canada." They told me good-bye and to have a good hike.

I headed back to the trail and continued my trek. Man, what a relief. What I was wondering about now was if those people really didn't know the PCT went right by their cabin? Probably not. I camped about an hour later after I found a small water cache. There was a note that a Christian School will put up PCT hikers and was located down the dirt road. The note had an arrow pointing in the direction of the school. It was way too late to bug anybody now, so I found a flat place just off the dirt road to camp. I cooked dinner and fell off to sleep. I'd had a long day. I probably covered a little over 25 miles that day.

Desert flowers everywhere

San Gorgonio pass, lowest elevation on the PCT in California

Mt. San Gorgonio

"Long Haul" at the Pink Hotel

Journey Four:
Solitude is Lost by SoCal Holiday

The next morning I got up early and headed out, down the trail. After walking a bit I realized I wasn't as far along as I'd thought I was. I finally reached the summit at about 10am. I knew then I wouldn't be reaching Big Bear today. I had a long way to go before I reached Van Dusen Canyon Road. Soon I reached Austere Camp and Deer Springs.

The area is in a place I've been to many times. Not only did I do my trek in 1978, I use to jog here along this trail that ran from Onyx Summit and Gold Mountain. A friend of mine had a cabin up here and I would come up here to visit him. We would cut ironwood and then I would walk and jog on this trail. In those days I had the running bug. I would enter all the 10ks and marathons that I could. That was more than 20 years ago. Man, how time does fly by. The rest of the day I marched down the trail. I began heading around Baldwin Lake, which has been dry for several years. At the other side of Baldwin Lake, I got a great view of the desert below. I stopped here and called Linda. I was lucky I got a connection, but I had to hold my cell phone in a certain direction or I wouldn't be able to hear her.

After a nice chat with Linda, I started out again, soon crossing Highway 18, which dives down into the desert. This was once an old stagecoach route. They would stop here to get water and other supplies before they headed on to San Diego. This place was hustling with Confederate miners during the 1860s.

Gold was discovered here by accident by Billy Holcomb and a group of cowboys from the Irvine Ranch, near the coast. Indians had been stealing their horses and would head up here to the Big Bear area, a few miles past the lake, over to the next valley, which is now Holcomb Valley. When Billy Holcomb reached the lake area, he saw a giant grizzly bear. They had chased the bear by the lake and over the ridge to the next valley.

As Billy and his men looked over the valley from the top of the mountains to see if they could spot that huge grizzly, one of his men looked down and across the huge slab of rock was a ribbon of glowing gold, about 20 feet long and 3 to 4 inches wide!

That's how gold was discovered in the Big Bear area and how the lake became Big Bear, because of the giant grizzly bear that Billy Holcomb and his men saw. The area where the gold was found is now called Gold Mountain; at one time 15,000 men were working this area and Holcomb Valley. Today there is a self-guided tour people can take and drive to numbered parts along the dirt roads, which will lead to the hanging tree, the saloon, and other dilapidated structures. It's no Bodie, CA, but it's still pretty cool. Pretty soon I arrived at Dobie Trail Camp, which had water and an old broken down picnic table. I decided to eat here and make the most of the cold spring water. I had chicken tetrazzini and cherry Kool-Aid with a Balance Power Bar.

After a pretty good nights sleep, I broke camp at about 7am and headed to Van Dusen Canyon Road. I tried to call the Best Western, the only motel listed in the AAA guide, but couldn't get through on my cell phone. Soon I arrived at the Van Dusen Canyon Road and headed towards Big Bear. It didn't take me too long to get out of the canyon. When I got out of the canyon, I called the motel, and to my disappointment, they were booked. I should have thought about where I might be on Memorial Day weekend and called before I left the Pink Hotel. I would still be able to shower because the Big Bear Fire Department would let the PCT thru-hikers shower there. There were also plenty of places to eat and a laundromat, all in close proximity to each other.

I headed down the road, following the PCT guidebook, making all the proper turns. I arrive at the post office first. I received my package and believe me, after the fiasco in Idyllwild, I was relieved when the lady in the post office gave me my supply box.

After putting my new supplies in my pack and throwing away three days of trash, I headed to the fire station to take a shower. A cool lady showed me where the showers were and pointed to the PCT register book, which I filled out. I began reading about the people; most of them left a week or so ahead of me, names like Lug-nut, Free Radical, Choo-choo, Bandana, the White Stag, Elk Man, and Strider, were only a few days ahead of me. For the next few hours I condensed my town visit quickly by washing my clothes and eating like a pig at

BJ's Sandwich Shop. I met a guy named Greg there, who was walking the PCT. He was pretty amusing as he decribed the PCT, that walking it was like walking a treadmill with a pack, 12 hours a day. He was kind of a strange guy. He had arrived in Big Bear the day before me and was heading out today.

I finally got everything together. My clothes were washed and I had enough food to get to my next pit stop, which was Wrightwood, three or four days away. Before I left, I pigged out at a pretty good Mexican restaurant and then took the shuttle bus back to Van Dusen Canyon Road, where the PCT crossed. I was heading west now, as the San Bernardino and San Gabriel mountain ranges run. It was now May 23rd, my 19th day on the trail. I had traveled just a little over 270 miles and was about two to four days behind my schedule, but who's counting? That night I camped somewhere behind Fawn Skin, ready to start descending slowly down to Holcomb Creek tomorrow.

The walk into Big Bear on those hot roads, with dirty socks, was causing a major blister. The problem with this type of blister is it can't really be treated very well. Tape just won't hold and the same goes for moleskin and second skin. I treated it with a triple antibiotic, so at least it wouldn't get infected. It sure was strange. I didn't have any blisters for 270 miles and a road walk to Big Bear and suddenly had a doozy and only on my right foot, nothing on my left.

Down the trail I went, trying to put less pressure on my right foot. A few miles down the trail I came to Holcomb Creek Crossing. I was surprised at the low flow of this creek for this time of year. There should definitely be more wa-ter. I had to get water here. I didn't have my breakfast. I filled up a quart of water and put my potable water tablets in the water to be ready to drink.

I headed down the trail. About 20 minutes later, I put a packet of Car-nation Instant Breakfast in and some Milk Man and shook the hell out of it. I then drank it down with trail mix and a power bar. So much for breakfast, man. It did fill me up, but it wasn't bacon and eggs, like I could be eating back in Big Bear. Then again I was making tracks. The Big Bear stay would have cost me another day. I was already behind schedule.

I could tell it was Memorial Day. The sound of dirt bikes, quad runners, and four-wheel drivers could be heard all over the place. So much for the wilderness experience. It wasn't long before I reached Deep Creek, which runs from Lake Arrowhead to the end of probably a 15 mile long canyon to Deep Creek Campsite below. This creek is really scenic. The trail skirts above the water almost all the way, leaving a thirsty hiker gazing down 300 or 400 feet and not being able to drink! The water also had a poor reputation for being drinkable. A person should always cure the water or filter it first.

Right after I reached Deep Creek, two guys on mountain bikes flew by me heading down the canyon. This was completely illegal of course. But what could you do. It was Memorial Day and people were everywhere. I'm sure the forest rangers were stretched to the limit.

A few hours later the trail finally came down to the creek. Next to the creek was a dirt road where a couple of trucks were parked. I needed some water, so I walked over to a pool of slow running water. This would be a great place for a rest and a drink. There were a few people there, so I said hello. To my amazement, it was Scooter and Toes! "Wow, man, what are you doing here?" They said, just walking the trail. I got the impression that they didn't want their two older friends to know that they must have hitchhiked to Big Bear to get here in front of me. So I said nothing to them, like how's the walk dudes or how did you get here already?

After a half hour of walking and then resting for three minutes, I said to them that maybe their pace was a little too fast. Maybe if they slowed down, they might not need to take so many breaks. They said no, that it was a good hiking pace and that it was comfortable. "Well whatever," I said, getting bored.

We finally reached the famous as it was infamous Deep Creek Hot Springs. Back in the 60s and 70s, two people got spinal meningitis here. In the last 25 years or more, there haven't been any problems. Man, I needed a bath. My feet were killing me. My blister felt like I was walking on a lump.

Then I noticed what I had feared, playing the Smokey the ranger game, a ranger came out between two rocks. He said, "Hello, can I see your permits?" "We're PCT thru-hikers, going from Mexico to Canada," Toes said. I opened the top of my pack and pulled out a permit. The ranger thought we should be further along. I told him that I left a week later than most people and another reason was because of the late snows in the Sierras.

The ranger said he was sorry to inform us that we couldn't spend the night there. I told him that it was getting late and we had to make camp soon. He said he knew we wouldn't be able to walk the six miles out of the canyon, but a couple miles ahead we will see a flat area where we could camp, not here. Oh man, there goes my bath and on my birthday too. The ranger said we could come back tomorrow and spend the whole day, but nobody was allowed to camp there. Scooter and Toes tried to get their two-cents in, but to no avail.

What a drag, man. I was pissed off. This Memorial Day weekend was really getting to be a drag. If we had arrived in the middle of the week, there wouldn't have been a problem. Memorial Day weekend did me in again, as it did in Big Bear. It was getting dark and we only had about an hour of hiking left. Down the trail we went, hoping to find a flat place to camp in this canyon.

We walked for about an hour. Scooter and Toes took the lead. "We want to find a spot, Wrong Way, and you're going a little slow'" said Scooter. I told them to take it easy, that it was dark and if they fell off the trail they'd be in dire straits. Off she flew like a runaway truck, and Toes, who is legally blind, following as close as he could. I saw them switch back and forth below me. We were heading back down towards the water.

With our miner-lights strapped around our heads, we arrived at a wood bridge. This is it, dudes, probably the flat spot, until we reach the mouth of this canyon. Scooter and Toes camped a short distance from the bridge. I camped at the north end of the bridge. Not the greatest camp site but at least it was a bit flat. I made an attempt to get some water, but to no avail. The cliff was too steep and the water too deep. Scooter and Toes had to put up their tent. I slept under the stars. The next morning I awoke at 6am and was hiking 15 minutes later. This was probably the earliest start I've had so far. I didn't wake up Scooter and Toes, knowing they like to sleep in. I probably wouldn't see them again, unless they hitchhiked ahead of me. A few hours later I walked out of Deep Creek. Deep Creek Campground wasn't much. Vandals had broken the picnic tables long ago.

I walked across a cement dam and after being lost for awhile, I finally stumbled back on the PCT. I crossed a creek and then started crossing rolling desert-like hills towards Silverwood Lake.

ECSTASY OF MISERY

Today was May 25th. I was now 56 years old. Perhaps today, at least, I could celebrate with a cold one, maybe at the lake. It was now about 10:30 when I arrive at Valley Creek Road. I was surprised to see a water cache there. There was a note that said the store on Highway 173 was closed! I was a bit disappointed. This small Ma and Pa store was only a quarter of a mile from the trail.

After having lunch, utilizing the water from the cache, I was off again, walking on a well maintained trail that skirted near the hills and wound its way to Silverwood Lake. It was warm but not too hot. I was still at an altitude between 4000 and 5000 feet.

A couple of rattlesnakes came across my path. One was three or four inches long! When I first saw it, I thought it might be a centipede. The other snake was about three feet long and he wouldn't get off the trail until I nudged it with one of my walking poles. Slowly the snake moved and slid off the trail. It seemed to be a bit upset about moving. Too much, I thought. I will never, unless I really have to, kill a snake, animal, or even one of those black beetle bugs you see crawling across the desert floor. Hey, this is their turf, not mine. I'm just passing through.

I drank water constantly in order to prevent dehydration. Finally the trail dropped down to Highway 178. The trail actually ran along the highway for about half a mile before it left the asphalt to dirt road and then became a trail once more. It was kind of confusing. I was lost again for about half an hour, before I found the trail again, heading towards Silverwood Lake.

About 20 minutes later, after a shadeless climb, I reached a ridge and out in front of me was Silverwood Lake. Boats were rushing about here and there, dragging water skiers behind them. I soon heard the sound of people below me as I walked along the edge of the lake. I began looking for a store there. Maybe there was one by the boat launch; there should be a store somewhere around here.

I quickly left the Cedar Springs Dam area and entered the Silverwood Lake Recreation Area. The lake looked good, but I still wondered where was the marina. After walking about half a mile, I found out that the marina was south of the lake at least a couple of miles from where I was heading. This was a bummer. If I was staying here for awhile, I would try to get a ride down there. But in a few hours it would be dark.

I had to follow the trail down to reach the picnic grounds, according to the trail guide. Oh well, not too shabby. There should be a lot of people there, according to all of the vehicles I could see from my view on the ridge. I'll first make a few friends down there, with the "I'm hiking from Mexico to Canada" rap and before I know it, someone will offer me a burger and a Bud! The trail started switchbacking down toward the lake.   It joined an asphalt bike trail that headed right to the picnic grounds. I walked into the park and headed right for the water fountain. There were people everywhere, kids running around and riding bicycles. The smell of great food was everywhere. But one thing wrong, they were all Mexicans. Hey don't get me wrong, the thing is I don't speak Spanish that well. My chance of a Bud and a burger just sank below the western horizon along with the sun.

I found a lonesome table and sat down with my water and prepared a meal of chili-mac and beef jerky. I felt like I was in a foreign country. One little dude, about eight years old, stomped up to me and asked me if I had a home! I told him it was in La Habra, CA, just eight miles north of Disneyland. The little guy started telling me that he loved Disneyland, and about a ride that he thought was so cool and how he took it over and over. Then all of a sudden his mom called him to get back over to where she was. The little dude ran off like I was poison or something. I couldn't blame her. I probably looked like a homeless bum, a vagabond for sure. I probably smelled like one too. I think I might have called my son back too, if I had been her.

It was now about 7pm and everybody started to make a sudden exodus from the park. I began gathering my stuff. I had to find a place to crash for the night. There wasn't any overnight camping here and with my luck, if I did try to camp here, I would probably get busted. So again like the last two days, I had to leave and find a campsite in the dark. As I was leaving, I couldn't help notice that trash and garbage were everywhere. What a mess. I couldn't believe it. People left crap all over the place. I was disgusted. It was almost like they wanted to pig out the place, like it was part of their agenda or something.

I found a sandy, smooth place along a wash, just northwest of the picnic area. I laid out my ground tarp, then my ground mat and then my sleeping bag. The crowd was leaving and for a while car lights flashed right above me. Thanks a lot Memorial Day! Thank God the three day weekend was over!!

As I lay there I had to reconsider what this holiday was about. It was a day to honor the soldiers that have fought in all our wars. Bless those brave souls. In honor of them, I put my anger aside. It was no big deal not finding a room in Big Bear or no burger or Bud in Silverwood Lake. At least I'm alive, laying under these fabulous stars. Though it sure would have been better if I had been able to get a hot bath and to be clean. Oh man, go to sleep and try not to get angry, it will only keep you awake. Tomorrow would be another day, with a Bud and a burger at Trail Inn.

The next morning I got my usual start on the trail by 7am. My right foot was really hurting. It had been bugging me for the last few days. I had been taking Motrin 600. I was able to acquire these about a year ago when I went to the doctor for a shoulder injury. I always carry Motrin, Aspirin, and Tylenol, which are good triple combinations for pain.

It was a slow climb out of Silverwood Lake Valley. I soon crossed Little Horse Thief Creek. The distance from Silverwood Lake to Cajon Pass was about 15 miles, so I knew tonight I would be at McDonalds or Del Taco. There used to be a great diner near McDonalds, called Tiffany's. The place was especially good for breakfast, but Tiffany's closed about the same time they started building a McDonalds along with a gas station and a small store. There was also a Comfort Inn in the same area along Interstate 15. Being that Memorial Day weekend was over, I had a good chance to get a room at the Comfort Inn.

The trail was well maintained. The terrain was of rolling high desert mountains. There weren't any trees, but plenty of high bushes and other chaparral. The PCT seemed to travel north of the old route, which traveled on top of Cleghorn Ridge. Hikers had nice views looking north and you could also see Interstate 15, heading over Cajon Pass Summit and off towards Las Vegas. This was always alive and noisy with thousands and thousands of travelers.

Journey Five: Cajon Pass to Agua Dulce

Before too long I found myself on a huge ledge, looking down at an incredible view of Cajon Pass. I could see Mt San Antonio and massive Cucamonga Peak with snow on top of it. Before these mountains, however, was a huge gorge and even an earthquake fault line. The Mormon Rocks and the Marmot Rocks also lay below. This was definitely Chato's land. On top of this ridge I gave my girl Linda a call to let her know that I should be at Cajon Pass in an hour or so. She told me if I get a room at the Comfort Inn, that it might be better if she and my parents came to see me there instead of trying to meet me in a couple days at Wrightwood, that Cajon Pass was closer and wouldn't interfere with my dad's golf game. I told Linda I would call her back if I was able to get a room, and also asked her to bring my Wrightwood supply package so I wouldn't have to go to Wrightwood, and would save time that way.

After the call, which came in great, I headed down, dropping into Cajon Pass. There were some nice looking cliffs and other scenery. The trail was easy to follow and before long, I reached a small creek that still had some water in it. The trail followed this creek all the way out to Interstate 15, with lanes of rushing, noisy traffic flying by. This is definitely a main artery of Southern California and the great southwest.

In this area is a monument dedicated to the railroad workers who built the tracks that traversed this very rugged area. Soon I was walking the asphalt road that traveled behind McDonalds and a gas station. About five minutes later I walked by McDonald's. Here I talked to a girl and a guy who asked if I was walking the PCT. I told them that I was and I was heading to the Comfort Inn, hoping to get a room, a shower, and to crash for a couple of days! They laughed, and the girl wondered if it wasn't too hot to be hiking. I said it was a little, but this was mild compared to some of the desert mountains behind the San Diego area. I told them so long and headed towards the motel, about a short half-mile ahead.

ECSTASY OF MISERY

My foot was really hurting now. The Motrin had worn off. The hot, flat pavement pressed against a bulge of burning skin on my right foot. I finally got to Highway 138, crossed over Interstate 15. Man, what a sight it was. It was Monday late afternoon and the holiday traffic coming back from the Las Vegas casinos was back to back. Wow, what a scene. I wondered how many of them were winners. Ninety percent will tell you of their big pull or their winning hand at cards, but the truth is probably about 95% of them are losers and you can bank on it.

I arrived at the Comfort Inn and they had a room, which was a great relief. I checked in for two nights. The price wasn't too bad for two nights. The place was really nice. I called Linda and told her that I had a room and gave her the phone number to the motel and my room number. This was important so my parents or Linda could call me back. It's cheaper if they call you. So I tried to make my first call short, mainly to pass on important information.

I couldn't believe how good a hot shower felt, as dirt rolls off your body. My head was past the itching stage, which was a sign that it's really dirty. I washed my hair three times, scrubbing my scalp and then rinsing it well. When I got out of the shower, my right foot looked more swollen than before. I sat on the bed and looked at the bottom of my foot. Man it looked hideous. I applied my triple antibiotic and put on some clean socks. From now until I leave this place I would try to put as little pressure on my foot as possible.

Next stop was Del Taco, a local Mexican fast food chain in Southern California. Not bad really, I got myself a giant burrito, a taco, and a monster Big Gulp and went back to my room to watch TV and munch down on my food. God it was good, real food at last. After eating, I did my laundry, which is one of the things a PCT hiker must do on town visits. After doing my laundry, I just kicked back and watched the tube for the rest of the night and fell asleep with the TV still on.

The next morning I awoke about 6:30am, used the bathroom, and crashed again, till about 9am. I got up, took a shower, and off to Del Taco for a small breakfast. I didn't want to eat too much because my parents and Linda were coming at about 11am and we were going to have lunch together. I thought about having a McDonald's breakfast, but the walk down and back was out of the question. I was trying to keep all the pressure I could off my foot. I walked on the side of my foot and walked with a bit of a limp, and it did help. I didn't take any Motrin because the pain would remind me not to put too much pressure on that area of my foot.

About an hour and a half later, my parents pulled up to the motel room. Linda came up to the door and I gave her a big hug and a kiss, as I did with my mom. My dad shook my hand and we sat down and talked for a while. They were really surprised at the weight I had lost. I probably lost about 20 pounds so far on this trip, in only three weeks.

After they brought in my food supply package as well as an assortment of other stuff that I might need, we decided to have lunch. We drove to Victorville and decided to eat at Marie Callendars. I pigged out on a great Chef Salad with plenty of Thousand Island dressing. After lunch, which my dad paid for, we headed back to Cajon Pass.

An hour later, my parents and Linda thought it was time to leave. It was a weird deal saying good-bye to them this time. It would most likely be a long time until I see them again. From here, I would be walking away from them. I would never be this close to home by highway as I am now. So after taking a bunch of pictures, they headed out, just in time to miss the rush hour.

I hung around the motel the rest of the day. I would lie down on my back with my right foot in the air, making the most of this layover day. That night I ate at Del Taco. It was strange, but the food didn't taste quite as good as the first day. In the evening, I packed my pack, getting ready for tomorrow. As I did, I watched Willie Nelson's birthday party on TV, and drank Bud. Later that night I ate a pint of Ben 'n Jerry's Chunky Monkey ice cream. Because I had taken a few naps during the day, I stayed up a bit late that night watching the tube. I finally fell off to sleep about 1am.

The next day was going to be a big day. I had to climb out of Cajon Pass and get as close to Guffy Campground as possible, because the next water supply was some 22 miles away! I turned my key in at the desk and to my surprise, saw a PCT register book. I quickly signed and dated it. I was also surprised to see that one of the last people to sign the register was Jenny B, from St Paul, Minnesota. Wow, she is human after all. She was now at least three days ahead of me.

ECSTASY OF MISERY

I left Comfort Inn and soon was walking down the frontage road to McDonald's. Some guy asked me if I was Raley? I told him that I was. He said his name was Steve and that next year he was going to walk the trail. He and his dad were sort of scouting the area out.

I had wondered how Steve knew who I was. He told me had been following my hike by reading about it in the Orange County Register. He said he thought I was doing pretty good. Steve had read how I made it to Big Bear and how I got scared by a caged grizzly. He thought that was funny. Steve asked how heavy my pack was and was shocked at how heavy it was.

I told Steve that I had to go, that it was getting hot. I told him that I might have to walk 20 miles for some water. He said there was a water cache that he and his dad saw at Swarthout Canyon Road. He said he saw about eight gallons of water there yesterday and he was going back there today and if I wanted he would stash more water there for me. I thanked him and said that would be great. Before I left, I wished him luck next year.

I left McDonald's and headed under the wash that tunnels under Interstate 15. The trail goes under the freeway and turns right and goes around some private property. It then heads west towards the Mormon Rocks. Right at first I climbed and then dropped into Swarthout Canyon. I had only walked about six miles or so and I was already thirsty. My thermometer read 98 degrees. I was drinking water as I went and hoping that the water cache I heard about was true. If it wasn't there, I would be hurting because it was still 13 or 14 miles to Guffy Campground.

I was soon walking in a valley. I crossed a dirt road and thought that this had to be Swarthout Canyon Road. Where's the water? About a hundred yards past the dirt road near a poor dripping spring and a trail for horses there was the water cache! What a relief. There were about five gallons plus my empty quart bottle that I sent with Steve and his dad. The sun was pounding down on me and would be for the next 12 miles or so. Once I was past the San Andreas fault zone, I would be in an alpine forest, which would be a little cooler and have some shade.

Now it was time to bite the bullet and start climbing my ass off. I would have to carry about 10 pounds of water and a pretty heavy pack that would sustain me with food, until I got to Agua Dulce. One thing I had going for me was fresh legs. A days rest can really put a spark back into a thru-hikers wheels. So up I went, steadily climbing. There wasn't any shade, only the usual desert chaparral. I could tell as I climbed into the San Gabriel Mountains that it was starting to get a little cooler as the elevation got higher.

Views of Cajon Pass became more spectacular. What an incredible location of energy. First you have Interstate 15 and then you have the railroad, with plenty of trains snaking through the torn up twisted earth. Then there's the potential of earthquakes and minor land movements, due to the San Andreas fault line, as well as the San Andreas rift.

The San Gabriels themselves can be treacherous mountains, especially if one ventures off the trail. John Muir once said that the San Gabriels were the most inaccessible mountains in all of California. This is because they are so steep with rocks that can make your feet slide. There are also bushes with stickers and cactus at the lower levels. Man however has conquered the San Gabriels with roads and trails, but it was a lot of hard work.

In the winter, the "Gabes" can have plenty of snow, which makes them more dangerous. There have been many people who have died in these mountains. I like them however – they seem to have only a few people in them during the late spring and summer months, even though millions of people live nearby. Another thing about the San Gabriels and the San Bernardinos is that the trails are always kept up great. The main reason is Boy Scouts earning their merit badges by raking the trail all the time with rock rakes, and even leaf rakes!

A few hours later I had completed the climb. I was back in the pines again. I sat under a tree for a while, munching some Power Bars and trail mix. Finally some shade. Thank you trees for the life-saving shade.

That night I camped just a short distance from Coblers Knob. The next day I would reach Guffy Campground and water. I had enough water from the Swarthout Canyon cache to do my cooking, cleaning, and drinking. I fell asleep that night listening to my tiny radio. Art Bell was on, rapping about UFOs and abductions. That's all I need, some dudes from outer space paying a visit. The way I smell right now, they probably wouldn't hang around too long!

ECSTASY OF MISERY

The next morning I started walking about 7:30am. By 10am I had finally arrived at Guffy Campground. There were a couple of dudes there. They looked like they may be thru-hikers. After introducing myself, I found out that they were in fact thru-hikers. One guy was named Paul and the other guy, a skinny looking dude, named Frog. Paul was trying to walk California and Frog was going all the way to Canada. "Well, where's the water?" I asked. Frog looked at me and said "There isn't any!" I couldn't believe it. The water had dried up.

I was pissed off. This was the first natural water for the next 22 miles. Paul said Wrightwood was only a few miles away and all down hill. I told him that I wasn't going to Wrightwood. Since I only lived 50 miles away, my parents brought me my supply box to Cajon Pass. Then Paul said I would have to trudge another six miles to Grassy Hollow Family Campground where there is definitely water. I asked how did they know and they said a forest service worker told them there was water there.

That was a relief to me, but I was still upset about the fact that there wasn't any water at Guffy Campground. I said to them that Acorn Trail to Wrightwood was in back of us. Paul said that there was a paved road at Blue Ridge called Highway 2 that they were going to hitchhike down to. Why walk if you can ride!

Frog and Paul headed off towards Blue Ridge and Highway 2. They were anxious to get to Wrightwood. I couldn't blame them. Wrightwood had some nice restaurants and I believe a pretty good place to get ice cream. For me however, well, I had to march to Agua Dulce. I had already stopped and had my rest. Besides, I was two or three days behind my schedule. Frog was amazing. He had left Campo eight days or so after me and he had already caught me at Guffy Campground!

At the present time, my biggest problems were the giant lump on the ball of my right foot, and my thirst. I was really counting on the Guffy Campground for water, but there wasn't any at all. The good thing was that I had some shade from the pine trees. It also helped that the altitude was over 6000 feet, which made the temperature cooler than the desert below.

Grassy Hollow Campground was six miles and I was 90% sure that water would be available there. My home town, La Habra, was only 60 miles away and I had come up here a few times in the last couple of years to catch a view and visit the ten foot bear that I had carved with a chainsaw for a friend in 1995. Chainsaw sculpture had been a hobby of mine. I was sorry that I was going to miss my bear, but if Grassy Hollow doesn't have any water, I just might head down there. The next water stop after that would be Lamel Springs, half way up Mt Baden Powel.

Down the trail I headed, a thirsty dude though it wasn't that critical. A couple of miles later, I was surprised to find a bottle of water along the trail. There was a note on the bottle that read, "Wrong Way, here's some H2O. I don't need it – Frog." Man, that was nice of the guy. I grabbed that water and drank it down immediately, getting it into my system as quickly as possible. It was refreshing. About a mile further I met a forest service worker and he gave me a pint of water. All right! I scored again! About three miles later I crossed Highway 2 and soon came upon Grassy Hollow Campground. Lo and behold there were water faucets all around. Yeah, running water.

I spent about an hour here, eating lunch and cleaning myself up. This was a nice car camping place, with a large building for campers to visit. I think there was a store and a small restaurant inside, but I couldn't tell, because the building was closed. A few people walked by. Then a couple with a baby in a backpack stopped to talk to me. They were from Wrightwood and they seemed interested about my trip. I asked them if they had ever seen a wood sculpture of a ten foot bear on Betty Street, near the main tourist section of Wrightwood. They said they had seen it and were surprised to find out that I was the guy who carved it. They were nice people.

Pretty soon, two other people came by. They were section hikers walking from Vincent Saddle to Cajon Pass. The girl had a bandana covering her mouth. I didn't need to ask her why. I knew the gnats were bad, ever since I got into the mountains from Cajon Pass, the flies and gnats have been a real nuisance. Backpacking has its ups and downs, flies and gnats being one of the downs.

It was now 2pm and I started to head out, full of food and clean from taking my splash bath. Which reminds me that these splash baths have been called Dundee Showers for the last seven or eight years. I think Ray and Jenny coined this phrase after camping at a campsite called Dundee, when they walked the ATP. However when my buddies and I hiked the Sierras back in the mid 60s, we called this type of bathing splash baths. We would make the water almost lukewarm. We would start with a head shampoo and splash the rest of the water over us, sorry Ray, you were probably in grade school at the time!

I grabbed my pack and off I went, heading up and out of the campground fully refreshed. Soon I hiked by Jackson Flat Campground. I remembered back in 1977, a year before I walked California, I was checking out the trail and met a guy who had met Teddi Boston, from Boston, Massachusetts, here at Jackson Flat Campground. I believe she was the first lady to walk the trail in one season, back in 1976. She went by herself and walked north to south. This always amazed me. It was fascinating to me that this guy had met her at Jackson Flat Campground. I had read about her in the old trail guide and handbook of the PCT.

Once more I started heading down to Vincent Gap and Highway 2. After crossing the road, the PCT began ascending to Mt Baden Powell. This mountain, named after the founder of the Boy Scouts, has an elevation of 9399 feet. I believe it might be the fourth or fifth highest peak in Southern California.

It was now getting late. I thought Lamel Springs would be a good place to camp. Somehow, however, I missed the cut off trail and found myself in snow, and plenty of it. The trail in places was covered in snow. So I would try to follow a small foot trail straight up, then catching the switchback trail at another location. The going was slow and exhausting. Then suddenly I found myself at the summit trail location. The summit trailhead was another 200 yards before you go to the peak. But I took the PCT heading west again.

The views on the summit of Baden Powell on a clear day were incredible. Views of L.A. and the coast to Death Valley's Telescope Peak and even the fantastic Sierras can be seen across the arid desert. Now, however, it was starting to get dark. I had very little water and still hadn't found a campsite. I marched on for another hour. After passing a patch of snow, I crashed on the trail. I used my stove to melt the ice before I cooked dinner. What a day. I was really on my way. My blister was hurting me quite a bit. But that's what thru-hiking is all about. You have to cope with pain. If it's not one thing, it's another.

The next morning I broke camp pretty early. I headed west, walking on a ridge heading for Little Jimmy Campground. I remember Little Jimmy Campground pretty well. I spent the night there in 1978. It was pretty nice and there was also water there. It was now May 30th. I felt that I was behind schedule, but who cares. At least I was still hiking and I have done well, walking over 300 miles. Wow, only 2350 miles to go!

The ridge walk was pretty nice and very familiar since I have hiked up Mt Baden Powell some three or four times on this trail. Usually I would head up Dawson Saddle Trail that joins the PCT near Windy Gap and from there, headed east to the summit trail. The mountains looked great, until I hit a burned out area. I then remember the fire that had hit here some seven months earlier.

I soon passed Windy Gap and the trail junction that led down to Highway 2 on the one side and Crystal Lake on the other side. The trail now began to drop down to Little Jimmy Campground, where I was planning to have lunch and tank up on water. A little bit further, I arrived at Little Jimmy Springs, where really cold water rushed out of a pipe.

About a hundred yards further was the campground and man, what a mess! The trash bin was supposed to be bear proof, but the bin was so stuffed with garbage and crap that the lid wouldn't close. Some bear obviously had powered the door open and pulled mass quantities of trash out. It's easy to dump the cans at vehicle accessible campsites. But when they have to walk a ways, it makes it much more difficult. Somebody should have taken better care of the trash bins.

I had a quick lunch here. Once again, I was heading down towards Islip Saddle and Highway 2. Down I went, making good time. About 34 years ago, Highway 39 came out from the south and joined Highway 2, but heavy rains in 1968 and 1969 caused a cave-in and rockslide that closed the 39 for good. The road now stops at Crystal Lake, about a mile or so away. One reason I heard why the forest service didn't want the road repaired was because of crowd control. Too many people could get up here too easily. Another reason was the discovery of Big Horn mountain sheep. They are on the endangered species list, especially in the San Gabriel Mountains.

The trail here joins the Mt Williamson Trail and climbs about a half mile to excellent views of Devil's Punchbowl. The rest of the day, I hiked at a pretty good pace. I must have crossed Angels Highway or Highway 2, three or four times. This highway, I'm sure, is used by many thru-hikers as a shortcut to make up time. In my book, it's kind of cheating. But I guess there aren't any real specific rules about walking to Canada. There are purists that follow the trail as much as they possibly can, and then there are hikers that are hell bent on just getting to Canada as fast as possible.

The rest of the day I headed west by northwest and then down Rattlesnake Trail to Rocky Creek. Here I ascended to the southwest Cooper Canyon. I crashed for the night. I wanted to get to Cooper Canyon trail camp, but I was just too exhausted.

While I was cooking my dinner, Frog appeared out of nowhere, hauling ass up the trail. "Hey man, what's happening?" I said. "How was Wrightwood?" Frog told me it was really nice and that he didn't have a problem getting a ride down there and back. I told him that I really appreciated the water he left for me along the trail and gave him his water bottle. He said he was going to camp at the campground about half a mile ahead. I told Frog that was my original goal too, but I just ran out of gas. He headed out, gliding uphill. I said, "See you later, stud". He yelled that he'd probably see me in Agua Dulce and how he heard that there was a real awesome place where you can stay, a good place to spend a layover day.

I couldn't believe it. The guy goes down to Wrightwood, parties for a day, and then catches my weary ass a day later. And by the look of his stride, I doubt he walked any of Angeles Crest Highway either! I decided that I'd better get use to it and put my ego back into my pocket and face it. I am an old man compared to him and still too fat. I have to realize that young people have an advantage. But I look at it this way: I have less to lose and more to gain by finishing this trail at age 56 than a slim kid of 24.

The next morning, I got going about 7am. My right foot was really hurting. The blister wasn't getting any better. I tried to wash my nylon socks out every night and also made sure to put antibiotic on the blister. As soon as I got something in my stomach, I took a Motrin 600.

Within 15 minutes, I came to Cooper Creek Campground, where I got some water. I was soon off again, climbing near Cloudburst Summit. Here the dirt road turned back into a trail and once again, for a short while, traveled beside Angeles Crest Highway. An hour later, with my foot feeling better due to the Motrin, I came to Three Points where it crossed Angeles Crest Highway and headed away from the highway. There was a water cache at Three Points, but unfortunately it was drained dry by previous hikers. So, on I marched. It was starting to get hot. The rest of the day I kept a steady pace. I really began to get low on water. Somehow, I missed Sulfur Springs. I believe I missed it because there was a separate trail that headed down to it, but it was a trail for horses. I should have taken it, but I didn't. Now I was really getting thirsty and hungry too.

I began climbing right after crossing Sulfur Creek Springs and dirt road 5 N 04. I was starting to get really thirsty and I didn't have any water left. I was getting quite concerned about this situation. Then suddenly, I came across a tiny flow of water dripping off a rock. I began to shout for joy. The water must have come from Fountain Head Springs, which was right above the trail and according to the trail guide topo strip map, about a quarter of a mile away. It took a little while to fill my water containers, but I was just thankful that the spring wasn't dried up, like it might be in a couple weeks.

After munching a Power Bar, I was off, happy as a toad, because I had that precious commodity, H_2O. The trail still climbed up and then curled around Mt Pacifico, which was 7124 feet high. It was starting to get late and I thought about staying at Mt Pacifico Upper Campground, but there still were a couple of hours of daylight left, so I headed on.

There was a small sign there that announced the new development of Mt Pacifico Trail Camp. That would be ready for trail hikers in the future. I could see the red plastic flags that outlined where the trail would be heading down to this future campsite. Now the trail began to pick up. I was sailing along pretty good, when I came to a flat area on a ridge. Here I found about 10 people camping. They were all young kids, and one adult. I started talking to these people and found out they were Boy Scouts from Hesperia, California. I introduced myself as Wrong Way and told the leader that I was going to Canada and had started at the Mexico border. This brought a wow from everybody.

I still had a good hour of light and I wanted to get down to Mill Creek Summit Ranger Station, where I was planning to camp for the night. The trail guide said that there was piped water there and picnic tables, which I like to sleep on because they kept you off the ground and you had fewer problems with ants. But then I was asked to have dinner with them. This was their last night out and they had a ton of food left.

That evening I ate well. All the peanut butter and honey, cheese, applesauce, and cookies I could eat. It was great. These kids as well as their leader were really nice! After telling them about my hike and the horrible weather I encountered near Mt Laguna, I set up my sleeping arrangement behind some bushes, using them as a wind block. That night I slept well and with a full belly.

The next morning I got up with everybody; we had breakfast of home-made cooked cereal, which was excellent. It had a good cinnamon apple flavor to it. The scouts couldn't break camp as fast I did because they had more things to take care of, like taking down tents. I told them that I would probably see them at Mill Creek Summit Campground. I soon found a water faucet coming out of a rest station. I filled my containers up to the max. It was getting hot and I wasn't sure where my next water supply would be, so I wanted to make sure that I had plenty of water. A few minutes later the Boy Scouts arrived. We took pictures of each other. They gave me some more applesauce and cheese. Just then one of the fathers of one of the boys drove up in a Ford Bronco. He brought some Gatorade. I love Gatorade. It had been my favorite drink on the trail. It not only quenched thirst, but provided energy and electro-lytes.

I said a final good-bye to my Boy Scout buddies and headed up a dirt road. My pack weighed a ton, laden with pounds of water. Messenger Flats Campground had piped in water early in the season, so I wasn't sure if water would still be available there. I was on a ridge, heading west. I started drinking my water as soon as possible because the weight was killing my shoulders. I think, somewhere around here, gold was discovered back in the 1870s. The mystery of the location of La Padre Mines was never solved. Many miners searched for it, but to no avail.

I was finally in some shade, which was provided by oak trees. The next five miles basically lacked views. It was hot and boring. I wore my head net because the gnats and flies were abundant. Sometimes a thru-hiker has to question his or her self on what the hell they were putting themselves through. This was one of those cases, for me at least. You have good days and bad days. Some days you just don't have it. You must think positively and forge on. Hikers that don't, will fail. And failure was not an option for me. This was a chance of a lifetime, and damn it, I'm going to see it through until I get to Canada.

All of a sudden, there was a noise that sounded like a horse or donkey sneezing or something, just up the trail! This wasn't cool. I stopped moving, waiting for what I hoped to be a horse or donkey coming down the trail. I didn't see anything. Then there was another loud noise that arouse from the silent forest of oaks and sycamores. What the hell was this noise? I waited about five or six minutes before cautiously moving up the trail. I didn't hear anything for awhile. Then it came again, but this time it came a bit below the trail. I kept moving for awhile and then heard the noise again. This time I recognized the sound. It was definitely the sound of a bear. Not a bear that was pissed off, but a bear that was playing or goofing around. I couldn't see a thing because of the heavy shrubbery and assortment of trees well down below, but I pictured a mother bear playing with her cubs. I felt relieved now. I knew I was too far south for it be Big Foot or something like that!

A few hours later I arrived at Messenger Flats Campground, where I found a water cache. I finally had skirted Mt Gleason, a definite landmark telling me that the San Gabriel Mountains were coming to an end. Here at the beautiful Ponderosa Pines, I decided to have lunch.

Things were looking up now. The heat of the day was at its peak and it would start to get cooler soon. I had plenty of water. North Fork Campground, which was about 6 miles away, looked like it was basically downhill. It was now 3:30pm and I decided to head out. My goal for the day was still 6 miles away. I planned to camp at the ranger station grounds which had water and probably a nice flat area to crash on. Down I went, back into the scrub oaks. There was a nice view of Soledad Canyon and what I believed to be the small community of Acton, down below.

The trail was great. Down below I could see the ranger station. I began to get a hot spot developing on my left foot. I couldn't afford to have another problem, especially on my other foot. I took off again. In a few minutes I arrived at the ranger station.

ECSTASY OF MISERY

Here I met a couple of people who I guess worked around the place. They showed me a PCT register, which I signed. One clown came up to me and asked if I was packing a gun. I asked what for. He said because of bears, and if he were me, he would be carrying a 45, that it was my God given right to carry a gun. He then said, "That's the only thing that will stop a grizzly in his tracks."

I tried to tell this jerk that carrying a gun was illegal and too heavy, especially a 45. I also told him that there weren't any grizzly bears in California or even Oregon or Washington. Bears were the least of my problems. Ants, mosquitoes, and gnats were my problem. The guy started to get really belligerent and said that I was crazy. I could tell that this redneck yahoo was drunk as a skunk and I felt like whacking him upside his head with one of my walking poles. Just about then the other guy inside intervened and pulled the clown away.

I really feel that one of the biggest dangers on the trail are gun-toting yahoos, though they are usually found near the roads and highways. The guy seemed to be messed up, who knows what his problem was. He looked about my age, so maybe he might have been in Vietnam or something else had messed him up. But whatever it was, adding alcohol to the problem was like tossing a match on a sage bush during Santa Ana winds.

After eating my dinner that night, I decided to move on. I didn't want to sleep there at a prescribed sandpit area, especially made for thru-hikers. I didn't like the vibes I was getting there. I walked about a half mile down the trail, and ended up crashing there for the night.

The next morning I awoke quite early. The sun was on me and heated up my sleeping bag. I bolted down the trail at about 6:15am, with the anticipation of reaching Agua Dulce today. Soon I was heading down Walter Canyon, a treeless gorge that probably had some water early in the season. Yerba Santa Bears, a blue flower that smells awesome were still in bloom, but they were definitely starting to fade away. Spring was over and the long, hot summer was just beginning.

A couple of hours later, I came to Soledad Canyon Road and the end of the San Gabriel mountain range! While walking along, I heard large footsteps behind me. It was another thru-hiker, trudging down behind me, but coming out of a rock enclave that provided some shade.

It was the dude that I met in Big Bear, named Greg, the guy that described the PCT like 12 hours a day on a treadmill. "Hey man, what's happening?" I said. He replied, "Nothing much, but it's sure getting hot fast." I told him that I was hoping to get to Agua Dulce today and how I heard that there was a cool place to stay there for free. "You mean the trail angels place," he said. I told him yeah, that was the place. Greg proceeded to tell me that he didn't stay at people's places, that he is doing a wilderness walk, and wasn't looking for charity. He went on to say that he kept himself clean as well as his clothes, and he still was averaging 18 miles per day. I told him that was great, man, but that I could use a hot shower and rest a day or two because my right foot is in bad shape.

I started to head over to a trailer park to get some water out of a drinking fountain. Greg said "Hey you don't have to go there, there's a creek down here." I told him the water down there was probably dirty and I wouldn't trust it. "I didn't say to drink it straight," he said. I didn't want to put iodine in it when I didn't have to. "I have a filter and everything," he said. Right away, I could see that this guy had an attitude.

It was cool of him to filter some water for me. So with this water, I made lunch and then headed out. Greg went to another part of the creek, where he kicked back in the shade. He had a pretty good idea by not walking in the heat. I could see that, but I wanted to get to Agua Dulce. It was now about noon and I had about 12 miles to go. After losing the trail a bit, I soon found it behind some railroad tracks. I now began climbing out of Soledad Canyon and wound my way up some barren rolling hills.

Towards the top of this climb, I came to some real interesting rocks. It looked like these huge rocks were poured out of a giant wheelbarrow. They were pinkish orange in color and had large rocks in them providing the mortar. These were amazing rocks and they stood alone. The rest of the terrain was smooth rolling hills, which were barren, except for wild grass, most of which had now turned brown in the early summer heat.

The sun was really pounding down on me. My right foot was killing me.

ECSTASY OF MISERY

I took another Motrin 600 and kept marching on. At one time a bad ass black crow circled my head. I thought this was pretty cool until he dropped a green slab of crow crap on my right shoulder. I yelled at the bastard, hoping he could take a hint and fly off. But he didn't, he just kept fluttering above me, squawking like he ruled the roost or something.

Maybe he thought I was going to die or something, and then he could pick my bones. There were a few times, I swear, he called me names like 'you yellow turkey' 'you turkey'. I started to wonder if I was having a flashback or if the heat was starting to affect my head! I kept drinking water, getting it in my system as well as making my pack lighter.

Finally I came to the top of a hill and down below I saw the Antelope Valley Freeway. According to the topo strip map, I was getting real close to Agua Dulce. A few minutes later, the bad ass crow flew off. I entered a tunnel that went right under the freeway. The tunnel had to be at least 200 yards long. The hole of light on the other end looked quite small. There was water running down the middle of it, so I walked with wide steps to avoid getting my running shoes wet. I soon reached the other end and felt a rather cool breeze blowing into the tunnel. I decided to rest here before going back into the sun.

After resting there for a bit, I heard a noise coming from the other end of the tunnel. I knew it was a hiker because I could hear the sound of his walking poles clanking against the bottom of the metal tunnel. Soon the silhouette appeared in the light. To my surprise it wasn't Greg but Paul, the guy I met with Frog near the Acorn Trail above Wrightwood. I greeted the guy with a friendly hello and told him I was resting here in the shade. He stopped for a minute and then took off, saying that he was on a mission, that he had to get to Agua Dulce. I told him that Agua Dulce was only three or four miles away and that he should take a break. He said, "No, I'm on a mission," and off he went. "Whatever dude," I said as he disappeared behind some rocks. Wow, another friendly guy! Oh well, to each his own.

About five minutes later I left, feeling a bit better. I was soon walking along Escondido Creek. There were a few times the trail took a few tricky turns. It would have been nice if Paul had waited a few more minutes because sometimes two heads are better than one. But the guy was a man on a mission! I walked by some more amazing rock formations. I now entered the Vasquez

Rocks County Park. The park was cool. There were awesome rocks and far out bushes, that had small signs that told you what kind of bushes they were. There also were places to camp at the park. But I was determined to get to town and it was only 2:30pm.

Walking out of the park, I came to Escondido Road, where I made a left and then a right onto Agua Dulce Canyon Road. This road leads right into town and it's the main street of Agua Dulce. As soon as I made that turn, I went by a house where a young guy and older woman were working in the front yard. They asked if I would like a drink of water. Since I was real thirsty, I said "Yes". The young guy handed me a black hose that had a ton of water pressure. I started gulping water like a mad man. I said, "Man, that's good well water and now I know why they call this place sweet water." I then talked to them for a short while about my trip.

When I noticed a pair of walking poles leaning against a fence, I said, "Hey, first class walking poles. Whose are they?" They said they must belong to the hiker who came by here a few minutes before I arrived. "They must be Paul's," I said.

Just about then, a brown jeep pulled up and two guys were inside. They yelled out "Are you a thru-hiker?" I said "Yes" as I walked towards the jeep. Then I heard the driver say, "Is that you, Wrong Way?" I looked at the driver. It was Frog. I asked what he was doing driving this jeep. He told me it was the Saufley's jeep. They told me that they would take me there, and that it was about a mile and a half from there. I decided that I had better take Paul's walking poles that he left when he got a drink of water.

I said good-bye and thanked the people who gave me the water. Off we went, heading back up the road towards the store, me, Frog, and a red-haired guy named Choo Choo. The store was one of those convenience stores, with limited supplies.

Inside I found Paul buying some drinks. "Hey dude, you left your walking poles." He looked shocked. He grabbed them and thanked me. He couldn't believe he had left them. I said, "Well maybe you were a little spaced out by the mission you were on!" He looked at me and I could see that he knew I was letting him know that he was not too friendly at the freeway tunnel.

ECSTASY OF MISERY

Paul ended up buying me a six pack of beer in appreciation for bringing his poles to him. Then off we went to the Saufley's home. "You guys will like this place'" Choo Choo said. They went on to say how Donna does your laundry while you take a hot shower! I said, "I'll do my own laundry, it probably smells pretty bad." Frog said that the rules were that Donna does the laundry. About a mile outside of town we came to this famous trail angels place, Jeff and Donna's home. There was a two bedroom house next to theirs , with a kitchen where most of the hikers hung out. Then in their large yard were an RV and three tents, where other hikers stay if the place got crowded.

I walked into the garage area where I met Donna, also called Saint Donna, by the thru-hikers who came through. She told me that I should go behind a curtain, give her my dirty clothes and to put on these extra clothes she had and then go and take a shower. When I told Donna that I was Wrong Way, she said she knew who I was and prompted me to look on the bulletin board. On the bulletin board was a story about me from the Orange County Register. I was surprised and asked her where she got the article. She said a guy brought it by a few days ago and that they had been expecting me. I asked her if she recalled who the guy was and she replied that she couldn't remember.

The shower felt really great, as trail dirt ran off my skin. I picked a cool bedroom to crash in. There was another room with a TV and a computer. Next to that room was a kitchen with a refrigerator stocked with food.

When I went outside to get some stuff out of my pack, Donna saw me hobbling around and asked if she could take a look at my foot. So I sat down and lifted up my right foot. She said, "Oh my God, that's about as bad a series of blisters I've ever seen." She asked if it was painful and I said that it was, especially when I start walking in the morning. I went on to tell her how after eating I would take Motrin 600, which seemed to knock the edge off of it. Donna said that she had a foot tub and that I better soak my foot in Epsom Salt. If my foot wasn't already infected, Donna said I should still put an antibiotic on my blister and wear clean white socks before I walked around. She also suggested that I should plan on staying there for two or three days.

That evening I checked out Jeff and Donna's Ford Taurus and ended up having dinner with Choo Choo at a great Mexican restaurant. Wow, I was in heaven, Mexican food and plenty of beers. Later on that night, I sat around with Frog, Choo Choo, Paul and a guy named Zeb, who was supposed to have walked 51 miles the day before! This kid, Zeb, was only 19 years old and had already walked the Appalachian Trail the year before, in a real fast time. He was probably about my height, about 5'11" – 6', and looked like he weighed 130 pounds. Not a muscle on the guy.

I asked Zeb where he walked from and he told me from where the road from Wrightwood joins the PCT to here, Agua Dulce. "You did this yesterday?" I asked. He said yes. Then I said, "Well you must have passed me up last night then." Zeb replied that I was probably camping somewhere. I said, "Not really, I was sleeping on the trail, man, just a half mile north of the North Fork Ranger Station". I then went on to say that he would have had to jump over me in the middle of the night! The only thing Zeb said was that he must have, and that it was real dark when he went through there. I dropped the subject. I'm not here to question people, but during my 4500 miles of backpacking and thru-hiking, I've heard a lot of bullshitters.

I was getting really tired, so I decided to hit the hay. Before I did, I prepared the foot tub, poured in some Epsom Salt and soaked my funky foot for about 15 to 20 minutes. It had been a long day and a painful one too. Tomorrow would be a day of rest.

The next morning I slept in until about 9am. I took a shower and ate some odds and ends that hikers had left around the place. A little later, I found out that Choo Choo had left early that morning. The problem there was that he owed me some money for the Mexican meal I had bought for him the night before. Oh well, perhaps he forgot. I know I wouldn't have forgotten, but that's me. A few hours later I used the Ford Taurus and had lunch at a coffee shop about four miles away. It was excellent.

The rest of the day I just kicked back and watched a little TV. There was a movie of the PCT called "Somewhere Along the Way" about two kids who walked the trail back in the late 80s or early 90s. They left with 60 pound packs on their backs. Before they knew it, they were walking in snow up to their butts in the San Jacinto Mountains, without ice axes! At the end of the journey they saluted the trail with a prayer and Kool-Aid. Too much!

That day a couple of people came in. A dude named "No Way Ray" was about my age. He was going to walk a section of the trail from the Antelope Valley Road, near Nenac School, to Mt Whitney. We got along pretty good. We ended up going to the Mexican restaurant. After dinner he asked me if I would do a favor for him. He thought since I was taking one more layover day, that I could drive his truck back from Antelope Valley Road, back to Jeff and Donna's place. I told him, "No problem, man."

After dinner we walked outside and to my surprise, there was Scooter and Toes. Who knows how they got there. But it was nice to see them again. They had already eaten, so I drove them and No Way back to the Saufley's. That night I watched Frog and Zeb tear little pieces of material off their packs. They were getting ready to take off the next morning.

The next morning I awoke at 6:30am and by 7am, No Way Ray and I were off. We took the Antelope Freeway to Lancaster and then went West on Highway 138, until the highway ended, where I dropped No Way off. I'm glad I decided to check the rear view mirror before I took off. I could see the dude frantically waving his hands. He even threw his Mylar coated umbrella up into the air. I stopped his Chevy truck, managed to get it into reverse and backed up to where No Way was. He said "Thanks for seeing me, Wrong Way. I left my camera." I guess checking the rear view mirror just in case No Way wanted to get my attention paid off.

I said good-bye again and drove back to the Saufley's and gave the car keys to Donna. I told her mission accomplished and how Wrong Way took No Way to nowhere! Donna wanted to know if I could drive the Ford Taurus to a garage about seven or eight miles away. The car needed the emergency brake repaired. She would pick me up afterwards in her new car and drive me back. I told her that I would be more than happy to do so.

That night, Toes fixed an awesome pasta dinner, out of the scraps of food left from the kitchen. This kid from Victoria, Canada, who is legally blind, sure could cook. He also could sing and play a fine guitar. I think he might have been a pretty good hiker, but his girl, Scooter, wasn't into it at all. I thought this might be the end of the line for them or at least it would probably be the last time I would see them. They were going to be picked up by some-body and were going to Disneyland in a couple of days.

Journey Six: Agua Dulce to Walker Pass

The next morning, June 4th, Frog and Zeb left and headed towards the Sierra Palomas. I was feeling very anxious to go. This would be my second full day, but I knew my foot would be so much better with another day's rest. I signed the register that day and read all the stuff other hikers wrote.

I was starting to get familiar with the names in the register. There was Huff & Puff, who always had a giant cartoon of himself, and Free Radical, one of my favorite names. There was Lug Nut, Batteries Included, Belcher, Wahoo and Lou, Elkman and the Herd, Billy Goat and Apple Pie. Also there was Prune Picker, Tea Tree, Special Agent, Luna, T-Bone, Bandanna, Northerner, Mercury Hatchet, Shutter Bug, and Cliff Hanger. These were some of the trail names of hikers walking the PCT.

One person listed at the beginning of the register was my hiking hero, Scott Williamson. His trail name once was "Let It Be". But since another hiker named Naomi had it first, Scott stopped using it. I had met this dude twice, first when I walked Oregon, then again in 2000 when I walked Washington. By age 29, he had already walked the ATP twice, the CDT twice, and the PCT some six or seven times.

Scott's goal was to yo-yo the PCT, to do the trail in one direction and then come back in the other direction, all in one season. He almost had it in the bag once. Scott had hiked all the way to Canada from Mexico and then back to Lake Edison. In Vermillion Valley, he fell in love with a waitress and stayed there about a week with her. While there, it had snowed like hell and Scott gave up and ended up going to Seattle with the waitress, without telling anybody.

There were trail angels waiting for Scott in Big Bear, but of course he never showed up. They worried that he might have perished in the snow. They were about to send out a search party. He finally called the Saufleys and I believe Saint Donna alerted the PCT Association. Many members and trail angels, like Meadow Ed, were very upset about this and I did not blame them.

Scott was still my hero. I hope he will be the first to yo-yo the PCT. It all depends on doing it in the right year. With the ever improving trail and LED burning flashlights that strap on the head like miners wear, young people walk at night like Zeb does. That's for the gifted few, however. In a way, it's quite stupid. How much do you really see or experience? I believe that towns and other small communities as well as places like the Saufley's are an integral part of walking the PCT. If Scott doesn't yo-yo the trail, somebody else will.

Today would be my last day at the Saufley's. I would be hiking tomorrow, no matter what. I was now five days behind my tentative schedule. My right foot still felt like I was walking on a cloud of mud, but with less pain. I had been soaking it every day and trying to stay off of it.

Later that day, one hiker arrived whose name was Jim, a tall guy about 40 years old. He had left Mexico on May 11th and was making good time. That evening, Donna took a picture of us, knowing that we would be heading out early the next day. I had dinner for the last time at the Mexican restaurant, trying to carb out as much as possible. I went to bed early that night and the next morning I headed out with my walking poles clanging against the asphalt.

The first five miles or so I walked on asphalt roads before I got to the trail. I was glad to have reached the trail, for a couple of reasons. One, I believe it's easier on my right foot and two, I finally felt that I had left Agua Dulce.

I was now entering the Sierra Palomas, which is desert-type mountains without trees, just chaparral. It was somewhat hot, but not too bad. The temperature was hanging around 85 degrees. At about 1pm I arrived at Bear Springs, where I had lunch and filled up my water reserves. An hour later I crossed Bouquet Canyon Road and began climbing higher into the Sierra Palomas. I was glad Bear Springs had water, though it looked suspicious so I made sure to cure it with iodine solution. Going to the Springs prevented me from having to go down to Bouquet Reservoir, which would have been a four mile trip.

That night, I managed to get as far as Green Valley Ranger Station in San Francisquito Canyon Road. I was able to get some water out of a tap here. I wasn't supposed to. There was a sign there that said that the water wasn't for hikers. It was also a hassle to turn it on.

A few minutes later and to my surprise, I found a water cache. There was a note near one of the five gallon plastic water bottles which read, "From Casa de Luna, please call this number if you need a ride to Green Valley and Casa de Luna." Casa de Luna in Spanish means "house of the moon". I had heard from the Saufleys that the Andersons were really cool trail angels, similar to Jeff and Donna. There was no way I could afford any more time off now. So, that night I slept behind a picnic table, near the water cache. I would have slept on the table but it exposed me to the road below. I wasn't sure that I was even supposed to be camping here at all.

The next morning I got up about my usual time and proceeded to climb out of San Francisquito Canyon back into the sun drenched Sierra Palomas, leaving Green Valley Ranger Station down below. At about noon I got to Elizabeth Lake Canyon Road. A right turn here and a two mile walk would take me to Lake Hughes.

In the old days, the trail went to Lake Hughes where one could get water and maybe some good food, but not any more. I've heard that there had been some problems with hikers and the locals here. This might be one of the reasons the PCT was relocated again. The rest of the day was really quite monotonous, with the sun pounding down on me and nothing but the same old flowerless chaparral.

Towards evening I was able to get water at Upper Shaker Campground, which was about a quarter of a mile off the trail. It was about 6pm, with a few hours of light left in the day. Because of the cool evening, I decided to hike on. I climbed out of the campground and headed back north on the PCT. I decided that I was going to walk until it was almost dark. A few hours later, and just past Saw Mill Campground turn off trail, I found a relatively soft flat place that looked down towards Antelope Valley.

I cooked my dinner here amongst the scrub oaks and was about to wash my pot when another hiker came down the trail. I yelled out, "Hey dude, it's getting really dark. If you want to crash here there is plenty of room." Then I heard, "Wrong Way, is that you?" I answered yes and then realized it was "Be There Now". "Man, you're walking late," I said. Be There Now said that he does that sometimes because it's cooler. He decided to take me up on my offer to stay there.

I asked Be There Now how he got his peculiar trail name. He told me he got it from Elk Man and his herd. Who in the hell is Elk Man? Be There Now went on to say that Elk Man was the leader of a group of people that he was a part of at one time and had given him the name.

I thought this sounded weird and asked if he is like a king or something and the herd is his flock? Be There Now said sort of, but it wasn't too cool to be traveling with them. Too many accidents happen a lot. One guy, Strider, drinks too much and they get lost a lot because they smoke weed. I agreed that would get you lost all right. You need all you're faculties when you're hiking around in these ungodly desert mountains

Be There Now said if I thought that Elk Man and the Herd were weird, that I should have met the Chaos twins. I found out that they were brothers that loved to dig holes, anywhere they could; they even dug a ditch in Wrightwood for $8 an hour. They both couldn't hike because they had iodine poisoning from curing their water too much. They had to see a doctor in Wrightwood and the doctor told them that they shouldn't hike for five days, not until the iodine extricated itself from their bodies.

I wondered how in the hell you get iodine poisoning? Be There Now said that maybe because they were super skinny dudes, probably about 5'11" or so and weighing about 125 pounds. Maybe they loved the stuff so much that they drank it in mass quantities. Be There Now went on to say that they both had reddish orange hair, so maybe it was the color that they liked. I laughed. Be There Now said that could be possible and went on to say that when he was walking the desert hills just north of Scissors Crossing, he rounded a corner and low and behold, they were sitting on a rock. They had a big joint and both guys had a bright orange bottle of iodine water. Maybe it tastes like orange juice. Be There Now chuckled. Oh my God man, that is really weird.

The next morning I got up a bit later than usual because the damn black ants kept crawling in my bag all night. I still got up earlier than Be There Now. But bad news! When I went to dig my morning hole I had the runs. Bummer! I didn't worry about it too much. I thought it would be temporary.

Several minutes later I headed down the trail. Be There Now was just starting to get up. Before long the trail switched to the sunny side of the ridge. The sun began to pound down. It was abnormally hot for just being 9am.

Suddenly I started having cramps and they didn't feel normal. I got my pack off as fast as I could and barely got my white butt out of my pants when I squirted all over the ground. This was bad news. About every 200 yards I had to go to the bathroom. I felt like hell and really weak. Be There Now passed me by. I told him I was sick. He asked me if I had any medicine. I told him that I had Imodium D but didn't want to use it right away because I wanted to be completely flushed out first.

Be There Now left and was off to the races while I was making constant pit stops. After about the tenth time of having to go to the bathroom, I started taking Imodium D. It was now time to try and stop it. I was afraid that I would get dehydrated.

I was trying to find some shade and finally found some under a rather tall bush by the trail. I didn't notice at first, but I sat near a red ant hole. Soon I felt a horrible burn right in the back, between my shoulders. There were red ants all over me. I quickly brushed them off, but it was too late for my back.

Now I was really miserable. I was weak from the pit stops. I was also lightheaded. The ant bite was really painful. My right foot hurt. My shoes kept getting filled with small rocks and it was 100 degrees! There was absolutely no shade either. My water supply was getting low. I knew that in a few miles I would be at Bear Springs Campground where there was supposed to be water.

I felt like I was going to die. I was so weak it was unreal. I wanted to rest but since there wasn't any shade, it didn't make any sense because all you would do is bake in the 100 degree sun. Finally I came to the top of the ridge and arrived at a dirt road, thank God. I looked across the road and was thrilled to see a four foot jack pine right above the trail. Shade, shade, shade at last!

I crossed the road and walked down the trail about 20 feet and sure enough there was shade that covered the trail. Quickly I took my pack off and took out my ground mat and laid it down as quickly as I could. I took out my water bottle and reached into the top of my pack and took a couple of the Imodium Ds and drank about a quart of water with them. I felt a little better.

ECSTASY OF MISERY

The pain between my shoulders was still intense, so I decided to take a couple of Motrin. Man, I never thought that an ant bite could feel this bad for so long.

After resting for about five minutes, I heard the sound of dirt bikes on the road above. I didn't think much of it. It was Sunday and I guess a few dirt bike riders were taking a pleasure ride. They were tearing up and down the road, kicking dust all about the place. Whatever blows their dresses up – I guess to each his own.

A couple of minutes later I heard them mumbling about something and then suddenly they were racing down the trail. As sick as I was, I rolled out of the way just in time to avoid being run over. The first clown screamed by, followed by two other assholes just missing my precious water bottle.

I couldn't believe it. I said to myself that maybe it was time to go home. I do believe I've had enough! I was sick, probably with giardiasis, a blister on my foot the size of a golf ball and a painful stinking ant bite between my shoulder blades, and now I nearly got run over by three motor bikes! To hell with the Pacific Crest Trail and the wilderness experience.

I laid back down on the trail disgusted with life in general. A few minutes later I heard a vehicle go by on the road above me. The vehicle turned around and came back and parked. Now what?

A man and a woman got out of the car and headed down the trail. They said hello and asked how it was going. I told them about my wonderful day. The lady thought that was terrible and asked if I had been drinking water. I told her yes, I had some water, but I had run out and now I was going to fill up my tanks at Bear Springs. They didn't think that I should get water there because it was smelly mud, cluttered with beer bottles and other garbage. Damn it, that's all I need. They told me not to worry because they have plenty of water, and then the man went back to the car and brought back two quarts of bottled water. "Oh thank you so much" I said. He said that he was glad to do it, after the day that I've had.

Then the two nice people headed down the trail on their short day hike. They had restored my faith in mankind. This was a lucky break. I started guzzling water and then had to get up and go to the bathroom again. This time I brought out my secret weapon, Flagyl, an all purpose drug that fought off giardiasis, dysentery, and any protozoa that had lodged itself in my gut. For this stuff you need a prescription and I was lucky enough to get one from the doctor who took care of my skin cancer that was on my back.

It was getting late now. I thought about staying the night near Pine Canyon Road, but after a Top Ramen dinner and a couple of Power Bars, I decided to move on for at least another hour or so. The cool air and the fact that the medicine was working gave me a bit of a lift.

So off I marched heading towards Jack Fair's place, which is now owned by Richard Skaggs, who became an automatic trail angel when he bought this place. In fact, I saw this place when I took No Way to No Where.

If Richard Skagg's place didn't work out, I could hitchhike to Lancaster and get a cheap hotel room until I recovered. After having giardiasis many times when I was in the Peace Corps in India back in the early 70's and once in 1978, I know you must rest and take Flagyl. Once you start taking the medicine you become weak and lose your appetite. I needed to take some days off now, but I really couldn't afford it. What a dilemma. That night I camped near a place just off the road, called Three Points.

The next morning I got up quickly, nature was calling me in an accelerated way. I barely got out of the sleeping bag. Immediately I took another stop-up pill, as well as another Flagyl. I choked down a Power Bar and drank the rest of my horrible iodine water. Off I went, down the trail feeling really weak and the medicines were making me feel lightheaded.

About an hour later I arrived at Richard Skagg's house. There was a Canadian and an American flag that waved in the breeze. In the front yard, baking in the sun, was a Rolls Royce and a red Ferrari. I opened the gate and walked by a couple of horses and a chicken pen. Along the side of the chicken pen was a small western town, which was a miniature movie set.

Before I reached the front door a guy of about 60 with a slightly bald head opened the door. He asked if I was a Pacific Crest hiker. I said, "Yes, and a pretty sick one too!" I told him I had dysentery. He looked sympathetic. "Why don't you go to the bunk house and lay down. Have you had breakfast?" I told him that I hadn't but didn't really feel like eating. "Wow you must be sick. Most hikers that come in are half starved." He asked me if I needed a doctor and I said, no, that I was taking Flagyl which takes care of Giardia. I guess he started feeling a little sorry for me because he told me to come in, that he had an empty room near the bathroom. It didn't have a bed, but that the rug was soft. "That would be cool."

I went in the room and crashed on the floor for at least three hours before washing up and taking another Flagyl. I felt a little better for the rest of the day. I even painted Richard's white picket fence that surrounds his front yard.

At about 2pm, Richard and I drove to a hamburger place down Lancaster Road. I bought the guy lunch, which seemed to impress him. He told me about his trip out here in the desert. The guy was sick of L.A. and the Hollywood scene and came out here where he bought some 50 acres and Jack Fair's place. He was going to fix it up and give it to his daughter someday. Richard's home was in Pacific Palisades, near the ocean.

After lunch the dude asked me if I wanted to go to the Home Depot in Lancaster. He wanted to pick up some building materials that his workers needed. I told him I would give it a try and off we went. I had popped some stop-up medicine an hour before. So I had some confidence about not going in my pants, at least for a few hours.

On the way to Home Depot, Richard started telling me more about himself. He wondered if I had watched the movie "Gone in Sixty Seconds". I said I thought I might have. He produced it; it cost him $250,000 and ended up grossing $240 million. "Not too shabby man," I said. He went on to say that he was semi-retired, which is why he was there in the desert fixing up this house. He would do most of his consulting over the phone. He's basically a lawyer for producers, directors, and some stars. A lot were very famous and what he said about some of them wasn't too flattering.

I was amazed. This guy was one smart guy and very energetic too. I told him that he looked pretty good for his age. Richard told me his success was simply to stay away from drugs and alcohol. So many talented people are destroyed by these two things. When one of his favorite producers and directors died suddenly, well, that did it for him.

At the Home Depot we picked up some bags of cement and other stuff.

As we walked through the store, everybody knew him. He would have a joke or something funny to tell everyone. We loaded the supplies in his truck and drove back to his place. On the way back he told me he knew about Jack Fair, who was another character.

That night, after soaking my right foot in some Epsom Salt and a special herb Richard tossed in that was recommended by a Chinese herbal doctor, I crashed in the empty room. I knew I needed at least one or two days off for the Flagyl to start to work. My foot was starting to get better and with a couple of days rest it would be 100%.

The following day was June 7th, a day of rest. Most of that day I painted Richard's picket fence. I didn't mind at all. It was a pretty nice day, not very hot. In fact it was kind of overcast. Painting gave me something to do. It was restful and sort of felt like I was earning my keep. Richard would walk around talking on his cell phone, rapping to some Hollywood dudes. There's a lot of money wrapped up in movie productions. If there's a delay on something, millions of dollars could land in someone else's pocket.

Later that day Richard and I went back to the Home Depot to get some building materials. On the way back from Lancaster, Richard and I thought of doing a documentary of the trail. I told him I would give him a call when I finished the trail, or I would still call if I didn't make it. We had a lot of laughs on the way back, but whether Skaggs was serious about the documentary I don't know. I really doubt it. He was Hollywood and he was a lawyer, a very difficult animal to read. That evening we had steak and beer for dinner, just me and Richard and his two workers. There weren't any other hikers around now and I felt that there was probably no one in back of me, which was a pretty funky feeling.

The next morning I got up at 6am and headed out. I had said my good-byes the night before and now it was time to punt. Soon I was walking by Nemac School. I reached the California Aqueduct and made a right turn. My feet felt really great, but my head still didn't feel right. That morning my bowel movement still wasn't quite normal. I had about eight pounds of water and food for two days, so my pack was a little heavy, but my legs were well rested. A mile later I made a left turn at the L.A. Aqueduct and headed straight north on perfectly flat ground for another four miles.

ECSTASY OF MISERY

The historic L.A. Aqueduct was just a pipe that ran along the road. It used to be easier to get water along the aqueduct. There were holes that you could put your cup to and even a couple of drinking fountains. But now they were cemented over, maybe because of the scare of terrorism.

The rest of the day I walked continuously. I stopped and had a half hour lunch break. I made sure I had plenty of water. I took my Flagyl and Imodium D. I was lucky that it wasn't very hot, maybe 75 degrees. This helped tremendously. I walked until 8pm that night and finally reached Cottonwood Springs and some water. After tanking up on water, I made camp about 100 yards away on a flat area.

That night I made my favorite, Beef Stroganoff. Later that night I took another Flagyl. I did really well that day. The cool weather and rested legs helped a lot. The stars that night were great, bright and beautiful. I did worry a little bit about the Green Mojave Rattlesnake that I heard was somewhat aggressive. Richard Skaggs and his two workers really threw the bull at me about this snake. They told me the snake would actually chase hikers down the trail! Looking at my facial expression, they got a kick out of it. "Yeah, real funny guys."

The next morning I arose early. I ate some sweet rolls that I had bought in a Lancaster bakery and popped some medicine and off I went. My legs felt weaker today, especially when I started to climb up into the Tehachapi and Mojave Hills. At Cameron Overpass, I made a left and started walking to the town of Tehachapi. This was my next re-supply station. I chose Tehachapi over Mojave simply because Mojave was my stop back in 1978, so I thought I would try another town. Both of these towns were about 10 miles from Cameron Corner. I started walking down the road, hitchhiking as I walked, but no luck. Soon I arrived at a Travelodge that had a restaurant and bar. I went to the restaurant first and had a great tuna-melt sandwich and a chocolate malt. I also had a small salad and French bread with butter too.

After dinner I thought I'd wash it down with a cold one, so I went to the bar and had a Bud or two. Here I got lucky and started talking to a guy about my trip. He and a couple of other people who were listening to my story were amazed. I mentioned that my next supply pickup was Tehachapi. A dude named Jack offered me a ride. He worked in Mojave but lived in Tehachapi. He ended up dropping me off on the other side of town, where I was able to grab a cheap hotel room for only $37 per night.

The next morning I slept in until about 9am. Hey, this is a long overlay; a day to rest my whole insides while I was taking that damn Flagyl. However I didn't spend all of my time resting. I found out where the post office, laundromat, and stores were, spread out all over the place. The post office was about a mile away, which I didn't mind; there was a great greasy spoon to go to. I eventually finished all of my chores and started to get ready for tomorrow's sojourn. That night I had an excellent Chef's salad at a fancy hotel up the street. I fell off to sleep at about 11pm.

The next morning I got up about 6am and went down to the Tehachapi Café where I ordered a breakfast of steak and eggs, hash browns, and a side order of buckwheat pancakes with some coffee and orange juice. I waddled back to the motel and at about 7:30 I headed out of town and headed back to Cameron Pass. I wasn't having any luck hitchhiking as I walked along the highway. I had walked about four miles before I got a ride by a trail angel named Bill. He would supply the water caches that were located at Tehachapi Pass. I thanked him so much. He saved me from a dreary six miles of walking on the road back to the PCT.

At Cameron Corners I filled my water bottles up, giving me one gallon of water. The next water was a long 16 miles at Golden Oak Springs Campground. It was now about 9:30am and getting hotter by the minute. I knew I had to get to Golden Oaks Springs that day or it would be a dry evening somewhere and a thirsty one too. The trail traveled along the road for a few miles and then cut north, switching its way up the side of the canyon. Then it leveled out a bit, heading north. It eventually joined a dirt road, which the trail traveled on for at least four or five miles before becoming a trail again.

Right after leaving the road behind, the trail went around a small saddle and suddenly a large bobcat sprang across the trail. I could tell it was a bobcat by it's short tail. What an athlete this cat was. It must have leaped 40 feet through the air, heading downhill. I wondered how the cat could land without hurting itself with the sharp rocks around the place. It was a thing of beauty, a natural athlete on four feet.

ECSTASY OF MISERY

There were some excellent views as I walked along these rolling Tehachapi Mountains. I could see Olancha Peak and what I believed to be Mount Jenkins. Yeah man, the High Sierras were getting closer. It was a sign that the Southern California desert mountains would soon become just an unpleasant memory. I was walking at a pretty good pace. I noticed my right foot was feeling great. It had finally healed. I was also pleased with my morning movement. It was normal after five days of diarrhea.

I had lunch at a shady flat area under an oak tree. I powered down some trail mix, sweet rolls, a couple Power Bars and a quart of water. I had only a pint left, but I knew Golden Oak Springs was not far away. After rounding the side of Cache Peak, some 6700 feet in elevation, I started going downhill and I soon arrived at a cement tub with water pouring out of a galvanized pipe. I had made it to Golden Springs.

The water tasted great, no need to cure it. I started tanking up because according to the guidebook, the next water was at Robins Bird Springs, about 18.3 miles away. I walked another three hours until about 8pm that night. I camped along the trail that had become a dirt road again. I made a turkey tetrazzini dinner and mixed up some butterscotch pudding. I fell asleep under the stars but not before I took my last Flagyl. I was finally over my Giardia problem.

I got a good early start the next morning; by 7am I was heading down the trail. I still had a heavy load of water. The trail was basically treeless, but so far it wasn't too hot. My problem now seemed to be my right shoulder. It aches most of the time, but it hurt more when I was carrying a lot of water. Pain was part of the backpacking experience. No one walks without irritations. Even the younger guys have their problems.

I moved at a reasonable pace. I kept drinking water so my pack would get lighter. I soon came to a forested area with plenty of shade and took a lunch break here. While looking at the map I noticed Jaw Bone Canyon which I remembered well from my hike in 1978. I also remembered Butterbret Canyon. I was walking well above these canyons now. In 1978 I must have walked a little further to the east and at a lower elevation.

The rest of the day I walked along sometimes in shade and sometimes where there wasn't any shade at all. Towards the end of the day I came to Robins Bird Springs and amazingly enough, there were a pair of red breasted birds chirping on a rock. They had to be robins. I guess that's how the springs got their name, ha. I filled up my water container and decided to have an early dinner. I might as well; that way I could get good use out of the springs.

After dinner and for the rest of the day, hiking was great. There were a lot of rolling hills and an elevation of four to five thousand feet. Wild flowers were all over the place. Pinion Pines were at the lower elevation.

I was feeling great. I think one reason that I was feeling so good was because I didn't have that Flagyl gnawing at my stomach. My appetite was coming back. I was also getting in better shape all the time, probably caused by my shrinking body fat. When I left Campo, I weighed about 220 pounds and at 5'10 ½ ', that was too much weight. In six weeks of hiking, I think that I was under 180 pounds.

At 7pm that night I decided to camp. It was a good day for me; I believe I walked well over 20 miles. Most of all however, I was in good spirits. At least, for now.

I think today I will be out of the Tehachapis and at the start of the Piute Mountains. There were some nice trees for a while. Then the trail started dropping. The PCT wound around on St John's Ridge and crossed St John's Mine. I crossed Kelso Road and went slightly around Mayan Peak. The trail then rolled north across the high desert, coming to a series of mines. There was the Donny Boy Mine, the Sunset Mine, and the Sandy Mine.

The gold mines were mainly closed caves. They weren't anything to get excited about. A few hours later, I found a huge Joshua tree that provided enough shade while I had some lunch. I was really hungry and since finishing the Flagyl, the hunger pains were more acute and more often.

I cooked a hot lunch in the heat. I had Shepherd's Pie with extra mashed potatoes mixed in for more carbs. I also had a Power Bar and a melted Snickers bar. I washed all of this down with a quart of water. I was now down to a half gallon of water.

I began to climb slowly up to a place called Wyle's Knob. There's a radio tower on top of the knob. It seemed a bit strange to have a radio tower like that, way out here, in no-man's land. The PCT traveled around the knob a little bit as it hugged a ridge. Then the trail descended down to Bird Springs Pass.

Here, to my surprise was the Paradise Hotel, which was just a large water cache with an ice chest that had ice in it! I couldn't believe it. There was a cold Gatorade, water, and even some Michelob beer. There was a plastic flamingo under a chemise bush. The place had a little register book, too. And reading a little, I found that the cache was put there by the Andersons of Green Valley.

The beer was great. I put down a couple when two hikers approached. I began rapping to them and found out they were Sweep and Clover. They were hoping to reach Canada. The guy, Sweep, was a medical doctor of internal medicine. He had either been in school or in practice for most of his life. He broke away from the medical group he worked with. Right now he was going on a super adventure. His wife or girlfriend didn't seem to say much and I sort of wondered if she was really into the trip.

They decided to camp near the cache. I decided to move on. I felt I could still walk for about another hour and a half before it got dark. So, I said goodnight to these young people who were from the east coast.

Before I scrambled off, I grabbed another beer, one for the road. I put the brew in the back of my pack and jammed up the trail. Those two beers went right to my head, and it didn't help that I had a rather empty stomach.

I tackled the trail with a smile and began to climb up and up. I kept a good steady pace, finally reaching the top of the hill. It was getting dark now. I was lucky to find a flat area just off the trail. I crashed under the stars. I really did quite well that day. Having covered well over 20 miles. That night I cooked some chili-mac and washed it down with lukewarm Michelob. Can't get much better than that.

Ants bothered me a bit that night but in general, I had a good nights sleep. I slept in a little the next day. I didn't get rolling until almost 8:30am. After walking for an hour, another hiker passed me by. His name was Solace and he was walking all the way to Canada. The guy sure looked like he could make it. He didn't have any body fat at all. He was six feet tall and weighed about 130 pounds. He had a small pack that didn't have a hip belt. I figured this guy was doing 30 miles per day and I was pretty much right. I talked to him for a while and then he took off ahead of me. I tried to keep up, but it was uncomfortable, so I let him go. Damn those 20-year-olds, they have those elastic muscles.

I kept up my pace and by looking at the map it looked like I had been hiking in the Scodie Mountains. The Piute Mountains and the Scodies are wilderness areas, land that will never be developed, which is a very long time.

A few hours later, Sweep and Clover passed me by. They were in a hurry to get down to Walker's Pass. They had some friends that were going to take them to Lake Isabella. I walked along with them on a dirt road that was used as the PCT. It was hard to keep up with them. They were going at a good three miles per hour pace. At McIver Cabin Trail junction we parted ways. I needed water and they didn't, so they headed down hill dropping into the Walker Pass area.

I headed down the McIver Cabin Trail and after about a quarter of a mile, I arrived at a well kept up cabin. There was a spring nearby and a pipe with water pouring out of it. I filled up my plastic water bottles. I had lunch on a picnic table that was just outside the cabin. There was a PCT register which I quickly signed, then left. A short time later I reached the PCT and started descending down into the valley below to Highway 176 and Walker Pass Campground.

As I dropped in elevation the day became hotter. I was glad that I got water at McIver's Cabin, that was a good call. The trees started to get smaller. There were Pinion Pines and then fewer trees and chaparral as I reached the campground. There was piped in water, bathrooms, and picnic tables. One campsite had about six to eight people.

After drinking some water and refilling one water bottle, a guy at the table called out to me, "Hey are you a thru-hiker?" I said that I was. The guy said, "Far out, so are we." I headed over to the table and introduced myself as Wrong Way. "Wrong Way, right on," the guy said. He was Strider and one of the other guys said that he was Elk Man and the herd. I mentioned Be There Now to them and they asked where he was now. I told them that I didn't know, that the last time I saw him was at Richard Skagg's place and he must be just ahead of us.

I asked them if they had started at the border. "Yeah, we left Campo on April 24th," said Elk Man. Then Strider added that they have been in pain ever since. "This heat has been killing us," said Elk Man. I told them that there wasn't much real hot stuff left because we'll be getting into the High Sierras soon and life will change.

I told them I was going into Onyx for a visit to the store, that I was a little short on food. Elk Man showed me a hiker's box they found. There was some food in it, but not much that interested me. We talked for a while. Elk Man was pretty funny when he had people around him. They were leaving today, but I guess they were waiting for the day's heat to withdraw. There were some heavyset girls there. They put their packs on and were going back into the Scodies. These girls were way over weight and had to cruise along in vehicles here and there.

One of the girls got me a ride and before I knew it I was at the Onyx store. I went for some ice cream right off the bat. A couple of Hostess fruit pies, that was really good too. The prices were high; I was startled at the total price. The people there didn't look too friendly either.

Back on Highway 178, I started hitchhiking back to Walker Pass Campground. I didn't have any luck whatsoever. It was incredibly hot out there standing beside the road. So I went back to the store and bought another Gatorade and took a break. I went back to the highway again and tried to hitch a ride, but my luck wasn't any better.

I was bummed out about this revolting development. I then heard a voice yelling out that there was a bus going back to Lake Isabella in about 10 minutes. He went on to say that I would be better off hitchhiking in the morning, and that the bus fare was only $5.

I thought about what the guy said, but I still tried to get a ride, right up to the arrival of the bus. I jumped on the bus, not sure that I was doing the right thing. Too late now, the bus pulled out, heading westward to Lake Isabella. I started talking to the driver and asked where the closest motel was that was reasonably priced. He said there was a place in East Lake Isabella.

The driver dropped me off at the motel and told me the bus leaves in the morning about 6:30am or so. I checked into the motel. The cost was 50 bones per night. Not too bad. The room was excellent. It had a nice shower and kitchen area and a big color TV. The motel owner gave me some laundry soap and I washed my clothes in the kitchen sink and then hung them up near the windows in the kitchen and bathroom. That way they would dry fast because of the warm desert wind that was blowing in.

After my wardrobe and my body were immaculate, I headed for the café, down the road a piece. Most everything was closed up, even the store. But not the 1950s style café. They had pictures of Elvis Presley, James Dean and Marilyn Monroe. Oldies but goodies were being played on one of those old juke boxes. It was "Do the Locomotion With Me" that was playing. "Chuga chuga motion If you got the notion." Anyway, I sat down at a booth by the window. I ordered a Chef's salad with a cherry coke and French fries on the side, with a whole lot of salt and ketchup, just for the carbs, man!

There were some bizarre people in the café. One guy, who looked older than me, looked like a spaced out beatnik. Then there was, I think, a mother and daughter talking about a car the daughter wanted. There was a normal looking couple and myself, "Joe Thru-hiker", waiting for mass amounts of calories to enter his half starved system.

The salad was awesome. It was nice and big, with turkey, cheese, egg, ham, lined up with your usual array of vegetables and plenty of thousand island dressing. I asked for more dressing, and offered to pay extra for the dressing. She said that she would be glad to give me more dressing and not to worry about it, and she proceeded to put down the plastic bottle of dressing. "Righteous, thanks!"

I gave the waitress a nice tip and waddled about a quarter of a mile to my hotel room. That night I watched some reality TV. That's about as real as walking the PCT. Walking the trail is kind of surreal. That might make a cool reality show. They could follow a dude like me or a couple, walking the PCT, and their crazy five month sojourn of the Pacific Crest Trail. What an idea. I could make millions of dollars with an idea like this. I should patent my thought!

The next morning I slept in longer than I wanted. It was about 8am when I finally got up. Man, that soft bed felt so good. I felt like I could lie there all day. I had a couple of muffins and coffee, which was the hotel's complimentary breakfast. By 9am I was on the road hitchhiking. Now I was ready to rock and roll.

After about 45 minutes trying to hitch a ride, a small truck stopped and picked me up. The older man was a semi-retired handyman. He was a funny guy, who liked to talk more than he liked to listen. He was especially cool when I told him I was walking the full length of the PCT. The old boy took me all the way to Walker Pass, even though it was a bit out of his way. I started out where I had left off, at the campground. I followed the trail a quarter of a mile and then crossed Highway 178 to a monument at Walker Pass. I looked to the south and for a minute, joyfully said good-bye to Southern California. It was now June 17th and I would finally be climbing into the High Sierras.

My Wrightwood Power Bear I carved in 1995

Agua Dulce, Home of the Saufleys

The Saufleys Home

Vasquez Rocks near Aqua Dulce

Walker Pass Monument, The start of the Sierras

Journey Seven: Goodbye Desert and Welcome to the Mighty High Sierras

At last I could say good-bye to the desert and those punishing desert mountains. It was sure easier in 1978. For one reason I was only 31 years old and when I got here I was in great shape, no body fat. I was also fortunate to just have missed the last heat wave of the season. Finally, the trail was easier and more direct. It was also flatter and seemed to lead you to places that had water, like Lake Hughes and other little enclaves of civilization. The only advantage I have now was a lighter pack and better footwear.

I looked to the north and the Sierra foothills as a new beginning. I was a week behind schedule, but maybe that would help a little bit, giving the snow ahead of me more time to melt. I was off walking at a good pace now. The celebration between my ego and super-ego was definitely over, as I felt the pain of an ascending trail.

A few hours later, after climbing nearly 2000 feet, I traversed around Jenkins Peak. This peak was named after Bill Jenkins, who was co-author of the Pacific Crest Trail Guide. The guy was one hell of a hiker and explorer for his time. A ridge stood out on the other side of a huge ravine. The rocks were grayish looking granite. It was the look of the High Sierras, although premature, it welcomed me. I was definitely in the Sierras at last.

I sat down here and had a bite to eat. I then made a phone call to Chuck Hinkle, my main sponsor. He wasn't home. I left a message that I had just entered the Sierras and that at last Southern California was done.

I took off walking, chugging down the trail, looking at the scenery. My next stop would be Joshua Tree Springs. This was a very important stop since I needed water. About 2pm I saw a small wooden sign that said "Joshua Tree Springs ¼ mile".

Below the sign, written on a piece of paper, read "Bear at Joshua Tree

Springs" and it probably would be best not to camp there. There was another note that said "Enter at your own risk!" Oh, man, the second note was the one that bothered me. I needed water. I was completely out. I wasn't sure where the next water source was.

I decided to go light. So I took my pack off and walked down the Joshua Springs Trail with just my water bottles. I didn't take my walking poles. The trail was pretty steep and led to a large gully, with sycamores growing all around. Then suddenly there was a large rustling noise and a grubby looking bear stood up and then quickly moved off into the brush. He was brownish blonde in color and looked like he weighed about 200 pounds. He didn't seem to be groomed well or really kept up. I just kept walking, glad that the bear seemed scared of me.

The Springs had water dripping out of a pipe into a horse trough. It took quite a while and all the time I was thinking, what if that bear was smart enough to circle around and make its way back to my pack? Of course that was taking into consideration that the bear would have noticed that my pack was off my back.

I stood there watching the slow running water dribble down in my water bottle. I contemplated this would be a drag. Anxiously, I waited for my last bottle to be filled. Where's the bear?

Finally the last bottle was filled and off I flew, jumping over an old deserted sleeping bag lying in the dirt. Did the bear scare somebody so bad that they ran off without their sleeping bag? I jammed back up the trail, climbing with eight pounds of water as fast as I could. I was huffing and puffing when I got back to the trail. Quickly I looked in back of a bush where I left my pack and it was still there. Man, was I relieved! If that bear had graduated from the University of Yosemite at Tuolumne Meadows, my food would have been gone!

I headed down the trail glad that I had enough water for dinner. Now I could walk as long as I wanted, which I did, until about 9pm that night. I camped right on the trail, not too far from a slow running creek. Even after getting a late start, I believe I had walked 20 miles that day. .

It had been a good day, leaving Southern California and its deserts and climbing right into the Sierras. Weldon to Belden is what they used to call the length of the Sierras, when the trail ran through the little town of Weldon. Four hundred miles of High Sierras was in front of me. Very few water problems would arise now. Now, however, snow, mosquitoes, rivers, and altitude could be problems. Oh, and don't forget the bears. But say good-bye to the rattle-snakes, at least for a while.

The next morning I got a pretty good start, hiking by 7am. Today was June 19th. I was behind schedule. I was hoping to have left Kennedy Meadows by the 15th, but I was still two days away. As the morning wore on, I was start-ing to get deeper into the Sierras. Getting water wasn't a problem. Most of the small streams were running. About noon time I arrived at the south fork of the Kern River. Here I stopped to have lunch. There were a couple of dirt roads heading off to the east and the south. After a good lunch I headed out again, past Fox Mill Spring. I had to get water here. Man, it was so cold and sweet!

I was now entering Dome Land Wilderness, named appropriately for huge domes. The trees were beautiful as I walked along at an elevation about five to six thousand feet. There were quite a few things to look at that day. There was Chimney Peak, Saw Tooth Ridge, Lamons Point. The scenery was now changing fast. That night I made it to Rock Basin where there was a flat area to camp, with plenty of water. As I lay in the sack that night I realized that I hadn't seen anybody in almost three days. Tomorrow would be a hard half day and then Kennedy Meadows and the Kennedy Meadows store and post of-fice. In 1978, I don't remember a store being there, just a large vacant campground. Things do change. Most likely, I will run into more thru-hikers.

The next morning, June 20th, I hiked along a pretty flat trail that rolled through Rockhorse Basin. The roaring sound of the Kern River could be heard intermittently from the trail as it rolled along about a quarter of a mile from the trail. The trail was lined with quite a few flowers, the white funnel-like flowers most abundant.

The trail soon joined up with the Kern River again, and ran right beside it. A few miles further, I came to the Kennedy Meadows area. I saw some buildings off to the right. The PCT trail guide said to keep on course until you reach a paved highway and turn right. The road will lead you right to the store and post office area. So I followed directions, for once, and I arrived at the Kennedy Meadows store at about 1pm.

ECSTASY OF MISERY

There were people all about the place and many looked like thru-hikers. The thru-hiker look was not hard to recognize. Then sitting on a picnic table was Elk Man, Strider, and the rest of the herd. "Hello dudes." "Hey it's Wrong Way, isn't that your name?" asked Strider. "You got it dude." I talked to them and found out that they had arrived at Kennedy Meadows that morning, at least those who walked, Elk Man said, as he looked at a few of the heavy girls that I guess were part of the herd.

Elk Man told me that the post office was inside the store and that I could take a shower for two bucks. He told me that it was sort of an outdoor shower, but it had plenty of hot water. I sat around with them for a while, then went and got my supply box. I threw out my old stuff and put my new food in its place. I then took a great shower. Afterward I bought some beers, in fact a couple of six-packs, some cheese dip and chips.

The herd and I sat around and I indulged myself for a while. Elk Man really enjoyed the cheese dip. He told me that the campsite was about two miles away, but that Strider's girlfriend was going to pick him up in a while and that I could have a ride to the campsite.

We sat around and ate a variety of chips, dips, and melted cheese dip, along with cold beer, ice cream, and candy.

A few hours later we were off in Strider's girlfriend's car heading down the road to Kennedy Meadows campground. We pulled up to the outer part of the campground and grabbed our packs and headed over to a picnic table. Standing beside the table was a pretty old guy, about my age. "Hey", he said. "So you're Wrong Way?" He then went on to say that he had heard a lot about me from Tony DeBillis, also from John and Millie. "That's right dude we walked Washington together." This guy was called Meadow Ed. Meadow Ed went around trying to get familiar with everybody.

There were quite a few hikers around. There was Solace, Bobka, Be There Now, a big girl named Stitches, Ray, Elk Man and the herd. They were really simple names to remember, real normal too. Meadow Ed said to get the fire going that we were going to have Chicken Fettuccini. About two hours later we were eating a great-tasting meal. Meadow Ed must have been a chef at one time.

After dinner and cleaning up, people were rapping to each other. I believe I was telling Bobka how my trip through Southern California was hell. I told him all the things that had happened to me, like Giardia, huge blisters on my right foot, 60 mph winds for three days straight, ruining two pairs of glasses, and then no supply package waiting for me at Idyllwild, and no water at Guffy Campground. But hey man, it's been some adventure. By 10 or 11pm, most everyone was in their sleeping bags. A lot of the people had tents. As for myself, I slept away from the campsite because of the ants. The next day would be a day of rest.

In the morning we had pancakes, bacon, and eggs. I needed plenty of carbs to keep my strength up. I was losing weight pretty fast. I left home weighing about 220 and according to the scale in the store, I was now 185 pounds.

After breakfast a lot of people headed to the Store. Elk Man and the herd came to a huge decision to go somewhere along the coast and camp out, while Strider's girlfriend took care of some business in San Jose. Then later they were going to hike some of Oregon. It sounded crazy to me. I think they'd had enough of the PCT. Elk Man had a numb foot and wasn't one of the strongest of hikers, having taken more than a week longer than me to get to Kennedy Meadows, even with all the layover days I had. They needed a few bucks for gas, so I gave them $10.

The rest of the day I just kicked back with Meadow Ed, who ended up being a real jack-ass. I had all kinds of stories about what the trail was like in 1978, but he just kept reading his book and listening to the Doors over and over. I think the big problem was that he wanted everyone's undivided attention when he tried to explain to hikers about the trail, such as for instance, Lake Edison.

Meadow Ed was wrong about the trail to the VMR Resort, so I corrected him. He didn't like that. I tried to be funny after that. "Hey dude," I said, "my girlfriend and I saw a ball of lightning at this lake", and pointed to the lake. "Really?" a few people asked. I told them that a huge ball of light went right across Mott Lake. It looked like a lot of sparklers tied together that had the sound of popping sparks. Meadow Ed looked pissed and said "Oh yeah, I suppose you think they're going to see this." I told him to go to the lake and wait and see, you never know. People started laughing a bit. But Meadow Ed was definitely irritated.

I believe it was my clowning around and the ball of lightning story that made Meadow Ed a really angry boy! Too damn bad. I'm not just out here to walk the PCT like some zombie. I'm also here to have some fun and if Meadow Ed can't handle it, then tough toe nails!

The next morning I got up real early. I was tired of the place and all the people, including Meadow Ed. I got up at 5:30 and by 6am I was walking, heading north once again. For the next three days I would be climbing into the High Sierras where the PCT would join the John Muir Trail. It then traverses one of the most beautiful landscapes in the world. The hiking now was easy. My legs were rested and even though I had a lot of food, I didn't need to carry more than a quart of water. Soon I traveled through Clover Meadow, after crossing the Kern River twice. I don't remember there being any bridges in 1978, but now there were two.

A few hours later, I came to the southern side of Monache Meadow. This meadow was the largest in the Sierras. I was kind of surprised that the PCT now seemed to skirt around the meadow. I think in 1978 I walked almost through the middle of it, but I might be wrong. Things can really look different when you walk in the opposite direction.

I was getting a little low on water when I reached the gauging station at the Kern. I stopped here at what was a newly constructed bridge. There were a couple of guys there, Solace and Mark that I had briefly met at Kennedy Meadows. They had left the evening before. I was surprised that they were not further along. Their excuse was that their packs were too heavy. Mark, the skinnier of the two, said he was eating more often making his pack lighter by the hour. Well, I guess that makes sense. So I sat down and made my pack lighter too.

Small birds were flying all about the bridge, where they had made small mud nests under the bridge. The mud nests must be really strong, because little baby Swallows could be seen popping out of the holes. "Is that too much, man?" Mark said. "Yeah that's too much all right." "I think it's safe to say that you better get your water upstream. It looks like too much stuff is falling out of the peep holes, or should I say poop holes!"

About an hour later I headed out. For a while I was walking in a perfectly flat meadow. I had left Solace and Mark who were still lying in the shade, trying to digest the food in their swollen stomachs. Both of these skinny dudes were faster hikers than me, but when you put a heavy pack on a skinny dude, well, it can have a profound effect on just how fast he can boogie. I figured they would be passing me up soon. They were probably right about eating to make your pack lighter. They both probably were only 2% body fat. A thru-hiker must do what's right for his/herself, because they are the only one who knows how their body feels under this kind of every day stress.

Back on the trail, I started slowly climbing out of Cow Canyon and entered South Sierra Wilderness. I now joined the Olancha Pass Trail. Soon the forest was gone. I was walking on a sandy trail once again. Not having any shade didn't bother me because the weather was fantastic. It was probably about 78 degrees with clean, clear, fresh air. God it felt great to be in the Sierras. Red flowers as well as some yellow and white flowers adorned the mighty PCT. I wished my girl, Linda, also known as Trail Perfect, could be here right now. I believe she would be inspired to the max.

About three hours later, I entered Golden Trout Wilderness. I was wasted. The last three hours I had climbed some 3000 feet. Trail Perfect wouldn't have been inspired by this stretch of trail. I was now at an altitude of over 10,000 feet.

Just after reaching the summit, I met a guy named Milo, who I had met at Kennedy Meadows. I sat down on a log near the trail rapping to this young guy for a while. We had to put on warmer clothes because the change of the temperature was extraordinary. Three hours earlier the temperature was about 75 degrees, but up here it was 52 degrees and dropping fast.

Soon Mark and Solace arrived. We all decided to head out, but each man was a different entity. Each man could camp where he wanted. Mark would have to go the longest distance since he was almost out of water. He may have to walk into the night until he reaches Gomez Meadow, which was probably six or seven miles away. Milo decided to camp right there, just off the trail. Solace headed out first, followed by Mark and then myself.

ECSTASY OF MISERY

The trail now began to head downhill and that was really nice. This was definitely the highest point that I had been so far, since leaving Campo at the Mexican border. I was surprised that the altitude had little effect on me, maybe because after 740 miles I was pretty much in shape.

That night, I walked well into the evening. I finally made camp at around 9pm. I was by myself; this was a pretty big day. I believe I had hiked at least 27 miles, as well as did a lot of climbing at the end. The reason why I did so well was not because of a light pack because I still had a lot of food. But I'd got a really early start and my legs were rested. This was one of the keys to thru-hiking success: a lot of hours on the trail and being completely dedicated to covering as many miles as one could.

The next morning my start was not as early as it should have been. I didn't get started until 7:30am. I was tired. I could have slept a couple of more hours at least. Down the trail I went. I was heading for fresh water at Gomez Meadow, which was only a mile or so away. My legs felt tired today and my right shoulder ached already. But it looked like another beautiful day. How could I get depressed? I arrived at Gomez Meadow and found one guy there. I saw him at Kennedy Meadows. I remember the dude's huge beard. "What's happening? How's it going dude?" The guy looked at me rather strange and finally mumbled. "All right, I guess."

The guy was definitely hard to talk to. I asked if he was going all the way to Canada and he said that he was.   He sounded rather despondent. He went on to say that he didn't start in Mexico and that he decided he didn't need to walk Southern California this time. He supposedly walked the trail back in 2001 and was doing it again, but without doing Southern California. I told him that I didn't blame him, how I had a hell of a time.

After telling me his name was Dan, he wanted to know mine. I told him Wrong Way. Dan looked at me in disbelief and said that wasn't a very smart name. I told him everyone can't be smart. Dan thought trail names were stupid. I said to him that maybe he was right but mentioned how I've had my trail name since the '70s, probably before he was born. I also said that I hadn't heard of another Wrong Way yet. Dan went on to say, yeah, because it's stupid and wondered why I would want to call myself Wrong Way. I tried to explain to him that it was sort of self-explanatory for a person who usually does things the wrong way.

While he was talking, I gathered up my water and started to head out with this strange dude following me. A short time later we arrive at Death Canyon. I remember this place well from my 1978 walk. It seems to always have water. The Canyon was green and lush with flowers and other forms of life.

Just past Death Canyon Creek, it becomes arid again. The soil becomes sandy, yet the altitude increases. Here I decided to have my usual late breakfast. Dan, the strange man in a strange land, headed out. I told him to have a safe trip and how I'll see him in the funny papers. He didn't like that too much, as he gave kind of a quick scowl and headed out. I took my time, letting the guy get his distance from me, then I left.

This area was one of my favorite parts of the Sierras. First, you really start to get higher in the Sierras and stay high too. The trail began to traverse the eastern edge of the Sierras. A hiker can look both east and west. Looking west you can see all the way across the Sierras. If it's a clear enough day, one can even see the Los Padres range of mountains near the Pacific coast. It's possible that on certain days in the past, one could see the Pacific Ocean, which is only about 200 miles away, as the crow flies.

If one looks to the east, he can see the desert below, Owens Valley to the north and the Mojave to the south. The White Mountains can sometimes be seen if you have the right angle. They of course are to the north and they are big dry-ass mountains. I don't know where you could get water there. That's probably why no one hikes there. Altitude measurements were taken of White Mountain and a very surprising development took place. White Mountain was about the same elevation as Mt Whitney, some 14,500 feet or so! Later, more accurate measurements were taken and Mt Whitney was found to be only about a foot or two higher than White Mountain. The White Mountains also border California and Nevada. They are just inside California.

I consider myself lucky to be a daydreamer. By getting into your own head, thinking about high school football days or college parties and distant girlfriends, these memories can make the time fly by. The bad part about it is you can fly right by the wrong trail junction. That's how I got my trail name "Wrong Way".

ECSTASY OF MISERY

Rounding a corner, there was Stitches, lying on a giant slab of white granite. She was fast asleep. Not a bad idea. A noon day snooze can do wonders for your spirits, especially if you didn't get a good night of sleep the night before. I would do this every so often. Even a cat nap of 15 or 20 minutes could make you feel refreshed. I said nothing so as not to wake her and traveled on starting now to look for water. I finally found it just off the trail about a third of a mile at Dutch Meadow Springs. The water was really cold and sweet tasting. I took about 15 minutes off, drank my fill, then filled up a quart bottle to go.

I got back to the PCT and began to climb. Once again I was looking for the summit of Mulkey Pass. About an hour later I was at the top. On top of Mulkey Pass, I really felt that I had now entered the High Sierras. What I mean by that is there are the Sierras and then there are the High Sierras! Mulkey Pass is the entrance to the High Sierras.

Leaving Mulkey Pass, the trail descends slightly. The hiking was pretty mellow. My right shoulder really bothered me. I couldn't understand why sometimes my right hand would go numb. I then would have to shake it. I wondered if it was my pack or my walking poles. Whatever the cause was, it wasn't a good feeling!

The temperature was now falling rapidly as I began climbing my way up to Cottonwood Pass. I remember in Agua Dulce, at the Saufley's house, that Scott Williamson had hiked all the way here before he had to quit because of heavy snows on this pass, which cancelled his 2003 opportunity to yo yo the PCT! There was virtually no snow now. Just a couple of patches in very shaded places.

It was getting late now as I got close to the top of the pass. Then in a rather flat place were four tents. The first one I noticed was Stitches, who must have passed me when I got water at Dutch Meadow. The other tents belonged to Milo, Mark and Dan, the strange man. To me this wasn't the best place to camp. It was too high. I felt like going on and trying to get to a lower elevation but friends are friends so I decided to stay.

On this night I decided to put up my tarp, because there was a constant 20 mile per hour wind and it was getting colder. I didn't have much time to socialize. After setting up my tarp, I put stakes in and then applied rocks to hold the tarp down better.

I had to get water, which was a quarter of a mile away. While making dinner I noticed that my food supply was getting low. I had been eating like a pig lately. I was hungry all the time. Looking ahead on my trail guide maps, I realized I was about a day short on food. I asked Stitches and Milo about it. They said I could probably make it to Kearsarge Pass, but that I would be one hungry sucker. I might have to pass up Forester Pass, which would take a ton of energy. "If I were you, I would head out at Trail Pass and hitch down to Lone Pine," said Stitches.

Oh man, I was not counting on this. My next supply box was at Independence, not Lone Pine! I guess I'll have to sleep on this and make my decision tomorrow morning. Stitches and strange man Dan both told me the Trail Pass was easy to get out of and also into the Sierras. This was a big surprise to me because I thought the only way out of here was Whitney Pass and that would be tough.

It wasn't 1978 any more when you hardly needed a pass and definitely not 1966 when Mike Stephany, myself, and a few other guys hiked up Whitney Pass. Backpacking in those days was in its infancy and Pacific Crest Trail wasn't even heard of. The big goal then was to hike to the John Muir Trail that ran from the top of Mt Whitney to Yosemite Valley, a distance of around 250 miles.

These things I kept thinking about as the temperatures kept dropping and dropping. I began to get real cold, so I put on my extra pair of pants and slipped my sleeping bag back into my bivy bag, Thank God I had the bivy bag sent to Kennedy Meadows,. My sleeping bag was only rated at 35 degrees when it was new and needed all the help it could get, and a bivy bag added 10 degrees or so to its warmth.

Soon I was putting on my spare smelly long sleeved shirt and everything else that I could and still I was cold. In the middle of the night, I woke up and had to do isometrics and ate my last candy bars to keep warm. It was now 17 degrees above zero. Thank goodness that wind finally died down and I got some sleep.

I didn't get going until about 8:30. I was the last person to rise. At least

ECSTASY OF MISERY

I didn't suffer too much getting up. Why get up so early anyway. From what I hear, that Trail Pass is only a short distance and the road and campsite were only three or four miles away. Supposedly the road connects with Whitney Portal Road. It then heads down the valley a few miles to Lone Pine.

So I headed down the trail towards the trail junction. There was only a quarter of a mile climbing and then all down hill. Before I knew it, I came to the trail junction. Without hesitation I took the Trail Pass trail and headed towards the campsite and road area. Here I had to get a ride to Lone Pine or it would be a super long road walk in the sun! I didn't have any doubts about going to Lone Pine, after last night. Because I ate my candy bars and some power bars, that keeps up your metabolism and keeps you a little warmer. I was now lower on food.

Just about an hour and a half later, I arrived at the campsite. I walked through the campsite and found the road on the other side. There were few people at the campsite. I believe it was Friday and more people would probably be coming today. But what about cars leaving. That might be a problem.

I began looking for Stitches. I was wondering if she got a ride. I asked one guy if he had seen a big girl walking through the campground or hitchhiking. He said he hadn't. There was a water spigot nearby. I took a long drink and then washed my face and arm pits, then applied some deodorant. I knew I probably smelled pretty bad. My last shower was at Kennedy Meadows Store.

After cleaning up, I asked a couple and their two young teenage kids if they had a seen a girl about 6 feet tall walking through the campground. But what I was really doing was hinting around that I needed a ride.

If you tell people in a manner where you don't sound like you're boasting that you're hiking from Mexico to Canada, they'll take an interest and sure enough they did. The man said, "Right after breakfast we are going down to Lone Pine to pick up some supplies we forgot to get for our hike to Guitar Lake. If you want, you can ride with us." I told him that would be great, and thanked him. These people were cool. They were both high school teachers. Their two boys and friend were quite talkative and amusing. I told them about my trip, the ups and downs, but how it's been a great adventure so far.

They shared a few pancakes with me, as I munched down on a Power

Bar. Soon we were ready to go. They told the boys to hang around the campsite and that they would be back in an hour or two. We drove off down to Owens Valley. About a half mile away there was Stitches, sitting by the road hoping to get a ride. I said "Oh there's that girl I was asking about. Is it possible to give her a ride?" Sure, they said and asked what her name was. I told them Stitches. The cool school teacher picked her up and off we went, descending into the valley below.

What a ride. The road was steep with a lot of curves. Loose rocks lay on the side of the road. This road probably needs constant attention due to erosion from the rain and wind. Not to mention snow. We really had a beautiful view of Owens Valley, the Alabama Mountains and the Eastern Ridge of the fantastic High Sierras.

About 20 miles later we arrived at Whitney Portal Road. We turned left and headed east right to Lone Pine. The people dropped us off, then Stitches started calling cheap motels to stay. I began noticing strange bearded dudes coming from the motel type place across the street. Then to my amazement, I spotted Scooter and Toes! Well, the search for a place was over, at least for me. This was probably the best place to stay for the money.

I was right. Forty bucks a night to stay in the hotel part, and sixty bucks for the motel, per night. I grabbed a room for forty dollars, so did Stitches. I was hoping that another thru-hiker would come in and I could share a room, because the room had two single beds. You had to share the bathrooms. There were two for the girls and two for the guys.

The first thing I did was to take a hot shower. I wore my Patagonia long sleeve shirt in the shower, scrubbing it as I scrubbed myself. These things dry so quickly, so I would have something to wear that wasn't dirty and smelly. After the shower, I went back to my room, and hung up my wet shirt in the sun drenched window. I turned on the TV and got my head back into civilization.

Soon my shirt was dry. I put on my running pants because they were black and didn't show dirt, and headed over to the Mt Whitney restaurant. I had the Giant Mt Whitney Cheeseburger, a salad, chocolate malt, and a ton of fires. I have to watch my diet! After that I waddled back to my room with a couple of brews, drank one, and fell asleep.

ECSTASY OF MISERY

About two hours later there was a knock at my door. I got up, like a walking zombie, and opened the door. Lo and behold it was Be There Now. "Young Stud, what's happening?" I asked. Be There Now said he needed a place to crash, and the lady downstairs said that maybe I would share my room. I told him sure, and would be 20 bucks a night. He said that would be great. I said I would be staying two nights and if he wanted to stay we could split the room tomorrow. He said that would be cool.

Be There Now would save me 20 bucks a night. He was a pretty cool young guy. That evening, I ate at a good Mexican-American restaurant. Later that evening I met Scooter and Toes walking down the street. We ended up going to McDonald's then and an ice cream place. They told me that Disneyland was a lot of fun. I didn't ask them how they got here. I know damn well they didn't hike it. I really felt that this would be the end of the line for these young Canadians. It would be too difficult to hitchhike up Highway 395 and try to enter the Sierras from any of these small places. They were all too far from the PCT. Most hikers wouldn't even be in these small towns.

Tomorrow Scooter and Toes were going to hitchhike up to Trail Pass and try it again. I told them that it was very cold the night before and how the temperature went down to 17 degrees. They said they had warm gear. I figured they would, being from Canada.

The rest of the evening I sat around in the lobby, watching TV and talking to the other hikers. Most of them had permits to hike Whitney. One guy there was "Molasses". I said "Oh your mom gave me a ride in Idyllwild to the Tahquitz Inn. She told me about the walk you were doing from the Cabazon area to the top of Mt Whitney." I told Molasses that his mom was cool and when he sees her, to tell her Wrong Way says hi. He said he would, and that it was nice to meet me.

That night I fell asleep watching the tube in my room. Be There Now came in from partying with Wheeze and Bobka, guys of his generation, and he turned the TV off. Around 4:30am I heard the horrible noise of Harley Davidsons below my window. People were talking in really loud voices. When they took off, they gunned their engines, as to let everyone in town know that they were leaving. It was like they were saying "Hey, hear us, look at us, we're leaving now. Have a nice day!"

That morning I slept in to about 9am. Why not get as much rest as you can. Be There Now slept until 11am. I couldn't believe it. After breakfast I went shopping for something warmer. I found a few things at the local sporting goods store, but the price was too high. I saw Bobka in the lounge area and he told me that they had a hikers box at the post office and he had seen a long sleeved flannel shirt someone didn't want.

I told him thanks and walked down there. I asked for the hikers box and sure enough, there was an old flannel, a bit torn, but still wearable. There were also some wool mittens. I grabbed both the mittens and the flannel. I believed I would be warm enough until I got to Independence, which was where Trail Perfect had sent all my stuff. I heard that the 17 degree temperature I had encountered was kind of a fluke. So the rest of the day I rested and ate a lot of good food and junk food too.

Scooter and Toes took off. They were going to hitchhike to Trail Pass, where I guess they were going to walk the Sierras a little. About three hours later they were back. They had gotten a ride to Trail Pass, and when they found out how cold the Sierra nights were, they turned around and hitched all the way back to Lone Pine!

Nobody could believe it but me. I was glad they decided to come back. They might have gotten injured and have to be rescued. Their hiking ability was not applicable to the Sierras. Once out there, it's a long way back to a road where they could hitchhike out, which is what I said to Bobka when we were sitting in the lounge and he said "They're Canadians, they should be use to the cold."

That evening was basically like the previous night. My pack was ready for tomorrows excursion. Sitting around in the lounge you hear about all the different characters on the trail. One of the most interesting is Ronnie of Israel , the guy who walked back and forth from Mt Laguna to Anza and back again with his buddy Florida Bob.

This guy walked the ATP the year before and got caught in a terrible snow storm. He managed to find one of the many shelters along the trail route, and was snow bound for about ten days. While he was snow bound it became real cold, so the guy insulated the cabin with his favorite food, Honey Buns!

ECSTASY OF MISERY

Ronnie loves Honey Buns, eats them all the time, and has been known to sleep on top of them for extra insulation and comfort from the hard earth. Every supply box he receives Honey Buns. He even manages to stop along the way and goes into stores to buy Honey Buns. Which is what he did when he left the trail and found a Raley's Supermarket that are located in Northern and Central California. The supermarket must have been well off the trail.

At Raley's Supermarket, Ronnie discovered a giant display of Honey Buns on sale. His buddy, I believe it was Florida Bob, wondered what he was doing. He reminded him that his pack was full of Honey Buns that he had received in his supply box earlier that day. Ronnie said something like that it's a beautiful sight to see all of those Honey Buns and how he would be dreaming of them for many miles.

It was characters like Ronnie that can really lighten the trail up for almost everyone. As far as I know, Ronnie was doing well and he was about nine or ten days ahead of me. I had a couple beers with the boys in the lounge and headed for bed. Tomorrow I would be back in the saddle again!

The next morning I got up pretty early. I had breakfast at the Mt Whitney restaurant. I had five eggs, three pancakes, hash browns, toast, orange juice, and coffee. They've always called that type of breakfast a Lumberjack or Wranglers breakfast. Why not call it a thru-hikers breakfast? Most thru-hikers are hearty eaters, especially because they burn up a lot of calories in a day from walking up and down hills. A male hiker who weighs 170 pounds can burn off more than 6000 calories a day.

After breakfast I was back on the road, trying to hitch a ride to Trail Pass. My first ride came about 40 minutes later from some people who were from Nevada.

The second ride came about an hour later from two campers going to Trail Pass Campsite. They were actually mountain bikers. The two guys were going to ride their bikes from Trail Pass to Lone Pine, while the girlfriend of one of the guys drove the van. That should be one hell of a ride, I thought. At 10am I arrived at Trail Pass, and then headed back to the PCT at about 11:30. I was at the trail junction and the fantastic Pacific Crest Trail.

It was good to be heading north once again. The hiking was relatively easy compared to the terrain that surrounded me. There were some great views of Mt Langley. A beautiful creek crossed the trail on a beautiful day. Down in Lone Pine it's probably 95 to 100 degrees. Up here it's a clear refreshing 65 degrees.

My legs felt very rested. My pack was somewhat light; there wasn't any need to carry water. I only needed food for about two and a half days. Foxtail Pines were abundant, and small meadow flowers were all over the place, along with butterflies and an occasional red breasted bird. I soon passed Chicken Springs Lake. There wasn't any need to get water or stop to eat. The breakfast I had in Lone Pine was definitely sticking to my ribs.

The trail was almost flat. I started to pick up my pace here. My goal for the rest of the day is to get as close to Forester Pass as possible. This area I believe is called Big Whitney Meadow. I remember it well from my 1978 hike. To my left somewhere is Siberian Pass and Mt Guyot, 12,300 feet in elevation.

I made it to Guyot Creek. The water looks so good and refreshing, so I pause for a drink, and suddenly a huge male deer springs out of some bushes only a few feet away from me. He tears off down the trail a bit and then disappeared behind a small ridge. Wow, you don't often see deer during the middle of the day. What a specimen he was! Shortly after this, I'm walking through Guyot flats, when I saw a red fox dart across the trail. The golden shining on his red fur made him look almost surrealistic.

The hiking remains easy, as I get along at about a three mile per hour pace. An hour later I arrived at Crab Tree Meadows. Now I know that I'm right behind famous Mt Whitney, the highest peak in the continental United States! The trail for Mt Whitney comes up next and now I have joined probably the most beautiful and most famous trail outside of the ATP, the John Muir Trail.

Now, do I want to climb Mt Whitney? No. For the simple reason that I've climbed it four times before. It would also delay me another day. I only had food for a couple days. Easy decision here. I bet up there somewhere above me there were thru-hikers heading to Canada. Most thru-hikers take the trail up there. I don't blame them. It's one hell of a fine view. If you stand on a high rock there, you become the highest person in the continental USA that is still touching Earth's surface.

ECSTASY OF MISERY

It's now 3:30pm and the temperature is starting to drop. I just hope it's not going to be as cold as it was at Cottonwood Pass. At least now I would have a long sleeve flannel shirt and mittens that I was able to dig out of that hikers box.

As I walk along I keep wondering who might be up there on Mt Whitney. Could it be Mark or Milo. Maybe strange man Dan. Maybe somebody in back of me before I took Trail Pass was up there, and spent the night at the Smithsonian hut at 14,495 feet! I hope they have some aspirin, man, for that altitude headache can be rude.

On down the trail I went. It was now 4pm, giving me four more hours to hike. It was important for me to get as close to Forester Pass as possible. Climbing up that sucker was a chore. I was sure there was plenty of snow up there. A couple of hours later I arrived at Wallace Creek, which was a great place to camp. But my goal was Tyndall Creek. If I can make it to Tyndall I would be set up for a midday assault tomorrow on Forester Pass. Checking out the map, it looked like Forester Pass was 5 miles. It was now after 6pm and I was incredibly hungry. Suck it up, man! I had to accomplish this. So, off I went, heading for Big Horn Plateau.

God what a beautiful walk. The sun was going down in the West. The definitions of the incredible Sierras were highlighted by the late afternoon shadows. Unbelievable!

The trail was rough but reasonably flat. While all the time I was cruising at a sustained altitude of about 10,000 feet, I was surprised that I didn't have any altitude sickness or headaches. I think the reason was that I was in great shape, especially for an old man. That night I hiked to about 9pm before I reached my famous creek, Tyndall, a creek that in 1978 I caught 20 golden trout in 15 minutes!

I had come here with my buddy Mike Stephany. Mike's feet got messed up because he had worn his dad's boots, which were a size or two too small for Mike. So I went fishing alone while Mike prepared for dinner. I had a simple rod and reel with a Super Duper Lure. Every time I would cast the Super Duper out into the creek and reeled it back I would nab an 8 to 12 inch golden trout.

Mike was really surprised when I brought back all those fish. He started cleaning them and gutting them and popped them into our mess kit frying pans. Doing this made Mike kind of sick. The smell of fish plus the altitude destroyed his appetite for the golden trout. I ended up eating all 20 of those little guys and man, were they good. Mike could only eat the mashed potatoes and beef jerky. But at least I did the dishes for the poor guy.

These thoughts went through my mind as I walked along, now almost in total darkness. Then I heard the musical sound of a creek with water falling over the rocks. I found a campsite rather quickly. There were a number of them spread along both sides of the creek. I immediately started preparing dinner, and then laid out my ground mat, insulation pad, and finally sleeping bag. I could hear a few people at another campsite a couple hundred feet away. I didn't pay any attention to them. It was too late to socialize, and I was tired. That night I fell asleep under millions of stars that one can see at 11,000 feet in the Sierras.

The next morning I slept a little longer than usual. I needed the extra rest. I wanted my legs to be as rested as possible because this is the day I would cross the Forester Pass, the highest pass on the whole Pacific Crest route. The walk to the pass is what we used to call a moon walk. There was basically nothing but white rocks, and patches of snow.

As I approached the pass, it looked insurmountable. There was plenty of snow. Snow itself is only one obstacle. The consistency of the snow really makes a difference. If it's shady and cold, it becomes like ice, dangerously slippery. If the snow is in the sun areas, it will be softened and one can sink up to the crotch. The hiking becomes exhausting. This is commonly called postholing. The best condition is somewhere in between.

I was approaching the great wall that separates Sequoia and Kings Canyon National Park. As with most of the high passes in the Sierras, the north sides of these passes get more of the snow. The south side gets a little less snow. The south side of the passes usually have more small avalanches than the north side. This is due to the sun softening the snow more quickly than on the north side.

I had to be careful since I didn't have any crampons or ice ax, just my walking poles. I knew, however, that quite a few people had already hiked the pass, which would give me plenty of places to put my light weight running shoes. Boots are better in the snow because you can kick into the snow creating temporary places to step. Crampons work great, but when you have 20 feet of snow and 60 feet of rocks, you have to take the things off and then put them back on. This can be a hassle.

While walking up the pass I put on my scratched sunglasses. It was better looking through scratched lenses than getting snow blindness. I began climbing about 10am. I was lucky the consistency of the snow was just right. I climbed steadily and deliberately trying to keep my breathing at a steady rate. At noon I reached the top. It was actually easier than I thought it would be. It definitely helps to be in shape and have a light pack.

The view up here was great. There were small unnamed lakes that were spread out on the south side and on the north side was Bubb's Creek; the altitude here is 13,180 feet. From here you are surrounded by 14,000 foot peaks, but you felt just as high as they were.

I remember in 1966 Mike found a pair of tennis shoes up here. His poor feet were being tortured by his dad's small boots. This really saved his trip. Walking in tennis shoes in the Sierras, whoever heard of that. I guess he was ahead of his time.

I stayed here for about a half hour looking at the views. I tried to make a call but couldn't get any service. Down below there were a couple of people making their way up at an extraordinarily slow pace. I decided to leave and let them have the pass for themselves. It was now almost 1pm and time to move on.

Down I went, trying to be as careful as possible. I slipped a few times. Once I fell, but I made the most of it and slid on my butt for about 50 feet cutting across two switch backs of nearly covered trails. Finally I see more rocks and less snow. The trail becomes clearer as I walk across a snow patch and rejoin the actual trail. All in all, I was relieved a bit to be down to Bubb's Creek.

It's here at Bubb's Creek that I saw my first High Sierra bear, way back in 1978. I remember in those days that small trout would leap out of the water, especially late in the day. It was 2:30 now and I decided to have lunch. I took out some macaroni and cheese and washed it down with some Bubb's Creek fountain of youth water! I have found it, I am Ponce de Leon. The fountain of youth is not in Florida, but right here at Bubb's Creek. Feeling younger already, I jam down the trail, heading for Vidette Meadow and Bull Frog Lake.

I arrive at the Bull Frog Lake junction at about 4pm. There is no camping here. One probably has to camp at Charlotte Lake or the Kearsarge Lakes. This is a very popular trail junction, as it was when I brought my brother and his buddies here in 1969.

That was a trip I shocked my brother and his friends by taking them to Rae Lake. They wanted to go to some far out place, so I brought them here. We stayed at Charlotte Lake for a day or two. We all popped some good Sandeous Orange, then climbed up to Mt Bago for a short day-hike. They all flipped out in total amazement. Hey, you know that was the sixties. I sure wouldn't do that now. One poor guy was so wasted by altitude sickness he nearly toppled over a cliff. That's not cool.

The rest of the day I hiked until I joined the Kearsarge Pass Trail. Here I had to make a right hand turn and head out over the pass to Onion Valley. Then I would hitchhike to Independence. If I had known about Trail Pass, I would have had Trail Perfect send my supply box to Lone Pine. But like I said before, I thought one would have to come out at Whitney Pass in order to get to Lone Pine. That was a logistic mistake on my part. Walking out at Kearsarge was definitely taking me out of the way. I was so close to Glenn Pass, which was my next major pass. But what to do. I must go to the Independence post office.

Walking on the Kearsarge Pass was like a little freeway of people entering the Sierras. Not until Mark and Milo went by did I finally recognize someone. We talked for a bit. They were hoping to get over Glenn Pass, and I was hoping to get over Kearsarge Pass.

About 7pm I got to Kearsarge Pass, walking with a group of young people who I caught up with. They were in bad shape. They had planned to crash for the night at the top of the pass. I told them it wasn't the best place to camp, but they were exhausted. I gave them the last of my water. I really didn't need any because I knew there were several lakes on the way down to the parking lot. There were a couple of snow patches there that could be melted for water.

After ten minutes I said good-bye to them and then headed down hill on a rocky trail. I was heading towards Onion Valley and the parking lot. I felt it was too late to hitchhike to Independence tonight. I remember there is a store down here, at least there was in the sixties. Here I could eat dinner, and sleep near the parking lot. In the morning I could hitchhike to Independence. For the next several hours I bailed down hill at a good three mile per hour pace. I finally arrived at the parking lot at 8:45pm. To my surprise, however, there was no store, just a parking lot. Thank goodness for that drinking fountain and man was I thirsty.

The next morning I awoke pretty early, maybe too early, because it took me a couple of hours to get a ride. I finally got a ride to Independence. The thought of getting into town meant having a great breakfast, which may have been one reason I woke up so early. Since it was Sunday, the weekend restaurants were open and I had a good breakfast with plenty of pancakes and syrup. I grabbed a motel room for 50 bucks a night. I would have to spend the night here because the post office was closed on Sunday. I took a hot shower and did my laundry in the bathtub. There was a pretty good little convenience store, where I could buy my laundry detergent and junk food. Gatorade was my drink of choice, and Budweiser was a close second.

Independence is a small place even though it is the county seat of Inyo County. In fact, it looked smaller and in worse shape than I had seen it last. Lone Pine and Bishop were the neighboring cities and I believe were doing well, especially Bishop. The author Mary Austin was born here. Like Lone Pine, a number of Hollywood films were shot here, including John Wayne's "The Shootist", which is my favorite John Wayne movie.

Towards the end of the day, while I was watching TV, I heard a knock at the door and lo and behold, it was Be There Now. He said, "Hey, you want to save some money and split the cost of the room?" I told him sure but he would have to crash on the floor since there was only one bed. I told him I'd charge him 20 bucks but I wouldn't charge him for a shower. Be There Now laughed.

That evening I went to the store to buy my dinner. My room had a microwave so I brought some frozen chicken and Mexican food that I could heat up fast. As I left the store a backpacker saw me and must have figured that I was a hiker. He wanted to know if I wanted to buy a bear canister. He would sell it to me for $45; they cost about $65.

This was a Garcia bear canister, the only official canister sanctioned by the National Park Service. There were other canisters that were lighter than a Garcia, but they cost around $150-$200.

I thought about it and pondered over it for a while. A bear canister would make me completely legal. I wouldn't have to worry about bears, ants, or rodents getting into my food. My pack was large enough to carry it. The negative part was that it weighed two and a half pounds. Should I or shouldn't I, that was the question. I finally decided to buy it. The hiker was happy. This would give him enough money for a bus ticket back to Santa Barbara, California, where he lived. Right after I bought the canister I started to get buyers re-morse. Two and a half pounds plus the added weight of warm clothes, I would be getting quite a bit of food, enough to get me to Lake Edison. I was going to have a rather heavy pack. I know that quite a few campsites have bear boxes where you could lock your food up for the night. Oh well. The damage was done. I would be doing my part, I guess.

I strolled back to my room and as I did I met Bobka, who took a bus from Lone Pine to Independence. Be There Now had a ride tomorrow to go to some rodeo or something up north somewhere. I had a feeling these guys, like Elk Man and the herd, were pretty much through with the PCT, at least for this year. I was surprised at the number of people that dropped out after getting to the southern Sierras. This was the most spectacular part of the trail. I think Southern California burned out a lot of people. For me, the thought of fresh sweet water that I didn't have to carry on my back inspired me, a little anyway.

The next morning was Monday so I was at the post office door when it opened at 9am. My box was there, thank God. That's something you always worry about. My down jacket was there as were my long johns and wool mit-tens. After breakfast I went back to the room and spent an hour and a half packing and repacking my pack.

Finally I was finished. My pack was heavy. The heaviest it had ever been since leaving Campo, excluding the time when I had to carry a lot of water. By 10:30am I was finally ready to go. I said good-bye to Be There Now, and Bobka, who were waiting for their ride. I grabbed my walking poles and headed out.

A few minutes later I was hitchhiking on Kearsarge Pass Road, standing under a tree for shade. There were virtually no cars at all going by, just a few locals that turned on their respective side roads going back to their homes, maybe coming back from shopping. I felt like I might be here a while before I would get a ride. Almost immediately, two young guys who were students in Berkeley, California, stopped and gave me a ride all the way to Onion Valley, and the trail parking lot! I was lucky how quickly I got a ride. I could have been there a long time.

About 11am I headed back up the Kearsarge Pass Trail and even though my pack was heavy, I made real good time. The guys from Berkeley left right after I did, but never got close to catching me. It seemed so incredibly different walking up this pass than in 1969, when I came with my brother and his buddies and walked up and down this trail. For one thing, the trail was much closer to the recess lakes. The trail now stayed away from the lakes, probably designed to keep the multitude of hikers from destroying the lakes. I don't believe that any of those lakes permit overnight camping now.

Only two hours after starting I reached the pass, which was close to 12,000 feet. I took a few pictures there and then out of the blue, Sweep and Clover appeared. "Wrong Way, how are you doing?" "Pretty good, dudes, what's up?" I asked. They went on to say they were heading to Independence and how they thought these mountains were beautiful. I then said that they probably didn't have mountains like this on the East Coast and they said, "Well not so high and barren, that's for sure."

Then Sweep mentioned how Solace was just behind them. I said "Cool, I thought that guy would have been well ahead of me." Solace had been traveling with them since Kennedy Meadows. They wanted to know what was in Independence so I told them nothing much but there was a pretty good store and a restaurant that was open about half the time and two or three decent motels. Clover seemed happy to hear that. They didn't ask about the prices. Maybe they didn't ask about the prices of the motels because Sweep is a doctor and they probably have more bucks to spend, unlike most hikers who are younger and on a tight budget.

I said good-bye to them and hoped to see them later. I was surprised to see they had gotten so far. I didn't think that Clover was really into the hike. I've heard that from other people who knew a little bit about them. Sort of like Scooter and Toes, Sweep was held back by Clover. I believed the long-haired doctor would go all the way if it weren't for her. But who knows, maybe he wouldn't even be here if it weren't for Clover. I think somebody said that they were getting married after this.

I headed down the trail and in a short time I met Solace. I said hi to him and told him I would see him probably again when he ever decides to haul ass. After Solace left, something came to me. I don't think he likes hiking alone. It seemed that he was always hiking with someone. That's cool, probably safer too. I guess I'm more of a loner. I sometimes feel my age scares the younger generation off. I'm old enough to be their father! Oh man, how did I get so old so fast? And why did I wait 19 years between these hikes. Man, I could have been a contender!

The trail now becomes an easy ridge walk as I head back to the PCT trail junction. The view is just beautiful and the bird's eye scenery is awesome. It doesn't get better than this.

Along the ridge here, I pause and have lunch. This new albacore tuna in a vacuum-sealed aluminum foil pack is great stuff. With it comes crackers, mayonnaise and chopped sweet pickles. It makes a great lunch. The only drawback about tuna is the smell. I'm sure the local bears can smell this a half mile away.

What I do with smelly food like this and candy wrappers is I wash them out making sure they're clean. Then I spray mosquito repellent on the wrappers and food containers. Deet is very rude to smell, but I figure that it must cut down on food odors.

Another thing I like to do in bear country is cook dinner in one place, then walk a few miles and camp in another area, if possible. Now, however, I carry a two and a half pound bear canister that I still have buyer's remorse over.

This little stream here is really far out. It comes directly from a patch of snow, about a quarter of a mile above me. The pure sweet water runs down over rocks and between bright green grass. The little waterfalls provide a musical tone to the whole affair. A little waterfall makes it easy to fill up your cup and drink that wonderful sweet stuff.

Lunch is over. It's time to boogie on. I pop my relatively heavy pack on and with rested legs I head out into the great wide open. About a mile or so, I join the mighty PCT coming out of Junction Meadows. Me, my pack, and walking poles heading for Glenn Pass. The trail now becomes a steep hill. My pace slows down but I stay steady as she goes, until it starts to switch back in the snow. Bummer. My pace now is less than one mile per hour as I try to negotiate snow piles and rocks. I'm not equipped for the stuff. Running shoes are horrible in the snow. I don't have an ice ax.

Two hours later I reach the top of Glenn Pass, at 11,978 feet high. At the top of the pass, there were two young guys heading out of the Sierras.

The dudes try to show me the way down to Rae Lakes, but it's totally ambiguous. The trail is covered in most places by snow. The oldest of the guys said, "You have to cut switchbacks." "Yes, it took us four hours to get here from Rae Lakes," the younger guy had said. They went on to tell me how they lightened their packs by giving away their army shovel and bear spray canister to a guy down there. They also left food in the metal bear boxes at Rae Lakes.

I told them good luck and how there was some snow that they will have to barge through, but it wasn't too bad. I said to them that they might consider camping at Junction Meadow tonight. It's a little too late to go out at Kearsarge Pass. The older dude said that they were going out at Cedar Grove tomorrow. They had been out there for almost a week and were really burned out. They did catch a lot of golden trout. I wished them good luck again, and to take it easy. We went off our separate ways.

One hour later I was down to Rae Lake. But not before falling seven or eight times. Not before sliding on my ass for over 150 feet and not before cutting my wrist on a sharp rock. My watch helped me from getting cut more, because the wristband took most of the blow. The snow was heavy due to the fact that a lot of areas were in shade most of the time. The snow up stream was just as dangerous because it was hard and old.

At the bottom, I was standing on some green grass and looked up at one of my favorite natural monuments. The Painted Lady of Rae Lakes. I remember my brother John took a picture of this back in 1969. It somehow ended up as the background for a Toyota car commercial. My brother is a professional photographer. He graduated from Los Angeles Art Deco, somewhere in Hollywood. I followed the trail past the first lake. The mosquitoes were getting real bad. I ended up following a footpath on the wrong side of the second lake. It didn't take long to figure out what I had done wrong.

I had walked back to the first lake, and crossed on a narrow piece of land that was in between the first and second lake. The two lakes looked bigger than I've ever seen them before. Probably because of the snow melt and the fact that I have never been here this early in the season.

I ended up camping by the second lake. It was now starting to get colder and darker. There were about seven or eight people there. A few were fishing and a few were preparing dinner. I asked them if it would be alright if I camped there, near them. They said it would be OK. I walked down to get some water out of the lake and discovered a bear box. Well, I guess my bear canister wasn't needed here. Two and a half pounds and $50 for nothing, so far.

That night I cooked my beef stroganoff and I'm glad I tried to use my new blue can of butane mixture because I discovered it didn't work! There weren't any threads on it to screw into my stove. What a bummer.

I would have to go with my Mountain Peak canister. I hope it will last until Lake Edison. It was at least half gone. By discovering this early, at least I could leave it in the camper bear box and not have to carry it all the way for nothing. If my fuel ran out, I could resort to my back up which was Ebbetts Sterno Tabs. I didn't have the right stove for that, but by adding pieces of wood to it, I probably could get it hot enough for cooking my dehydrated and freeze dried foods.

That night I hit the ground about 9pm. I tried to listen to my miniature radio, but got absolutely no reception. It got pretty cold that night, but nothing like the 17 degrees at Mulkey Pass. What helped was that I had plenty of warmer stuff, including that home made down jacket, leftover from the exploits of 1978.

ECSTASY OF MISERY

The next morning I got up about 7am. After putting my useless fuel cartridge and some food that I didn't need into the big bear box, I left about 7:30. Now it was time to begin, my legs were not as rested as yesterday. My shoulder hurt quite a bit. I had a pretty good size cut on my left wrist and a large blister on my right hand, between my thumb and index finger. I believe I got this from goofing around with my walking poles. Getting bored, I flipped them high in the air quite a few times and I guess that's what caused it, but I'm not sure.

The hiking was pretty easy for a while and I made pretty good time. A series of lakes went by. One lake didn't have a name and then there was Dollar Lake. Just past Dollar Lake, I stopped for my usual breakfast. I would mix a quart of powdered milk into my wide mouth polyester bottle which only holds a quart. So I mixed three fourths of a quart because I would also add a packet of Carnation Instant Breakfast and shake the hell out if, making a shake. Today it was chocolate malt. I then chug it down with a power bar, a breakfast bar, and some trail mix. This stuff hits my gut like a canon shot sometimes causing a little pain. But it's fast and sticks to the ribs.

With breakfast accomplished, I headed out again. Today would be a big day. My goal was to get over Pinchot Pass. I had about 15 miles or so before I get to the top of the pass. Then I should go another five miles or so to get down from that 12,130 foot pass to a lower, warmer elevation, such as Kings River.

That would give me a good 20 miles for the day. Anytime I can get 20 miles in this terrain, I'm very happy. Soon I got to the south fork of the Kings River and somehow turned in the wrong direction and headed southeast down a pretty good trail which soon got worse. That gave me a clue that I wasn't on the John Muir-PCT. I lost about an hour. I was angry with myself. I have to keep my eyes on the trail guide and the compass a little bit more.

From here the trail heads north and ascends in elevation, continually following the beautiful and lively King Creek. Water rushed down in many places and then the trail travels above the trees. Moon land is here again.

The pass should not be far off. But I wonder how much snow would be there. I jump over small babbling creeks that are bordered by grassy areas with tiny dwarf pines. The weather started to get a little colder and the air gets a little thinner. Pretty soon I'm looking at the pass.

It wasn't where I thought it would be. It's loaded with snow. So I have to take it slow. Finally I leave the last part of the creek, which is half frozen water. Moving slowly, I start following switchbacks as best as I can.

Then the snow becomes deeper, but there were plenty of postholes to step in. The snow, at this time, was soft from the warmth of the sun. This makes it less dangerous, but a little harder physically to get through. There are a few places that are kind of hairy, but for the most part, the pass is pretty passable. If it was any worse than this, a hiker should have an ice ax and know how to use it. Finally I can see the top or at least I sure hope it's the top. Huffing and puffing, I'm just a few yards from the summit and then the top. Yeah. Pinchot Pass!

The views from these High Sierra passes are really special. On top of moon land one looks down to half frozen lakes, white rocks, and snow. At lower elevations, the meadow starts to be followed by green grass and small pines to larger pines. There are lakes all over the place.

From the top of any pass, it's always a good idea to study your map. Especially when the pass is loaded with snow. One general landmark was Lake Marjorie. The trail went right along its east side, so head for the lake if you can't find the trail. Sure enough, the trail disappeared on me and I cascaded myself downward, heading for Lake Marjorie. Suddenly there was a noise. A loose rock had fallen above.

It was a hiker who had kicked a stone. As the hiker came closer, I could see it was Greg, or as I called him, Mr Natural. "Hey man, glad to see you." Greg said, "I can't stop and talk. I only have food for two days and I have to get to Lake Edison." I told him that maybe I could help him out a bit. But he said for me to keep my food. "I'll make it."

Off Mr Natural went, in search of his wilderness experience. Maybe he ought to try some jeep trail out of Nome, Alaska or something. What a funky dude. What surprises me is how come he's always passing me. He says he doesn't stay at motels, trail angel places or hostels. But he's always coming from behind me. It's weird, especially with all the layover days I've had.

ECSTASY OF MISERY

Down towards Lake Marjorie, I went jumping from rock to rock and wading through snow. Soon I joined the PCT-John Muir trail and Lake Marjorie. I'm back in tree land. Moon land is just another memory. The trail starts switchbacking down and crosses the King River twice. Just past here and right before I get to Upper Basin, I make camp along the river under some trees. There was another hard but beautiful big pass to be conquered and that was Mather Pass.

The next morning I awoke at 6:30. But like a wuss, I didn't get out of my bag until 7:15. I left about 7:45am. The temperature is about 40 degrees this morning. But it really starts to rise quickly as the morning sun finally shines upon you. Suddenly, it's a perfect 65 degrees. Mosquitoes have been a hassle lately. I wear my running pants and long sleeve Patagonia shirt, doused in Deet which really eliminates lot of the problem. I've learned to sleep quite well in my mosquito head net. It also keeps ants and other crawlies from hiking across my face. On bad nights I'll coat my head net and my ears in Deet. That works great, though putting up with the smell can be rather unbearable.

Now I'm heading up the trail on a slow continual climb to Mather Pass. Upper Basin has a ton of water everywhere, including bunches of small lakes and ponds. Now the trail sharply ascends in elevation. It's moon land all the way, as the PCT-John Muir trail switchbacks through the snow, including one tricky looking snow infested hairpin turn. I could see people on top looking down towards me. Will he make it or not, which I imagine is what they're thinking. Careful to take it really slow and not make any needless moves, I arrive at the top. Yea, Mather Pass is done. Another major High Sierra pass is accomplished!

What a view. The sky a sweet blue, snow capped mountains everywhere. Way off down the trail was Upper Palisades Lake. For a while, I talked to the young people who were there. There were about eight guys and a couple of girls. I did most of the talking. They wanted to hear about my trip.

After an hour on the magnificent pass with an elevation of 12,100 feet, I headed down saying goodnight to my laughing buddies. I hope they went on their way, down the south side of Mather Pass, because it wouldn't have been cool to take note of my descent. Several times I fell. At times, the snow was up to my crotch. The snow's consistency was too soft from the relatively warm summer day up here. I slid, I rolled, I crashed and burned. I finally went into a controlled slide on my ass for more than 200 feet. I tried to break with my walking poles, but with no real success, using my feet first. My butt cheeks were totally frozen.

I didn't know where the hell the trail was, just the general direction. I simply headed in that direction, bounding over brownish orange boulders. Finally the ground leveled out a bit and I took a short break, sort of gathering my wits. My feet were pretty cold. The wet snow had given them an ice cold soaking. My knees seemed to be OK, so I headed on. Hiking can really warm up the feet and start the process of drying. Running shoes dry quickly, but in the snow, they really suck!

A few more yards and I found the trail. Slowly, the sharp descent became a gradual descent all the way down to Upper Palisades Lake. The Upper Palisades Lake was moon land with giant thousand foot cliffs around the backside of it. Snow surrounded the pair of lakes that was near the cliffs. There were a couple of small waterfalls that fell off ledges in the lake.

After passing Upper Palisades Lake, I came to Lower Palisades Lake. There were snowy cliffs around the lake, but also green grass was abundant. On a large rock next to the trail, a guy was fishing. As soon as he cast in his line and started reeling it in, he would get a strike. Then a golden red trout would fly out of the beautiful blue water. I sat and watched this guy for a while, as he caught fish after fish. There were fish actually jumping out of the water, trying to snag mosquitoes.

I put down my pack to take a break before heading on. It was about 6pm but I knew I had about two hours of sunlight. That guy kept pulling out fish, so I walked over to where he was fishing. Another guy comes out from behind some giant rocks. His trail name was Snickers and his buddy was Mountain Goat.

Mountain Goat reeled in and said, "Well, that's the limit, 10 trout." I talked to these guys for a while. They were hiking from Cedar Grove to Mammoth, at least that was where Mountain Goat was heading. Snickers was going to Tuolumne Meadows. He was section hiking the PCT. He was about 45 years old and Mountain Goat was 37. We found a pretty good campsite on the top of those huge rocks.

Snickers and Mountain Goat put up their tents. No place to put a tarp, so I just put down my ground cover, my thermal rest and sleeping bag. I slept pretty well that night. It got cold, down to 23 degrees. But I had the down jacket, which I would put between my bag and me covering my shoulders. Also thick wool socks, two pairs of pants, a couple of long sleeve shirts and wool cap, which is a must. I usually put on my head net to keep ants away, but it was so cold, those big black ants were not active.

I was caught off guard; these guys like to get up early. At 6am, they were sitting around. I had to hustle to leave with these guys; it did give me an early start. By 6:30 we were hiking. It was cold. The sun hadn't had a chance to come down between those huge granite cliffs.

A few minutes later, we're heading down the Golden Staircase. I've always remembered the Golden Staircase. In 1978, my brother John and I hiked from South Lake over Bishop Pass and southward, coming out at Independence. The Golden Staircase was a highlight to us, golden rocks, with incredible crashing water. The tremendous energy caused spray and if there was any wind, you could get wet pretty quick. Now, the trail moved away from the water. It wouldn't surprise me if some day someone doesn't get killed in the rushing torrent of the creek. Many times if a trail followed a waterway too closely, that trail is in jeopardy of becoming extinct.

Mountain Goat was the fastest walker of the group, that's for sure. He was always out in front. He was pretty fast at going down hill, but slowed down going uphill. We headed along the Palisades Creek, basically downhill. We came to the junction of Palisades Creek and the Glacier Creek, a big body of water that comes together in a turbulent body of water. This would probably be a good fishing spot.

On down the Palisades we went. This was the first time that I had walked with anybody for any length of time, on this whole trail. It wasn't bad. They kept a good pace, especially downhill. When I was young, I really ripped down hill and if my pack was light, I would actually jog. Now at my age, it's a stupid thing to do. Your knees take a real beating, as well as your shoulders. The dangers of spraining an ankle or getting shin splints really increases. A fall can terminate your trip. Having to get rescued is not only another possibility but also expensive and embarrassing. I tried to convey this to the guys, but no one listens to anyone else up here too much.

A few hours later we arrived at Big Pete Meadows and there were other people there. There was an old guy that looked older than me. His name was Cliff Hanger. I said, "Oh yeah, I've seen your autograph a couple of times." He introduced the others. There was Shutter Bug, from Nova Scotia, Sun Burn from England, and Steady from Oklahoma. Cliff Hanger was from Alabama. "Cool," I said. "I'm Wrong Way from LA and I'm heading for Canada, all the way in one play."

Snickers, me and Mountain Goat decide to have lunch and rap a little with these people. They had started in Mexico on April 24th and they were hoping to go all the way. Cliff Hanger was 64 years old, unbelievable. I asked him if he had seen a guy name Cruising Carson, who is 62 years old. He said he hadn't but knew of a guy called Billy Goat, who was 62 years old, who was well in front of them. The four of them started to leave, having finished their lunch some time ago. I told them that I'd see them down the line and now there was one more major pass being Muir Pass.

After a few minutes we left. I figured at our pace we would definitely pass them quickly, but not so. That group ambled pretty good, even that old man, Cliff Hanger. The hiking was still pretty fast and beautiful as we crossed through Evolution Valley.

During this beautiful trip through one of the High Sierras prettiest meadows, we had to forge a couple of swollen creeks. I just walked through it with my running shoes on. Snickers and Mountain Goat put on sandals. Not a bad idea, then when your feet dry, you can put your running shoes back on. To me, that's kind of a hassle. Once on the other side, I would try standing on a rock with my toes pointed downhill, letting the water drain out. If one starts walking right away, in about half an hour your shoes are 80 percent dry.

That evening we got all the way to a small lake, where the run off water comes from 11,595 foot Helen Lake, named after one of John Muir's daughters. The lake lies right below Muir Pass. This pass is the last major pass in the High Sierras. There were a couple of campsites along the way, but some section hikers took them. So we marched on until we found some choice camping sites just above a tiny lake.

There were some twisted and dwarfed out Fox Trail Pines there that provided a bit of a wind block. In between the small trees were quite a few places to sleep. It was pretty cool. We decided to crash here for the night. It was now 7pm. The next day we would be in perfect position to attack Muir Pass early. I could tell already that there was going to be a lot of snow to cope with.

A few minutes went by. Cliff Hanger, Steady, Shutter Bug, and Sun Burn came hiking toward us. Mountain Goat yelled to them, "Hey, there's all kinds of room for more people up here." Cliff Hanger looked a little relieved and said that was great news and how he was about spent for this day. There were seven thru-hikers here now. This was a little strange to me because I'm use to traveling by myself and camping alone and now all of a sudden there were seven hikers in one place. Pots and pans were brought out from packs and everyone started preparing their dinner while there was still some daylight.

Three more people were seen coming up from below. A red haired guy with dreadlocks. Wild Man, this guy had bright red hair alright. Just behind him was a tall thin young girl hiking in a skirt. Most everyone said hi to them as they looked back at us and just kept walking up the trail. Finally the third dude arrived and he looked familiar. I then realized it was Dan, the strange man. You couldn't miss him with his wide brimmed hat and his full beard. Cliff Hanger yelled out to him that there was one more place to camp here. Dan, the strange man, said nothing and kept hiking. Cliff Hanger kind of looked at the rest of us as if to say 'what's that dude's problem?'

For me, camping with everyone is a blast. Cliff Hanger was pretty funny and Steady had a nice personality. I didn't know if Steady and Cliff Hanger were a couple or not; she was quite a bit younger than him. I figured Sun Burn and Shutter Bug were definitely a couple, even though they slept a little ways apart.

Listening to the conversations that night was informative and entertaining. I heard stories about Shutter Bug's climb up Mt Whitney and their struggles through the Southern California desert. I laughed and threw in some amusing things myself. Some of them also knew people that I had only seen on the trail registers. Like Yogi, Billy Goat, and Mercury, who were all walking the trail two years in a row! "Man, that's nuts," I said. I couldn't imagine anyone doing the PCT two years in a row, especially Billy Goat, who was 64 years old! Names like Scooter and Toes came up as did the Chaos Twins.

I asked if anybody had seen Cruising Carson, but no one had met him. I then asked about Jenny B, but no one knew her either until I told the story about me resting under the 10 freeway near Palm Springs and the Pink Hotel with her and Scooter and Toes. I mentioned how she skipped many places along the trail because she didn't need to get resupplied.

Then Shutter Bug and Sun Burn thought I was talking about "Long Haul". Sun Burn asked if she was kind of short, with dark hair and a dark tan and a few muscles. Shutter Bug looked on with curiosity about his vivid description of Jenny, or I guess, is now called Long Haul.

That night at about 10pm, everyone was finally quiet and most were sleeping. These last few days have been awesome for me. The weather was fabulous, the landscape insurmountable. Good hiking friends and a story about the thru-hikers of 2003 was starting to emerge.

I had a few problems of course. My blister on my right hand, which I had lanced with my tiny knife and applied triple antibiotic to so as to prevent the blister from getting infected looked pretty ugly. My right shoulder was hurting quite a bit. I didn't know if it was from my backpack or my walking poles. At least my feet and knees were doing fine. I have to be thankful for that.

The next morning I got up quite early. I had to go and dig a hole. I was probably the first guy to leave camp. I knew the rest of them would catch up with me shortly. About 100 yards away from camp I had to cross quite a large icy creek. It looked pretty tricky; a lot of the rocks had ice on them. I had to be real careful.

One thing going for me was that the water was down in the morning. The water flow in this creek would be twice as strong in the late afternoon. The sun melts the snow as the day goes on, so early morning hours are the best time to forge creeks and rivers. On the other side of the creek I had to follow rock ducks for a while, because the trail was not distinguishable. Soon I was above at Helen Lake. I could see Dan the strange man still sleeping in his bright blue bag.

The sun was starting to come out now. The white fields of snow lit up with a golden tinge. I began climbing more and more; it got steeper and steeper. I couldn't find the trail for a while. I had to double back here and there to find it, as well as looking at the trail guide.

Soon I saw Shutter Bug moving up behind me. "Having problems, Wrong Way?" I said that I was and she told me to follow her, that she was pretty good in the snow. She asked if I had any sunglasses and If I did to put them on. I told her I did have glasses but they were scratched. Shutter Bug said to put them on anyway, so I won't get eyestrain. "Good thinking, Lincoln," I said. So I let the fabulous Shutter Bug go ahead of me, in her knee high gaiters and lightweight snow boots.

Shutter Bug had a global positioning unit or something like it, because she knew pretty much where to go. Shutter Bug said, "This is what I teach back in Nova Scotia, backpacking and snow camping. I'm an instructor." I said, "Excellent, just instruct me out of this mess and I'll be most obliged." At one point we rested. I was huffing and puffing like crazy. I think it freaked Shutter Bug out a bit. She thought I was going to have a heart attack. I told her not to worry, that she should have heard me back in the day when I ran marathons and stuff. I recover quickly.

We rested there for a few minutes. Then Dan, the strange man, came marching up, using the snow prints to keep up a good pace. He actually stopped and rested a bit, even though the guy wasn't out of breath at all. Right after that Sun Burn came up the hill. He was breathing pretty hard, but he was going at a pretty good pace.

Sun Burn said, "We must be extremely close to the pass now," as he looked at his map and his altimeter. He went on to say we were at 11,900 feet and have about 50 feet of elevation to go. Shutter Bug asked where Cliff Hanger and Steady were. Sun Burn said they were having a difficult time getting over that creek, but he looked back and saw that they made it.

A few seconds later Cliff Hanger and Steady appeared about 200 feet away, looking great. With that we all started heading up to the pass. Dan the strange man had left a few minutes earlier. He probably didn't want to be part of the group.

Suddenly I turned a slight corner and there it was, John Muir Pass and the John Muir Hut! Yeah, time to celebrate another High Sierra Pass, accomplished. This pass according to a lot of experts is considered to be the last pass of the actual High Sierras. Muir Pass is the last 12,000 foot pass on the PCT.

The hut is really made nice. I like it a lot better than Mt Whitney hut. There's a book here for anyone to sign in. We looked at all the thru-hikers names that signed the book. I wondered who this "Free Radical" dude was and this guy Huff and Puff, who draws a mean cartoon of himself! We all took pictures of the hut with all of us in front of it. There were quite a few of us. Steady, Cliff Hanger, Shutter Bug, Mountain Goat, Snickers, and myself. Dan the strange man was nowhere to be seen. I guess he just kept going at the pass.

After about 20 minutes, most everybody bailed, dropping to Evolution Basin, but not before reaching large Wanda Lake. This is another lake that's named after one of John Muir's daughters. The trail ran along a creek for the most part. There were lakes after lakes. As the elevation got lower, the trees got bigger and the place became more green. This was unbelievably beautiful Evolution Valley. There were a couple of nice lush meadows, but there were nice lush mosquitoes to go with these two meadows. Colby and McClure Meadows were certainly a welcome change from moon land.

So down hill the group went looking for greener pastures down below. I saw Mountain Goat fishing at Sapphire Lake and as usual, he was doing real good. It didn't take long for him to catch fish nor did it take him long to go ahead and catch up with the group. The guy could really fly.

The 37 year old kid had climbed a lot of High Sierra peaks. He was thin and light at about 5'9" and weighed 135 pounds. He was the perfect size and bone structure for an endurance athlete. He had mentioned to me that he would like to hike the PCT in one season.

I told Mountain Goat that I believed he would be a great prospect. But the PCT isn't all High Sierra wonderlands. That there was Southern California and the hot, dry spots in both Oregon and even in Washington. He seemed to understand that he had never been on a prolonged trip like hiking the PCT for five months.   I told him he could walk it in four months, but faster than four months, well, I really believe you are cheating yourself.

After talking to Mountain Goat, I started back down the trail with Snickers. Soon we passed Cliff Hanger, then Steady, but never caught Shutter Bug. Sun Burn had made a speech at John Muir Summit that he was getting off the trail for a while, to think about his life and this trip. He had darted off the pass after spending just a few minutes there.

I had the feeling that he might have been put off by Shutter Bug, but I can't be sure. On the way down from Muir Pass, Cliff Hanger told me Shutter Bug had two boyfriends back in Nova Scotia. One guy was real good looking and the other guy was so-so. The so-so guy has the bucks. I would go for the bucks myself, because it's just as easy to love a rich guy as a poor guy. But then again there's more to it than money and looks too. Cliff Hanger asked "Like what?"

I said "Like maybe he doesn't like thru-hikers." Cliff Hanger thought that was trivial, that there's not many people who like thru-hiking and you can't thru-hike all your life. I told him that I didn't know about that, ask Brice Hammick of Oregon. He's still hiking and he's in his eighties. He's a Triple Crown winner, hiking the ATP and CDT as well as the PCT probably a couple of times. Just then Mountain Goat sped by us and as he did, told us that we should stop at Evolution Meadow tonight. He had caught ten fish. Trout tonight!

So on I ambled, down a nice trail that was relatively flat. That evening, we all camped at Evolution Meadow. We had a giant fish feast. At least four or five of us did. Some people, like Snickers, didn't like fish. That's cool, more for me. Just like fresh meat, it was a solid protein, which made me, at least psychologically, more fit for the trip.

That night everyone else hit the sack early, but me and Mountain Goat built a fire. Snickers gave Mountain Goat instructions not to make the fire too big because tents or tarps might catch fire, even though there wasn't any wind and everyone's shelters were well away from the fire. Oh well.

Mountain Goat and I talked about religion and God, stuff like that. He had to pause for 15 minutes in order to walk behind a tree and talk to God! That gave me more of a chance to dry my soaked running shoes in the heat of the fire. We rapped until about 10pm, when we decided to turn in. After all, it was one hour after "hiker's midnight", which of course is 9pm.

The next morning I was second or third to get up. Since I didn't have a tent or tarp set up, I was able to break camp in 20 minutes and was off to the trail, which was about a hundred yards away. I turned and faced everybody. "Good-bye, kids, see you in Vermillion Valley." Then I purposely headed down the trail going the wrong way. Immediately I heard Cliff Hanger yell out, "You're going the wrong way, Wrong Way." "You mean it's this way," I yelled. Most everyone was laughing now.

Down the trail I walked, only to be caught and passed by Mountain Goat. "Praise the lord, dude. I'm going to walk your God-fearing ass into the ground today, buddy." A startled Mountain Goat said, "We'll see," then he rose to great expectations and flew down the trail, like daddy long legs. Now Shutter Bug passed me by, a slight blow to my ego. It wasn't too severe, because of the simple fact that girls are excellent hikers. Jenny Jardine walked the whole PCT, north to south, in just 94 days.

Girls have endurance, I've seen it many times, whether I was hiking or running a 26-mile marathon. The best long distance swimmers have been women. So don't feel too bad, man, or remember that you're 56 years old, old enough to be their parent. In fact, I bet I'm older than their parents!

This excuse always made me feel better. The older you are, the less you have to lose, the more you have to gain. So now I hiked keeping my downhill pace but watching behind me now and then for Cliff Hanger. No excuse if Cliff Hanger, the ancient one, passes me. Could my ego rationalize that one? No, maybe, I don't know? So move it man, he could be right around that small ridge you just passed.

Down and across the Goddard River and then Sanger Creek to the beautiful but mosquito-infested Keys Lakes. A beautiful day and a beautiful walk. The trail starts to climb again. I pass Shutter Bug. Cliff Hanger is just in back of me with Steady. Snickers and Mountain Goat are up in front.

Now that I was going up hill, I figured I would catch the fading Snickers. I would probably see Mountain Goat on top of Seldon Pass. Sure enough, I did and I got the feeling that Snickers didn't like it. I was surprised when the pass appeared. It seemed so much easier than any of the passes in the Sierras so far. Somewhere before the pass, we all entered the John Muir wilderness.

At Seldon Pass, I was surprised to meet Mark and Mike. "Hey, dudes, fancy meeting you here. I thought you guys would be at Lake Edison by now." They said that they had slept in that morning and didn't start hiking until 10am, which was a nice break.

Soon after I arrived Shutter Bug reached the pass, then came Steady and Cliff Hanger. "Hey, Cliff," I yelled out. "Not too much further to go to reach the pass. Just about a mile and 1,000 foot climb." I heard him moan a little. He said that I shouldn't psych him out. "No, Cliff," said Shutter Bug, "the pass is right here where we're standing. Don't listen to Wrong Way." The rest of the people were on Cliff's side of course. They said, "Yeah, Wrong Way, that's cru-el." So Cliff Hanger scores again and I look like a funky monkey!

Seldon Pass is 10,900 feet. It's similar to Mulkey Pass and Cottonwood Pass of the southern Sierras. The pass had a few patches of snow, but it wasn't a problem whatsoever. After resting for about a half hour, I decide to head down with the first part of the group, including Mountain Goat and Snickers. Quickly, after going down the north side of the pass, I arrive at Marie Lake, a beautiful high lake with some vegetation around and patches of snow.

Mountain Goat decided to try his luck once again. I knew he would catch up, so I headed down the trail. My goal was to get to Kip Camp or at least close to it. From there it would be a three or four hour walk to the ferry. The ferry takes backpackers twice a day, from the far end of Lake Edison to the Vermillion Valley resort, on the other side. It's about a three mile ride.

So down Bear Creek everybody went, but not all together. Each man was on his own. Snickers, myself, and Milo make it to the junction of Hilgard Creek and Bear Creek. Mountain Goat shows up a little later, just as it was get-ting dark. The dude has scored again. Marie Lake was good to the lad. He caught six golden trout. "Fish tonight" he yelled. "Alright," I bellowed. He started preparing those golden beauties right away.

Mountain Goat cooks the fish in a small plastic bag. Inside the bag he puts some oil, spices, and a dab of butter. Then he puts that bag in his cooking pot, with water. The dude then boils the water for about four or five minutes.

The fish are then pulled out of this cooking bag into everyone's eating dish. The bones of the trout slide right off, as does the skin. Beautiful pink meat is left. Wow, unbelievably delicious. Clean up is a breeze for the Goat and he is finished in no time.

That evening me and Mountain Goat were talking about the size of the universe and stuff like that when the obnoxious snoring of Snickers subsides. He tells us that we're keeping him awake, that we're talking too loud. Reluctantly, Mountain Goat said alright. I said, somewhat mockingly, now it must be 9pm, the hikers midnight hour. I think the guy was a bit jealous or something because Mountain Goat and I had made friends, or something like that. I'm starting to realize that this guy doesn't have much personality, that's for sure.

The next morning we all get up around 6am. We were walking at 7am. We flew through Kip Camp. Vermillion Valley was on our minds. We had a good chance to get that morning ferry. I wasn't really paying attention when Snickers and Mountain Goat, who were ahead of me, took the first trail. The problem was that it was the horse trail that comes out near Lake Edison's Dam area. I was wondering why the trail was so torn up and had so much horse crap on it.

About two miles down we realized our mistake, but it was past the point of no return. We would just have to follow it down to the road and the dam area. About one hour later, we reached the road where there was as small parking lot of hikers and riders. As we got to the dirt parking lot, we noticed a new white Ford pick-up and a couple of people walking towards it.

I said hello to them and the guy said hello back and said that we looked like we've been hiking for quite some time. I said yes, from Mexico. He thought we were thru-hikers. "Well, at least he is," said Mountain Goat. Then Snickers said, "I am too. But I do it in sections." I think Snickers wanted to be in the limelight. You could tell by his fat waist that he wasn't a thru-hiker. More and more I felt like this guy was some sort of wanna-be.

We rapped to this guy for a bit. He and his girlfriend were very nice. We told them how we had taken the equestrian trail by mistake instead of the foot trail that led to the ferry. "Hey, if you guys want to sit in the back of the truck, I'll take you guys down to the store." We told him that would be great. Little did he know that this was our main intention of talking to the guy in the first place.

We all jumped into the back of the truck and off we went, down a bumpy, dusty road that led to the other side of the lake and Vermillion Valley Resort. Fifteen minutes later, we turned a corner and there it was, the resort, and who do I see first, sitting outside drinking a beer? None other than Cliff Hanger! "Hey, ancient one, how did you get here so fast?" Cliff Hanger said they had walked until 9pm the night before. They arrived here about 10am this morning.

Cliff Hanger told us that the food is great here, a little expensive, but damn good. Alright, let's eat. So me, Snickers, and Mountain Goat went inside and powered down some giant cheeseburgers. Even Mountain Goat indulged in a burger, though he's basically a vegetarian.

On the other side of the small restaurant sat Milo and Greg or Mr Natural, as I call him. "Hey," Mountain Goat said, "look, Snickers, there's that rude guy that wouldn't talk to us because he was low on food." I just laughed a little and told them that's what he says to everyone. I told them how the guy is looking for a wilderness experience except Greg won't stay at any trail angel places but seems he likes to party at places like this. That big dude, with the curly blond hair is Milo. He started out in Mexico, but had to get off the trail for a week or so, because of a wedding back east. He's cool though, he wants to go all the way, but money is a problem.

We started pigging out on our food. It was great. The first drinks are free for all thru-hikers. Even for Snickers and Mountain Goat, who weren't hiking to Canada, the cool owner said don't worry about it, and gave them free drinks as well.

The store was set up for backpackers and fishermen. They were hip on stuff that thru-hikers needs. They even had a propane canister, slightly used but at a great price. I bought that right away, knowing if I didn't, someone else would. I was happy to get this canister, because after cooking my dinner last night, my stove petered out.

The tent cabins were only $5 a night. They had four cots in each tent. The room was simply a 20x20 foot wooden cabin. Half the sides and the roof was a thick brown tarp. So Snickers, Mountain Goat and myself shared one tent cabin. There was an extra cot. But a few minutes later it was occupied by the couple we saw going up Muir Pass a few days ago -the dude with bright red hair and his wife or girlfriend who hiked in a skirt. After talking to them for a while, I found out their names, Wookie and Island Mama.

After securing a bunk, I headed to the showers which were over near the store. As I walked by the back of the store, I saw Milo washing dishes. "Hey, man, did you get a job?" Milo said yes but instead of being paid, he had an open tab at the restaurant. "That's cool, man" I said as I walked by. I liked this kid, Milo, who was probably in his late twenties. The guy was low on money, but he was trying to get as far as he could. If the dude had bucks, I believe he would definitely make it to Canada, for he was a strong hiker.

The shower felt great and only cost me $2. It was sort of an honor system deal. After the shower, I walked around the other side of the building and found Shutter Bug, Steady, and Cliff Hanger. They all had cabin rooms, which were about $40 per night.

I met Steve, who was married to Steady. Steve wasn't walking the trail, but supporting his wife by driving on dirt or jeep roads wherever he could to intercept her. He would give her water or food or whatever she needed. He also gave food, candy, Gatorade and water to thru-hikers as well. Steve had a regular size SUV 4-wheel drive with two big ice-chests on the back. He was a real estate agent in Oklahoma.

Steve mentioned that he and Cliff Hanger would be heading for Fresno early tomorrow morning. I asked Cliff why he was going home. He said that his mom was real sick and it didn't look good. I told him that I was sorry to hear that. He knew this would be coming sooner or later and how his mom was 95 and has had health problems for some time. I told him that it had been fun hiking with him. Cliff Hanger said to me to be sure to walk the right trail, "North is north, and south is south."

I told Cliff Hanger that maybe our paths will cross again some time. He said maybe, that in fact he might be back this season. "If things happen back in Alabama like I think will happen, I may rejoin Steady and Shutter Bug north of here, maybe with a heavy heart, but with relief that her bedridden days are over." I said I'd see him later and Cliff Hanger said to me "Happy Trekking,

Wrong Way." I left Cliff's cabin and went to do my laundry with a load that Mountain Goat and Snickers shared with me.

That evening I walked down to the Lake Edison shore and watched the sun go down over the lake. You know walking the PCT in one season takes a lot of planning, a lot of grueling hard days and luck. Being gone so long, anything can happen.

There are family ties and things that can happen to loved ones back home. Life doesn't stop for you. You are just departed from your usual grind. There are weddings, funerals, accidents, and all kinds of family problems that can pop up, grab your emotional strings and put you back into the fray. Also personal injuries, hair-line fractures, chronic foot pain, etc. So luck is definitely a factor and even though I feel high and free on the PCT, things can always happen the wrong way!

That night after having a few beers and visiting a few camp fires, I hit the hay about 10pm. Right after I get in my bunk, I was awakened by a family that had mass quantities of motorized toys. They had dirt bikes, quad runners, and trikes, all towed behind their camper somehow. They had a powerful flash-light that continually bounced across the canvas tent cabin.

The kids were jumping, screaming, and fighting with each other. The mother was angry with the father. The teenager had his boom box to Green Day, a punk rock phenomenon that already had their day. It didn't last too long because the father told the teenager to turn that shit off.

This went on for several hours. During this time Wookie and Island Ma-ma came in and crashed together on their bunk. Soon the motorized family clan of motorized mouths fell silent. For just a short time I was relieved, until Snick-ers took over the noise brigade, with ungodly amounts of snoring. It was unbe-lievable! Even Mountain Goat started to snore. Were they having a deep sleep snoring contest? Maybe, I don't know. It was so bad that I would rather hear the motorized family start up again. At least they were more interesting and somewhat comical.

The next morning I awoke about 6:30am, my usual time that I arise on the trail. This day would be basically a layover day since I had planned to take the 4pm ferry back to the trail. I got up, went to the bathroom, and went right back to my bunk. Mountain Goat, Snickers, Wookie, and Island Mama went to breakfast. I slept, trying to recover from the noisy night before. At around 9am, I finally got up and went down to the kitchen for a giant breakfast. As I walked by the kitchen, I noticed the cook and some of his helpers carry a wild pig carcass to the large barbecue pit. Inside the restaurant, I asked the waitress what was going on. She told me that they were going to have wild pig barbecue today, in honor of Independence Day.

Holy Smoke. This was July 4th. I had forgotten all about it. July 4th also signified to me that I had now been on the trail for exactly two months. It took me two months to get to Lake Edison. Oh man, I wasn't even close to being half done with California. I felt that I was more than two weeks behind schedule.

The problem with being late was simply getting to Washington too late. Washington is the wet state. It's also the state I fear the most. This was because the later in the season it gets, the worse the weather can get.

The biggest fear with the weather is not just the miserable rain, but the snow, also called the big dump. The big dump can end the hiking season. How terrible would it be if I got my ass all the way up to Stehekin or so and the big dump hits and I have to quit. Wrong Way never made it. He got to within 100 miles but the big dump engulfed him and he failed. 2,550 miles for nothing.

My god, this could happen to me. One thing I had thought about was plan B. If I was running late, I might just take a bus ride to Canada. Then go east to Manning Park and start at the northern terminus of the PCT and head south to Ashland, Oregon.

This was called flip flopping, an official word used on the PCT, maybe even invented on the PCT. Flip flopping is done mainly on really snowy years, especially in the Sierras. Hikers march to the Walker Pass or Kennedy Meadows and then get a ride to Canada where they head south, back to Kennedy Meadows, thus avoiding the heavy snows of the mighty Sierras.

This doesn't help much if the Washington Cascade Range is laden with snow. I guess another alternative would be to go from Kennedy Meadows to Cascade Locks on the Columbia River, which is the border of Oregon and Washington, and then hike to Canada. From Canada, take the bus back to Cascade

ECSTASY OF MISERY

Locks and hike south, back to Kennedy Meadows.

The one thing I like about flip flopping is that I would finish my hike in Ashland, Oregon, where I had started my thru-hiking career 25 years ago, back in 1978, when I walked California. Another thing is I would most likely see Washington earlier in the season and hopefully, under better weather conditions. Flip flopping was an alternative move I could do if I felt I had to and it took a little pressure off me.

A few hours later I was having lunch with Milo, Mark, Steady, and Shutter Bug. I brought up the subject of flip flopping. To my surprise, that's what Shutter Bug and Steady were probably going to do. Cliff Hanger, in fact, introduced the idea to them some time ago. By flip flopping, one could extend the hiking season a month or so, just get Washington done with. We sat around eating cheeseburgers and chewing the fat, no pun intended, talking a bit about Cliff Hanger. Both Steady and Shutter Bug hoped he could get back on the trail somewhere up north. They planned to keep in touch with him while he was in Alabama.

At about 3pm that day, I started to gather my things together. My clothes, even though washed, still smelled a bit. I think the load of laundry we did together was overstuffed. Once I was packed up I walked down to the lodge to sit around and wait for the boat. That wild pig sure smelled good. They were starting to serve it up, but at $14 per plate, I felt it was a little too pricey. At 4pm, Mountain Goat, Snickers and I with about 15 other hikers got aboard. We crossed the large blue Edison Lake to the other side and back to the mighty PCT.

While crossing the lake, I was really impressed with the modern day ferry. It was more like a speedboat. I couldn't help but remember a 1979 trip I made with Linda (Trail Perfect). We crossed this lake with about 10 other hikers. The boat then was half the size and twice as slow. The scary part was that it was pouring like hell. White lightning bolts slammed into a tree, which started on fire and it even struck the lake right in front of the ferry.

I squatted down and sat on my heels as to avoid a possible lightning strike. Then the driver of the ferry had everyone sit on the floor. I could see it in the newspapers, "Twelve people and a ferry boat operator drown as lightning strikes boat in electrical storm." Man, was I glad when that boat finally arrived on shore.

Before I knew it, we were docking at the far harbor near the trail. There were about a dozen hikers waiting to go back. This included Bobka and Be There Now. They were still in the race. "Alright, dudes, glad to see you." "Hey, Wrong Way. What's up?" I told them that I was heading out to Red's Meadows and my continual race for the northern terminus. They wanted to know what Vermillion Valley Resort was like. I said that it was dynamite! It had good food and cheap bunks. "Try that Black Forest Pie, man, it's outrageous."

A couple of minutes later, the boat was loaded with return hikers, including one girl who decided to return because she met a guy that she had previously hiked with. The boat took off and the driver who owns the resort yelled out "Thank you and be sure and come back to see us. There is a road that you can take. If you hurry you can still get your 30 miles in." That guy ran a good resort and had a great sense of humor too. The Vermillion Valley Resort is definitely hiker friendly. It always has been and if this guy stays on, it will continue to be a good place for hikers.

I headed up the connection trail that leads to the PCT. About 20 minutes later I reached the junction and headed north. It was about 5pm and I figured I had about three hours of hiking left. Mountain Goat and Snickers just took off when I was talking to Bobka. Gee, they couldn't wait for a few seconds for me. I believe little pudgy boy Snickers didn't like me or my political views. He can kiss my ass. The clown is definitely a wussy. The trail traveled through Quail Meadows and then to a trail junction with the Mott Lake/ Blue Jay Lake trail.

This trail led to high adventure for me and Trail Perfect back in 1979. We took a five day trip to Mott Lake because my brother told me how great the fishing was. I thought this would be a good way to introduce my girl to the High Sierras. I never thought that I would experience one of the most remarkable freaks of nature.

The fishing was poor, but the lake and surrounding area were beautiful. We only had to share Mott Lake with one other couple. That was cool, even though the other couple ran around naked, but that's not the remarkable freak of nature I mentioned.

While getting ready for dinner on our second night, Trail Perfect blurted out "What's that?" I looked up just as I was about to light the fire. To our amazement there was a ball of fire moving across the lake. It was traveling about four to five miles per hour and making a cracking sound as it went. The best description of it would be about six or seven sparklers tied together and moving at a slow speed, across the lake. It must have traveled several hundred feet and then suddenly burned out! We were amazed. What could it be? There was no one else at the lake at the time.

When I got home from the trip, I told my brother and others what we had seen at Mott Lake. What it boiled down to was that it was ball lightning. Ball lightning often is said to appear before a storm, often along solid rock cliffs.

Both things were true at Mott Lake. About three days after seeing the ball lightning, when we were leaving, it stormed. Just like I previously mentioned about when on the ferry as we floated to the other side of the lake, lightning struck a tree in the Devil's Punch Bowl area, causing the place to catch on fire.

What a trip that was. How many people see ball lightning in their lifetime. Some scientists believe that ball lightning is impossible. But if it wasn't ball lightning, then what the hell was it. The two of us will never know. We were both glad to have experienced the beautiful and colorful event.

Passing Mott Lake Trail Junction I headed uphill continually until I reached Pocket Meadow. I thought about camping here but I still had a good hour of hiking before it got dark, so I might as well go for it. About an hour later, I climbed a steep rise and a relatively flat area. The mosquitoes seemed to flutter about. I was about to camp when I heard a familiar voice. It was Mountain Goat. I had caught up with them. So that night the three of us camped together once again.

The next morning we arose earlier. We all broke camp at about 6:15am. Our goal was to do 20 miles. If we could do this, Red's Meadow could be reached the following morning. The problem was that Mountain Goat had to be home Sunday evening to go back to work on Monday. He lived 300 miles away in Paradise, CA.

So up we climbed, past Silver Lake and then Silverwood Pass. At 10,900 feet it was a breeze compared to the usual passes. Down the trail we jammed past tiny Squaw Lake and then Tully Hole and Lake Virginia, where we stopped and had lunch. Cascade Valley rolled out before us and was incredibly beautiful, with Fish Creek rolling down into it and through it.

After lunch we headed off again. My shoulder was giving me pain again. The blister I lanced which was between my thumb and index finger had not healed yet. In fact, it freaked people out who took a look at it. I had a feeling, however, that it would heal in time. Cuts and scrapes like this take a lot longer to heal up here at high altitudes. The cold wind and other elements slow down the recovery time.

From Lake Virginia on for the next few miles were pretty good hiking. Popular Purple Lake is next. There were a few campers hanging around its edges. We hauled butt and camped at Deer Creek, three or four miles past Duck Lake Trail Junction. We covered about 20 miles that day in the Sierras.

After having an early dinner, I came up with the idea of walking until dark. We still had about an hour left of daylight. Mountain Goat and Snickers weren't into it. They were wasted. I still felt pretty good. I was definitely in good shape. I hope so. I figure that I was at around the 800 mile mark.

The next morning, we all got up early and headed down the trail to Red's Meadow. Soon we got to a burned area, probably a fire zone of ten years ago that definitely smoked this area. About 8am we arrived at Red's Meadow. Red's consisted of a store and a restaurant. It also had a horse corral, not far off.

We met up with Wookie and Island Mama who had left Vermillion Valley the same day we left but had taken the morning ferry at the restaurant. We sat across from them. They looked a little irritated because they had not received their breakfast yet. They had waited nearly an hour. The excuse was that the grill had to be warmed up.

No way did we have the time because the Goat had to leave Mammoth as early as possible. It was now Sunday, July 6th, and he had to be at work Monday. He had a good 250 miles or more to drive to reach home. We said good-bye to the long-haired Wookie and his girl or wife - I don't know if they're married – and then headed to Red's Meadow's famous hot springs.

ECSTASY OF MISERY

The hot springs haven't changed since 1978. There's an enclosed area with a single pipe of hot mineral water. There are five or six of these antique looking shower booths. The hottest waters are closest to the actual hot springs. I got one about in the middle. I was lucky the booth I got had soap in it. We had been in such a rush that I couldn't find my soap. I would have enjoyed a longer bath, but we were in a hurry. We went over to the parking lot and climbed in Mountain Goat's car, with no room to spare, and off we went to Mammoth.

I've been told several times that Mammoth is LA's resort. Skiers from the LA area flock to Mammoth every year to slide down these snowy hills. They spend a lot of money here, not just skiing or snowboarding, but on food and lodging,. Many of them go home with cuts, scrapes, broken legs, sprained ankles and sore muscles. I'm sure it's a real blast but the cost of the latest equipment fads and all the rest make it a little clickish for me. It looked like a lot of trees had to be removed for all these people to slide their asses down these barren hills. All in all, I guess it's cool for people to have fun and resort owners to probably get rich.

A short drive down hill and we were in Mammoth. In the center of town there was a giant metal skeleton of a Mammoth. It looked pretty cool. The place was pretty crowded. Tourist buses were parked all over the place. We headed more towards the center of town, where we stopped and pigged out at the local Subway sandwich shop. It was OK, but I would have preferred a greasy cheeseburger place where I could really have piled on the calories and maybe wash it all down with a thick chocolate malt.

Mountain Goat was really concerned with his weight. The dude was already too skinny. He was basically a vegetarian I think and didn't want mayonnaise or any sauce on his already calorie-robbed Subway sandwich. He washed it all down with a diet soda. Oh, my, section hikers are quite amusing at times.

After lunch we headed to a supermarket because Snickers wanted garlic mashed potatoes like the package I had given him the day before. Even though the Goat was anxious to head home and we had rushed through the mineral bath, Snickers took his sweet time picking out trail goodies. I found some imported cheese from Spain smoked in applewood.

Finally we left the incredible giant Raley's Supermarket and headed back to the big resort area where I said good-bye to Mountain Goat and wished him well. He gave me a big hug and then he left.

Mountain Goat was one of the nicest characters I have ever met on the trail. I hope his dream of walking the PCT in one season comes true. He would be a success at least as far as hiking ability is concerned. He had a good personality. Mountain Goat was very religious but he didn't push the Christian thing at you. He seemed to pray and discuss things directly to God which he would do almost every day.

I made a quick phone call home to my parents and Trail Perfect. I couldn't believe how I got a cell phone connection. They must have an astronomer close by. Everything was fine at home. Trail Perfect told me that my monetary funds I left her were drying up quickly. I told her to get some money off my dad. She had found some Lipton side dishes in packaged dinners that she was going to send me. These were much cheaper than the regular backpacking dinners and maybe we could save a few dollars. That sounded good to me, as long as I had my instant mashed potatoes to add to the concoction I would be alright. After the phone calls, Snickers and I climbed on the bus that went to Red's Meadow and back again to the mighty PCT. The next step would be an official supply box at the post office in Tuolumne Meadows, which was a few days away.

So Snickers and I headed north once again, towards Donohue Pass. After Donahue Pass it is a pretty quick walk down to Tuolumne Meadows camp and store area, at least that's what it looks like on the map. What is interesting at this area of the trail is that a hiker actually has two choices that he or she can make. They can take the traditional PCT route which is the PCT-John Muir route or take the Pacific Crest High Trail.

The traditional trail and the high trail split apart at Red's Meadows. The traditional PCT and John Muir trail heads north through Devil's Posts Pile National Monument, past Rainbow Falls and Minaret Falls and then right through Agnew Meadows. The two trails then join once again at Thousand Island Lake. If one takes the high trail, he is usually headed out of the town of Mammoth. That's what the high trial was really designed for. It didn't matter which trail a hiker takes, both trails are considered official.

ECSTASY OF MISERY

Having come from Mammoth, we took the high trail. I'm glad we did. I've already walked the PCT-John Muir Trail, but never the high trail. I was taken aback by the views. Ritter and Banner Peaks were beautiful. Down below were awesome sparkling lakes. I felt a little like an airplane circling over one of the most beautiful places on Earth. My favorite rock formation in the Sierras has always been these rock-like little dudes, the Minarets. Shadow Lake lies below like a dark blue pearl, majestic as hell. I'm glad I had an aerial view of this place.

At Thousand Island Lake, we take a break and have some munchies that we bought in Mammoth. The Ansel Adams Wilderness is definitely another highlight of the dynamic Sierras. This lake of a Thousand Islands looks just like its name. The islands are made of rocks that jut out of the water, looking like miniature islands in a sea of bright blue.

Soon we were on our way again climbing a small pass called Island Pass. At Island Pass I ran into a guy on a rock looking down towards the valley that we had just walked. The guy's name was Amigo. He was looking for his brother, Tread Lightly. Me and Snickers, the silent one, tell him we haven't seen anybody in a red coat but we weren't really looking either. The guy looked a little concerned. He asked us if we would tell his girlfriend Dragon Fly that he still hasn't seen Tread Lightly and that he would be back in about 15 minutes after getting his message.

So Snickers and I headed out and in about 15 minutes we reached Dragon Fly sitting on a rock, waiting for Amigo and/or his brother, Tread Lightly. She tells us thanks and we head out, steadily climbing to Donahue Pass. About 7pm we found a flat area with plenty of water and made camp for the night.

Right after we stopped, a girl passed by us. I said hello and asked what her name was. She said it was "Detour". She was going from Walker Pass to Canada, at least she hoped she could. She was leaving the trail at Tuolumne Meadows for about a week to go to a wedding.

I told Detour that leaving the trail for a week would be a nice break. But she said that the lost time was crucial and how she wanted to get out of Washington while the weather was still nice. I didn't want to sound too negative, but told her that there wasn't any nice weather in Washington, especially after September. You should always count on rain, fog, and wet weeds, and just hope that the big dump doesn't hit. That can put an end to anybody's trip. "Oh, thanks for the tips, Wrong Way. See you guys later in Tuolumne Meadows," she said. Then off she went at a blistering pace.

Snickers was amazed that a girl would be walking alone. She was the first one we saw. I told him that it's not quite that uncommon and told him about Jenny or "Long Haul" that I had met under the 10 freeway near Palm Springs. Snickers said "yeah but where is she now?" He sounded like he kind of doubted my story. I said, "according to the last trail register, she's about two weeks ahead of me!"

After dinner, we saw a helicopter cruising around slowly. It was definitely looking for someone. Now and then you could see two tiny heads in the cockpit. They cruised over to us and checked us out and then headed in another direction. "Hey, I wonder if they're looking for Amigo's brother, Tread Lightly." Snickers said he doubted it, that it would be way too early to report him as a missing person. I told Snickers that he was probably right, but that they were obviously looking for someone and I hoped he has warm clothes because it was starting to get cold.

The next morning I awoke to Snickers giant farts. I had made sure that I didn't sleep within 20 feet of the guy because of his ridiculous snorings, but I didn't count on his atomic bombs.

Soon we were up and off, heading out towards Donahue Pass, a place that I always remember as a beautiful pass and not a terribly hard climb. It proved to be just as I remembered. We were up on top at an elevation of 11,056 feet before we hardly knew it. The views were outstanding. Lyell Canyon Creek ran below it and after a couple of pictures, we headed down into the valley, entering Tuolumne County.

I remember this area well from my 1978 trip. It just got through storming the night before and I was lucky to have shared a tent with a guy that was hiking from Crescent City to Mt Whitney. I gave the guy some of my dinner which he never had tried before. He got sicker than hell. It was pretty bad. Reluctantly I left the next morning. He reassured me that he would be all right so I left. I've always wondered if that guy had made it to Mt Whitney or not.

ECSTASY OF MISERY

When I got up to the pass, I met two dudes that were heading north. One guy was from Colorado and the other was from Georgia. They didn't like each other too much, at least that's the drift I got.

When the dude from Colorado offered to smoke a joint with me, the guy from Georgia got pissed, said a few things to put us both down and jammed down the trail. The guy from Colorado thought this was amusing. I don't promote smoking on the trail, because it can really make one go the wrong way! I went ahead and had a smoke and then floated down the trail, passed Thousand Island Lake all the way to Red's Meadow. The trail wasn't hard to follow back in 1978 and was in excellent condition, as it is now.

Now I followed funky, boring, Snickers down the trail to Tuolumne Meadows. There was some snow, but not much and soon we were back in the trees and out of lunar land. The trail was now almost flat and soft. We were doing a three mile per hour pace.

The Lyell Canyon Creek flowed in the meadow and becomes very lazy and deep. Pools that were probably 10 feet deep sparkled with pure clean slightly flowing water. We stopped and had lunch at one of the pools. Then suddenly I heard a noise and to my surprise, Milo and Solace came marching up to us. They said that's what they were thinking about, lunch. So we all sat around and ate together.

Milo and Solace told us that they had a visit last evening from a helicopter. We said that a helicopter had buzzed us too. "It more than buzzed us, it landed!" A ranger got out and asked them if they had seen a guy walking alone, probably in a green jacket. "We told them no, and they told us we were too close to the creek and that we should move back." The guy looked irritated, Solace said. Milo said that he probably wanted to be back home watching the Giants play baseball or something. I told them that he could have written them a citation. They said he would have it if was in his jurisdiction, and besides they were over 100 feet from the creek.

Suddenly there was a splash and Snickers had jumped in the freezing water of Lyell Creek. He dunked his head, then got out quickly. "Man, that's got to be cold" said Milo. "You must need a bath pretty bad to jump into that!" Snickers just got out and started drying off. I had to give the man credit for that. Not a bad idea, except that Tuolumne Meadows probably has showers. I think I'll wait for a little hot water.

We were just about to leave when about a dozen young campers or hikers came by. They started telling us about the bears that raided their camp the night before. "Didn't you have bear canisters in camp?" One of the young girls who seemed to be the spokesperson for the group said that they all had their own bear canister. "Then how did the bears get a hold of the candy bar?" "Well we left a few of them out and I guess a bear or two came by and noticed them and took off."

Then the female spokeswoman said that it was only two or three candy bars. It was no biggy. I told them it was a big deal, now they have helped train as well as keep the attention of two more bears that will be causing problems for other campers around here. The bears will be hoping to be rewarded with more candy bars or whatever. The young hikers didn't seem to care, they were more interested in buying coffee from us, but we didn't have any for sale, so off they went.

Down the trail we all headed, now understanding why bears in this area are so much of a problem. Hell, they have their own college here. It's called the University of Tuolumne Meadows. Bears enroll quite innocent and end up getting masters degrees in the five claw discount.

About 3 in the afternoon we arrive at Tuolumne Meadows. Snickers grabbed a $70 per night cabin tent. I found a space at the PCT campground for only $2. There weren't any showers, but the bathroom had hot and cold running water, which is perfect for a splash bath and head shampoo. Right now however I'm going over to the fast food hamburger place to pig out.

I got in line and ordered a High Sierra double cheeseburger special with a chocolate shake. Outside there were tables for people to eat their food. They seemed to be filled with hikers, most of them were day hikers, your basic backpackers. Some were thru-hikers that included Solace and Milo, Detour, Snickers, Mark, Wookie, and Island Mama. I went out and found an open place and started eating like a starved pig. I listened to different conversations from the hikers: the latest bear story, a developing blister, mosquito complaints.

One story blew my mind, and that was the name of Tough Old Broad. A guy asked me if I knew T.O.B. I told him that I had met her when I walked Washington in 2000, coming down to Stehekin. She blew my mind. I couldn't believe a woman her age could or should be out doing this type of hiking, especially alone. She must be 80 years old or older.

The guy who was talking about Tough Old Broad introduced himself as Lost and Found. He went on to say that he met T.O.B. when he was walking up Mission Creek near Big Bear. She told him she usually did abut 10 to 12 miles per day. She's already hiked Oregon and Washington and now she's section hiking California. I wonder how far she's going this year? Lost and Found thought she was going as far as Cajon Pass. "Wow, I hope Tough Old Broad makes it. In fact I'm going to giver her a toast right now." With that I raised my chocolate shake. Lost and Found raised his beer as well as a few other hikers at the table. One girl yelled out behind me "Hats off to Tough Old Broads." I looked behind me to see Detour, probably on her third or fourth beer.

After eating, I went to the store and bought some Gatorade, beer, chips, cheese, and Oreo cookies. I then left the store and walked back to the campsite. It was too late to get my supply pack at the post office; it was almost 5pm. I took a sponge bath in the bathroom. I also washed my hair which I lathered up 4 times. Now feeling quite good, I went back to the PCT campground where I slept like a baby that night.

The next morning was July 9th. I was definitely two weeks behind schedule. At least I was finally done with Southern California. Tuolumne Meadows is the official dividing line of Northern and Southern California. Half of California has been done, but it took me two months and five days to do it, a bit slower than I thought, but at least I'm still hiking.

My messed up right hand was still looking bad, but not infected. My knees were fine. My right shoulder was really giving me a problem. While walking with Cliff Hanger's gang, Shutter Bug told me she also has a shoulder problem with the same model pack that I had. She had sent it back and bought another ultra light pack that agreed with her. This is an idea that I might try if this shoulder problem persists, and I have a feeling it will.

Today is going to be a day of rest and eating and rapping to thru-hikers. Yeah, a day of rest is good for you and especially me, because of my age of 56.

Older people, especially over 50, should take the rest days seriously. Walk as little as possible and stretch at least two or three times a day, but slow and easy.

I like to soak in a hot tub, if possible. Drink plenty of water. Make sure to eat some vegetables and fruit. Be careful on the junk foods, especially if you're older. Eat a lot and eat well. Once in a while you can have a half gallon of ice cream. If possible, try to keep these urges to a minimum.

At 2pm a small bus comes by the store. Hikers are encouraged to take their showers at the lodge during this time so that people staying in those tent cabins won't be over crowded in the morning or evening. So I bought a #3 ticket and grabbed a free ride in the shuttle to the showers, which were near the lodge, about a mile away.

The showers were still pretty crowded, but I managed to get a pretty good soaping. This was my first shower in four days since I left Red's Meadows. After my shower I rode back to the store on the shuttle. This time there were just a few people on the bus, which gave me a chance to ask the driver questions about different things. She was pretty funny.

Snickers finally left that afternoon, going back home to Sacramento. He barely introduced me to his wife. I had to walk over next to them so he didn't have much choice. I felt like I might as well introduce myself since Snickers used my phone to call his wife two or three times. His kids were cool, smiling and stuff. His wife looked at me like I was Charles Manson or something, at least that was the feeling I got. They all got into an SUV and drove off to some place in Yosemite Valley, so Snickers could recover from his 90 mile ordeal. "Jumping Yuppies and New Born Puppies". That dude was one dull sucker.

That evening, Wookie and Island Mama arrived at the store area. I sat near them eating chips with cheese sauce and downed a High Sierra Pale Ale. I heard them say that they were going to hike down to Yosemite Valley to check it out and then take the bus back. One of their goals was to finish the John Muir Trail that actually starts in Yosemite Valley.

They were concerned, however, because they didn't have a bear canister. For me this was a perfect time to unload the two and a half pounds of weight off my back. I was out of the high country and things would be warming up, and getting rid of my extra warm clothes and this canister would really save me some weight, so this was a great opportunity to get rid of the canister.

I yelled out to Wookie that if they wanted a canister, I had a Garcia, if they wanted to buy it. "No, but what if we used it and mailed it back to your home? You wouldn't have to worry about mailing it or trying to sell it." I thought it over and what the hell, it sounded pretty good,. So, I gave them the address of my girlfriend, Trail Perfect, and shook hands on the deal. Take it. So Wookie and Island Mama took my Garcia bear canister. They were smart to do that. Both the bears and forest rangers down there would be a scary combination.

The second night there I went to one of those campfire shows the park services put on. It was okay, but a lot of it ruined by small children that got bored fast. The ranger talked about the local animal life, including bears, mosquitoes, and ants. The kids cried and a few of them got in arguments and the mosquitoes bit me many times. I was glad when Ranger Rick was through with his show.

I headed back to my camp and crashed for the night. Tomorrow will be a travel day. Yep, Northern California here I come. The next stop would be Echo Lake Resort, some seven or eight days away. I would have to carry at least 16 pounds of food.

The next morning I got up at 7am and went to the store to buy some last minute junk food. I then went to the grill and had breakfast. Milo was sitting there, so I sat down and had breakfast with him. He told me something kind of interesting. He said that at Sonora Pass you can take the highway east about 15 miles and you'll get to Kennedy Meadows Camp. Another Kennedy Meadows with a post office! I asked Milo if he knew the address, but he couldn't remember. His package was mailed from home last week. He said I could call the PCT Association, that they should have the address. "Thanks, man, for the tip". With that, Milo got up and took off on his northern quest. Money was the guy's problem. If I were rich, I'd turn the guy on to enough money to reach Canada.

I went over and used my cell phone to call the PCT Association. I had to stand in a certain area and hold the phone a certain direction to get a good connection. The lady was cool and gave me the address.

I walked over to the dumpster and pulled out my cardboard box that my food had just come in yesterday. I put half of my food in the box, the other half in my pack. I went to the post office and bought a label and sent the package by Priority Mail to the Kennedy Meadows Campground post office. The box had about nine pounds of food in it. Without the extra food and bear canister, my pack was 11 pounds lighter. This would help my trip through the so called vertical Sierras and all the way to Sonora Pass.

It was nearly 10am by the time I was ready to leave. I went over to the store and bought some Gatorade and a few more candy bars to take along with me. The Gatorade bottle would be my next wide mouth plastic water bottle. I had lost my 20 year old bottle, sliding down Mather Pass. Empty Gatorade bottles worked great to fix those instant breakfasts I like.

At the store, I met Shutter Bug. She had just arrived from Mammoth. They had stayed there a couple of days at a cabin owned by friends of Steve, Steady's husband. Now they were going to spend some time in Yosemite Valley. She asked me if it were true that one can cover 30 miles a day in Oregon. I told her yes, it's a pretty flat state. But if you're running late, you can flip-flop at Ashland. They had Steve with his SUV so transportation wouldn't be a problem. You could see she was a little concerned about being behind schedule, just as I was.

I said good-bye to her after asking about Cliff Hanger. She didn't have any news of what was happening to him. So at 10:15am I left the Tuolumne Meadows area and headed down Highway 120, to the fantastic Pacific Crest Trail, on my continual quest for the Canadian border.

My back felt pretty good. My legs were rested and the huge sore on my right hand was looking a lot better. I still had an aggravating right shoulder. But that's thru-hiking. There's usually some pain or two that's always there. Highway 120 is also called the Tioga Pass area. If one goes east far enough, he or she will come out of the Sierras at Mono Lake and the small town of Lee Vining. If you head west, you will come out of the Sierras at Yosemite Valley.

Getting ready for Muir Pass Left to Right: Mountain Goat, Shutterbug, Steady, Sun Burn, Snickers and Cliff Hanger

Two old guy's at the hut on John Muir pass
Wrong way and Cliff Hanger

Journey Eight:
Tuolumne Meadows to Donner Pass

Just past the junction of Highway 120 and the PCT, I began walking on more of a dirt road than a trail. This was because tons of people walk this part of the trail. The PCT here is not the John Muir Trail because it runs down, as I mentioned, to Yosemite Valley.

The PCT now joins the Lake Tahoe-Yosemite Trail, which runs all the way to the Lake Tahoe area. Walking down the huge wide trail here, I pass the imposing Lembert Dome with a great view, and take a picture of Cathedral Peak.

While walking along, I have to pause at the different historical signs that spring up everywhere. Old time settlements and other historical sights run along the multi-branched Delaney Creek. I'm feeling really good right now. The weather is perfect. The golden meadow of Tuolumne stretches out to the west of me, connecting beautiful sculptured mountains that touch the bright blue sky of the mighty Sierras.

For a few hours I hike along the Tuolumne River and then start to climb a little. I could hear the sound of cascading water. About 100 yards further, I reach Tuolumne Falls and a foot bridge. This is definitely worth a picture. There are a few people here, but not as many as I had thought there would be. Maybe it was because the weekend is over.

Back on the trail, the PCT parallels the Tuolumne River all the way to Glen Aulin High Sierra Camp. This camp is huge. It has a store and cabins. I remember it well when I did my Ebbetts Pass to Tuolumne Meadows walk back in 1997.

I had taken this walk, which was a north to south hike, because I had missed this in 1978 due to the rude September storms. I didn't have a tent or tarp, not real smart! The camp looked bigger now. I went into the dinky store and bought an over-priced lemonade.

ECSTASY OF MISERY

I started rapping to the guy in the store about my trip and he gave me free lemonade. He asked me if I had a bear canister. I told him that I used to, but that a couple was using it down in the Yosemite Valley and then sending it home. "Oh man, you should have one of those here. The bears are pretty bad." "Well, I plan to be 10 miles north of here by sunset and I don't cook and sleep at the same place." The guy went on to say that they have bears there almost every night!

A few minutes later I was back on the trail, heading north up Cold Canyon. The trail seemed to be easy to walk along Cold Canyon Creek. A lot of the walking was through a large flat meadow.

I was surprised that I didn't see anybody until I got to Virginia Canyon Creek, where I met the first hiker of the day and that was Grunt. I had met him at the PCT campsite at Tuolumne Meadows. This guy had been off the trail for a couple of weeks. He had to fly back east to upstate New York for a wedding. Grunt had left Mexico way early, at the end of March. He had to definitely hike a lot of snow to say the least. I think it was his thing. His hardest climb was Mt Baden Powell that had a ton of snow on it. It even snowed on him while he was walking.

We sat down together and made dinner. I think he was surprised that I had caught up with him. He told me his legs felt pretty good, but he was worried about being stiff and sore tomorrow. I told Grunt that he might want to take it easy for three or four days, until he got into his groove.

Grunt said that he wished he could, but that he had to be at Burney Falls Memorial Park in two weeks. He had a couple of friends that wanted to hike with him from there to Ashland, Oregon. "Dude, you're going to have to knock out 30 miles per day or better." Grunt said he knew that and then asked if I had any Motrin. He thought he would need it to help him sleep. I said no problem, that I had an abundance of Motrin 600. So I gave him about eight to ten of these white wonders. The guy was happy, so we headed out for the last stretch of trail for the day.

I hadn't looked at the map, but Grunt said that we have 1200 feet to cover in just over one half mile and it doesn't look like there's any water up there either. "What? You've got to be kidding?" So to make matters worse, we had to haul water. This is going to be a workout.

So off we went and we sure enough started to climb. Grunt was in back of me. But then he said, "Is this your pace?" like something was really wrong with it. He took off at a torrid pace. The guy could really move, especially for a big guy. He probably will be sore tomorrow, pushing up hill like that.

I kept my slower pace, pushing it only a little bit. It's no time to get a leg strain or injury. Canada was a long way off. Grunt was a pretty strong hiker but at 28 years of age, I wasn't really impressed. When I was 28, I could have smoked the guy easily. Too bad we can't turn the hands of a clock to 28 years from now and see how fast Grunt Boy would be then.

A half hour later and a pretty mean climb, the trail leveled off a bit and there were some pretty good campsites. There was also water. A small spring ran down off the trail. "Oh man, we didn't need to bring water up here!" I said. Grunt said that it was better safe than sorry.

We set up our camping spots. I just laid out my ground mat, cushion and bag. I haven't used my tarp in weeks. It's too bad. That's extra weight I could have saved, but if it had rained, I would have been in trouble. In fact, the last time I set up my tarp was Mulkey Pass. That night it got down to 17 degrees. Grunt had a tree hammock. I've seen one before – they're pretty cool, I guess. Grunt liked his, but he wished he would have bought a bigger one. The thing only weighs a pound and a half. You don't need flat ground, only two trees anywhere between seven and twelve feet apart.

The hammock can be cool because it keeps you off the ground. An adjustable tarp hangs over you, and if the wind blows the rain from one direction, then you can adjust the tarp accordingly. It looked to me in a heavy wind that this thing may be a little difficult, especially if it's a gusting wind. Then a hiker might swing back and forth, hell it might cause bad dreams. I would like to try one some day, but not now. I'll keep my body flat on the ground, thank you.

The next morning Grunt held to what he said he would do. The guy actually got up at 4:30am and by 5am he walked out of the campsite and headed north to Miller Lake. I heard the guy getting ready in the ice cold dark. I have to give him credit for that. That's the way you get 30 miles a day and even more.

ECSTASY OF MISERY

At 7am, I finally crawled out of my sack. It was nice now, not as cold and dark as it was when Grunt got up. It made more sense to get up a little later when it's nicer. One problem however is that Grunt has probably walked five or six miles by now, and I'm still here in the same place.

As I stated before, getting early starts are great, as long as you walk late too. PCT thru-hikers must dedicate long hours on the trail day in and day out. And when there is a layover day, celebrate, baby, celebrate. I believe in layover days especially for senior hikers like myself. It can help keep an old hiker out of injury problems. Most of the time an old hiker should have a few dollars more than a young hiker, so it works out and we all know old guys party better anyway!

A short walk downhill brought me to my first lake in this section. Miller Lake was kind of pretty, but not too deep. After Miller Lake, the PCT ascended again and then drops into Matterhorn Canyon. I've heard that there's a peak called Little Matterhorn, but I'm not sure where to look for it. This is one of the problems with topo strip maps. You just don't get the big view at all. But like the Rolling Stones say, "You can't always get what want, but if you try, sometimes you get what you need." A topo strip map is all you really need and be sure you also have a compass.

Up and down I go as I travel past Matterhorn Canyon, the vertical Sierras, like a roller coaster. Now the trail levels out a bit and then I start climbing to Benson Pass. At Benson Pass I'm very surprised to find lingering snow patches at an elevation of 10,140 feet.

From Benson Pass, I ascended into a large meadow and a slow running creek. The trail would descend sharply at times. I then arrived at one of my favorite little Sierra lakes. The beautiful Smedburg Lake is a blue liquid jewel. Here at the lake I decided to have an early lunch. Oh boy, I still have plenty of junk food from the Tuolumne Meadows store. A smashed Twinkie, a melted Three Musketeers and some Oreo cookies, too. How about a sugar rush to get out of this little Smedburg Lake area ? No problem, but where's the trail?

Backtracking a little bit I find the trail again and now notice ducks up the side of a granite hill and past Volunteer Peak. The trail now heads down sharply once more to the famous Benson Lake. This lake is often called the Riviera of the Sierras.

I take the short trail down to the lake. The forest here is rich and tropi-cal-like. The trees and bushes finally break into a magnificent sandy beach. The lake is huge and has dynamic cliff surroundings, with a few small waterfalls cascading down. I saw a few backpackers along the lake. I wondered what the fishing was like. But there's no time for that. Thru-hiking has its disad-vantages.

After a half hour of rest and a few pictures, I head back to the trail. It's almost like walking through a jungle to get back to the trail. Once back on the trail, I head out and I'm soon walking another canyon divide. The trail hugs and crosses Piute Creek for a mile or two.

A young couple passed me on the way up. They're heading down to Ben-son Lake. They ask what it's like. I told them it's awesome and so is Smedburg Lake. They told me there's a flat area to camp after I reach the first little recess lake. I told them I wanted to get over Seavey Pass today.

I can't believe it. I am not in shape? I've only hiked 950 miles so far, how could I not be shape. The reality is that the last 25 miles have been both steeper uphill and downhill than I have navigated in some time. Another thing is my age. My legs are in shape for specific movements. Once I change that movement, my specialized walking muscles become disturbed and soreness sets in. The soreness is minor, however, and it really doesn't affect my hiking to any degree.

The hike out of Stubblefield is not as rigorous as the other canyon. Be-fore I knew it, I arrived at Wilma Lake and a junction with the Jack Main Trail to Hethachi.

The creek here is more like a slow running river, with clean clear sand at the bottom. It's a perfect place to clean up. I end up taking a bit of a bath and a head shampoo to boot. The stops with both bath and lunch take about an hour, but man, do I feel better. A couple of young hikers go by me. We talk about the mosquitoes, which are pretty heavy in Grace Meadows, but not nearly as bad as they were a few weeks ago.

Grace Meadows is definitely one of the most beautiful meadows in the Sierras. It's long and lush, passing between Kendrick Peak, Chittenden Peak,

ECSTASY OF MISERY

Keyer Peak, and Bigelow Peak. It's a great place to see deer scurrying about and other wildlife. The hiking is easy and breezy, except for the all time party pooper, the irritating female mosquito. Only the females bite for blood!!

Finally I arrived at Dorothy Lake, my destination for the day. There were a group of about 10 people camping near the lake. So I chose to camp just off the trail, about 300 feet above the lake with a perfect and a nice view of the lake and the cliffs around it. Plus, there were a lot fewer mosquitoes than down by the lake. It was a little bit of a hassle getting water, but after that I fell asleep under a great array of stars.

Popping out of bed early on a cold morning can be difficult, but it's something you have to do every morning. It's a constant battle to get up early, and your reason on earth overrides your laziness. Therein lies one of your powers of thru-hiking, the early start. Today I got an early start. One long 24 miles can get me to Sonora Pass. My food was getting low. At Sonora Pass, I'm a short hitchhike west to Kennedy Meadows Number Two, as I call it. This place has a store, restaurant, and showers. I could be there tomorrow. Roll those stones, baby, I'm coming in, jumping cheeseburgers!

At 6:30am I was on the trail, climbing a little bit to get over a small ridge. I had read about this last section of Yosemite, how the geological terrain changes from granite landscapes to volcanic landscapes. I guess this terrain will dominate for the next 500 miles, until I get to Castle Crags State Park.

In fact, I've just left Yosemite and entered Toiyabe National Park and one can definitely see the change in terrain and rock structure. Leaving Dorothy Lake Pass, the trail starts to drop past a couple of small lakes named Stella Lake and Harriet Lake. It's another beautiful day in the Sierras, not a cloud in the sky.

My pace is pretty fast, as I'm feeling my oats this morning. The Tahoe - Yosemite Trail – PCT glides along slowly downhill to Walker Meadows. A few packers go by and we exchange pleasantries.

Soon I arrived at West Walker River and crossed a cool bridge. I have lunch as I battle a few mosquitoes. My head net of Deet has really been a lifesaver the past few weeks. The long nylon running pants are mosquito proof, my Patagonia long sleeve shirt isn't but applying 100% Deet to the shirt keeps most of them off me. My beard also helps a little. I am able to apply Deet to my beard and not to my skin. Those little bastards are a pain, but I think with fewer lakes now, the mosquito problem should subside a bit.

After lunch, which was my last Lipton dinner, I crossed the steel bridge and started to head up Kennedy Canyon, where I now enter Emigrant Wilderness. I'm a little concerned when I enter official wilderness areas, due to the fact that trail crews are not supposed to use chain saws. Falling trees have to be cut by old-fashioned handsaws.

Even though I am an environmentalist, I think this rule is ridiculous. Walking these so called wilderness trails, one comes across a lot of downed trees. This is of course because the time and hassle it takes to cut a section of them out of the way of the trail.

The problem lies in going around them, under them, or over them; going around them creates a new trail. Sometimes hikers will create two trails when some hikers go left around the tree and others might go right. These new trails end up causing erosion problems. Even a quick thunderstorm can bring water pouring down to the actual trail and washing a portion of it out.

Yes, a chain saw is a bit noisy but so is the distant noise of jets zooming overhead. There's no way of isolating noise any more. This is the 21st century, not the 18th. The noise of the chain saw is compensated by the incredible amount of cutting it can do in just a short time. Keep a new or sharp chain on them and a trail crew dude can fly through these logs. I believe everyone would be happier.

Some of these people that make these decisions do not hike. I say send them out here and let them negotiate these falling trees and maybe they will change their minds, especially if they fall on their fat butts trying to get around one of these large fallen beauties!

With that thought pounding in my head, I started the long gradual climb to Sonora Pass. Sometimes it's actually good for me to get pissed off. It seems to give me energy and helps me to escape mentally from the tediousness of the trail.

I definitely go off on tangents about people, other hikers, and some of their bullshit on how fast they can walk, politicians and their lies, and even teachers and coaches I've had. I think it breaks up the monotony of these crazy melodies and lyrics that play over and over in one's head. The dumber the song, the more you hum it. "Come on, do the Locomotion with me, chuga, chuga, motion. If I got the notion, then come on, do the Locomotion with me!" Oh my god, I'm going insane. Please, anybody, help me!

After lunch I started the cruise through Kennedy Canyon, continually ascending towards Sonora Pass. Gradually the trees and vegetation disappear. I was in moon land once again. The rocks being more volcanic were not blinding white as they were in the previous 200 miles of the High Sierra. That was nice because I didn't need to put my scratched shades on.

The trail at this point became steeper until I came to a trail junction. There was a sign that read "take the stock trail this way and foot traffic another direction." I thought about that for a minute and decided I would go with the foot traffic trail. This way I would avoid people on horseback and road apples along the way.

I started climbing steeply, in fact, very steeply. My pace was slow and sometimes my feet would slip on the loose rocks. Upward and upward I climbed as the cold wind picked up. The views were excellent as I stopped now and then to catch my breath and look down at the stock trail that contoured its way slowly uphill.

After another quarter of a mile I reached a large snow bank and the PCT disappeared into it. There was no way I could walk straight up it without an ice axe or crampons. So I walk alongside of it for about 50 yards until the snow subsided a little. Then I made a diagonal cut across it until I reached the ridge.

Twenty minutes later I was on the ridge and looked down at the fabulous view to the south. In the other direction the trail headed north and was somewhat level. It didn't head steeply down like most passes do. In fact, that's what is unique about Sonora Pass.

Where exactly is the actual pass? Could it be here? Could it be the highest point in the next eight or nine miles before one reaches Highway 108? Or could Highway 108 be the actual pass, even though it's a good 1500 feet lower? Officially it must be the highway pass because that's where the big sign is. This is definitely the longest pass in the Sierras.

There was a young guy up there on the ridge. I rapped with him for a while. The kid had a wooden guitar he was carrying, but no pack. He was waiting for his two friends below to climb up. You could see them way down below taking small baby steps, inching their way up the pass. They were smart enough to take the stock trail, at least. I said "later dude" and headed out on a ridge walk that promoted great views of Kennedy Lake and Leavitt Lake below. I decided to make a cell phone call to my parents. I was able to get through for a few minutes before losing the connection. The cell phone, so far, was next to worthless in the Sierras. Even on the high passes I wasn't able to get connections.

The PCT switched to the eastern side of the long pass and I was finally able to get out of the cold wind. I remember in 1997 when I hiked from Ebbetts Pass to Tuolumne Meadows, Sonora Pass was so cold and miserable with winds of 60 to 70 miles per hour. I'm glad it wasn't that bad now. On the eastern side, I had to travel across three or four large bodies of snow, which is kind of rare to have so much snow in the middle of July.

I thought about Cindy Ross's book and how she had taken a long fall on Sonora Pass. I tried to figure out where she could have tumbled. There were a number of places. One thing about Sonora Pass is that it can be dangerous. Snow can hang around for a long time. The reason for this is its many shaded areas. Mt Whitney can usually be negotiated easier in late spring than the Sonora Pass can. That's because Whitney is exposed to the sun in more areas than Sonora Pass.

I was glad to get to the northern end of the pass. I looked down and could see Highway 108 passing below. If you go west on the road, you can get to the town of Sonora and the gold country area. If one goes right, you will eventually get to Highway 395 and Bridgeport. I knew by the time I got down there I would have just enough time to cook a meal, and to set up a camp site before it gets dark. It's too damn bad, because if there were a pub down there I would celebrate 1015 miles completed on my quest for the Canadian border.

After a few pictures of the pass and Sonora Peak, I headed down, dropping in elevation with each step. I ran into more snow patches that were more irritating than difficult. At one point, there was an unofficial trail junction that looked like it would get to Highway 108 pretty quickly, but I decided to stay with the looping trail that steered me into more snow piles.

Finally, I reached Highway 108 and the actual vehicle part of the pass. After a short walk the trail and the road led me into Sonora Pass Campground. The place had picnic tables and pit toilets but no water. Only a couple of people were there in the campground. I camped at what I thought would be the least windy place.

Pretty soon I started a conversation with my two neighbors, who were really nice. I asked them where the nearest water was. I kind of knew, but it doesn't hurt to ask. They told me across the road where I had just come, but if I need water, they had more than enough. They said they were going for a walk and to help myself. That was a cool break, because I didn't want to go back a quarter of a mile where I had just come from.

I grabbed a gallon and cooked up a meal of mashed potatoes with minute rice, brown gravy and some noodles that had spilled at the bottom of my pack. I found some crushed up apple chips and threw them in too. Whatever is left from the night before, like Milk Man powdered milk, got tossed in to help thicken it. It isn't the most wholesome diet, but it does fill your gut.

That night I crashed quickly. Sonora Pass and those cold winds always gave me a workout. It will give anyone a workout. Even the best hikers are human and walk on two legs.

The next morning, July 13th, I got up to another beautiful day in the Sierras. Oh yeah, it's town day, well almost like a town day. I was hoping that this Kennedy Meadows campground had the amenities I needed. I began jamming stuff in my pack and 15 minutes later I was on Highway 108, trying to hitchhike the 16 miles to the campground. There were very few cars coming through, but enough to give me a little hope. There was no way I was going to walk down there. I had a nice little area of road rocks that I would throw at a tree or any object that would make a good target. This seems to help kill some time.

Then all of a sudden I see two figures with backpacks coming down the hill from the lower end of Sonora Campground. Right away I recognize the two figures. It's Solace and Beaker Boy. "Hey, dudes, what's happening?" "Wrong Way, are you thumbing it out?" I told them I was, that I was going to Kennedy Meadows Campground. One of them said "Aren't you about 200 miles off?" I then told them what Milo had said about the other Kennedy Meadows Campground that has a post office, store, and restaurant.

This stopped the trekkers right in their tracks. Solace said that he would like to get some bacon and eggs for breakfast. Beaker Boy said he would like to stop and have breakfast too. I told them that the campground, according to Milo, was about 16 miles away. They wanted to know if Milo was here now and I said no, and that he had told me this at Tuolumne Meadows. I thought it would be a good idea to send part of my supplies to Kennedy Meadows Campground to lighten my pack.

So now Beaker and Solace and I were all trying to hitchhike. Right away I knew this was not a good idea. Three funky smelly thru-hikers all trying to get a ride was much tougher, but I didn't say anything at first.

We talked about our equipment, especially our packs. I told them that my pack was killing my right shoulder and I could see why. The strap didn't go over my shoulder, as it should. Solace noticed it too.

Solace wanted to get another type of pack with a hip belt. His pack was really light, but most people need hip belts. Hell, they only weighed a few ounces. They keep a lot of pressure from digging into the shoulders. The idea of not having hip belts was made somewhat popular by Ray Jardine. But you have to remember that Ray Jardine had Jenny Jardine split the weight up between them. And with no vehicle assistance, at least that's what Ray said in his last PCT trek, he probably had friends bring them food at different locations along the trail.

After a half hour of no luck, we agreed to split up. Since this was my place first, Beaker and Solace moved down the road. About 10 minutes later a young couple stopped and gave me a ride. They were on a short camping trip. I waived at the two thru-hikers as we drove by. I think they were happy I got a ride. Chances are better now that they would too.

Down the winding road we went, the two people asking me questions about my trip and me telling them everything that I could. They wanted to help me out, so when we got to the campground they took me all the way to the store and restaurant, which was a good mile off the highway. This was one enormous campground. There were quite a few campers here. Giant motor homes and tent campers cluttered the area. The young couple told me it's popular because of the fishing and the trails that you could either walk or go by horseback.

The two kids dropped me off at the restaurant. I rushed into the café and ordered the Paul Bunyan breakfast. It was great, the waitress was cool, and the price was very fair for a place up in the mountains like this. By the time I finished, Beaker Boy and Solace had arrived. They too got a ride all the way to the café.

After eating I went to the store, which also doubled as the post office. There were a number of people there so I waited my turn. I told the man at the store that I was hiking the Pacific Crest Trail and that I had a package sent here for me. The guy said okay, just a minute, and he went to back to look for my package. "Raley?" he said. I said yeah and then spelled it for him R A L E Y. He disappeared for a few minutes. This was always a nervous time for me.

A few seconds went by and then what seemed to be forever, the young guy finally came back emptyhanded. "Sorry, guy, but there's no package for Raley." "Hey dude, I sent it Wednesday morning from Tuolumne Meadows, which is only 70 or 80 miles from here. It should have been here Friday or so."

The guy in the store said that he was there on Friday and saw the mail come in and believed there were only two packages that arrived. When I asked what about the other days, he said that the mail only gets delivered there once a week. I told him that he must be kidding, and he said that he wasn't, as he headed back to the cash register. I was freaked. I needed three days of food and this store was tiny!

I began examining the wooden shelves in the store. I was surprised to see that it was outfitted pretty well for dried food and wasn't priced too high. I grabbed three Top Ramen, mashed potato mix, powdered milk, candy, and I couldn't believe it, they had Lipton dinners. What luck! I also picked up some Oreo cookies and beef jerky. I hoped this would see me through to Echo Lake Resort. The kid in the store said he would send my package back to the return address. That food could be used later on in a future supply box. I thanked him and left. The total bill was only $28. Not bad at all.

The shower cabin had men on one side, women on the other. It was pretty clean. The shower was great, plenty of water pressure and hot water. Oh man, it felt good to get five days of trail dust off of me.

After showering I was able to use the camp's little laundromat. I washed all my dirty stuff, even my Pendleton. This time I let it dry naturally. My last Pendleton I had thrown in the dryer and the thing shrank to half its size. It was a real source of amusement to Meadow Ed at Kennedy Meadows, in the Southern Sierras.

By the time I got all this stuff done it was 1pm and hey, why not have lunch, you're already here. So I pigged down an enormous cheeseburger, potato salad, fries, and a fantastic chocolate shake. About 1:30 I headed out and walked the mile out of the huge campground.

On Highway 108 I was concerned because not very many cars were going by. It was now late Sunday; most of the traffic had come and gone. Suddenly I got an idea and called my girlfriend, Linda Robison, alias Trail Perfect. "Linda, what's happening?" I told her that I had called Eric Carpenter and that there would probably be another story in the paper soon. I asked her if she could have Gordon of Gordon's Easy Trails send me a new backpack and Ridge Rest to Echo Lake Resort.

I told Trail Perfect that my shoulder was killing me and sometimes I have to take Motrin to keep down the pain and that this pack, called the Go-Lite Gust, was very popular on the trail. It was cheap and only weighed 20 ounces. I told her the Sierras were coming to an end and I was lightening my load as much as possible. She said that she would call Gordon to make sure he has one in stock. "Thanks, honey, later."

Not long after the phone call I got a ride by a young woman, of all things. Man, I sure wouldn't pick me up if I were a girl alone. I think she was also a thru-hiker. She took me back to Sonora Pass campground. I felt really lucky to get a ride at this time of day. My trip down there was a success, except for my package. But I was rested, clean, and full of carbs for the hike.

Beaker Boy and Solace were just leaving to hike the trail. They were going to get in an hour of hiking before it got dark. I was too, as soon as I arranged my pack and stuff. But then I saw three old friends on the other side of the campground. It was Amigo, Tread Lightly, and Dragon Fly.

ECSTASY OF MISERY

I went over to where they had their table. "Wrong Way, what's up? I thought you would be further along than this." I had to remind them that they were ahead of me. They said that they had gotten a ride from Dragon Fly's brother to Bridgeport; he lives just outside of the town, on a ranch. "Oh man that sounds cool." They said they had all kinds of good grunts, like huge salads, hot dogs, chicken and steaks. "We have more food than we can eat." They would be leaving tomorrow, as I would be.

That night we had an awesome barbecue and a lot of laughs. These three characters were from Chico, California, not far from here. I'm not sure what Amigo's brother did for a living, but Amigo was a school teacher. About 8pm, a harvest moon appeared on the horizon. It was huge and amber in color. I was amazed. It was one of the most beautiful moons I've ever seen.

The next morning I arose about my usual time. Amigo was already up and talking to an old white-bearded dude on the other side of the campground. I broke camp in about a half hour. We all pretty much met at the trailhead. Tread Lightly headed out first, then Amigo and Dragon Fly. I followed and right behind me was this old white-haired dude in a straw hat. Up the switchback we all went at a pretty crispy pace. I usually go at a slower pace, but I had to keep up with the crowd.

About halfway up I took a short pit stop. And lo and behold the funky old guy passes me. "Hey wait a second, buddy, how old are you, and how can you haul ass so fast?" "I'm 62" he said. "My god you're older than me." He said that age is only a mental state. I said "yeah, that's what I'm worried about, my mental integrity." The guy didn't laugh; he just kept jamming up the switchback trail. I followed him and was able to keep up, but I was pressing it a bit. An hour of this and we all had climbed out of the pass. Sonora Pass lay behind and below us. It was time to venture north, back into the great wide open.

It was here at the first flat spot I congratulated the old dude. I found out that his name was Cloud Walker. He was from Virginia and had walked the Appalachian Trail twice. The guy was definitely fit as a fiddle. He was now doing sections of the PCT, working his way to Canada. This section he was going from Sonora Pass to Belden on the Feather River. That's where his wife was going to pick him up.

So we all headed out, except Tread Lightly, who was way ahead of us somewhere. An hour later we went by Wolf Creek Lake and Sonora Peak. The trail pretty much followed the Carson River for the next seven miles. Soon I passed Stanislaus Peak. I was alone now. Everybody was walking at their own pace. I had taken lunch early and everyone passed me. But a few hours later they all had their lunch and I passed them once again.

The PCT had now entered Carson-Iceberg Wilderness. This was not one of the most popular sections of the PCT. I remember in 1997 when I walked through here the place was loaded with cows and several times I almost got lost, taking a cattle trail instead of the PCT-Tahoe-Yosemite Trail. There weren't any cows now, but they must have been through earlier because I could see plenty of road pies along the trail.

The problem with cattle is they dump anywhere, often into creeks or embankments which drain into lakes. The water then can become polluted and before you know it, you end up with a good case of the runs.

This happened to me in 1978 while hiking through the Marble Mountains of extreme Northern California. I drank from the creeks freely. There were cattle and unfriendly cow boys everywhere. Ten days later I had to bail out of the mountain just south of Mt Lassen at a place called Horse Thieve Flat.

That night when the runs hit me, it was violent. I was sweating pretty bad too. The dreams I had between bouts of diarrhea were really weird. In one dream a giant white horse without a rider came hauling ass out of the forest and was about to run over me when I woke up in a panic. It was very real like.

I found out later that Indians used to talk about dreams of horses galloping at them or around them. The story was handed down through generations. Did you see the horse? If one said yes, it meant this guy was one sick Indian. I was fascinated when I read this in an old folk lore book of the wild west.

The rest of the day I hiked alone. I guess I was out in front of the others. My pace was not fast, but I was steady at it until 7:30pm. That night I crashed at Wolf Creek.

The next morning I got up at 6:15. Before I headed off, Cloud Walker passed me at 7am. We walked together for the rest of the morning, until about lunch when Cloud Walker takes his one hour siesta, not a bad idea really, a casual lunch and a short nap.

This is where I passed by him again. The other three guys were still behind me. Cloud Walker told me that they take a lot of breaks and have all kinds of good food. But good food can weigh a hiker down. It's all up to the hikers. Many hikers don't consider food as weight. They will put anything in their packs. Jars of peanut butter, a jar of grape jelly, stuff like that. That sounds great to me right now, but I still wouldn't want to carry all that weight.

That's why I really try to pig out on town days and layover days. Get the good out of those days because leaner and meaner days are going to follow. I've been told that a male hiker weighing 170 pounds covering 25 miles per day needs at least 6000 calories per day. That's one reason that Snickers candy bars are so popular. One king size Snickers has well over 500 calories. They taste pretty damn good on the trail too. Damn, I think I'll sit on this log and have one right now. Too bad it's not a king size, just a regular one.

The rest of the day I hiked pretty much alone. A few section hikers came and went. It was pretty much just a hello and good-bye scenario. I knew that my four friends were probably just behind me.

Golden Lake was the first real body of water that I came to. It looked like a shallow lake with willows surrounding it. The trail then seems to climb in and out of gullies, and then it passes a small creek and heads in a more northern direction. A few hours later, after a day of vigorous hiking, I reached Wolf Creek, and like in 1997, I decided to camp here for the night. I was expecting my friends to show up, but they never did.

The next morning I left camp at 7am and headed up the trail. Today I would cross Ebbetts Pass. Not much to Ebbetts Pass, except that my parents had dropped me off there in 1997 when I walked to Tuolumne Meadows. It was here that I bailed out in 1978 when a three day storm hit. I was under a rock for three days and nights just past the pass, about six miles north of it. I was very interested in seeing the rock once more, taking a picture of it and giving it a kiss. This rock saved me from a lot of misery because I had no tent or tarp, just a long rubber raincoat called a kahula. Every once in a while over the past 25 years I thought about this rock and always wanted to visit it some day.

At Wolf Creek Pass I had my usual late breakfast and then immediately

Amigo, Tread Lightly, Cloud Walker, and Dragon Fly passed me by. I knew those guys were close. They also camped at Wolf Creek, but at the second branch. There were three tributaries which joined together and flowed into Elder Creek that flowed out of Asa Lake. After breakfast of Carnation Instant Breakfast, a fruit bar, and a chunk of cheese, I headed out and almost immediately passed small but pretty Asa Lake.

The trail soon traveled through sagebrush and views of a few lakes below. It then enters a forest of white bark pines and a meadow with snow patches in the shade. Old cow dung lies just a few feet from the snow, reminding me that the days of crystal pure drinking water were starting to come to an end. A few miles later I pass Nobel Lakes and Nobel Canyon Creek. Two hours later at about high noon I reach Ebbetts Pass.

Ebbetts Pass has a small road that goes through it. Where it goes I don't know for sure. My California map that I carry is almost like a strip map itself. I cut it up into sections to save some weight.

As I mentioned before, Ebbetts Pass brings back memories of that terrible storm, called Hurricane Norman, back in 1978. The storm came out of Mexico and killed 12 people in the High Sierras. They weren't equipped for it. The weather can be rough, wet, and even a pre-season snowstorm can hit in September.

Well, I wasn't prepared either. I didn't have a tarp or tent, just a raincoat. Then this rock appeared out of nowhere, maybe 50 feet or so above the trail. It was sort of hollow underneath and it was dry. It also blocked a really cold wind that blew out of the south. With my two-pronged walking hoe I was able to re-landscape it a bit. It was pretty comfortable.

For three days and nights I stretched out under the rock. I would listen to my radio. I would only get one station during the day, but at night I could get 10 or 12 stations, including stations from Colorado, LA and San Francisco. I was starting to get a sore throat so I started taking some antibiotic pills.

On the third night I fell asleep and the next morning I woke up to a beautiful blue sky and a winter wonderland. It had snowed about three to five inches. I headed out immediately, slowly trying to find the trail.

As the day wore on the snow melted pretty fast. By the time I reached

ECSTASY OF MISERY

Ebbetts Pass the snow was gone.

Wow that happened 25 years ago and here I was again, heading in the opposite direction and no longer a young man. Yep, just like Jerry Garcia from the Grateful Dead said, "What a long strange trip it's been."

I crossed the highway and only went up the trail a short distance when I ran into my buddies once again. They were having lunch and a good one at that. They had fresh fruit and a few vegetables. Heavy stuff to carry, but they weren't in a hurry.

I believe Cloud Walker had to be in Belden by a certain date. His wife was going to pick him up and they were going to drive through Mexico or something. Cloud Walker was ready to go and I had eaten my late breakfast just a short time ago, so we were ready and off we went, a 56 year old and a 62 year old phenomenon. We both walked about the same pace, so that was cool.

I told Cloud Walker about my pet rock and that I wanted to stop and take a picture of it. I wanted Cloud Walker to stay with me so he could take a picture with me under the rock. "Oh I can handle that" replied the white-bearded dude with the straw hat. So off we went, past Upper and Lower Kinney Lakes and onto Raymond Meadows. We passed quite a few people. I couldn't believe how popular this place had become. Probably because of the beautiful volcanic peaks and rock formations that were everywhere.

I knew my rock lay near a creek. I didn't know if that creek was Eagle Creek, Pennsylvania Creek, or Raymond Creek. Reynolds Peak and Raymond Peak tower over most everything. But it was the view across the open canyon that interested me the most. It looked familiar. It should be, because that's what I gazed out at for the three days I laid under the rock.

Shortly after traveling through Ray Meadows, Cloud Walker and I began seeing large volcanic rocks that had rolled down from the high volcanic ridge above us. These rocks began looking more and more like my rock, but none of them were, at least so far.

Cloud Walker was into it too. He would ask me now and then, "Hey, maybe it's that one." I kept looking, still no recognizable pet rock. At Pennsylvania Creek things looked very familiar. My hopes were up as I walked away from the creek. I thought for sure I would see my rock, but no such luck. My memory from 25 years ago didn't remember so many of these big volcanic rocks. Could there have been a rockslide or two during the last 25 years? I don't know.

By the time I reached Raymond Creek, I knew that something was wrong. I could tell by walking the other side of the valley that I had passed the rock. Cloud Walker started reading the guide book maps to see if a pretty, cool campsite would be coming up in the next six to eight miles. It was now late afternoon.

Cloud Walker then read the part of the trail guide that took in where we were. He read "Now if you look several hundred feet below you, you can see the old PCT below, winding around undulating gullies. This trail was abandoned for a new higher trail in the early '80s." "Hold it right here. That explains it. We walked above it! Damn it to hell anyway. I bet it was just down from the trail at Pennsylvania Creek! Shoot, man. Oh well, you can't always get what you want. Someday I'll make another shot at it, but for now I just don't have time. The Canadian border is a long way off."

Cloud Walker and I then headed out towards the Twin Blue Lakes area. We passed a series of lakes as we hiked along at a quick pace. First we came to Summit Lakes, then the upper Sunset Lake. We finally stopped at Tamarack Lake where a couple was camping with their dog "Rough Guy".

We needed water so Cloud Walker let me try his water filter out while he talked to the two young people about bears. Cloud Walker was really concerned about bears. I heard him tell Amigo about it after we climbed out of the Sonora Pass area.

The couple said that they don't sleep at the same place that they cook at. "Yeah, but other hikers don't know that and sometimes they camp where you ate; that can mean trouble," Cloud Walker explained.

I'm saying to myself, why tell these young people about that. Is he trying to freak them out? I doubt it because they have Rough Guy. Everyone knows that a dog will keep a bear away. Bears don't like dogs at all, especially a big dog like Rough Guy. What he was really saying is that now we couldn't camp here because they had cooked here about an hour ago. Ridiculous. Cloud Walker definitely had a bear phobia.

ECSTASY OF MISERY

So we hiked out of Tamarack Lake, even though it was almost sunset, and headed once again to the huge Twin Lakes. Soon we came to a dirt road and immediately saw an SUV coming our way. We waved and the driver waved back. He looked at me and then smiled. The guy parked the SUV and out jumped a guy who looked familiar. "Wrong Way, what are you doing way up here, you're doing great." I said that I have been hiking pretty good, even though my shoulder is hurting and told him I was getting a new pack at Echo Lake. I really don't have any excuses, especially now that I'm walking with Cloud Walker who is older than I am.

Finally it dawned on me who this person was. It was Steve, Steady's husband, who drove Cliff Hanger to Fresno. "How are the two girls doing?" Steve said they were doing pretty good and were about three days or more behind us. He also said that Sun Burn was coming back to the trail. Steve offered us some goods from the car. I had a cold Gatorade and a Mounds bar, but Mr Organic only took a few crackers. We said "Later" to Steve and bolted down the trail. It was now getting pretty dark.

The cool campsite Cloud Walker was talking about never materialized. We ended up camping on some flat rocks. I decided not to cook because it would freak out Cloud Walker. So I ate Top Ramen in its cold cubical form and washed it down with water. Cloud Walker was even worried about the crumbs on the ground. "Leave those to our black ant buddies, man." But Cloud Walker had to kick dirt on them so they were partially buried. "Whatever dude, I'm hitting the hay."

The next morning Cloud Walker woke me up stirring around, getting ready in the dark. I was sort of dozing off when I saw the guy standing a few yards from my feet wondering if I was going to stir. I could see him, but I squinted my eyelids so he would think I was still sleeping. Then he headed out. I fell back to sleep for about an hour and got up after the sun warmed the place a little.

Today would be a day to get as close to Echo Lake as possible. It was nice to hike by myself again. I really didn't mind at all. I headed north, past Lost Lake. The hiking was moderately hard, but I made good time. There were excellent views of the Twin Blue Lakes. The trail had changed quite a bit since 1978. In those days it actually went much closer to the lakes. In 1978, however, a huge storm started to develop here. I remember it blew up here with winds around 60 or 70 miles per hour.

I arrived at Carson Pass and Highway 88 at 1pm. I stopped at the forest service information station. I was hoping they sold cold soda or at least candy bars, but no such luck. The lady could only offer water and the PCT register to sign. I read the register quickly and saw Cruising Carson's name for the first time in 500 or 600 miles.

The usual people were in the register. Choo Choo and Long Haul seemed to be traveling together now. Free Radical, Mercury, Billy Goat, Prune Picker and Apple Pie sounded like a couple. Then there was T-Bone, Leprechaun, Huff and Puff and others. No Cloud Walker however. Then there was Milo. Milo had a cool poem, it was kind of sad. It looked like he was leaving the trail due to economic reasons.

I wrote my name and then split down the highway where the PCT continued on its journey north. There were some cool historical markers, one about Kit Carson. On the other side of the highway there was a large parking lot, with pit toilets and a trash can. The trash can was of interest to me as a place where I could unload all my empty wrappers and other trash. It's a good idea to do this. It cuts down on the smell of certain things like old candy bar wrappers. It also lightens the load. Soon I was back on the trail heading up and climbing out of the pass.

After a few miles I was crossing through a wide sloping green valley. It reminded me of old California, with rolling green hills. Soon I passed and crossed the upper Truckee River. The river was more like a creek, as it wound its way down towards the valley below, then picked up tributaries and became much wider. When one is walking the PCT, he crosses rivers that started out as creeks.

I was looking forward to arriving at Showers Lake. Here I remember getting a fresh cooked trout by some campers I had befriended in 1978. Right around 4pm I arrived at the lake to find quite a few campers stationed around it. I decided to make dinner here by this beautiful lake.

I thought I'd make a couple of Top Ramen dinners because that's all I had. I reached into my plastic trash container, and to my horror there was nothing! Evidently I had left my food on top of a parking pillar while I dumped the trash out into the trash can at the parking lot at Carson Pass! No food, man, I had blown it. I put my stove back. I was completely blown away. What a drag, no food and I was hungry. There was nothing to do now but bolt towards Echo Lake, some 15 miles away. Down the trail I flew trying to figure out if I could make it to the Echo Lake store some time tonight. But how late does it stay open?

The trail after Showers Lake climbs quite a few feet before it levels off and traverses a side of a ridge. Then it heads north in an easy to hike terrain towards Echo Lake. I was flying along now. My pack was light and I was giving it all I got to get at least as close to the Echo Lake Resort store as I could.

The last 5 miles of the trail was a knee thumping descent. Down, down I went, practically jumping from rock to rock. This descent seemed to go on forever. I finally got to Highway 50 and Echo Lake ski area. I thought for a bit that this place may have a small restaurant or a store, but no such luck. There was probably a restaurant but it probably is only open during the skiing season.

Crossing Highway 50 I continue towards Echo Lake. It's now dark, nearly 8:30. I take a short break and take out my Pacific Crest Town Guide and discover that the store closes at 8pm. I'll have to wait until tomorrow before I can eat. I decide to camp at the next flat area. As I travel by quite a few cabins, most of them were dark inside. They were probably cabins used by families during their vacations.

Finally I find a place to crash along the trail, a kind of funky place, but it's now 9:30pm and pitch dark. Down goes my ground cover, my thermarest and my bag. I put my Pendleton on to keep warm because my sleeping bag has lost its loft. I then put on my head net which I sleep in every night. It's a must for me since I don't have a tent. It helps to keep the bugs off my face. The head net is one of the most valuable hiking friends I have. I take off my hat and put it next to me, then my watch, compass, lighter and flashlight.

I look up at the stars for a while and slide my head net over my face and fall asleep. It was a big mileage day for me, having covered close to 30 miles. I know that sometime this evening I had to have passed Cloud Walker somewhere along the way. It doesn't matter, tomorrow is civilization day with real food, ice cream and rest. God I am hungry.

The next morning was July 17th. It's kind of overcast, something I haven't seen for a while. The great weather I've been having was starting to change. After walking for about a half mile I reached Echo Lake Resort parking lot and then down a very short trail, I arrived at the store. The store was open. It probably opens early because of the fishermen who like early starts because the trout feed in the morning. This is when most fish are caught.

The store is geared more for fishermen than hikers. They have Coleman butane fuel, but it is sold in the big canisters which are used by car campers and such. The girl in the store was nice and I think she knew by looking at me that I am a Mexico to Canada thru-hiker. We have a gaunt look about us and I'm sure a certain scent too. I buy some chocolate milk and a pastry even though I'm not hungry any more. It is weird my hunger seems to have disappeared. I'm beyond hungry, more like numb now.

The girl tells me that they do have cabins for rent but you had to spend at least two nights. It was $160 for two nights, too much for me. She then suggests that I go to the Berkeley Youth Camp facility about a half mile down the road. She said that they have tent cabins that are very reasonable.

I thanked her and asked when the post office opened. She said that it opened at 11am and closes at 2pm and that it was right beside the store. I said I'd be back later and left heading to the Berkeley Youth Camp. I walked up a short trail to the parking lot above the store and then down the highway. Man, I'm tired. My feet took a beating coming down out of the highlands to this place.

About a mile later I arrived at the Berkeley Youth Camp. I was directed to Tom who ran the place. It was weird. There were a few buildings, including a cafeteria and bathrooms. There were regular wood cabins and tent cabins. I finally found the guy and asked him if he had a place to crash. He did have one tent cabin left. It was 40 bucks a night, including meals. "Great, man, I'll take it."

Tom said that bathrooms are the long wooden structures and they also have showers on the other side of the toilets. "That's the cafeteria, we eat at 8am, 12pm, and 5pm every day. The only thing you have to do is get along with the kids." I said "No problem," and asked where they were. Just then a giant recording of Reveille hit the air waves .

Young kids suddenly rushed out of cabins and lined up on the basketball court. A couple of camp counselors came out and started telling the kids some of the events of the day like a nature walk and swimming lessons.

Tom told me if I wanted breakfast it would be best to get to the cafeteria 10 minutes early and get served early before the maddening crowd gathers.

I quickly went to cabin 42, the one I rented. I left my pack there but made sure I kept my valuables including my money and credit card with me. I wasn't sure about the place with these kids. Their ages ranged from 9 to 13 years old, both boys and girls. I really didn't have time to clean up before breakfast so I tried to sit as far away from people as I could.

The camp was different from the YMCA camps I went to as a youth. These kids ran wild. Several of them had boom boxes with that hip hop jive and some playing rap. The breakfast was great. I ate quite a bit, but not as much as I thought I would. I believe that my stomach had probably shrunk some.

After breakfast I jammed back to my cabin and got my soap and stuff. Then I headed to the showers and scrubbed up really good. It was great. While heading back to my tent cabin I didn't see any kids. I guess they were off somewhere having a good time. The next step was laundry but instead I fell asleep in my cool cabin. I didn't wake up until 11am. Oh boy, only an hour until lunch time. Hey man, this is the life.

My tent cabin was incredible. It looked out to South Lake Tahoe which was about 10 miles away. I could just see the southern part of the lake and the casinos on the Nevada side. What a view with a cool breeze blowing into the tent to boot.

When I looked in the mirror before going to the showers, I was shocked to see that a big portion of my lower lip was caked with dried blood. I remember that I had neglected to apply Chapstick on my lips and they had cracked horribly. While waking up in the morning I accidentally stuck my thumb hard against my lower lip and it had bled like hell.

If I see a small mirror in that nearly worthless fishing store, I am going to buy it. That way I can at least look at myself before I come to civilization. A mirror can also double for a signaling device if one wanted to be noticed by aircraft, etc.

After lunch, which I got to early and looking and smelling a lot better than before, I made the decision I would stay one more day. That way I wouldn't have to walk to the store and back. Today I would just do my laundry and rest. Tomorrow I would go to the store and post office as soon as the mail gets there at 11am. I should be getting my food parcel as well as my new backpack, a Ridge Rest gound mat, plus new shoes. By just resting today would also give the mail service one more day to deliver the stuff. It's only been four days since I ordered the pack and Ridge Rest at Kennedy Meadows Camp. Today is the day to wash, rest, eat, and communicate with home. My cell phone worked great here.

After washing my clothes in the bathroom sink, they came out nicely. I had hot water and plenty of soap. Dinner was at 5pm and I wisely got there early and dived into the fried chicken. The food was good here and the kids were amusing, so full of energy and stuff. The boys here were silly and more immature than the girls at this age. I tried to sit away from them, but even so I was pretty much in the middle of their antics. After dinner I headed back to my cabin and rearranged my drying clothes. That night I listened to talk radio and fell asleep probably around 11pm.

The next morning I got up at 7:30 and hustled to the cafeteria and ate a huge breakfast that included pancakes with blueberry syrup. They were awesome. I chose blueberry because I thought of those blueberries in Washington growing right along the PCT.

Washington is still a long way off. Oh man, will I make it? Time is going by fast now. It's already July 18th and I still have almost half of California to conquer. After breakfast I went back to my cabin and actually fell back to sleep. I couldn't believe it. My body needed the rest.

The post office opened at 11am and I was there sucking down a real Gatorade. I gave my name to the postal girl and she said to my joy, "Oh yes, Mr Raley. I believe we have two packages." That's always a relief at those places.

I sat down on a rock in front of the store and opened my boxes. The first box had both my Ridge Rest sleeping mat and my new backpack. The other box was my New Balance All Terrain pair of shoes. I put my old bag and thermarest into the box that my new stuff came in and mailed it back to my parents.

I took off my old shoes and tossed them into the trash can. I put my new shoes on and they seemed fine. If anything they were slightly loose. It's better a little loose than too tight. That's the way with New Balance shoes: they're usually made a little wider than other running shoes.

I gathered up my stuff and headed back to the Berkeley Youth Camp. I was really anxious to load up my new pack. The new pack only weighed 19 ounces and had some 3800 cubic inches. It was basically a glorified stuff bag with one large pocket in the back of it. The main thing I was worried about was how the straps fit on my shoulders. I was pretty sure I would miss my thermarest, but it weighed 22 ounces. The Ridge Rest weighed about 10 ounces. Between my new Go-Lite pack, called the Gust, and my new Ridge Rest, it saved almost 3 pounds of weight.

Back at camp I put all my stuff in my new pack. My Ridge Rest worked great as a framework for my pack by rolling it up and then putting the rolled up mat in my empty pack. I would then let it unfold and it becomes a frame, which gave my pack form as well as kept it open. This made it easier to load. My clothes went into a trash bag and my food into an acrylic net bag. Most of my tools and other odds and ends went into my pocket. My stove, lighters, and eating utensils went into a special lightweight bivy bag. The most important thing is that my new pack felt very comfortable. The straps rode across my shoulders very evenly. I was one happy man.

A few hours later I was back in the front of the line at the cafeteria. My last dinner was a good one. I discovered that this was the last night for the Berkeley Youth Camp kids. They were going home tomorrow. They were going to have a dance at the new main lodge. I didn't think too much about it. About 8pm that night I heard the music blasting out of the lodge. It was basically hip hop with some rap mixed into it.

I decided to check it out, so I put on my new shoes and headed over to the lodge. Man, what a mad house! The music was blasting and there was a major light show going on. The kids were swinging their tee shirts around in circles above their heads. At the same time they were screaming something that I couldn't understand. It was kid rap. I'm too old to understand any of this.

The leaders in the front who were setting the pace were two black camp leaders. I guess they were going crazy too. One leader had a mouth full of green lights that flickered in his mouth. I couldn't believe it. The music just kept going on endlessly. The kids kept jumping around and swinging their shirts. After about 15 minutes of continuous action I was starting to get tired of watching and headed back to my tent cabin.

About half way back I heard some folk music and stopped to listen. One of the lady counselors had a guitar and was playing a Peter, Paul and Mary song, written by Bob Dylan. Not bad. The girl had some talent. But she had a very small audience. The hip hop had it beat in the ole popularity poll.

I got back to my cabin a minute later. The sound of music was way off in the distance now. Oh boy, those kids sure know how to have fun. About 11pm I fell off to sleep, ready to face the next day with a smile. It was a travel day through the incredible Desolation Wilderness.

At 6am I got out of the sack and grabbed my pack which I had prepared the night before. After a quick trip to the head, I was on my way. It had been a great stay. It turned out to be a pleasant surprise because my first impression of the place with all those kids had me freaked a little. How can a thru-hiker get more than this place for $40? Where you can get a nice tent cabin overlooking South Lake Tahoe, with three excellent meals a day, plus the good bathrooms and showers? The most important thing was that all the kids seemed to be supervised pretty well. I think if I had a kid about this age, I wouldn't mind if he went to a place like Berkeley Youth Camp.

Down the highway I walked with well-rested legs and new shoes. The new pack on my back felt good, although it would take a little time to get use to. For one thing there was only one pocket. My other pack had six pockets. I was reasonably happy so far with the hip belt. It seemed to work taking pressure off my shoulders.

Shortly after arriving at the PCT I noticed that the trail rocks hardly penetrated any pressure on the bottom of my feet. These New Balance Trail Runners I am wearing are heavier than my other running shoes, so they felt pretty good. I'm ready to go, so up the trail I went. I made a left turn and started walking north once again. I've just finished another section of the trail guidebook. I just left Section J and entered Section K, Echo Lake Resort to Interstate 80, a rather short section that finishes at Donner Pass. Today was now July 19th, less than two weeks until August, the last true summer month.

So down the trail I hiked, feeling good. A few day hikers passed me by. This area called Desolation Wilderness is probably the most crowded section of the PCT. This is due to two basic reasons. One, it is easy to get to, and two, it's incredibly beautiful with the most dense amount of lakes in the Sierras.

After the first Echo Lake, I soon pass Upper Echo Lake. It had cabins lining its sides. It looked like the only way to get to Upper Echo Lake was to either walk or go by boat.

Soon the Echo Lakes are just memories, as the trail slowly climbs and passes Tamarack Lake. My god, just how many Tamarack names are there? Tamarack Peaks, Tamarack Creeks, Tamarack Lakes, and Tamarack Campgrounds! Oh and how about Tamarack Flats! At home there is a Tamarack Street. I knew there was a Chief Tamarack, but I don't know much about him except that he must have been one hell of a chief to have all these places named after him!

The trail levels out now and soon I reach famous Lake Aloha. I pause here to take a break. I started talking to a couple that was on a day hike. I told them about my trip so far and they were amazed. The lady ends up taking a picture of me. I have a bite to eat and head out again, amazed at the beauty of this place.

Towards the end of the lake I met two young women, probably in their early twenties. They were both interested in my pack. They asked me if it was comfortable and how much it weighed. I told them that so far so good and that it weighed only 19 ounces. They couldn't believe it. How could packs that big weigh so little?

After talking to them for a bit I headed out once again. It seemed like I just couldn't get going for the day. If I wasn't stopping to talk to somebody, I

was stopping to take a picture. I wonder if the Appalachian Trail was like this. I've heard it is a trail to meet people with some 2000 or more people trying to walk it each year, as compared to 400 or so thru-hikers on the Pacific Crest Trail.

Heather Lake and Susie Lake are soon passed and finally I start feeling more alone as the day hikers' scene is past. Late afternoon is approaching and so is Dick's Pass. I'm surprised to see that snow is still located in shady areas around 9200 feet. From Dick's Peak it's just a downhill trek past Dick's Lake.

At Fontanelli's Lake I decided to prepare for dinner. I'm really hungry and although it's still early, I decide to eat here and camp later. A double package of Top Ramen chicken flavored noodles will do with some sharp cheddar cheese, and finish it off with a large Snickers bar for dessert. Should I eat that Honey Bun pastry or save it for tomorrow?

Just about then I heard a noise and right in back of me appeared Wookie and Island Mama. "Hey man, what's happening?" I asked. "Fancy meeting you here. How was Yosemite?" "Hey, it's Wrong Way," blurts out Wookie. They said that Yosemite was great and mentioned that they had sent my bear canister to the address I had given them. I told them that my girlfriend told me a few days ago that she received the canister. They asked if I were camping here and I told them no, that I was just eating here and that I figured I could hike another couple of hours. "All right, let's go." Stuffing my Honey Bun back into my bag, I headed out with them.

I found out quickly that they haul ass. I wasn't going to keep that pace, especially after just eating. It was amusing watching them hike. The super long red headed Wookie would lead and Island Mama would follow in her short skirt and sandals. She would break stride every once in a while to jump over a piece of wood or any obstacle that came her way. Their packs were light because they shared different things that couples can share. There is definitely an advantage that couples working and getting along with each other can benefit with lighter packs.

I let them go. It looks a bit too fast a pace for me at this time. What I can't understand is why I'm always either passing them or they are passing me when they have a faster pace than I do. From Fontanilla Lake the trail seems to descend gently towards Middle Velma Lake and then seems to level out.

Soon after passing Middle Velma Lake, the Tahoe-Yosemite Trail breaks off from the PCT. These two trails have often coincided with each other all the way back to the Tuolumne Meadows area. From here the Tahoe-Yosemite Trail climbs over Phipps Pass and then dives down some nine miles to Meeks Bay, Lake Tahoe.

Evening is starting to arrive now as I try and get my last few miles in before it gets dark. Since Middle Velma Lake the mosquitoes have gotten thicker and thicker, as I enter the El Dorado National Forest. There are a lot of slow sluggish creeks and slushy pools of water. It damn near looks like a swamp sometimes.

The mosquitoes are so bad that I promptly apply 100% Deet to my beard, neck, and long sleeves. This holds the little bastards off just a little. I finally find a place to sleep in a viewless overgrown mosquito infested forest. I'm glad that I've already had dinner because I wouldn't want to cook with all these damn mosquitoes around. I had a pretty good day. I definitely had covered over 20 miles. In fact, I probably hiked more than 24 miles.

The mosquitoes were the worst I have ever seen, even in the Sierras. I understand why the Pacific Crest Trail Association would like to put a ridge route trail above this swamp. The forest was too thick, there weren't any views, and there was a constant barrage of fallen trees that lay over the trail. While lying on my back thinking about this and other things, the constant buzz of female mosquitoes dissipated and I finally fell asleep, with my head net on, of course.

The following morning I was up at 6am trying to break camp as fast as possible in order to beat the mosquitoes. They usually start feeding around 7 or 8am. I guess I owe those little buggers thanks for an early start because I was rolling at 6:15. It's one of the earliest starts I've had on this trip.

Down the trail I headed hoping to get out of this swamp. My next destination would be Richardson Lake. Soon I left Desolation Wilderness and crossed back again into El Dorado National Park. Richardson Lake was just about a mile from there. I stopped there for water and decided to cure it with potable water, which is an Iodine solution. I hate using this stuff but this lake had a dirt road to it and there were car campers around. When I see a road with accessible lakes like this one that many people visit, it's always best to filter, boil, or cure one's water.

The lake was kind of funky with a road running all around it. People were hanging around making noise and calling each other names. Wow, it reminded me of that saying I've seen on bumper stickers and coffee mugs "Are we having fun yet?" Fun is a weird thing. It is happiness, excitement, amusement, or just a break from the norm.

This trail, the mighty PCT, is not actually fun because it's a hell of a lot of work. It was a break from the norm, but after almost three months on the trail, it is my norm now. Is it relaxing? Hell no. Is it comfortable and content? Hell no.

Hey wait a second. Don't worry about those car campers having fun. Maybe you should ask yourself "Wrong Way, am I having fun yet?" Fun, fun, fun – Fun is a funny word alright. Maybe one should try to be more comical on the trail, think up jokes and all, because being comical is being funny and funny is just a longer word for fun!

A short distance after leaving Richardson Lake I found a rock to sit on and have my usual late breakfast. My water now has been treated for 20 minutes and supposedly that's how long it takes to kill all the bugs that can cause incredible intestinal disorders, and I've had enough of that stuff already.

After breakfast I scurry around Sourdough Hill and begin to head in a more northerly direction. The terrain becomes drier and the forest was a bit thinner. This is a nice change, for the mosquitoes have completely vanished.

The trail crosses quite a few dirt roads. It then starts to ascend in elevation. Barker Pass is probably the culmination of this elevation rise. A few hours later I reach Barker Pass, which actually has a well-groomed road going through it, Highway 3. There are a few people hanging around, just past the trail crossing.

One lady has a giant bull mastiff dog, about the size of a year old black bear. I went over and started up a conversation with the lady. "Wow, I thought your dog was a bear for a second." She laughed and said that I should have seen the huge black bear that had just walked by there a few minutes before. She said, "It was about three times the size of my dog, Spoiler." I asked where the bear was heading and she said, "Right down the trail where you'll be heading."

The lady told me that she was waiting for her husband that had walked a small adjacent trail up and around a big rock looking structure that was above us. She then told me that there was a great view of Lake Tahoe up there. I told her thanks, and that I thought I would head up there and take a few pictures.

So off I went, not only to check out the view, but also to give that giant black bear a chance to mosey out of this vicinity. It was just about a five minute walk before I reached the top. To my delight there was a fantastic view of the fabulous blue alpine lake, named by the Indians as Tahoe.

What a beautiful shade of blue Lake Tahoe is. On the south side I could see the Nevada and California border, highlighted by the fancy casinos. I was glad to be a bit north of it now and felt honored that I could see it again from the Pacific Crest Trail, just like I did back in 1978.

One other person was there. I knew it must be the husband of the lady with the big dog. "Nice view," said the guy. I said "yes" and asked him about the huge bear. He said that it must have weighed 500 pounds or more and told me how they all yelled and banged some pots at him, but he couldn't care less. "Wow, I guess he probably has a mind of his own."

A few minutes later I was on my way when I noticed spelled out with rocks along the side of the trail read "PCTA Members, This Way". An arrow pointed the way down the trail. Hey, this ought to be interesting. I noticed that the trail had just been worked on. The chopped down weeds were still fresh looking. About a mile ahead I ran into the PCTA members. I talked to them for a while and learned they were from the San Francisco area. They had a few extra oranges on them and since they were heading out of the mountains today, they gave me two incredible tasting oranges. I ate them both in five minutes.

With the PCTA members gone, I walked down the trail for about another mile and decided to make dinner a little early. I had some good water and a patch of snow. The snow patch would provide ice for my lemonade mix. I could make a lemon slush. I began boiling the water and cooked some macaroni and cheese. It came out perfect. Man, it was great. The lemon slush was so good that I must have drank a quart and a half of it.

After dinner, as I was cleaning my pan and putting stuff away, to my surprise, who came down the trail but Wookie and Island Mama. "Hey dudes, what's happening?" "Nothing much, Wrong Way. Are you eating again?" Wookie asked. "You're eating every time we see you." I said that it seems that way. We talked about their trip to Yosemite and some other things. Island Mama is very shy and doesn't talk a lot.

Wookie and Island Mama looked like they really wanted to amble, so I told them that I'll see them later. "Alright Wrong Way, see you up ahead. You always catch us anyway." I told them that I didn't know how, that they levitate up hills while the rest of us have to walk. They laughed as they hauled ass off into the sunset. I finished cleaning up and headed off. I soon began walking a high ridge that didn't have any trees. The sun was now starting to sink out of the western sky and its rays lit up the grassy barren ridge that I now walked.

I could see Wookie and his girl way down the trail, probably a half mile in front of me. It's simply surrealistic, that's all I can say. The sun, the sky, and the ridge with a little thread in it that wound around on the rocks and parted the golden green grass as the PCT made its way north.

The hiking was easy because the trail was nearly level. I was kind of excited because Whiskey Creek was only a few miles ahead of me. Whiskey Creek was where I camped in 1978. I remembered a heavy but short rainstorm hit here. All I had was a bivy bag. Goretex had just been introduced as a miracle fabric that would keep you dry but at the same time would stop you from sweating like a stuffed pig inside it. This time the bivy bag worked. The rain lasted only 10 or 15 minutes but I never got wet.

The next day I met a guy that was also camping, but he had a first class tent. This guy was a real trip. I spent part of the next morning listening to the guy rap abut bears, especially grizzly bears. He had lived in Alaska for 10 years and he had bear story after bear story to tell. The dude made me nervous afterwards for a time as I reflected on his bear stories.

I finally arrived at Whiskey Creek but only at the trail junction. The Whiskey Creek campsites were about a quarter of a mile off the PCT. This wasn't the case in 1978. The trail has been changed again. I still had over an hour of daylight left so I decided to move on towards Granite Chief.

For a short while the PCT scoots along the side of Whiskey Creek and then comes to Whiskey Creek Springs. I don't remember this in my 1978 trip. I fill my platypus water containers, making sure that I will have enough for dinner and a morning drink. My morning drink of water has taken the place of coffee. Right before I leave camp I try to guzzle at least a pint of water. It lightens my load and helps prevent dehydration. It's like my morning ritual now; even if I'm not very thirsty I still down a pint and sometimes a quart at a time. Get the water in your system before you start out.

For the next hour and a half I climb out of the Whiskey Creek basin area towards Granite Chief Wilderness. Towards the top of my climb, which was almost directly in front of what I thought was Granite Chief, I made camp. It's now 9pm and dark. The next morning I arise at 6am and leave camp at 6:20am, a good start. Today may be a town day. I'm thinking of heading down to Truckee when I get to Donner Pass. The problem is that I'm running out of cooking fuel. Besides that, I'm of course out of real food. Maybe a giant cheeseburger with fries and a chocolate shake or how about a major pizza with some dark, rich, brown beer!

Within a mile after I started I reach the famous Squaw Valley skiing area where the Winter Olympics were held in 1960. This place doesn't look like much now. Only the ski tower and the motionless ski tram seats waving in the wind give an indication of the popular winter sports place.

I soon round a corner and I see a guy and a girl arguing. I can't hear exactly what they were saying but they don't look too happy. The girl takes off down the trail. Like Island Mama she is wearing a skirt but longer, just below her knees. The red headed guy goes back to his campsite. I follow the girl about 40 yards figuring that I would soon catch up with her, but I don't. The sort of heavyset girl can hike!

Not more than 10 minutes longer, the girl in front of me meets up with a young guy that had been ahead of her. They start talking to each other. I pulled up and introduced myself. The girl's name was Belcher and the real thin kid was Leprechaun. They had started in Mexico and both were at the kick-off party. "Well, no wonder you hike so well. I thought at first you might be a local until I followed behind you and saw how fast you hike." She said that the guy back at camp was her boyfriend, Puck.

Pretty soon all three of us were hiking down the trail, anxious to get to Donner Pass. A few miles later I heard Belcher and Leprechaun yell out, "There he is, talking to two girls." I asked who he was and Belcher told me that he was Batteries Included. All three of us went up to Batteries Included and joined in on the conversation about the usual stuff. The two girls were day hikers going from Donner Pass to Squaw Valley and I guess Batteries Included was turning on the charm. The dude did have a far out straw hat that was pretty big, almost like a sombrero, but not quite as stiff and when Batteries Included talked or moved his head, his far out hat would bounce and gyrate around. I think Huck and Tom owned these types of hats, back in Hannibal.

I stood and listened to this alien rap from another generation for a while until the subject of mosquitoes came up and black beetle bugs one sees all the time scurrying across the PCT. I came out and blurted out how the bugs had turned my beard white! And man, did I get a laugh from those two girls. Batteries Included didn't laugh, I think because I stole the limelight for a while. A few minutes later Batteries Included, Puck, Belcher, and of course yours truly, Wrong Way, were off again walking past Tinker Knob and drawing closer and closer to Donner Pass.

The terrain was basically rolling hills with some trees, but there were more bushes and grassy areas. The PCT then leaves a crest and passes near Benson's Hut and then climbs up to Summit Valley. There the trail disappears in a huge snow patch, the only snow around for miles. I noticed right away that this is a ski area. It's still here because at one time a ton of natural snow fell and man made snow. This place was Donner Pass Ski Resort. I knew I was close to Highway 40 and Donner Pass. Every bit of the next half mile was uphill until the trail switchbacked down granite rocks to the highway below.

Down on the road, me, Puck, and Batteries Included hiked back in the shade of a giant billboard advertising the ventures of skiing at Donner Pass Summit. The facilities were closed now and wouldn't open until winter. We sat there waiting for Belcher to come walking down those granite rocks. She was probably with Leprechaun.

ECSTASY OF MISERY

Batteries Included and Puck wanted a telephone to call up a trail angel that put hikers up. I just wanted to hitchhike down to Truckee and buy some fuel. My next stop was Sierra City and the trail guidebook said that the store had limited backpacking supplies. It mentioned they had Coleman butane. That was always a bad sign because Coleman fuel was in the big five-pound canister, good for car campers only.

Finally Belcher came down the trail. She had fallen behind at the giant snow patch on the other side of the ridge. Leprechaun was not with her. According to my new found friends, Leprechaun was having foot problems.

After a few more minutes I decided to try my luck in hitching a ride. I really didn't want to visit any trail angel at this time. Puck and Belcher were definitely not getting along. It seemed to me that Puck was being kind of mean to Belcher. But I really didn't know why. It was none of my business anyway. So I got out on the highway and put out my thumb. I really got lucky. The third car that came by stopped and gave me a ride. I think Belcher, Puck, and Batteries Included were amazed at how fast I got a ride.

Mather Pass Palisades Lake below and what a great summer!

Journey Nine:
What the Hell Was It, A Dude From Outer Space?

The two people, Darla and Jim, gave me a ride all the way down to Truckee, right to the Mountain Hardware Store. They were impressed with my walk and wanted to know all about it. Since I had told my story to so many people, I had a well-rehearsed story line by now. I had them laughing and amazed at the same time. Practice makes perfect!

I said good-bye to my transportation friends and went into the store. I found what I was looking for. Now I had enough fuel to last me for a couple of weeks. Right next to the hardware store was an actual outdoor recreational store. I thought about going in and looking at stuff, but I didn't really need anything. I thought I would probably gross out some city packers with my acute body odor. I guess that's a nice way of saying B.O. baby! So instead of a fancy backpacking store, I cruised across the street and walked into a much more important and necessary place of business. Mountain High Pizza and Beer Palace!

It was here that I parked my bony butt for two hours powering down beer and pizza and watching the San Francisco Giants play the St Louis Cardinals. There was a bathroom where I washed up a little. It was the first time since Echo Lake that I saw my bearded face. I considered it a job to eat as much pizza as I could in order to pile on the carbs. High Sierra Pale Ale was my beverage of choice. A few hours later I hobbled out into the 90 degree heat and began hitchhiking back to Donner Pass.

I had great luck getting a ride down here, but just the opposite getting out of here. Even though there were mass quantities of vehicles going by, no one stopped. Did they think I was a drunken bum now instead of an adventurous PCT thru-hiker or what?

The road temperature was so hot that I went inside a small store and bought a couple of bottles of spring water. The label on the bottles cracked me up. The labels said that the water was Lake Tahoe filtered spring water and it was in a pint flask, just like a whiskey flask. On the front was a naked girl dressed up in a devil costume with two horns on top of her head!

I went back to the road and started hitchhiking again. My luck had not changed. There was still a steady stream of cars, but no one even glanced at me. I felt like I had become invisible. I think most of the people were heading home after visiting Lake Tahoe, Reno, or Carson City. It was Sunday now and the weekend was over. It looked like families, which wasn't a good recipe if there is more than one person in a car.

I decided to start walking. I felt that if I could get back to Highway 40 which goes by Donner Lake and then up to the summit, that I would stand a better chance because the people were about to get on the freeway and then traverse the Sierra range into the California valley below.

I walked for about a mile. I took the Highway 40 cut off to the memorial park and lake. Sure enough, there was less traffic. I soon managed to acquire a ride back to Donner Pass. The guy who picked me up was a paramedic. He said he picks up any backpacker heading for the pass. His name was Jim and he was also a backpacker. We talked about the Sierras a bit and general things about backpacking. We soon arrived at Donner Pass. I bid the dude farewell. I might have had a long walk if Jim hadn't picked me up.

Jim drove off in his green Saturn and I soon noticed that the ground was wet everywhere as I joined the trail and began walking once again. I saw hail stones between rocks that hadn't melted yet. I soon met up with a couple, a young guy and his chick. They told me that one hell of a hailstorm hit here about two hours ago. I got lucky when the storm hit; I was having pizza and beer and watching a baseball game on TV. Good timing on my part.

I climbed a ridge that leveled out to a muddy trail heading for my destination for the night, which was Peter Grubbs Hut. About 40 minutes later I reached the freeway. I walked under it and through a giant drainpipe. The trail then passed a small lake where some Mexican kids were trying to catch something that dwelled there.

Leaving the noisy freeway behind, I began climbing towards Castle Pass. I remember this area well, for my mother and my girlfriend met me here in 1978. Back then the trail went down to Soda Springs in the form of a jeep road.

Now the trail goes directly to the pass.

The hikers in the good old days stopped at Soda Springs and they would bring their orange Tang or Kool-Aid mixes and use the springs, which actually produced soda water. A mixture of Tang would produce orange pop; a grape Kool-Aid would work well for grape soda! Down below I think I could see the same dirt road that my mom and Linda cruised up to meet me, but I could be wrong.

At Castle Pass I met two couples, neither of whom I had met before. One couple was Dave and Brooke and the other couple was Jeron and Godia. They were all in their twenties. Brooke and Dave had taken a week off and visited Las Vegas with Brooke's parents, so they were just starting up again. Godia and Jeron had started at Walker Pass and were just trying to get as far as they could.

I told them that I was planning to stay at Peter Grubbs Hut for the night. I had stayed there way back in 1978 and I was anxious to see the place once more. Brooke and Dave headed out first and I went second, then Jeron and Godia followed. I was interested in Dave and Brooke for they had started out at Campo a week earlier than me and also they were loaded down with some good-looking fresh food that Brooke's parents had given them. I was hoping to cash in on some of this stuff at Peter Grubbs Hut.

Soon the trail dropped into Round Valley and then came to the cut off trail to the hut. I was the first to arrive. I was surprised at how much bigger the place was now than it was in 1978. It now was two stories, with kitchen cabinets and cooking utensils. There were solar powered lights that had timers on them so if you didn't wind the knob back they would go off. This was a good idea. If the lights were on during the day the solar energy would go to waste and the light wouldn't come on at night when they were really needed.

There was a small door on the second story to facilitate entry to cross country skiers during heavy winter snow packs. The bottom floor would be packed in with snow so a skier could just climb the ladder and climb into the hut from the second floor.

Jeron and Godia soon arrived right after I had retrieved water from the local creek. After settling in for a while, Godia began looking through the animal

-proof food shelves. It was the usual stuff. What caught my attention was the Country Time Lemonade mix.

Wow, I got an idea. While getting water out of Round Valley Creek I had discovered a lonely snow patch. It's time for a lemon slush, dudes. I ran out the door and took my wide mouth Gatorade bottle and filled it with snow. I also filled a plastic bag with the white stuff. I mixed up a strong solution of lemon mix with cold creek water and then added snow to it. Man, before you knew it, we had a lemon slush! It was unbelievably good. I ended up drinking a couple of quarts of it.

After dinner Jeron and Godia went up to the second floor to crash. After writing in the journal and reading everybody's name from the Class of 2003, I hit the hay. I decided to sleep in the older part of the cabin. It seemed more historical, I guess.

What a day it had been. I woke up at Granite Chief, marched 12 miles to Donner Pass, thumbed it down to Truckee, filled my belly with pizza and beer, thumbed it back to Donner Pass, missed a hailstorm, and then ended up at Peter Grubbs Hut slugging down a couple of quarts of ice cold lemon slush. Man, that's what I call a cool day.

The next morning I woke up early. Today was Monday, July 21st, and I began to worry again about my progress. In just 10 days it would be August and I still had damn near half of California to go. So off I went heading north, hoping to reach Sierra City by tomorrow.

It was another beautiful day. In fact, it was pretty warm. I looked at my compass that had a thermometer and it read 74 degrees, and it was only 8:00 in the morning.

Near the bottom of Basin Peak there were a couple of small springs. I had plenty of water. It was a bit early to have breakfast so I marched on, past Paradise Valley which had another slow moving spring. I didn't stop for breakfast until I reached Rock Creek which flowed out of White Rock Lake.

I stopped here and made my usual Instant Breakfast power drink. I then ate a fruit bar or two and was about to munch on a Power Bar when Brooke and Dave strolled by. "Hey dudes, what's happening? Where did you stay last night? I thought you were going to Peter Grubbs Hut."

They had decided to camp elsewhere and since they had spent a week in Las Vegas they were anxious to pitch a tent. Dave yelled as he turned a corner and crossed Rock Creek on a fallen log bridge. I told them that was cool and how I was hoping to get hold of some of their fancy store bought food. "Maybe next time, Wrong Way." Then they were gone. That's one reason they probably stayed out of the hut, guarding their grunts from Jeron, Godia, and me. A few minutes later Jeron and Godia cruised by. Oh man, everybody is passing me. It's time to jam. So off I went, again heading north to Sierra City.

The trail started to climb now and I soon had some excellent views looking both north and south. To the north I spotted what looked like the Sierra Buttes. They looked great and right below them was Sierra City. The PCT then traveled over barren ridges of strange looking vegetation. The view below of French Lake and Meadow Lake sparkled in the sun.

The temperature was getting warmer as time went on. I kept drinking my water. My water was getting lower. My thermometer now read 90 degrees and to make matters worse, the forest had disappeared. The hills were covered by the flat broad leaf things that looked pretty cool but did not give any shade. Down below I could see the English River, which would soon flow into Jackson Meadow Reservoir.

My water supply had just run out and now I was definitely looking for water, but there was none. Soon I passed Jeron and Godia who were sitting under a ledge of rocks that provided some shade. We just waved, fanning our faces expressing the absurd heat. I kept hiking along hoping to find water. Finally I found a running creek as I descended down hill. It was a bit of a hassle. The water was running pretty hard and bouncing over rocks so I just drank it down without curing it.

After a short break and plenty of water, I headed out and soon arrived at the southern end of Jackson Meadow Reservoir. The trail was rather level now and the heat of the day was giving way to a more moderate temperature. I soon came to a sign that told a historical perspective of the reservoir. I then heard the noise of speedboats tearing across the lake, some pulling skiers behind them.

A little further I reached an asphalt road. A sign read "East Meadow

ECSTASY OF MISERY

Campground, one tenth of a mile". I could camp here for the night, but it's only 5pm. I still have at least three hours of daylight left and I want to get as close to Sierra City as I can, so I decide to forge on. Another sign reads "Pass Creek Campground", but I continue on. A few cars pass me by as I head northwest. I rejoin the PCT and then arrived at a nauseating display of pine tree butchery.

Huge trees along the trail have been cut down. The place looks like a war zone. In between the terrible destruction are small creeks running down the hill. The map shows that they are a series of springs coming out of the earth.

I believe it's time to eat now, for I'm starving. There's plenty of water to clean up and cook with. The place is pretty ugly because of the tree murder, but beggars can't be choosey. If I eat here I can still walk for another hour or two and draw closer to Sierra City.

After dinner I head out, now starting to climb out of Jackson Meadow area. An hour later I reach what is called Bear Valley. The going is slow because of all the beautiful trees cut down by the lumber companies. The trees fell across the trail. Sometimes I am able to crawl under them, sometimes over them, but never around them because of the length of the trees and the steep terrain.

Darkness starts to set in. It's time to stop and crash for the day. As I walk I'm continually looking for a flat spot. Finally I spot a large logging road which dead ends at what looks like an Orange County suburb cul-de-sac, without homes.

As unnatural as it is, I might as well use it because it's flat. I walk down about 50 yards from the trail and pick out a spot. I put down my ground tarp, mat, and sleeping bag. I hit the ground with a thud and immediately take off my shoes and rub my poor dogs. What a day. I believe I walked some 25 miles today. Tomorrow is a town day. Sierra City is an official package place. I know a place that has great cabins and excellent food. After swatting off a few black ants, I fell off to a pretty sound sleep.

Suddenly while I was still asleep, I hear the sound of someone or something walking! I open my eyes. I still hear the noise of a biped coming towards me in the dark! The first thing I think of is that it is probably a backpacker walking late and he noticed the flat area like I did. One problem, I don't see a light, at least so far.

I'm starting to freak out. I decided to sit up and reach for my headlight. Immediately after I sit up, the biped starts running away. By the time I got my light, it was too late. I couldn't see a damn thing!

I hiss out as loud as I can. This is what I do at home to stop catfights that are outside my bedroom window. I let out a major hissing sound. The sound of feet running fades away as whatever it is goes back into the forest.

I'm really freaked now. What in the holy hell was that? I'm baffled to the max. Could that possibly be an animal, like a deer or a bear? I don't think so. It was definitely a biped. I'm thinking to myself should I get up and move out of here? Could that thing come back?

Then out of the pitch dark, the whole area lit up. The light seemed to be coming from the back of me, so instinctively I turn my head, actually hurting my sore shoulder. Then incredibly I see what looked like a shooting star or something, breaking up in the sky. One piece seems to take off away from me and then followed the curvature of the earth and disappeared. The blinding light around me also subsides immediately and the place is dark once more.

I couldn't believe it. I was totally dumbfounded. What in the hell is going on, man? Maybe I should get up and get the hell out of here. But where would I go? I'm tired, my headlight needs new batteries. I lay there wide awake contemplating the whole incident.

I'm thinking to myself could it have been a visitor from another world who was flying over this area of forest devastation and he decided to land around here and check out the scene. Maybe the dude lands over there in the forest and comes walking down here to get a better look. I pop up and scare the crap out of the guy, he then turns and runs back to his ship and takes off. I don't look around until his ship turns to follow the curvature of the earth and then disappears. Then at the same instant the light around me goes off!

Oh man, that's too damn much. That can't be true. It's just too far out. Over and over, I run this through my mind. No that can't be, but what was that light and what was that noise coming at me and why didn't he have a flashlight? For another 10 minutes I just lay there, bewildered. A few animals were making some type of noises. Maybe they were still frightened by the loud hissing. Has earthman and spaceman disturbed them once again? Or am I going psycho?

One thing I have to do is either get up and walk out of here or go to sleep. It makes more sense to go to sleep. So I grab a Motrin 600 and pop it down with a glass of H2O. While I waited for the Motrin to kick in, I noticed the time that this incident took place: 11:25pm, July 21, 2003. I was surprised it was so early. I thought to myself, a spaceman walking up to you in the dark forest is sure a good way to ruin a thru-hiker's sleep!

I must have fallen asleep soon after that, and the next thing I know there is a huge noisy sound of motorized machines whirling through the air. It's Apocalypse Now, man, with Marlon Brando! I roll out of my sack and look up behind the local tree and see a couple of orange helicopters bounding through the air. One copter hovers over the earth and drops a cable with a hook. There a Mexican dude wearing a hard hat who seems to be overseeing the matter pointed to something on the ground.

The copter drops down and then up. Wow, he's got a tree log on the closed hook and off he goes, like an orange dragonfly, with the tree trunk dangling below him.

I grab my camera and take a few pictures. As I'm doing this, I'm starting to remember what happened the night before. Was it real or was I dreaming? No, I'm sure it was real. One thing for sure, it's time to get out of this messed up place. It's now 6:45am and I'm already hiking at a brisk pace. I sure don't know what happened, but I do know one thing for sure, at least I'm still alive.

About an hour later the trail starts to descend down Milton Creek, towards the Wild Plum Campground, which is probably a couple of miles from Sierra City. I remember Wild Plum Campground very well in 1978; I spent the night there. There was a young couple and the guy was an egomaniac who wasn't interested in my hike from Ashland, Oregon, to this place. He was only interested in telling me about a farm he worked on. We had a little campfire going and I swear he fell asleep talking about himself.

The next morning I will always remember because I walked up the trail, a portion of the PCT that was supposed to be finished in 1978, and ended up following orange tape and not the trail at all. I had to double back to Wild Plum, go to town and ask how to get to Little Grass Valley and La Porte. That was where the trail went through in those days. Down the trail I went, dropping now into the River Gorge of Sierra City.

An hour later I reached Wild Plum Campground and walked through it heading for the highway that heads towards Sierra City. At the far end of the campground, which has definitely grown since 1978, I reached the service road that leads to the highway. I decided to get a drink of water here at the last campsite. The water was cool, not cold. There was hardly anyone in the campground so I decided to take an outdoor shower under the water spigot.

First I took a head shampoo and then washed my upper body. One guy drove by and gave me a wave. Then with no one in sight, I took off my running pants and ducked my whole body under the spigot and scrubbed down everything with a small bar of soap.

It was great. An outdoor shower under the pines! After putting my clothes back on, except for my socks and running shoes, I jumped in again and washed my smelly shirt and grubby running pants. What the hell, it was a warm day anyway.

I left the campsite, one clean and soaked guy, and headed for town a happy man. The two mile walk was very comfortable. The wet clothes kept me cool and by the time I reached Sierra City, they were almost dry. Besides that, I smelled pretty good too?.

Sierra City was a pretty cool little mountain community. I guess it has grown a little since 1978, but not much. As I walked along I thought about the previous night. It played in my head over and over again as I entered town. I was planning to let people know about it too even though they might laugh or think I was a nut. I was going to tell the story.

The first place I got to was a small restaurant that Linda and I had eaten at a couple of years ago when we took a car trip to the Gold Country. The place was closed however, and so was the tavern across the street. Man, just my luck. So I strolled down to the store and the post office to at least get a cold Gatorade and perhaps something else that might look good.

In front of the store was a couple that was easy to recognize. The dude's long red braided hair glowed in the afternoon sun and beside him, his tall female partner. It was Wookie and Island Mama. "Hey dudes, what's happening?" "Wrong Way, it's you again." I told them that I had just got in and all the local cheeseburger places were closed for the day. They told me that I ought to try Harrington's down the street about a quarter of a mile and that they had a great breakfast there. "Oh I guess I'll head down there. I'm starving."

They were going to head out in a few hours after it got a little cooler. They were anxious to get to Belden. They had some friends who were going to pick them up and take them to the coast where they knew of a good place to go surfing. "Surfing" I said, "Don't you guys get enough exercise walking this roller coaster of a trail?" They said they needed a break and were taking a week off. "Well I guess you can afford the time to do that, the way you guys levitate over those hills." "You always say that, Wrong Way, but we can't seem to pass you for very long, because here you are again, the same old guy with just a longer beard." "Hey thanks for the compliment." I told them that I'd see them later and that I was heading for Harrington's. I thought I'd get a cabin for the night. My girl, Trail Perfect, and I stayed there a couple of years ago and it was pretty nice. "All right, later dude." I said I had something I wanted to tell them about what happened to me last night, but it's a long story and I had to get something to eat first.

I arrived at Harrington's and the place was looking great. But the restaurant was closed. It would open again at 6pm for dinner. I was a little upset. The lady who worked here said she could make me some toast if I wanted. I told her 'no thanks', and that I'll just go to the store.

I rented the hikers special cabin for only $50 a night. It was a great deal. It had a soft bed, a good shower, and a view of the trout pond that was stocked by Harrington's so people would be sure to catch some trout before they left town.

I got cleaned up and headed back to town and to the post office in order to pick up my supply package before they closed at 3pm.

Wookie and Island Mama were just heading out. Before they took off down the street, I told them about the spaceman visit. They thought the story was really cool, but they thought that I should keep it to myself or people will think I'm half a bubble off. I doubt if I can keep their eyes to the skies. I laughed as the two characters disappeared down the highway.

A little later I met a guy named Popcorn who was taking four or five years to walk the PCT. He was actually working his way to Canada by taking odd jobs. After rapping to Popcorn, I headed to the post office which was next to the store, and picked up my package. I got there just in time; it was going to close in four minutes.

I walked back to the cabin and began opening my supply box. I then began working on my backpack. It was time to lighten my pack even further. I cut off all excess material on my pack. The pad on the back wasn't needed because the Ridge Rest ground mat gave the pack enough of a form, so I removed it. I cleaned the loose debris in my pack pocket, throwing it out. I cut my ground mat nearly in half, saving quite a few ounces doing so.

I decided to send my cell phone ahead of me to Old Station, along with the charger. The biggest decision was to send my walking poles back home tomorrow. I felt that these poles, as much as I liked them, were hurting my right shoulder. It was a rough decision but I decided to do it. I spent a couple of hours figuring out how to lighten my pack. I think I probably lightened the base weight by at least a couple of pounds.

After dealing with my pack and scrubbing everything, especially my cooking utensils, I went out to the trout pond and started rapping to a couple of tourists. I decided to tell one guy and his wife about what happened the previous night. I wanted to see their expressions.

I was surprised that they took it rather seriously, at least the way their body language portrayed them. The guy looked at me like I was telling the truth. He then said that about 12 years ago, his sister and brother-in-law came up somewhere near Sierra City and they saw a flying saucer over a lake. They were very serious and still don't like to talk about it. "Oh man, that's heavy," I said.

Personally I just can't believe what I saw and heard was a space dude and his ship. But the light and whoever ran off without a light, man, I just don't know what to believe!

A few minutes later I saw a guy reading the Sacramento Bee and asked him if there was anything in the paper about a celestial light or comet that was seen the night before. He checked and didn't see anything. I sat outside talking to people here and there. I watched some young kids fish in the artificial trout pond. Each kid caught two large German brown trout.

The diner was about to serve food so I made a call on the pay phone using my calling card. I called my girl, Trail Perfect, and told her my story. She felt it could have been an animal or someone. But I told her it just couldn't be, what about the light all around me and what looked like a space shape hauling ass into the great wide open? She told me that there had to be some explanation. We talked for a bit longer and before we hung up, she told me to call my parents since it had been a while since I talked to them.

After talking to Linda, I went in the diner and had a great southern fried chicken meal, followed by apple pie a la mode. Before I left I mentioned my story to the waitress who was taken aback by it. People seemed to believe me, but I think they all had thought that there was a logical explanation for it. A few thought that I was just dreaming and some noise woke me up. I knew that I wasn't dreaming. That evening I watched television and finished my laundry washing it in the sink and hanging the stuff all over the place.

About 10pm I was channel surfing, which is one of my favorite sports, and I came across an old Twilight Zone re-run with Rod Serling. I started to watch it but it freaked me out and I turned the channel back to the Tonight Show and then fell asleep with the TV on. I was glad that I wasn't sleeping in the forest alone tonight.

The next morning after a great breakfast of steak and eggs, I headed down to the post office to send my bivy bag and walking poles home. While in the post office, I started talking to the postal clerk, again telling my well-polished story of the intruder from outer space. Then to my amazement she came up with an incredible explanation of what probably happened.

The postal clerk told me that I probably got caught up in an incident between two factions, the lumber companies and Greenpeace, plus ELF. Greenpeace noticed that many of the trees that were cut down were well over the 30 inches in diameter, which was one of the guidelines signed by President Bush in his proposals to thin the forest out. There were also large trees that were cut down next to a federal trail. They also said that the logger roads were too wide. After Greenpeace arrived, the militant organization called Earth Liberation Front (ELF) arrived. It was probably ELF that crawled under the trucks and dumped their oil out. This act caused two expensive truck engines of the lumber company to be totally wasted.

I stood there listening to her story quite intently. She said that both ELF and Greenpeace have camps out there and their members watch the logging company work every day and that I probably got caught up in that.

I started to put the pieces together in my mind. The logging company parked their equipment, probably down the road from where I was sleeping. Then perhaps one of those guys from ELF marched down the logging road where I was and woke me up. Yeah, and that's why he didn't have a flashlight. He didn't want to be seen by the guards at the logging company's storage yard.

When I heard the footsteps and bounced up hissing like a wild cat, it scared the hell out of the guy. Then he hauled ass back to his camp and told his compatriots what happened. They lit up the area with a floodlight, probably to see who in the hell it was. After only a couple of seconds, they turned the light off figuring that I was just a backpacker. They probably didn't want their position revealed.

Then the strange part is when I immediately looked around and I just happened, by sheer coincidence, to see a shooting star break up in the atmosphere. Holy moly that was it! I told the lady, oh man, thank you so much. I finally have an explanation that I can live with. She smiled and said she was happy she could help me. I then left the post office and headed back to the cabin to get my stuff. It was time to leave Sierra City.

Desolation Wilderness near Echo Lake

Journey Ten: Sierra City to Belden, Goodbye to the Mighty Sierras

A few minutes later I headed back down the highway taking one last look at the quaint little village called Sierra City. The temperature was about 85 degrees when I reached the trailhead. I know I was in for a climb, for above the town of Sierra City is the awesome peak called the Sierra Buttes.

About a half mile up I turned a corner and scared the hell out of a lady hiker. She thought I was a bear! She passed on some information I really hadn't thought much about and that was water. I did have about a quart on me, which was really not enough. Thanks to that lady I knew the location of a spring that was still delivering water near the trail. I was lucky. It's definitely time to get my head back into the trip. The spaceman thing is settled now, so I better concentrate on what I'm doing.

The PCT makes quite a few switchbacks as it climbs out of the Highway 49 area and then contours around the beautiful Sierra Buttes. Way down below me I can see portions of Sierra City as I head north. The temperature has cooled about 7 degrees as I reached an altitude of over 7000 feet. A couple miles further I reached two small springs and I drank like a pig and filled up my tanks. The next water could be many miles off and with the time of day now being 2:30 in the afternoon, I might even have to camp with this water!

The rest of the day I hiked with a rather heavy pack due to four days of food and a gallon and a quart of water. The hiking was pretty mellow, however, and I made good time on my rested legs. God, I love this hiking along with great views and great weather. This is the life, man, I'm in bliss. Belden here I come.

Soon the trail joined a jeep road and shared this road for about a mile. It's kind of scary when the trail does this, especially when there are no PCT emblems or posts in view. There have been times in the past when I have had trouble finding the trail and have hiked some frustrating negative miles. I was feeling really uneasy about this road too and then finally high up on a tree with, of course, many bullet holes in it, was the PCT emblem. That emblem can be a beautiful thing to see sometimes.

The PCT now breaks away from the dusty road and travels past Poker Lake which has a few structures along the shore. It's now getting kind of late as I stroll above Deer Lake which lies about a quarter of a mile and 800 feet below the trail. Since that is the last water for a while, I hike down to it and make camp there.

For the first time in a long time the sky is getting dark with clouds. I decide to set my tarp up between two trees, just in case. That night I ate some beef stroganoff and fell asleep listening to the chatter of happy kids in another camp. I sure hope they wash their dishes and don't leave smelly food out. That's all I need now with a full pack of food to be hassled by a big bear.

The next morning, July 24h, was another beautiful sunny day. No sign of those dark clouds anywhere. I was walking at 7:30, not the best start. I did have to put my tarp in my pack, but that's no excuse. I definitely have to start getting earlier starts. In seven days it will be August and I'm still pretty deep into California. The idea of flip flopping was becoming more of a reality in my thinking.

It took a sharp climb to get out of Deer Lake. I already could tell that my legs were not as rested as yesterday. After getting back to the ridge, I started making good time. At Summit Lake, I decided to have my breakfast.

While I was eating I heard footsteps behind me. Upon looking behind I was surprised to see Solace, Jeron, and Godia. "Wow, you guys caught up to me!" "Ya, Wrong way," said Jeron. "We only spent a couple of hours in Sierra City." I asked them if they had stayed at Wild Plum and Solace said that they did and how it wasn't a bad place to stay for a couple of bucks. I told them that I dropped a bundle in Sierra City, and how I needed it after having quite an experience.

I went on to tell them about my visitor from an unknown planet. But followed it up with my newfound explanation I acquired at the post office. The three hikers really enjoyed my story but all three agreed that I had been caught up in a scene between the loggers and the environmental groups. Solace, in fact, said in a couple of campgrounds, while digging a hole, he saw what were probably stations for one of the two groups. I quickly finished my funky break-fast in order to hike with the group. Then off we went, once again heading north to Canada.

The pace was pretty quick, but was soon slowed down by Godia's feet. According to Solace, she was having a hard time. I mentioned to Solace that Leprechaun was also having a rough time. Solace told me that Batteries Includ-ed and Leprechaun had passed by him last night at Wild Plum. Oh good, I guess he is doing okay then.

Soon we traveled around beautiful Gold Lake that lay some 1000 feet below me. I told the group that back in 1978 the trail ran down to Gold Lake and then you had to follow the highway to Sierra City. I remember in the old trail guide they were already plotting out a route over the Sierra Buttes, but I don't know when they finished it.

The rest of the day we hiked together with intermittent stops for Godia's feet. We were able to get water out of Wilson Creek where we all stopped to have lunch. A few hikers passed us by heading south to Sierra City. They all had dogs. "Great for chasing all the bears," they said. I said that's a good idea, that maybe I'll just bark if I see one.

About an hour later I found Godia and Jeron camped alongside of the hill on a pretty flat area. There wasn't really any room between the high plains chaparral to crash for the night so I decided to go on for a little while longer. They told me that Solace was just a little bit downhill.

I said good-bye and headed out and after hiking for almost a half hour I found a really great spot just before the trail started to descend. I made my camp between mountain bushes, with the golden sun setting in the west.

The next morning I broke camp pretty early. The sun hit on me early and that always promotes an early rising. So off I went for another day of great adventure. Before leaving I checked the trail guide and noticed that Bunker Hill was the name of this baldheaded mound of earth.

My toe, as usual, hurt quite a bit. I had a turned in toe nail that continu-ally puts pressure on top of the toe itself. I'm not sure, but I think this condi-tion is called Morton's Toe. After I do a couple of miles the toe seems to warm up or something and the pain eases up a little.

Around 10:30am I arrived at what is called Chimney Rock. It's pretty cool but nothing to get excited about. The rest of the afternoon was rather easy hiking, except it was a bit warm. It was in the neighborhood of 90 degrees.

Around Fowler Peak I notice I was getting low on water, but it looked too troublesome to get to the water so I continued on. Soon I ran out of the stuff and I was beginning to be sorry that I hadn't gone down and filled up a tank. It seemed to get hotter as I started to drop into the Feather River Canyon.

Down I dropped, switchbacking back and forth as I dropped in altitude. I was very thirsty but not worried for I knew the Feather River lay at the bottom of this gorge. Now and then I could hear the sounds of crashing water. It soon became a steady sound. The foliage seemed to change; it almost looked like a tropical island.

I soon came to a series of springs. I stopped at a good running spring and filled my belly with water and then filled my tanks. All of a sudden I came to an opening with a great view below me. There it was, the middle fork of the Feather River.

I remember in the old days there was only a rickety log bridge. Now, however, there was a beautiful steel bridge. The bridge stretched high over the river. It presented an awesome view of the water below. Incredibly beautiful white water cascaded down rocks, forming perfect blue tranquil pools. Along the north shore, tucked back into the trees, were fantastic looking campsites, but not a soul around. I considered stopping here to camp but it was only 1:30 and I would lose a half day of walking.

The creek setting was spectacular. First there was a small waterfall and a beautiful pool of water with flat rocks that were perfectly level, and colorful rocks that adorned the bottom of the pool. There was a perfect place to park my butt, too, with a small flat rock in front of it, great for a granite table.

I had lunch here that included a whole package of lemon pudding. It came out great. I let the mixture harden with most of the pack in the ice cold water. I wasn't in any hurry. As I sat and rested, the pudding firmed up. Oh my, what a great treat. It was probably the best tasting pudding I've made on the trail.

I was back on the trail about an hour later, climbing out of this gorge. I climbed and climbed. The trail never seemed to flatten out much or go down-hill. It was just hour after hour of climbing with most of my water tanks filled with water.

To make it even more strenuous, I soon began to encounter fallen trees that laid over the trail; trees all over the place. It looked like well over a hun-dred trees were on the ground. What ever happened to trail maintenance?

Most of the trees weren't too huge, but some of them did cause me some problems that added to the difficulty. It was now close to 7pm and I was still climbing. I couldn't believe it. Before long I would need a flat place to sleep instead of on a tilted trail.

It wasn't until 8pm that I finally emerged on a ridge that led to an open place that was flat and sandy. It was the perfect place to crash for the night. The sand was firm but still soft. I was far enough from any water to eliminate mosquitoes, gnats, and flies. I had a great view of a golden sunset.

That night I had chicken a la king, raisins, trail mix, and chocolate milk. I decided to try and call Trail Perfect and the reception was excellent. I had a bit of a problem falling asleep due to the bright moon shining in my eyes. The moon can be very bright in the mountains because of the fact that there is no obstruction from fog, haze, or smog. I took a couple of Motrin and that put me away. I don't worry about sleeping out here because I know I can always take a siesta some time during the day. That alone is a blessing that keeps me from worrying about sleeping, because worrying can cause insomnia.

The next morning I headed out again. I soon passed a look-out rock which had a cool looking figure about two feet high that seemed to look out over the valley. There was a cute little minaret that some hikers or perhaps an artist placed there. The area finally marks the end of a 2700 foot and seven mile as-cent from the steel bridge over the middle fork of the Feather River. There was an excellent view of Spanish Peak. A mile further I crossed a dirt road and got blasted by a blob of dust caused by a jackass in his horseshit four-wheel drive.

Sometimes I think that four-wheel drives are the big reason why the PCT in 1978 was so much more of a wilderness experience. These vehicles are usu-ally owned by young people that constantly go where they shouldn't. Wherever these vehicles get to you, you can be sure of finding litter and destruction of the terrain.

Twenty or thirty years ago this wasn't much of a problem because there were so few four-wheel drives. Now, however, with the exploding growth of California and the popularity of four-wheel drives, some once beautiful nearly virgin land is laid to waste.

I remember that in the 1950s and 1960s trucks were sold basically for work. In today's world, millions of these "macho trip play-mobiles" are sold. "Hey look at me. I'm going to tear up the side of the hill. Want to make a bet that I can make it?" Or how about those damn commercials on TV that show a four-wheel drive pig machine crashing down a streambed and parking right next to an alpine lake.

People laugh and sneer at me sometimes when I bring this up but they haven't walked the length of California twice, in 1978 and 2003, and the comparison between those 25 years is shocking. What's going to happen in the next 25 years? I'm not completely against four-wheel drives because many people really need them. But the vast majority of them are just a status trip and ego display.

Take for instance the new Hummers that are so popular. It's just a knock-off for the actual Hummers that the armed forces use. These monsters suck down gasoline in vast amounts, making the demand for oil even greater and causing the price of gas to rise higher all the time. So we all pay for it one way or another in gasoline prices, smog, and parking spaces. "Hello, you're occupying far too much space, man." What the hell, it's just the Earth anyway.

Bitter as hell, I make my way down the trail and soon find myself at big Creek Road that leads to Bucks Lake. Here I had to make a decision: should I walk the two and a half miles to Bucks Lake and Bucks Lake Lodge, or should I head on towards Belden.

In 1978 the guidebook really recommended stopping at Bucks Lake Lodge. The food was supposed to be great. I went in the place and ordered a spaghetti dinner. I waited for over an hour for my meal. In fact, I damn near fell asleep waiting for the food to arrive.

Wow, what a disappointment. The spaghetti sucked and wasn't hot.

There wasn't much of it and the waitress was a crab apple. The price of the meal was $7.45. I can still remember that today. In 1978, $7 was a lot of money, probably like $15 now. It was the worst place that I ate on my whole California trip.

Today, however, I knew that the place had probably changed and after 25 years, there were probably new owners. I sure could use a good meal, man. A cold beer and a cheeseburger sure would be great. So I decided to give it a chance. If I didn't get a ride within 15 minutes, I then would head up the trail.

So I walked up the road and waited for a car to come by that was heading west. The second car that came by stopped, and off I went. The kid driving was also a backpacker. He was a college student that was off for the summer. He was going to meet this friend and they were going to hike around Spanish Peak. A few minutes later we arrived at Bucks Lake Lodge. It didn't really look familiar because in 1978 I had arrived here just after the sun had set and I was so tired and bitter about the food and service that I bolted out of the place and made camp somewhere in the dark.

I said good-bye to the young guy and walked inside. There was a bar on one side of the place. The restaurant was pretty much on the other side. A pretty nice-looking young girl gave me a menu. There was a great view of big blue Bucks Lake. There were quite a few boats on the water.

The place wasn't an Italian restaurant any more. I ordered the Bucks Lake special power cheeseburger, fries and coleslaw, with a couple of High Sierra Pale Ales. I also ordered a dinner salad, leafy greens sounded quite delicious.

Within 20 minutes the waitress brought my food and it was huge, fries all over the pace, and a great double-decker cheeseburger. My salad was awesome. I poured blue cheese dressing all over it. I pigged it down like a starving immigrant.

After a great meal I talked and joked with the waitress who mentioned to the owner of the place that I was hiking the PCT. He was really interested in my trip. He told me that his grandmother actually knew John Muir. In fact, they had a letter written by John Muir.

The owner's grandmother died a few years ago. Now he and his wife keep the letter in a bank vault. I told him that was great. I also told him that it was a good lunch. He told me it was an honor that I stopped by. I was kind of shocked. "Don't other thru-hikers come by?" The man said not really. In the old days the trail ran close to this place but I guess now that you have to hitch-hike here, the hikers don't want to since Belden is only a day or so away.

After bidding farewell, I walked out of the lodge and back to the road. There was a trash bin nearby. I then took some time tossing my wrappers out and cleaning out my pack. Soon I was back on Big Creek Road, heading for the trail, hitchhiking as I went.

I was not having any luck at all. So I started walking at a faster pace and finally after an hour, I got a ride from a young lady. This was the second time I had gotten a ride from a young lady. It surprised me because I looked like Gabby Hayes, not a thru-hiker. Maybe that's what it was; they felt sorry for this old bearded man. The ride lasted only a few minutes because I had walked most of the two miles back.

The trip to Bucks Lake was really worth it this time. I felt refreshed and ready to hike until dark. I climbed out of the Bucks Lake area and then started to level off. I made great time. That evening, I camped just a little north of Mount Pleasant where a stream crossed the trail. I got water here and found an excellent place to crash for the night.

The next day would be town day. I was about seven or eight miles from Belden town. Belden was a well-known stop for PCT hikers because it had the Belden Store and the main body of the rushing Feather River.

In the old days the Sierra Mountain Range was considered to be from Welden to Belden, which is actually Walker Pass to Belden. One thing for sure, however, the Sierras were now in back of me. I had walked their total length somewhere around 400 miles. It felt good too.

The next morning I slept in just a little. I didn't break camp until 8am. I felt since this was a town day anyway, why not get rested for it. As I left camp I momentarily looked for my hiking poles. Then I remembered that I had sent them home. It's been really weird hiking without poles. I really felt kind of na-ked at first. I definitely recommend them, but at the same time my shoulder has felt better lately. I don't know if it's because of the absence of the poles or the lighter pack.

The poles had caused some numbness in my right arm. I did feel kind of free sometimes without the poles. For instance, I was able to swat mosquitoes or flies off of my face. Climbing over downed trees like the ones just north of the middle fork of the Feather River was a little easier, too, without the hiking poles.

Down the trail I ripped until I turned a corner and noticed a honey colored bear playing alongside Clear Creek's grassy meadow area. It was a rather small bear and I named him teenage bear because of his tumbling antics. The bear was rolling in the grass and then would sit on his haunches and swat at mosquitoes.

The bear looked like he was in good health, unlike the only other bear I saw way back at Joshua Springs. It seemed strange that one bear appears when I first entered the Sierras and then one when I finished the Sierras. I watched the bear play a bit but I had to make tracks so I coughed a couple of times and teenage bear hauled butt off into the forest. Wow, that was a cool experience to start off the day.

The trail starts to widen out as it cuts along a pretty much treeless terrain. It then drops into the Feather River Gorge. Tons of switchbacks zigzag down the side of this canyon as the day gets hotter and hotter. A rattlesnake suddenly appears in front of me making me put on the brakes. He curls up a bit but then stretches out and without making any sound he slides off the trail. A few minutes later I crossed some railroad tracks and make my way on a flat dirt road that changes into a paved road which takes me to a group of buildings and Belden Store.

I entered the store and there was no one there. I started looking for munchies. There was not much of anything, not even ice cream. A couple of minutes later a man enters the store and asked me if I needed help finding anything. "Yeah, where's your ice cream?" I asked. "Sorry, no ice cream, but maybe in a couple of days we'll have some coming in." I grabbed some Oreo cookies and a milk to hold me over.

I asked the man if the restaurant was open. The guy said not yet, but maybe in a couple of hours. It's already 11am, so there goes breakfast. I then asked the dude if there is a cabin available and he tells me no. I asked him how much are they and he said $90 a night. Wow, I'm thinking to myself, that's way too high for those funky little things.

"Are there showers available?" I asked. "Yeah, $4, $5 if you need a towel." The man said. Again, it's high, but I take him up on that and he gives me a towel. He then tells an older guy to show me where the showers are.

We walk abut 150 yards down the highway and the old dude points to the showers. Then the old guy goes on by himself and sits under a garage sign that read, "Joe's Auto Repair and Towing Service." I went up to the shower stall and it was locked. After trying to get in, I called out to the old guy sitting under the sign and told him the place is locked. "No problem," he said and he brings over a steel shimmy type tool, sticks it into the crack of the door and breaks it open. "Who needs a key?" he laughs. "Yeah, you definitely don't."

This place was starting to get real comical or real sad, depending on how you want to look at it. The shower was pretty dirty inside, but it seemed to get me clean. While I was drying off I reached into the pocket of my pack and pulled out a piece of paper that Wookie had given me back in Sierra City. It was a youth hostel that two trail angels had just opened up and it had their phone number written on it. I might try this number because this place was becoming a bad joke.

After my shower I felt much better. I headed over to the restaurant and was told that it would probably open in an hour or two. It was now almost 1pm. Well there goes lunch.

I had had enough of this place, so I went back to the funky worthless store and asked if I could make a local phone call because my cell phone was dead. The dude hesitated for a bit and then said okay. He asks, "Who are you calling that is local?" I told him of the hostel that is supposed to be near here in Belden. "Wait just a minute," he said. "There's no hostel here in Belden." I said let's find out and let me call the number. Then the jerk said that he would make the call. "Hey, whatever, man." I was trying to be as nice as possible.

The clown called the number and someone on the line told him that this place was a hostel called Hikers Heaven. The guy was now amazed and gave me the phone.

The voice on the other end is none other than Solace. "Hey Solace, how do I get to this hostel, man. Please rescue me from this cuckoo nest." Solace tells me to walk down the highway the same way I did when I first got off the trail. Then go down about a mile and I'll see a little sign that says Hikers Heaven. Go to the house on the right which adjoins with another house.

The house on the far right was the owner's place and the house to the left is for hikers. I asked how much and Solace said it was free. "Wow, dude, I'll be right there." Solace said that he might be at the café when I get there, that the café has dynamite ice cream shakes. He said the owners were at church so to just make myself at home. I gave the phone back to the worthless storeowner and bolted out of the store to the highway and headed down the road.

I hadn't gone too far when I noticed a group of hikers heading my way. Soon I could recognize them as Batteries Included, Leprechaun, Puck, and Belcher. "Hey dudes, what's happening?" "Wrong Way, it's you, you're still alive." I told them that I was heading to the hostel.

They said it was about a mile down the road and that it is a pretty cool place. The people who own it were from Minnesota and bought the place to fix it up. It was free and they also had an excellent breakfast that was free. Someone mentioned that Solace was there or at the café down by the forks. "Forks?" I asked. "Yeah, it's where these two rivers join up," said Puck. "Actually," said Belcher, "It's where the north and middle fork of the Feather River join up."

Puck looked slightly bugged that Belcher knew what two rivers actually joined. I could tell there was still tension between these two people. Belcher blurted out how they were going to Belden Lodge to see if they could rent some inner tubes and float down the river. They had heard that you could do that. "Well good luck, I'll see you guys in the funny papers." "You're in there," said Puck, "Homer Simpson." "Why you young whippersnappers, you should have more respect for your elders." They laughed and then headed towards Belden Lodge.

I headed down the highway. My God, it was hot. It was now early afternoon and getting hotter by the minute. I finally reached some cabins, but no Hikers Heaven sign. A few hundred yards later, however, I found the place and walked up a dirt driveway.

There were a couple of sleeping bags hanging over a wooden deck from the second story. I climbed the steps and knocked on the door, but no one answered. I opened the door and yelled hello, still no one answered. I could tell that I was at the right place because camping gear was all over the place. I took off my pack and sat down on a chair for a while and then went to the kitchen and took an ice cold Coke out of the refrigerator. For the next hour or so I just sat around, my sleeping bag hanging from the wooden deck fence.

About an hour later two figures marched in. It was Brooke and Dave. "Hey dudes, glad to see you." "Hey, Wrong Way, what's up? You made it." I said, "So far so good." Brooke said that they just ate at the café which had great food and shakes.

I was kind of surprised that she talked to me because she's pretty shy. Maybe Brooke was starting to get to know me. They went on to say that Solace is there pigging out. It was now 4pm, close enough for dinner so I thought I would head over to the café. I still couldn't believe how hot it was.

Dave said the thermometer at the café had read 112 degrees. They were going to leave when it got cooler. "Okay dudes, I'll see you later."

So off I went to the café and I ended up having a great experience. I ate a huge cheeseburger with tons of fries and a great chocolate shake. It was just like how they made malts back in the '50s, with plenty of malt in it. As I was leaving, I met Solace. He was spending the night. He had arrived there at 9am that morning.

After eating like a pig while trying to stuff as many calories down as I could, I walked back to Hikers Heaven. Batteries Included, Belcher, and Leprechaun were there now. As we talked, Jeron and Godia arrived and Godia looked wasted. Jeron said that Godia's feet were killing her. We all sat around talking for a while. I told Leprechaun, Brooke, and Dave about my encounter in Sierra City. They were amazed but all agreed that I probably was caught between two warring factions!

Dave and Brooke got their stuff together and left. Jeron, Godia, Batteries Included, Leprechaun, Puck, and Belcher went to eat at the café. It was now 7pm and I was already getting hungry again. So was Solace. We walked back to the café and this time I had a huge Chef's Salad, trying to balance out my diet from the heavier meal I had earlier.

That night we all sat around rapping about our trips. We also met the two people who own the establishment. It seemed that Jeron and Godia may want to quit their quest to walk the PCT. Godia's feet were evidently killing her and to tell you the truth, I don't think she was into it. Jeron was, but he was in love with her, I guess, and it looked like the end of the line for these two.

Leprechaun was really hurting too. His plan was to go to the highway that was just 25 miles north of here and then hitchhike to a town called Chester and buy some new shoes. Leprechaun definitely had it in him, like Batteries Included, and a number of other thru-hikers I had met. He had already hiked the Appalachian Trail the year before. On that trail he didn't have any foot problems so it can happen to anybody, I guess.

The next morning the lady who ran Hikers Heaven cooked us a great breakfast. She said that she was heading to the post office at noon, that it didn't make sense to go much earlier since the post office is only open from 11am to 2pm every day.

Batteries Included, Leprechaun, Puck, and Belcher all left around 9am before it got too hot. Solace and I sat around talking about stuff. Of all the hikers on the trail so far, Solace was the guy I always ran into. He would go ahead and I would catch up. It seemed weird too, because he traveled faster than I did but it seemed that he always had to have someone to hike with. That's okay. In fact, it's not a bad idea for safety sake.

Solace knew a lot about equipment. When he checked out my tarp he couldn't believe it. "Wrong Way, this tarp is way too heavy," he said. I told him that tarps are lighter than tents. "Not yours. It must weigh two pounds. It's not impregnated nylon," he said. "What the hell is that?" I asked. Solace said that it's just a real light material that is now used for both tents and tarps. He said that I probably could order one if I have a credit card. I told him I had a Visa card.

Solace and I looked through a Camp More order book and finally found one. I couldn't believe it. They had three different size tarps: 6 x 8, 8 x 10, and 10 x 12. The 8 x 10 would be perfect for me. It only weighed 13 ounces!

ECSTASY OF MISERY

According to the scale at Hikers Heaven, my 8 x 8 tarp weighed two pounds and 15 ounces. I would save two pounds in weight. I called the place up which was located in New Jersey and had a toll free number.

It was a little bit of a hassle but finally got it done. The new tarp would be sent to me at Burney Falls State Memorial Park. I thought that would be better than Old Station because it would give the company and the mail service a little more time. With the weather outside at 110 degrees I knew I had at least five days of warm weather ahead of me. So I decided to send my old tarp home when I got to the Belden post office. I was pretty happy about my purchase. It only cost me $75 and it definitely was an upgrade on my equipment.

At 11am we rode off with the cool lady that ran the hostel. Jeron and Godia came too. They wanted to mail some stuff. As for the trail, they were through. At the post office I picked up my package and sent my tarp home to Trail Perfect.

I thanked the lady for all the hospitality including the great breakfast and dynamite blackberry muffins. "Thank you, Wrong Way, please be safe and have a great trip."

Just before I left, an old pickup came by the post office and a thru-hiker named Chance popped out of the back of it. Godia ran up and said, "Chance, hey Chance, it's nice to see you." Chance looked like he was in his 40s.

Off I went heading steadily uphill in ungodly heat. It had to be well over 100 degrees. I was now heading into Section N, titled in the trail guide "Highway 70 at Belden to Burney Falls State Memorial Park, 134 miles". Soon I passed Indian Creek where I took a long drink of water. Man it's hot. I've got to make sure I'm hydrated.

After a couple of hours of climbing I reached a little flatter terrain and then arrived at William's Cabin but I couldn't seem to find the cabin. A few miles farther I passed by a few rustic backcountry campsites which I think must be Myrtle Flat Campground. I could camp here for the night but decided to walk on a while before I flop down. I make sure to load up on my cooking water for the next water will most likely be Poison Spring, some seven miles from here.

Journey Eleven: Belden to Burney Falls

For the first time on this trip I didn't select any of the food, Trail Perfect did. The reason was that I really didn't know I would get this far. From now on all my food, except what I buy out of some stores, will be bought and sent to me by my girl, Linda Robison, or now better known as Trail Perfect.

From what I can see as I check out my food bag, she has a lot more variety than I had, including plenty of candy and some great trail mix. Yep, there's my raisins. They supply plenty of energy and even keep you a bit regular too. Wow, these are weird looking candies. They're probably her dad's contribution to my traveling kitchen. He kind of likes strange candies. The Lipton dinners now have taken the place of the usual backpacking meals you find in your local sporting goods stores. They are about half the price or less and plenty good too.

Well, in a few days I'll be passing through Lassen, where it could be cool or hot. In fact, it could be really hot if I step into one of those boiling hot pools! What a trip this has been. Man, what's the date anyway? Holy crap, it's July 28th. In a few days it will be August and I'm still a long ways from the Oregon border. It seems a sure thing that I'll be flip-flopping at Ashland, Oregon, if I'm ever going to make it to Canada before the big dump.

The next morning I'm off early, about 6:30am. That's not too bad, it's one of my earliest starts. By 9am I get to Poison Springs. Here I made breakfast, my usual power shake and some pretty cool fruit bars. I head out, and the trail starts climbing and then starts to level out around Sunflower Flat. It's a warm day even at 6000 feet; my compass thermometer reads 85 degrees! Around 11am I arrive at Cold Springs. Even though it's early, I'm hungry so I stop and take lunch. The spring water is so good. I make sure I drink plenty of it. I fill up my water tanks with about one and a half gallons of water. The next water looks like a scary distance away.

My pack is now loaded down with 12 pounds of water. Damn it, I was just getting use to its light weight. No big deal. I'll probably drink this H2O up before long. The hiking is pretty level now. Even with a rather heavy pack I'm making good time, until I start to climb Humboldt Summit.

Right after the summit I reach a road that heads down to Robber's Roost. This rings a bell for me. It was here 25 years ago that I got horribly sick on bad water that I had drunk in the Marble Mountains. It took about 12 days for the Giardia to develop and it was here that night that I thought I was going to die. I must have gone to the bathroom 25 times that night. It was pretty much un-controlled diarrhea.

The next day I was able to limp down this dirt road to Lake Almanor where I got a ride with a hippie dude to Greenville and stayed at the Greenville Inn and recovered after seeing a doctor. This took five days of my trip.

On this day I barreled down the trail, guzzling water and eating almost continually. It was a warm but beautiful day and soon my water started to dis-appear. It was still quite a ways from any dependable water.

It was evening when I finally came to a small trickling spring. It was about 9pm. Thanks to the Gods for this spring because I was really getting thirsty and hungry. I spent the night near the spring. I camped a couple of hundred yards away from the water to avoid animals, gnats, and mosquitoes that came by for a drink or three. I probably had my longest mileage day of the trip so far. Judging by the trail guidebook I had covered at least 28 miles.

Before I fell asleep I thought of all the thru-hikers I have met so far on the trail and wondered if they were still on the trail. People like Shutter Bug and Steady, Be There Now and Bobka. I know Beaker had to leave the trail because of foot problems, Sweep and Glover, Frog. Did Cloud Walker make it to Belden? Who knows?

How about Wookie and Island Mama, were they still surfing? Then what about Greg, is he still seeking a wilderness experience? Or is he off the trail? How about Cruising Carson, is the guy still hiking? I haven't seen his name in any PCT registers since Peter Grubb's Hut. You pretty much know how the peo-ple ahead of you are doing because you can catch their act in the PCT register.

The next morning I had a hard time getting out of the sack. This was probably because of the 28 or 29 miles I did the day before. I finally left camp at about 8am and headed north once again. The trail here goes through private land. The signs along the side of the trail continually warn hikers not to leave the trail. The place is kind of flat and ugly and you can see by the cow dung that this is cow country. Soon I pass a private road and then come to Highway 19. If one goes east from here, he comes to a town called Chester. This is where Leprechaun said he was going to depart and buy another pair of running shoes for his painful feet.

I sat down and read the trail guide for a bit and noticed that there were two restaurants to the west and only about two miles away. In fact, St Bernard Lodge lies only one and a half miles away and the Black Forest Lodge only two tenths of a mile further.

Wow, a chance for a great lunch. Should I do it or should I not? Jumping cheeseburgers, yes I should. So I headed to the other side of the road and put out my thumb, but no luck. It seemed that cars would come by in bunches and they would be backed up behind a slow moving vehicle like a piss tuber or a truck. I started walking and thumbing. I ended up walking all the way to St Bernard Lodge.

I saw the big white building as I rounded a curve and I started walking at a faster pace. One thing I noticed was there weren't any cars parked in front. It wasn't long before I found the place was closed on Tuesdays. Oh man, that's a drag, but the Black Forest Lodge is only two tenths of a mile from here.

So off I went, and when I rounded a corner I noticed a Pepsi sign on the ledge just above the highway on the opposite side of the road. Below the sign in smaller letters it read "Black Forest Lodge, open for lunch". All right, now I was a happy dude. A few seconds later I could see the lodge. My pace quickened. It was about noon and I was getting very hungry.

As I approached the lodge I noticed there was only one vehicle in the parking lot. I soon found out that the doors were locked. Damn it to hell. I was pissed off like an agitated adolescent. This can't be. My cheeseburger and shake were now just a dream. I had already walked two miles out of the way to get here and if I don't get a ride back, which is uphill, I will have just walked four negative miles.

I found the hours to the place on the second door. It read, "Open 11am to 9pm Monday through Friday, except Tuesday from 5pm to 9pm." Damn it to hell once again. What luck! It was 12:30pm and I would have to wait until 5pm, four and a half hours at least before I could pig out. No way. I can't do it. I guess I'll have to walk back. I was bummed out, but decided to look around the lodge anyway.

There was a guy in the back who was about to start a lawn mower and I started rapping to him. His wife's family owned the place and he worked there too. I told him my story and he said, "Come on, I'll give you a ride back to the trail." He went inside for a second and brought out a bottle of ice cold water and gave it to me. I thought that was really nice.

The man said this happens from time to time on Tuesdays; hikers head down here and are bitterly disappointed. He wished that they could put a sign up near the trailhead stating what time they are open, but it changes a lot. In winter they were nearly always open due to skiers and stuff. Rick took me back to the trail and wished me luck. I thanked him for the ride and then with an empty stomach I headed north again on the mighty Pacific Crest Trail.

The going was pretty flat and there were enough trees to give me inter-mittent shade. A trail sign on the side of a tree read "Stover Camp, 3 miles". The trail guide mentioned that there was a spring there.

After starting out again, it didn't seem like it took too long to arrive at the campsite and spring. As I did, a deer was actually following me. I believe that this was the first time I ever had a deer follow me. He made a few weird noises, so I gave him my bullet whistle. I found a rifle bullet cartridge a few hundred miles back and by blowing on the open end at just the right angle I could make quite a loud noise! I brought the bullet cartridge along because I felt it might come in handy at night to scare bears and especially make a male deer go away. So I gave the cartridge one hell of a blow and that funky deer took off like a scalded dog!

Now at peace, at last, I gathered water out of a spring that was delivered by a plastic pipe. I went back to the side of the trail where there was a perfect log to sit on. Then I noticed a sign beside the trail which read "Canada, 1325 miles north" and right below it on the same sign read "Mexico, 1325 miles south", with an arrow pointing the opposite way! Wow this is great. I have come exactly halfway, half of the trip completed. Yahoo! It's time to celebrate. I cooked up a hot meal, which is something I don't usually do at lunch, but I was starving. It was time to reflect on my last 1325 miles and to psych myself up for the next 1325 miles.

After lunch I headed out, with a full belly of food. I had eaten up all my longhorn cheese. The rest of the day I headed for a snow peak called Mt Lassen, which I remember from my hike back in 1978. Lassen was like a miniature Yellowstone, with bubbling pools of mud, hot lakes, creeks, and sulfur smelling mud. It was a landmark to me, which meant I was getting into extreme Northern California.

At the north fork of the Feather River (it seems I just can't get away from one or another fork of that wandering Feather River) I tanked up on water. I wasn't sure where the next good water would be. I started to climb and a mile further came across a sign reading "Domingo Springs, one fourth of a mile". Not needing any water, I forged on.

Soon I was walking along the side of a pretty steep slope. When the trail became hard to follow it slanted downhill a bit and went right under a bunch of downed trees. I tried following as best I could but the butchered trees got in the way.

Now there were trails going in different directions. Most of these trails were probably cattle trails. I forged ahead but soon realized that I was definitely off the trail. I could go back to the Domingo Springs area and try again, but after studying the guide book I decided that the most likely trail was above me.

Down below I could see Stump Ranch Road and the PCT traveled basically parallel to this road only to the ridge above me, at least I hoped it did. I headed almost straight up hill. It was hard going.

I almost gave up and was about to back track when I could see what looked like a flat spot running along the side of a hill. I didn't know if it was the trail or a jeep road but at least it was flat looking from what I could see from down here. I was real tired of this incredible steep climb. I finally got up there, my running shoes sliding backwards half the time. I reached the area and it looked like a well-maintained trail. After walking a few hundred feet I saw the white diamond hammered to a pine tree, and was I a happy dude.

ECSTASY OF MISERY

It was starting to get darker now as the sun was setting. I figured on about another hour of hiking before complete darkness set in. I found a small creek with running water cascading down over the rocks. Boy was it hard to get to, and walking back up hill was a real drag. My legs were tired from the full day I had, plus the steep walking trying to locate the trail again. I had to move on because the terrain here was not very adequate for a good nights sleep.

I got my headlight out and prepared for some night hiking. After about 15 minutes I came to the border sign of Lassen State Park! All right! Lassen at last. A few feet away was a big flat register cover and after opening it, there was a register with all the thru-hikers of the Class of 2003 that had come just before me. There were quite a few people who had signed in on this one. But there wasn't a Zeb or Cruising Carson. I haven't seen them in quite a while.

The most interesting thing was the under side of the large metal cover that was written on with a Sharpie pen. It said, "Please no more livestock on the PCT. The trail is bad enough as it is. More horses will wreck it even more. So keep your damn horses off. You're not John Wayne, so cowboy up!" It was signed below "Free Radical".

I laughed my ass off. Well done, dude. After walking this part of the trail for the last couple of hours you just can't blame Free Radical from being upset a little.

A few minutes later I saw some flat areas down below the trail and decided to crash there for the night. It was a very dirty forest, to say the least, but beggars can't be choosers, especially the old exhausted ones. It would have to do.

It was a scary place. I kept hearing sounds all around me. Mosquitoes were a problem too. Willow Lake was not too far off and all around the lake area and the meadow below was like a swamp. This didn't surprise me too much because of dead wood lying all over the place. I popped a couple of Motrin 200 and probably fell asleep around 11pm.

The following morning I was hiking by 6:30am. Two miles later I arrived at Boiling Springs Lake. What a scene. Steam covered the hot water which was nearly boiling in the early morning chill. Along the edge of the lake were boiling blue pools of sulfur-smelling water and in some places were the pre-historic bubbling mud pools. Oh man, just like One Million Years B.C. but no Raquel Welch. I stayed here for a few minutes and took some flicks and then headed out once again.

Before I knew it I was at Warner Valley Campground. The new PCT had pretty much skirted around the park. The old trail that I walked in 1978 was so much more scenic. There were geysers and all kinds of stuff. If I had time I would have taken a side trail, but since I was behind schedule and the fact that I've seen all these things before, I elected to forge on. I suggest, however, that PCT thru-hikers or section hikers should take these alternative routes!

The PCT now headed on the opposite side of the valley, Warner Springs Lodge directly opposite. In the mid-day heat crickets rushed around and disappeared again in a hot marsh pit. A half mile towards the east I reached the campground which had running water, picnic tables, and flush toilets in the bathrooms, with sinks. A perfect place to wash up for my morning rituals and prepare an exotic breakfast.

After breakfast I headed out. I crossed a road and through the campground following the PCT emblem markers. I came across two guys having breakfast at a picnic table. They were really cool. I told them about my hike. They gave me some great tasting coffee and delicious pastries. After talking to them for 15 minutes or so, I decided to leave. The two cool dudes gave me two awesome oranges and a pastry to go.

From the campground I finally joined the trail once more and climbed out of the area rapidly on a sugar and caffeine high. Soon the trail leveled out at Flatiron Ridge and I headed to Coral Meadow stepping over mass quantities of road apples. I followed the trail along Grassy Swale. More trees appeared waving in a cool golden morning breeze as I went along White Firs, Jeffrey Pines, Incense Cedars, and Sugar Pine. By the time I reached Swan Lake the caffeine and sugar high had worn off and I seemed to be back to my grumpy self.

The Pacific Crest Trail soon edged around beautiful Lower Twin Lake. Here I ate one of those navel oranges and pigged down another pastry. Just past Lower Twin Lake I came to a trail junction with an alternative route that traveled by at least four Alpine lakes. But being a purist when I felt like it I stayed with the PCT which took a flat and boring sojourn around these lakes and headed for Badger Flat where my next water source was located.

The hiking here was really flat and exceptionally fast and slightly down-hill. I hiked at a fast three mile per hour clip. It was hot, about 85 degrees.

At Badger Flat I gulped down a quart and a half of H2O, ate a couple of power bars and was off again, all within 10 minutes. A couple of miles further I left the National Forest boundary and here I signed in a new trail register. Inside I read the usual quips from the usual expressive thru-hikers. I noticed many were looking forward to Old Station's Indian Red's Pizza.

I had 11 miles to go before Old Station. I was surprised because I didn't figure to hit Old Station until tomorrow. Due to an early start and a lighter pack I was really making great time in the rolling hills type of terrain.

I knew by walking this same trail in 1978 that the next 11 miles were basically downhill. It was now 4pm and hopefully the pizza place would remain open past 8pm. So off I went on my own mission for a cheesy slice of pizza. I started hauling ass down hill. In fact, I put my hand behind my pack to secure it as I started jogging at a pretty good pace!

A couple of miles further I heard the sound of rushing water. I knew immediately that this was good old Hat Creek. In 1978 the trail was Highway 89 all the way from Burney to somewhere around here. Past Emigrant Ford I flew along a dirt road. A quad runner that some clown had driven using the trail as if it were a jeep road now marked the trail. Like there aren't enough dirt roads around this thinly treed forest?

Manzanita and Tabasco brush bordered the PCT for a while running through a thin forest. Soon I passed a car camping place with a couple of cars but not people. I flew down a soft trail, still rattled by the quad runner. I didn't care at this point because the trail was well marked and the scenery was bleak.

The mighty PCT hugs Hat Creek which looks more like the Feather River. This is probably because of the tremendous amount of snow that has fallen this season. Here it is the last of July and the creek is huge.

Wait a second. I'm looking at my watch and I accidently pushed the date button. Oh no, it's August 1st already, the last real summer month up here in the North Country. I am definitely going to have to flip flop. Watch the trail man, damn near flip flopped over a rock just now.

Many times hiking on soft almost flat trails I have nearly fallen or twisted an ankle. The reason is I get confident and don't watch closely where I'm putting my feet. When I'm on rocky trails that are tight and funky I watch more closely where I put my feet, especially while hiking in running shoes.

The trail veers away from the fabulous Hat Creek. The sound of rushing waters fades away. In a sort of man-made forest of all the trees which looked like Lodge Pole Pines, they are all the same height and distance from each other. Now the sound of Hat Creek emerges again and soon I'm probably within a quarter of a mile from it, at a place called Big Pine Campground. There are a few cars, but again, no people.

By now my pace starts to slow as I hit soft sand. It was almost like a Southern California beach. The trail firms up and joins a dirt road. Dig it. I believe I'm at Old Station! Yabba dabba doo! The trail now heads one way. The road is parallel to the trail and then slides to the west. After looking at the guidebook I decide to take the road. It should go right into Old Station's Hat Creek Resort.

From here the road led right to an RV park. Across from the park I could hear and see Highway 89. A short time later I had traveled to the other side of the park. There I saw a small building with Old Glory blowing in the breeze. This had to be the post office and it was. But of course it was closed since it was almost 7:30pm.

Across from the small parking lot was the store and restaurant. Of course I entered the restaurant as soon as I could. I left my pack behind the door outside of the place. I walked to the back of the restaurant as far as I could away from other people because I knew I must smell pretty bad. After ordering a southern fried chicken dinner with a couple of High Sierra Pale Ales, I went to the bathroom and washed up the best I could. The meal was really good. Of course, I was so hungry, most anything would have tasted good.

With dinner over, I headed over to the store and bought a giant double-decker ice cream cone. I was filled to the brim now and headed outside and saw Dave and Brooke. They had arrived earlier that day and were camped with Puck and Belcher. They told me that they were going to spend another day here. Tomorrow they were going to visit some caverns. I asked them where they were camped and they told me just around the corner a ways. I said "Cool" and that maybe I'd see them later. From there I went to the pay phone and called my girl, Trail Perfect, who would in turn call my parents and let them know I had reached Old Station.

After making my call I walked down the highway where Dave and Brooke were camped. I couldn't find them. I was very tired so I found a field between Highway 89 and some residential cabins. I crashed between a couple of trees in order to make myself obscure from the sight of others. My legs were so dirty that I washed them with my washcloth and water before crawling into my sleeping bag.

I couldn't believe I was actually here. This morning I was on the opposite side of the Lassen National Park and now I was in Old Station with a belly full of food. I decided to look at the trail guide and get a mileage count. Yep, a new mileage record for the trip: 30 miles in one long day. Tomorrow I would take it easier, have a good breakfast, wash my clothes, and hopefully take a hot shower.

I fell asleep quickly but around 5am I was woken up by drops of rain hitting my sleeping bag. I couldn't believe it. This hadn't happened since way back near Mt Laguna, behind San Diego! There was nowhere to tie my tarp up but thanks to the Gods the rain suddenly stopped. I was very relieved and soon fell fast asleep once again.

The next morning I got up kind of late. I didn't get to the café until 8am. I had the Lumberjack Special. Afterwards I found out where the showers and laundromat were and used both of them. By 10:30am I had eaten, showered, and washed my stinking clothes just in time since the post office opened at 11am and closed at 3pm. I needed to get my stuff, have lunch, of course, and head out.

The post office was just a small place. Thank goodness my box had arrived. I proceeded to go through my white trash compactor bag and throw out some of my old wrappers. After I completed this task I asked the postal lady, who was very nice, where the PCT register was. She brought it out from under the counter and gave it to me.

I read through it as usual. I read about everybody in the Class of 2003 who were ahead of me. Ronnie from Israel was still about a week ahead of me. Long Haul and Choo Choo looked like they were an item now. I laughed a bit because I told her she would find some guy somewhere along the way. No Zeb or Cruising Carson, but there was Huff and Puff with that wild cartoon face of his.

There was White Stag and his dog Shizz, which by the way is a make believe dog. I guess the guy needs a pet to walk with. Shizz probably protected him from all the critters in the forest. Not a bad idea, because walking along can be scary and a little dangerous too. Quite a few people were just ahead of me, but just of late I had gained yardage on them.

I wrote my name in the register. I tried to say something cute. I mentioned to the lady in the post office that I had hiked through here in 1978. Then she said that they have registers dating back to 1975. "You actually have 1978?" She said that she did and if I wanted to see it. I don't know if I'm in there or not. Walking north to south I might not have even known that there were registers. "Here it is," she said.

I started to read through it. There were only 10 or 15 names. I wasn't in there. I looked for my real name, Robert Raley, because my trail name had not yet materialized at that time. No, I wasn't in there. But a very familiar name appeared. It was the first thru-hiker that I had ever met. His name was Brian Jacobsen.

I had met Brian heading south out of Seiad Valley. He was heading north. He had started out in Campo and had taken five months to get to where he was! He had gone through one of the worst winter snows ever. This was 1978, preceded by two years of drought not only in California, but the whole Pacific Crest.

I couldn't believe the guy. I found out later by another hiker that Brian was the real deal. I talked to him for a while and looked at his ancient trail guide that wasn't even up to date. He said he started out on the trail at Castle Crags but had lost it and pretty much walked to the Marbles by jeep roads. He had completely disregarded the John Muir-PCT through the Sierras and had just gone from valley to passes, through 60 feet of snow or more. He used snowshoes, crampons, and cross-country skis to do so!

Some days Brian would only cover 10 miles or less. His pack weighed 80 pounds or more. This guy was only about 5'7" and probably weighed 140 pounds. He had left on March the first, not unusual for those days. In fact, that was the cushion: leave in early March, giving you seven months or more to make the distance before the big dump. The big dump would probably mean very little to this guy with his snow hiking ability.

I had met Brian on July 17th on top of the ridge right before it drops in Seiad Valley. He wanted to know two things. One, where was Oregon, and I pointed toward the southern Siskiyous about two days away. I said, "See those mountains right over there? That's Oregon." Man was he excited. He wanted to get out of California so bad.

The other question was, "Do they have ice cream sandwiches in Seiad Valley?" I told him they sure do and that he might want to buy the economy pack. He laughed. I took his picture and he left, heading north and I walked spellbound towards the south. I guess Brian Jacobson and Scott Williamson were the two most amazing hikers I have ever met on the PCT. Honorable mention would have to go to Brice Hammick, a hiker and a trail builder out of Oregon.

Well, it's time to leave. I told the cool postal lady this nostalgia stuff is starting to get to me. As I started to close the book I saw "Warning" in red letters. "Don't eat at Bucks Lake Lodge. Forget that spaghetti meal. There's new management and the place is lousy. Don't waste your money." Wow, a mystery has just been solved.

I left the post office and headed down Highway 89 and not the trail. The reason for this was I wanted to visit Uncle Remus' Café. It was another PCT eating establishment landmark going way back to the first pioneers of the trail. As I got about 100 yards down the road I heard a voice call out, "Hey Wrong Way."

I looked around and to my surprise it was Solace, my recurring buddy from way back to the Tehachapis. I walked back to rap with him and tell him the latest. I let him know that Puck, Belcher, Dave and Brooke were here, but had left the trail somewhere to check out some caverns. Solace said he would probably spend a layover day and head out tomorrow. So off I went, north to Uncle Remus'.

Although the day started with some intermittent raindrops at 5am, the sun was out now and it looked like another great day. A few hours later I could see some buildings ahead. I knew this was the old stomping ground of many ancient thru-hikers. The first place I came to was a small store with a gas pump out in front. At the store I grabbed a few candy bars and then headed down the road to the famous little restaurant.

To my surprise the place was closed. It looked pretty run down. The sign read "Uncle Remus." The place needed painting. I looked inside and saw the old wooden tables and chairs stacked up on each other. Antique items hung from the ceiling. It was an eerie feeling, so I walked back down the road to where a few other buildings were. I crossed the highway to a restaurant which looked like it was open.

It was 1pm now, so I figured I would have another late lunch for the day. Two older couples ran the place. The prices seemed reasonable. I ordered a beef sandwich with a salad and a chocolate shake.

Towards the end of my lunch I asked the fellow about Uncle Remus' and he told me that a lady had bought it about two years ago and ran it into the ground. The food and entertainment slowly got worse and no one came much. She then sold it to a young couple and I believe she lied about how much she had grossed the year before. The couple bought it with enthusiasm but found out how many repairs were needed.

Also, old customers didn't come back. In fact, the whole Hat Creek Rim Valley doesn't get as many vacationers as it used to. The town council was trying to figure out a way to draw people to the area. I told the guy that I had noticed that all the campgrounds along the river were practically empty and this is August, prime vacation time. He said "A family can come here any time now, even in August, and always get a free campsite. I think the thing that hurt us was a two year drought and the river became a small creek and was soon fished out."

Well, it was interesting to hear the story of Hat Creek. I do remember when I last came through here it was jumping with campers. Now it was time to make tracks. I said good-bye to the older couple who ran the place and headed down the road. A short walk took me to a junction in the highway. Highway 89 kept heading straight to the town of Burney. A sign on the highway read, "22 miles to Burney."

Man, it would be so easy to head down that highway instead of the Hat Creek Rim Trail, but this is a trail that I have never traveled. It was a must for me to do so. I walked about a quarter of a mile on Highway 36 and joined the trail. It seemed to me to almost be like a desert scene.

The trail began to slowly gain in altitude and finally a few deciduous trees came into view, but no pines. After a couple of hours I had pretty much climbed to the top of the rim.

Here at the rim's summit there's a highway rest stop with a cement over-look and some coin operated telescopes. There was a great view of Mt Lassen and the whole Hat Creek Valley. Hat Creek got its name back in the 1800s when some cat lost his hat and his compatriots named the creek Hat Creek, and the name stuck. I talked to a family here for a bit. They offered me a bottle of water which I accepted and needed.

The hiking was pretty flat now as I was on top of the rim. The trail head-ed east for a short time and went around the top of a canyon. A spring lay far below which created Lost Creek which ran to the west. On I walked, enjoying a late afternoon hike and an excellent sunset. I was lucky to be walking while the temperature was cool because I know from reading about the Hat Creek Trail that it can be very hot.

There were also no trees because of fires. The absence of trees of course provided no shade from the sun. I just kept barreling down the trail, making excellent time. It was now about 7:45pm and I started looking for a flat place to crash. At about 8pm I found a pretty good place that was flat and sandy. Here I stopped for the night and prepared dinner. As dusk set in I no-ticed that the sky was starting to look black.

I really didn't worry about the way the sky looked too much, but in the back of my mind was the fact that I didn't have a tarp. My new tarp was at Bur-ney Falls State Park; at least I hope it was. I fell off to sleep about 9pm.

At about 1am I was awakened by the sound of raindrops hitting my sleeping bag! I was definitely concerned and hoped it would stop in a few minutes like it did yesterday morning. I got out my lightweight poncho and put it on. I rolled up my bag, tucking it under me as best I could.

I was still hoping that the rain would stop after a few minutes. About a half hour went by but the rain kept coming down. I was now freaked out. Another half hour went by and still it was raining. I was protecting everything as best as I could, but my back was starting to kill me. Now I had to make a decision. I couldn't just keep sitting up like this. It was starting to get very uncomfortable.

I had to go. I had to start walking and as quick as I could I put my shoes on and gathered up my stuff. I got a little wet doing it. Thank God the rain wasn't coming down in buckets. I strapped my light across my head. It needed a new battery. I was angry over this because I had plenty of opportunities to buy new batteries at the Old Station store, but neglected to do so. Finally, off I went into the night, edging my way down to the trail and then headed north into the dark rainy night.

I actually felt better now that I was moving. My back was stiff. It felt better when I leaned back and stretched it out a bit. The rain was coming down pretty good. I still had hoped that it would stop. Most of the time these summer rainstorms last an hour or so. This rain had been going on for over an hour.

My pace was slow due to my lousy headlight batteries. The trail was in pretty good shape but it could have been better because every now and then I would trip over some obstacle.

My feet were pretty much soaked now. I wasn't too cold as long as I was moving. I figured my pace was less than two miles per hour. It was better to play it safe than sprain an ankle in the dark. Man, that's all I needed. The cheap plastic poncho was doing its job, except there was little protection for my arms as the backpack straps pulled the lightweight plastic back and pinned it to my armpits and chest.

For the next three hours I worked my way along the Hat Creek Rim Trail. At one time I saw a strange animal near my feet. It was really weird. It kind of looked like a big rat with an owl's head on it! It seemed to be a couple of feet from me. I wasn't totally scared of it either. Wow, have I discovered a new animal up here in the rain on Hat Creek Rim, Pacific Crest Trail? I doubt it with my lousy light; a deception could easily take place.

I kept looking at my watch. The time was creeping by and the rain just wouldn't stop. Pretty soon I could see some kind of structure that was probably a mile away. It looked like a house covered in Christmas lights. If it had been closer or I knew some way to get there I would have gone there to seek shelter. But then again, I might be trespassing.

Slowly but steadily I cruised down the trail and began looking for the sky to get lighter. With better light I could see the trail and start making better time. The rain fell steadily. There were a few times that it slowed down a bit, but it would immediately pick up again.

It was now 5am and there wasn't any sight of increasing light. I was bored and pretty miserable; this was getting really old. Where was the sun? When would this miserable rain stop? Come on…..it's August 2nd. Continual rain like this isn't supposed to happen during this time of year. This was not a thunderstorm; there wasn't any sign of lightning anywhere, just a steady, monotonous rain fall.

I really didn't know where I was. It's too difficult to stop and check out my map due to the constant rain. Just about everything that shouldn't get wet is in my plastic trash bag. I don't have a pack cover and my backpack is already soaked. I just want the sun to come out so at least I can see where I'm going. Finally the eastern sky started to get a little lighter. It's about time. It's already 6am.

An hour later I put my headlight away. It's now 7am and I can see the trail just fine. My pace is quicker now with the improved visibility.

I now have trouble keeping my eyes open. I'm so sleepy, I can't believe it. I have to trudge on; there's absolutely no shelter from this storm.

It's now 8am and I have arrived at a water cache. Some guy named Amigo had put plenty of water out. Water, however, isn't what I need, but I drink all I can and felt nauseated after drinking it. The trail seems to be going downhill now. I believe I am getting off this forsaken ridge. More trees appear, not pines, but broad leaf trees. I'm starting to notice that these trees are partially dry underneath. I'm hoping now that I can find a large thick tree that can give me some kind of shelter.

About another mile down the trail I find it, a large weeping willow tree that looks dry underneath it. The thick branches hang downward towards the ground where the water seems to run off it. It's dry under the tree, but of course there are cow patties everywhere.

I spend a little time scraping the cow patties away with my feet and then I lay my ground mat out and dive down on it. I put my ground tarp over me to keep the occasional cold drops of rain from falling on me.

Oh man, this is pretty comfortable. I made a pillow using my clothes and almost immediately fell asleep. About an hour and 15 minutes later I wake up. I can't seem to sleep any more. I'm anxious to leave. I feel great now as I walk down the trail. I'm not sleepy any more. That tree was a godsend.

The damn rain just keeps on falling as I'm now trudging in mud. I have to watch it because it's slippery. Animals have roto-tilled the trail up as well as left souvenirs on it. Add water to this mixture and you have ugly goo. Many times when possible I walk to the side of the trail for better traction.

Onward I go into the never ending rain. No views and no sign of clear sky anywhere. The hiking is somewhat flat. I believe that the trail has curved to the west a little bit. I'm definitely off the rim now.

I soon crossed a paved highway. One car speeds by, maybe heading to Burney. My California map was so tattered that I tossed it out at Old Station. I have a bit to eat here and noticed that no other car has even come by. I'd better leave. Down the trail I head, hoping this damn never ending rain stops.

At last a long skinny lake appears below me. This must be Baum Lake. I go around a large power house. There's a dirt road that has a wooden house on it. It probably belongs to the electric company. For a minute I think about breaking into it, but I'm not that desperate yet.

One mile further I cross Crystal Lake and for a short time I go the wrong way, following the lake shore to the west. Soon I double back and walk along the other long body of water heading in a more northern direction. A short distance later the trail curves away from Crystal and Baum Lakes and slides a little to the west.

About two miles later I cross Highway 299. I think about hitchhiking here but to my joy, the rain has started to ease up a little. On the other side of the road is a sign that read "Burney Falls State Park, 11 miles". All right, this is good news. It's now 1:30pm. I can probably get there in the early evening. They have cabins there for sure. I hope to god one is available.

The hiking was basically flat and fast. I kept at least a four mile per hour pace, much faster than my usual pace. I wanted shelter. I was too tired to be tired, just plain numbed out. The weather eased up some, then clouded up and got darker once more as late afternoon drew near, I only took one break during this time and that was for a Big Hunk candy bar and a few swigs of water.

Finally I came to an overlook and I could see a huge lake stretching out in the distance. It had to be Lake Britton. I knew I had only a few miles left. About an hour later, at 6:30pm, I reached Burney Falls State Memorial Park.

I was elated. I had made it. Now it was time to visit the visitor area and find some shelter for the night. It all kind of reminded me of another Rolling Stones song, "Gimme Shelter". Yeah, give me shelter or I'm going to fade away. I remember in 1978 that the tourist stuff was right next to the falls. I can remember buying ice cream there with many other tourists on a hot dry day. Hot and dry sounds really good to me after walking 17 hours in the rain.

I jammed across Highway 89 and followed the trail until I found a couple of signs: "Head Camp – ½ mile, PCT Camp – ½ mile, Burney Falls – 1 mile". Nothing about a visitor center, restaurant, or cabins. I was kind of perplexed but I head down the trail towards these three things.

After walking at least a quarter of a mile I found Head Camp. It consisted of a large flat area with a wooden fence around it. There were three or four large walk-in tents about the place and some pit toilets. There weren't any people around.

I walked down the trail looking for what was called the PCT Camp. I wonder what fellow campers would be camping here. I never could find the so-called PCT campgrounds. This didn't bother me too much because I felt that my thru-hiking friends were probably in cabins or motel rooms nearby. I kept walking at a quick pace because now the rain had picked up and was coming down real hard.

Soon I heard a noise of crashing water. I had made it to Burney Falls. The trail led down to a huge wooden platform that circled the falls. This wasn't here in 1978. Back then you could go right down to the falls if you wanted.

I walked the wooden decking a short distance looking for the ice cream place and Visitors Center, but saw nothing. Wow, I was starting to freak out. What in the hell was going on? What should I do now? The only thing I could think of was to retrace my steps. There was still Head Camp with all those expensive tents. I could roust somebody out of one just to give me information.

So off I went back to Head Camp. The rain was coming down in buckets. It was now close to 7pm and it wasn't getting any lighter. Twenty minutes later I was back at Head Camp. This time I wasn't shy. I walked to the center of the whole place and shouted, "Hello, is anybody here?!" No answer. I yelled out again, "Hello, I need help. I've been walking in the rain now for 18 hours. I just want to know where the Visitors Center is."

There was still no damn answer. Man, this was just plain freaky. I was starting to shiver now and I knew I could be getting into the first stages of hypothermia. I had warm clothes in my bag but I didn't want to put them on in the rain because if they got cold and wet I would definitely be in trouble.

This is time for desperate measures. So I went over to a tent and looked inside. I was hoping that it would be vacant, but the whole bottom of the tent was mattress and little kids toys. I wished I could stay there. I checked out another tent and it was filled with people's belongings.

I moved on heading back to where I had come from. I was also worried that I couldn't hear the highway any more. That's bad, because at least with a highway I could possibly get a ride to the town of Burney, which was about 14 miles away. One problem with that was who in the hell would give me a ride now since it was getting dark.

Before I left Head Camp I checked out the bathrooms for at least some shelter. They were smelly pit toilet deals, gross. I even thought of getting in a large metal bear box, anything for protection from the continuing heavy rain. I was freaking out even more now.

ECSTASY OF MISERY

I was mad as hell over this whole situation. In fact I had to calm myself down. I decide to hike back to Highway 89 and approach the park in a different way. If worse came to worse I could try to hitchhike to Burney or any other place that could give me shelter.

So I followed the PCT white diamonds back to the road. When I got there I decided to get my trail guide out and read for any clues on what to do. The sounds of an occasional vehicle zooming by on wet payment increased as I neared the highway.

I got under a large pine tree that was dripping water like crazy. I then took off my sopping wet pack and dug into the plastic trash bag and pulled out the trail guide book.

I opened it and started reading. The rain was coming down hard now and the trail guide book was getting wet as I read. Right then, however, I discovered a possible answer to my misery. The trail guide read, "Northbound hikers, turn right. Southbound hikers, turn left. The main entrance is about one-eighth of a mile."

I couldn't believe it. All I had to do was follow the guidebook from the very start. This definitely plays into the old adage that a little knowledge can be dangerous.

Down the road I went until I saw some large brown rocks piled up on each side of an entrance road. It was more than one-eighth of a mile, but who cares. It looks like help at last.

I walked to the road and came up to a tollbooth where cars pay to get into the park. In the booth was a cute little blonde lady. I walked up to the booth and spelled out my case. I said to the lady, "Where are the cabins? I've been walking for 19 hours in this miserable rain and I could be coming down with the first stages of hypothermia."

The lady was very sympathetic. She told me to go over and get some hot coffee and to get out of the rain. I asked where the coffee was and she pointed over to a place next to the sporting goods store. Oh wow, the camping store was still open. I can get my new tarp. The lady asked if I had been traveling without a tarp or tent. I said I sure was and how I sent my old tarp home at Belden and had my new tarp from Camp More sent here. I told her how it was 112 degrees in Belden and I didn't think there would be 24 hours of rainfall within five days. I asked for five good days of weather and nature only gave me four days. The lady said I should get my supplies since the store closes in 20 minutes. Then she said, "I'll see if I can line up a ride for you to Burney City." "Oh, thanks so much. I really appreciate that."

I went over to the store first and walked in. It was a pretty nice place. A couple of people were there asking about different things. I believe I disturbed the peace a little by walking in dripping water like a sieve. I took off my soaking pack and put it on the floor. Water and mud were all over the place. I walked up to the counter and asked for my two packages. The two ladies in the door kind of gave me a quick look over and left the store quite quickly. The stark reality of what thru-hiking can be sometimes chases people right out the door. Probably my smell was none too pleasant either.

My food supply box was there as well as my new tarp, a day late and a dollar short. After receiving my stuff I went to a corner of the store and took off my wet stuff and put on some dry clothes. I asked the people if they had a mop so I could clean up the mess I made. The young man said that he would take care of it and that it looked like I'd had a bad enough day as it was. I told everyone my story: how I walked the PCT and walked 19 hours in the rain. I believe it eased the fact that I had messed up the floor.

After that I went outside and around to the other side of the building. They were out of coffee so I had some hot chocolate. Just as I was about to take a sip a guy came over and asked me if I was the hiker that needed a ride to Burney. I said that I was and how I needed a ride bad, that I had been through hell today. He said that he and his wife and brother and sister-in-law were going down to Burney for dinner. "You can come along if you want." I said, "I sure would. I need to get to a hotel." The man said he would be back in 10 or 15 minutes. I thanked him and told him that he was a lifesaver.

Everything was turning up roses now. I was one happy guy. A few minutes later the people came by and picked me up and off we went to Burney Town, a place that I had been to 25 years ago. But a place that I wouldn't be going to if the weather had been nicer. The people were really cool. I think they were a little flabbergasted as I told them my story. I definitely have a tendency to talk too much sometimes, which I told them, plus I haven't talked to anybody in a couple of days.

What was also strange; these people were from Brea, California. Brea is a city right next to La Habra, where I live, and where my sponsor, Chuck Hinkle, has his tree service and palm tree sales business. What a strange coincidence. It's a small world, that's for sure, a small world with a long trail.

The people drove me into Burney where there was a series of small hotels. I guess a lot of people would call it a motel now. They dropped me off at the Shasta Pines Motel. They had a room for $60 a night. An Indian guy owned the motel. I told him that I had spent two and a half years in Orissa, India, back in the early seventies. The guy didn't seem too impressed. I said goodbye to the people and tried to show them that I was one happy guy, which I was.

I walked down to the end of the place. Maybe they were putting me at the back of the bus, I'm not sure. My room was pretty nice. I had a color TV and a microwave. The place was AAA rated so it was pretty clean, too.

The first thing I did was to take off my funky wet clothes. The next thing was head right into the shower, with plenty of hot water to thaw me out. This had to be one of the greatest showers of all time. I was just grateful that I was here. When I go back to Burney Falls State Memorial Park, I'll definitely have to thank that lady who was so instrumental in getting me a ride down here.

After showering, I felt quite thawed out and decided to prepare myself a Lipton dinner. I had so much food. I was going to have to ditch some. I hadn't had much in the last day and a half. I believe I had walked well over 30 miles and if you include walking around Burney Falls looking for shelter, it was probably more like 35 miles in 19 wet miserable hours. It was after 10pm Sunday and I doubted much was open. While cooking my grub I took out all my wet things from my pack and spread stuff out so it would dry. Tomorrow would be a laundry day.

After dinner I called home and left my phone number so they could call me back, which is cheaper than me calling them. My mom called back and was happy to hear from me. I told her my ordeal about the summer rainstorm. She thought that I might have been in some rain because she had heard the weather report from the Weather Channel at home. Linda, "Trail Perfect", called after getting the phone number from my mom. I talked to her longer, telling her all about the crazy weather and that I would probably be here for two nights.

After talking to Linda I wrapped up about everything I needed to do, so I turned on the TV and kicked back on the bed watching the news and other TV junk. It's been hell the past few days. I had hiked some 100 miles during that time, plus hitching a ride 14 miles back south again to Burney Town. Some time around midnight I finally fell asleep. My 56 year old bones and muscles were finally getting a comfortable rest.

The next morning, after getting up for a bathroom visit, I slept in until 9am. It was August 3rd, Monday morning, and I was in Burney, California, USA. The first order of the day was breakfast. On the way to breakfast I paid for another night. I could tell by the way I was walking that I wasn't going anywhere today. This would be a day of relaxation, with the usual laundry chores.

The breakfast was good, steak and eggs with a short stack of pancakes. While walking back to the motel I noticed a sign on one of the food joints that had a bar and all you can eat barbecue ribs every Monday night. Well, I know where I'm going for dinner.

I went home after this and grabbed my laundry and got it washed. Then it was time to reload the new supplies into the pack. This food would have to last to Castella, in the Castle Crags area. I would go through the infamous Section O.

While I was doing laundry I heard someone constantly yell out, "Indian tacos, come and get your Indian tacos!" So after my clothes were dry I headed back to the motel and then stopped and bought an Indian taco. The price was good: $3.25 for a taco and a soda. I went back to the room and wolfed it down. It was too bland. No spices, no heat. The taco looked more like a pizza. It would have been much better if it had some salt, cilantro, or Tabasco sauce, to say the least. But for the price you got a lot of carbs, that's for sure.

The rest of the day I just watched the tube and slept quite a bit. When I get to these towns I try to make the absolute most out of a rest day. Evening came so I headed over to the pizza bar and had the all you can eat barbecue rib dinner. Oh man, they were great. I had about 12 of them, with some beans and macaroni salad. I downed it all with a couple of Buds. The rest of the night

ECSTASY OF MISERY

I spent in my room with some chips and Ben and Jerry's Cherry Garcia.

Later on in the evening I packed my stuff up and got my pack ready to leave tomorrow. I planned to take it easy, sleep in a little, take my last hot shower, and finally I'll get a great breakfast. After that it will be time to hitch a ride back to Burney Falls State Memorial Park.

Tomorrow I would just ease back into the trail. Maybe going 12 to 14 miles will be enough tomorrow.   If I were 25 years old like most of these kids I would go ahead and get an early start and shoot for 20 miles or more. You have to learn to listen to your body and if it's stiff and weak, a days rest is definitely a good option to take.

The next day I got up at about 8am and took a hot shower. From there I took off down the street and powered down a big breakfast. After that I went back to the room and grabbed my pack and hit the road. Burney Town sure had been good to me. My legs felt very rested now.

It took about 45 minutes to get a ride. The guy asked me if I were a backpacker hiking the trail. I told him yes and got in his car and then off we went. He asked me how far I had hiked. I told him that I started in Mexico and I was hoping to make it to Canada. The guy was really cool. He was an electrician that had moved from Redding, California, which he called the big city, to the country. It was hard at first but he built up a good clientele. This guy took me all the way to Burney Falls since he lived a short distance from there. I bid the guy farewell and thanked him for the most helpful ride all the way to the falls.

I was just about ready to put my pack on when I heard, "Wrong Way, you're still kicking." It was Dave and Brooke walking up from the falls. "Hey dudes, what are you doing here?" They wanted to know what happened to me. They had read my statement in the PCT register back at the Amigo water cache.

Dave thought it was funny and started laughing his ass off. I said, "It seems funny now, but believe me dude, it wasn't to me then." I then told the hellish time I had after getting to this place in a pouring storm. Dave still thought it was amusing but I don't think Brooke did.

I asked them if they were just kicking back here for the day. They said they were waiting for supplies and hoped they would be there at 2pm when the mail got there. Well, my mail did get there, even my "a day late, a dollar short" impregnated tarp. They both laughed. "Well, see you youngsters up ahead. I'm sure you will catch me. I'm just planning to do 14 or 15 miles today."

"Okay, later then."

Forest Service worker that saved me at Burney Falls State Park

Look to the sky's you thru hikers

for the "Big Dump" is coming!

Should one flip flop at the

"I Hop"

or go all the way in one play?

If the big dump stopped the

Donner Party

It can stop you, ah what to do?

Journey Twelve:
Burney Falls to the Border Tree

Down the trail I went and headed past the noise of the falls and dam area. Section O was waiting for me, the notorious Section O. A section that many hikers have skipped and instead followed Highway 89 all the way to McCloud before joining the trail south of Castella and Castle Crags Campground area, just off of Interstate 5. Soon I was at the end of the lake. Then the PCT climbed up rather sharply at first, but not for long and then ran up to a dirt road just above the lake.

Somehow I had got off the trail already. Not a good way to start the infamous Section O. When I put my backpack on I looked up and down the dirt road. I discovered the PCT again running downhill and crossing the same dirt road that I was standing on.

I was back in the saddle again, and off I went at nearly a three mile per hour pace. Walking down the trail I got into my own thoughts, some were of back home, some from high school. It's called getting into oneself, at least that's how I see it. It's good to do sometimes, but one must also watch out for tricks and twists in the trail.

So far the trail is in pretty good shape. The hiking was pretty easy and the weather is great. I still can see muddy areas along the trail that were caused by that last rainstorm.

I decided to stop at Peavine Creek. It's not easy getting water out of this creek because it's so incredibly overgrown with bushes and trees. I got some water near the little bridge area. Since it's so close to a road, I decided to treat the water with my potable water tablets and make orange iodine water out of it.

This is one of those non-scenic places to camp. There's water but it is on a dirt road junction of three or four jeep roads. What I'm sleeping on is a small dirt road that runs along the side of the creek. I'm sort of in a canyon, boxed in, no view, and I will have an uphill hike in the morning to get out of here. The next morning I got a pretty good start and was off climbing uphill out of the creek area. I was heading now for Red Mountain. These were pleasant hills, not spectacular, high, running possibly to 6000 feet.

This area has had a problem getting volunteers because the centers of population, like Sacramento and San Francisco, are a long way off. Also this area has almost always been logged. There are a lot of logging roads to cross over. Trail markers disappear here. Logging companies and backpackers have little in common.

Now as I think about this, I begin to enter lousy trail land. The trail goes through some Manzanita that hasn't been cut back in some time. The trail comes to an intersection with five or six logging roads, but no sign of the trail!

Now it's time to put down the pack in a safe place and walk off with the map to find the way back. The combination is usually successful. Then pop your pack on your back. This also gives your shoulders and back a little break. The problem here is it is time consuming and frustrating. For about three hours, I put up with having gone probably a quarter negative mile trying to find the trail, though it wasn't anything serious.

Then suddenly the trail became more maintained. Now I can make a better and more pleasant time. Bushwhacking is not a lot of fun, especially for the hikers wearing shorts. One thing that helped me and other hikers is the use of ducks, usually four or five piled rocks stacked on top of each other. I don't really know why they're called ducks but I've always thought that from a distance they often look like ducks.

A few miles later I take a short lunch break and started eating trail mix, power bars, and some cheese, and then wash it all down with water. Suddenly I hear the sound of a rock or two being kicked on the trail.

Well there they are again, Dave and Brooke. "Wrong Way, you're making pretty good time." They said their mail had arrived at 1pm. I told them that I had a three or four hour jump on them and they still caught up to me in about 24 miles. Because of their youth, I like calling them the Young and the Restless.

We talked for a bit and then headed out together. "Hey, have you seen

Solace?" Dave said that he was up in front of us, that he had left that morning before they saw me. Dave said that Solace looked pretty sad when he read what I wrote in the register at Amigos water cache about not having a tarp.

I told them that it was Solace who had told me about the new lightweight nylon tarp. "Solace helped me order it, but it was my decision to send my old tarp home. At least I could have sent my new tarp to Old Station instead of Burney Falls." Then Dave said that Solace might have to go home because of some family problem, but he was hoping to finish California. That's a drag. I thought he would finish because he sure has the ability. I was a little surprised that he wasn't further ahead.

Down the trail the two youngsters and myself hiked at a pretty good pace. I had to push it just a little in order to keep up. We traveled a well-kept trail, with Manzanita and other thick bushes lining the trail. This was probably one of those heavily lumbered areas where the trees never seemed to come back.

A few minutes later Dave and Brooke said they were going to scout ahead and find a good camping site before it got dark. Then they kicked into another gear and jammed off into the great wide open. I would catch them. They usually won't hike in the dark too much, but I will.

The trail now and then would bring one into view of Mt Lassen way off in the distance. It still had some snow on it. The setting sun lit up the snow on Mt Lassen and it looked like sparkling gold. The trail went around the hills in a sea of green shrubbery. A few miles later, near dark, I arrived at a place where a graveled lumber yard road was what provided a flat place to sleep. This was where I found Dave and Brooke.

It wasn't much of a camping spot, though it was flat and not like gravel; it was nice to sleep on. I hope a car doesn't come by; it's late. I really doubt that would happen. I joked around with Dave and Brooke, and Brooke actually said a few words too. I put my tarp up. The sky looked sort of overcast. I don't trust it any more. The dry months have possibly come and gone now. I made a pretty good meal of chicken with rice. That night I slept like a baby, but in the morning rain began to fall. Thank goodness I put my tarp up. I fell right back to sleep.

ECSTASY OF MISERY

The next morning Dave and Brooke left a few minutes earlier than I did. It was still a good start for me. As long as I start hiking before 7am, I'm pretty happy with that.

I started out behind the young couple and then headed up over Pigeon Hill. The trail was now in excellent condition. I'm just hoping that the few miles of bad trail was totally behind me at this point. Just past Pigeon Hill Brooke and Dave had already made a breakfast stop. After a quick hello and a few humorous comments, I jammed. Off I went, back in the lead, for a while anyway.

An hour later the trail crossed upper Bear Creek. Here the trail travels along the creek for a couple of miles. Then it pulls away from this creek and catches Butcher Knife Creek. I'm starting to be a little impressed with this section. It was actually prettier than I thought it would be.

At Butcher Knife Creek I took a half hour break and made lunch. I had tuna out of those aluminum foil type packets. They're pre-drained and are an excellent addition to my eating entrees. In the middle of the feast Dave and Brooke went by. "Caught you again, old boy." Then the Young and the Restless hiked on. Dave and Brooke don't know it but they now have a private trail name. The Young and the Restless from the TV soap opera, of course.

After lunch I sprang into action and started heading northwest. My next destination was Castle Crags. The PCT looped around the creek's little canyon and then headed back out again, following Bear Creek and a road 300 feet or so below the trail.

Soon the trail crossed Centipede Creek where I made myself some lemonade. God it was good. It's always good when you're thirsty. I started hiking again but I hadn't gone more than a third of a mile when I started hearing the rush of a large body of water. After crossing a road and a bridge I came to Ash Camp. The huge creek or better described as a small river was McCloud Creek, and it flowed out of McCloud Lake, which was just a couple of miles away.

I stopped and took a picture break and headed out following the river of water for a couple of miles until it slanted to the south at Ah-DI-NA campground. For the next few hours I was just hiking and digging it. There were views off and on of Lassen Park with its white lingering snow. The trail worked its way around a treeless bend and there it was, Mt Shasta, still spotted with snow on its eastern side.

The trail actually goes around Shasta like a horseshoe and the beautiful peak will be seen off and on for another three weeks. Shasta is a peak that you see early and stays late. A few minutes later I caught up with Dave and Brooke who were also taken aback by Shasta.

After a short climb we walked through a thick bushed out ridge and then Castle Crags. The lightly colored Crags looked beautiful in the late afternoon sun. "What's that, Wrong Way?" "That's Castle Crags down there, and at the bottom of the steep valley we're walking into is the Sacramento River." Interstate 5 and Castle Crags State Park, Castella, is just a little south of the park. Dunsmuir is just to the north.

There used to be a famous trail angel whose name I can't remember, but at the park they have a free campsite for PCT hikers named in his honor. He used to take hikers to Dunsmuir where there was an excellent pizza joint. Then everybody would pig out. "What's the guy's name and what happened to him?" asked the normally silent Brooke. I told them his name finally came to me, it was Milt Kinney, and that he died five or six years ago. I never got to meet him on either of my two California walks. The first walk I was too early and now on this walk I'm too late.

While we were hiking down the trail Dave and Brooke told me they were going to pick up speed so they could make camp a little bit early tonight. "Don't mind me. I'll just walk until I flop." Off they went, shifting into gear to hit about a four mile per hour pace. I just kept my 2.2 pace going and I will keep it going until I find some flat area. With the Young and the Restless gone, I could walk in peace, not having to entertain them. I can get those two laughing easily. I hope that isn't why they jammed ahead of me, trying to regain their sanity.

I followed them at my own relaxed pace and started zigzagging down the trail of bright green mountain brush. The day was ending now and it looked like Squaw Valley Creek would probably be the place tonight.

Soon my poor old dogs got me to Squaw Valley Creek Bridge. On the other side of the creek was a familiar tent: none other than Dave and Brooke. I marched on down. "Hey dudes, what's happening?" They said they were going to camp here for the night, though there was one problem. It looked like that was the only flat spot. They were right; only the bridge itself was flat. The other alternative was that I could march for about a half mile. The guidebook says there's a road there so there has to be flat ground somewhere.

Now it was getting dark and then a raindrop hit my hat. It was time to move. I dug for my tarp and with Dave's help, we put the thing up, tying the ends to the handrails of the bridge. We were sure to make it to where the water would have a place to drain.

The weather did hold off just enough to allow Dave and I to put up the tarp. Dave was showing me some cool knots when he had to jam back to his tent because the sky had just opened up. Rain pounded down on my tarp. At first most of it ran off, but the rain came down so hard that a lake pocket was just above my head. I pushed the tarp up from sagging and water ran off, splashing on the edge of the bridge. Most of the water ran off in Squaw Valley Creek. The rain pounded pretty good for about 15 to 20 minutes, then suddenly subsided.

The rain was over for now and now it was time to check out the damage. The rain had not gotten to me directly but splashing water from the bridge had dampened my sleeping bag. That would be easily fixed by placing my ground mat over my sleeping bag. This would keep my bag from getting wet.

I really didn't need a ground mat on the bridge but I would hold it over me at intervals of heavy rain. If I used it as a blanket the rain would not soak my bag.

Suddenly the rain hit again, though not as hard as before. The ground mat worked well, and five minutes later the rain stopped. A small breeze drifted by and the sky was clear. The amazing stars were lodged in their usual format.

Now, that's a summer rain: short but sweet. It gives everything alive a nice drink, cleans off the rocks and dampens the trail, which helps to keep the dust down. Hey, that's what a summer rain is all about. Does this mean that the trail will close earlier this year? I'm still in California, never-ending California, and then somehow I fell asleep.

The next morning was overcast and because I was hanging over Squaw Valley Creek in a canyon of sorts, there wasn't any sunshine. It was really cold however, and I was about to bolt out of my cocoon while the Young and the Restless walked over from their camping spot to the trail. I gave them a wave that I was okay and they took off down the trail.

No problem. I popped out and even with my tarp up, I broke camp and was hiking in 20 minutes. The bridge worked for me, but I don't recommend it. First of all, you can block the way of other hikers or animals, maybe even a bear. Yipes! I'm glad a bear didn't think about barreling his or her way across the bridge.

A couple of miles further on, mostly uphill on a wet trail, I found the Young and the Restless finishing their breakfast. They looked at me questioning whether I would be pissed off again like I get sometimes, but I came on with a smile and said, "The best night of sleep I've had in a long time." "Oh yeah?" said Dave, with a little relief in his voice.

I told them that the tarp worked with the first downpour and that I got slightly damp from the splashing water, but I was ready with the ground mat for the second round. But it really never happened. "Yeah that was a cool rain." I said that I agreed but it makes me wonder a little. We have had a lot of rain in the last four or five days, and it makes me wonder what is going to happen in Oregon and Washington.

We still had a couple of weeks at least before we get out of California. Dave remarked that you couldn't tell, that these are summer rainstorms in Northern California and it doesn't really pertain to Oregon and Washington. I said, "Yeah maybe not, but I'm still thinking about flip flopping." I went on to say how we all are running at least a couple of weeks later than is suggested. Last year you could have walked up until November in Washington, but this is a different year and you never know.

Dave and Brooke then took off. I grabbed a couple of fruit bars, ate them and headed down the trail a few minutes later. The PCT now began to descend into the valley below which was definitely a mainstream artery for the West Coast, also Interstate 5, and plenty of railroad ties and finally the Sacramento River.

The trail pretty much dropped into the river valley. Low lying trees appeared, such as sycamores, elms, and willows. A few hours later I reached the bottom and chose to walk south to Castella. Castella has a pretty good store, at least it did in 1978. Castle Crags Park is full of campsites, including Milt Kinney Campground that's reserved for thru-hikers. The walk to Castella was a couple of miles but it seemed longer because of anticipation of some good ole store bought food, including ice cream of course.

Finally I reached what looked to be the center of town. I have to cross under Interstate 5, the river, and the railroad tracks and then make a couple of turns and I'm there. Near the post office were Dave and Brooke, or as they are now known to me, the Young and the Restless.

After going into the store and buying a big bottle of Gatorade and chips, I walked over to the post office and started rapping to Dave and Brooke. I noticed that their supplies were almost completely reloaded into their packs. "Man you guys are fast, with having your packs almost reloaded." I was walking at a really quick clip to get here.

They said that they got a ride as soon as they got to the Castella Road. I said that was good but we'll have to hitch or hike back now and resume the trail there.

I asked why since it just goes to the park and then up and over the crags. I said, "I believe you can catch the PCT from this side of the park." "Yeah but we're sort of purist and I think we should probably push on." I told them okay, but there's a nice store and restaurant here and most of the day was gone. Just as I said that two people, a long-haired guy and a girl, walked through the parking lot. To my surprise it was Sweep and Clover. "Hey, what are you guys doing? I haven't seen you in a coons age."

Sweep and Clover sat down and began to tell us that they were basically doing bits and pieces of the trail. They would hike a few days then travel by rental car and catch the trail up ahead of it. It sounded interesting. Dave and Brooke along with Sweep and Clover seemed like good friends. As they rapped away I went to the post office before they closed and secured my supply box outside.

I started taking out my trash and restocking my pack when Sweep said that he heard that Shutter Bug and Steady are going to meet Cliff Hanger in Belden and then head north to Canada again. Sweep mainly was talking to me, knowing that we had all hiked together.

I asked Sweep how far behind they were from me. Sweep said, "I think they're probably at least a week behind you, don't you think, Honey?" Clover agreed. I then told them that I was seriously thinking about flip flopping at Ashland. That's what they were going to do according to Sweep, the young doctor, but instead of Ashland, they were going to do it here at Castella and then take a bus to Vancouver then to Manning Park.

"Well dudes, who's into downing a couple of cold ones?" I said with conviction. Then the couples turned cold on me. I believe the women were definitely against it. They seemed to wear the pants. I said "Later" to the young couples.

Wow, the guys can't even have a cold one at this cool bar beside the store. Things have changed in the last 25 years. Thru-hikers of old would have united and had a couple of beers with Wrong Way. I feel sorry for them, especially the doctor. Without that girl I believe he could have done the whole PCT instead of hit and miss, but whatever.

The bar was pretty cool. Hanging from the ceiling were old antiques. There were only a few people there. I ordered the Castle Crags cheeseburger special with a salad. To drink I had a Sierra Nevada Pale Ale. Again, a beer I don't drink at home because it's too strong. But here on the trail it's the bite that you want.

A few minutes later I was munching on a cheeseburger when a guy in a hat comes in the bar and ordered a Moosehead Canadian brew. I heard the guy rapping here and there to people. But what freaked me out was he actually pulled off one of his legs. Oh man, a plastic leg!

After a while and a couple of beers later, I started conversing with the guy. He lost his leg when a bunch of bikers jumped him, beat him up and threw him on the railroad tracks! The train came, ran over him, broke his jaw and took off his leg. I asked how he was doing with the plastic leg. He said it took about six months to get use to it but he really likes it now.

The guy had been a surveyor for the government before he got wasted and he gets some money every month. "That's good but what do you do in all your spare time?" "I walk down mountain creeks until they become lakes or rivers." "Excuse me dude, but did you say that you walk down creeks with the plastic leg?"

The dude told me that he gets a friend to take him to the creek source. A lot of them are not too far from jeep roads. Then he would hike down the creeks. "In the water with one leg?" He said yes, that he loves it, going down a cold stream into a bigger body of water.

I told him that was kind of strange. He said some people feel that walking from Mexico to Canada is pretty weird. "Yeah," I said. "I guess it's pretty weird but it's also a great adventure." We sat around drinking beer. He would buy me one, then I would buy him one. I was a bit sauced but still in control. I said good luck with the creeks. "Yeah, watch your step in Canada. They don't like us anymore, you know."

Down to the store I went and bought some fried chicken and some other stuff and headed over to Castle Crags Park. I hiked down a rock-lined trail to a campsite with trucks and giant camper shells. I crashed on top of the nearest picnic table and fell asleep for at least a couple of hours until some oversized RV tried to get in his parking spot.

What a scene. This guy was going back and forth with his headlights blinding me. Because of all the noise and his bright headlights, he should've been held responsible for being a public nuisance and disturbing the peace!

I slid out of my sack and walked over with all my stuff and slept on the next campsite table. I heard someone say "We made that hippie move." I then heard them laugh. It was now 10pm and I have to put up with this crap. I felt like screaming out, "Are you camping or building a suburb?"

I mean does this clown have to bring his entire home with him? For the next hour at least the place was taken prisoner by this huge monstrosity. "Hey honey, turn a little to the left. No, that's too far." "Well, honey, I can't see out here." "Okay that's enough."

Oh my God. What a hassle. Finally there was silence, except for the noise of Interstate 5 below. But that was a pretty steady hum of engines, like a creek I guess, unless the one-leg creek walker makes his presence. What a day. What's going to happen tomorrow? Who knows? But I do know that I want to leave around noon, if possible.

The next morning was August 8th and here I was in good old Castle Crags. First I grabbed a shower at the bathroom shower stalls. Then I went and pigged out, built up the carbs because they will be burned off soon. I had some excellent pastries and hot coffee. Then I had some freshly grilled chicken and some store made coleslaw that was excellent.

I sat outside and called Eric Carpenter at the Orange County Register. I told him where I was but that there might be a slight wrinkle in my plans, how I might flip flop at Ashland, Oregon. Ashland was a good spot because it was where I started this thru-hiking gig on the mighty PCT. Eric said "You have to do what you have to do."

After talking to Eric Carpenter and Trail Perfect I decided to head out. It was about 11am and all my chores were done. I was stuffed with excellent store prepared food. It was now time to bail, heading into a western direction towards the Trinity Alps, the Russian Wilderness and of course the dynamic Marble Mountains. First I went back to the store one more time for a double scoop ice cream cone to walk into the great wide open once more. Down the parking lot I started and then quite a climb to near the top of the Crags.

Just as I took a few steps I heard, "Hey you, buddy, are you a thru-hiker from Mexico?" I said that I was. "Well hello, I'm Madame Butterfly. I walked the whole trail back in 2000." I was taken aback with this little girl's statement about walking the trail. Man, that's when I did Washington state and actually finished the PCT as a section hiker. She didn't seem too impressed.

Taking over the conversation I mentioned that I thought I might flip flop at Ashland and avoid the late summer Washington weather. I feel that the season is getting late, plus I'm at least two weeks behind my original plans. Then the cute girl who was probably only 4 feet eleven inches and 90 pounds told me that she didn't finish the trail until October 27th. "October 27th." I said incredulously. "You could still hike at that late in the season?" She said "Yes, it was miserable, but we just kept on and finally we made it."

I thought that was unbelievable. When I walked in 2000 I had finished the state on September 3rd and the weather looked bad at that time. She said just keep going, don't quit, and you'll probably make it. Even if it snows it will probably melt in a few hours. "My name is written down at Calahan's Restaurant. I'm a trail angel of sorts." Then she disappeared into the store.

Wow, was this an omen. I just got through talking to Trail Perfect and Eric Carpenter about flip flopping. I thought my decision was made, but now I'm confused again. Oh well, Ashland, Oregon, is still a long ways away. I'll figure it out by then.

Walking across the park I began to head up a service road that becomes very steep. My progress was incredibly slow. My pack felt like it was full of lead. I began to chug the half gallon of Gatorade Frost. The heat and the climb were bugging me to the max. I followed the Bob Hat Trail and joined the mighty PCT on top of the Crags. A short distance later I stopped at Winston Creek where I was going to have to make some decisions, including one about my pack that had too much food in it.

The section called Section P goes from Castle Crags to Etna Summit. Etna Summit, however, is 10 miles from Etna. It would require a hitchhike to get there. A lot of hikers bypass Etna and go straight on into the Marble Mountains. Then it's another 55 miles before you reach the Seiad Post Office. The only problem with this is that one must carry eight days worth of food. For me that's 20 pounds of grunts. I decided right then and there that I was going to Etna town, which had an excellent "Hiker's heaven hostel".

It was time to ditch five days worth of food I didn't want and I dumped it, far from the trail, of course. I spent probably a half hour dumping stuff and eating some things too.

I then popped my pack on and headed down the trail. My pack felt slightly heavy, but reasonable now. I jammed down the trail trying to make up for some of the lost time. The rest of the day I seemed to be climbing in and out of creek beds. Most of them are dry. On one occasion I rounded a corner and there's this skinny looking guy sitting on a log.

So being the friendly dude that I am I asked the guy his name and he told me Carston, like Johnny Carson, but just plug a "t" in there. It was his first day on the trail. He told me that he was German, educated at Hong Kong University and now was teaching on a teachers exchange program. "Hey that's all right, man, far out in fact." I told him that I remove tree stumps in the Los Angeles area. I think that freaked him out a little, although maybe he really didn't understand me.

I walked until 8:30 that evening before I crashed pretty close to a small trickling stream. Since the rainstorms, I'm careful to set my tarp out and make sure there are a couple of trees, obstacles I can strap my rope on just in case the rain comes down. I fixed my heaviest meal, dessert, and a drink for dinner, still trying to lighten my pack. Tomorrow would be a full day. I've got to make tracks.

In fact, the time is flying. Tomorrow is August 9th. I've been walking this trail since May 4th, well over three months. The time seemed to go slowly then, but now the days of summer will be history pretty soon. A hiker must just hang in there. That's not too hard to do for most trekkers that have gone this far, for they are in great shape and past being homesick. It becomes a new life.

The rest of the day I traveled on fairly easy terrain and a well maintained trail. I try to keep a good pace, eating my heavier stuff such as trail mix and cheese and those tuna snack packs as I go. I was able to get some water out of Porcupine Lake and then head on for a few more miles. I ended up camping near Deadfall Lake.

The next morning I got up with the sun. It was a golden morning and the hiking was one of beauty. There were quite a few springs and creeks that ran softly through flowering meadows. The PCT continues it's almost imperceptible descent gradually seeing fewer white firs and red firs and started seeing more Jeffrey pines and Manzanita.

I hiked along in beautiful weather. The temperature was probably 64 degrees. I think 64 degrees is the perfect temperature for me. Many people like it hotter than 64 degrees, but for me, 64 rules! I would be perfectly happy if it never got warmer than 64 degrees. I also think the warmer weather brings out more insects, flies, ants and mosquitoes. When it rains and gets a little colder and there's a breeze, the mosquitoes take a hike. Where they go, I have no idea?

At Bull Lake I'm treated to a great view of Mt Shasta hanging above Bull Lake. Even Little Shastina is shining in the sun today. Today is a day of laziness for me. The hiking is easy, but I feel like just sitting around by a cold spring in a soft warm sun rather than hiking my butt off. It's weird. I keep yawning even though I slept pretty good the night before.

While sitting on my butt in a perfectly divine meadow I hear a sudden noise and I see two hikers, a guy and a girl. They walk by me and say, "Hi, how's it going?" I tell them good, but that I just don't have any energy today, especially since I only had a half-day of walking yesterday. The girl said that they have had days like that too. They were also heading to Canada. The guy asked me what my name was and I told them it was Wrong Way. They said that they hadn't heard my name before. I told them that it was because they've always been ahead of me. "We're Wahoo and Lou; we'll probably see you later, Wrong Way." Then off they went.

Not long after talking to Wahoo and Lou the trail drops down to Highway 3 at Scout Mountain Summit. Then there's a climb to make up for the descent and now I enter the Trinity Alps Wilderness, going around a ridge and a beautiful view of eastern mountains soon to be conquered. There the Trinity Alps and soon the Russian Wilderness will implode on my world and finally after heading north again, I still have the dynamic Marble Mountains.

My laziness has finally left me. Now the sun is softer. I had my lunch a couple of hours ago. I now arrive at the Eagle Peak area and there at least a half dozen springs pop up. I pound away at the trail and reach Carter Meadows Summit where Wahoo and Lou appear. It looked like they were through for the day.

I talked to them for a while and ended up telling them the "space man of Sierra City" tale. I'm getting quite good at it now, after telling it so many times. "That's pretty weird, Wrong Way," said Lou.

Both of them seemed very busy fixing up their campsite and preparing dinner. They wanted to get a very early start because they were going to try and do 35 miles tomorrow. This would get them to Etna Summit where they could hitch a ride early the next morning to spend the rest of the day at Hiker's Heaven in Etna.

So I bid them farewell and headed up the trail until it got pretty dark. Here I put my tarp up in a dirty forest. I don't trust the weather like I could in Southern California and the Sierras. The last few rains have definitely got my attention.

Early the next morning I heard Wahoo and Lou go by, crashing through the forest on their way to Etna Summit. They went by me at 6:30am. I was hiking at 7:30am. Forget the 35 mile deal. I kept ascending for a while, wondering how far ahead Wahoo and Lou were.

I soon found myself in the Russian Wilderness. I wanted to have breakfast at Bingham Lake but couldn't find the trail that goes up to it. It looked like a real time-consuming hassle, so I decided to head on. I found a clear looking spring just a little ways further on and I stopped and had my traditional meal of a rich supply of powdered milk and a Carnation Instant Breakfast mix. I drank my super morning concoction along with a fruit bar, a granola bar, and a couple of bites of trail mix. Now I'm ready to boogie again.

I soon get to a great big beautiful canyon that looks like it should be located somewhere in the High Sierras. At Payne Lake I find some cool camping spots. I check my trail guide and find out that I'm some five miles from Etna Summit.

This would be a good place to camp, and then I would only have about five or six miles to do the next day to reach Etna, a pretty good day for me. I feel that I have hiked just over 25 miles for the day.

I wondered about Wahoo and Lou. Have they reached Etna Summit? Probably not. They will probably have to walk at night a bit. That was pretty rugged country we traveled through. It would have been better for them if they had done 35 miles yesterday.

The next morning I slept in just a little bit. I didn't get out of the sack until 8am. By 8:30 I was hiking. It looks like another great day as I walk along on a super good trail that eventually curls above Little Smith Lake, with granite cliffs around it. It almost reminded me of an emerald embedded in stone. The trail from here begins to descend down to Etna Summit.

The trail begins to open up a little and I get views of the mountains up in front of me. I'm now traveling in a much more northern route than before. I make a gradual turn and am now looking at Mt Shasta from the west. Looking west I see the coastal mountains, which can't be too far from the Pacific Ocean.

In front of me lies the Marble Mountain Wilderness, which I have visited twice in my life: first in 1978, and then a few years later with my brother. I tried to hike through them but was surprised to find that the winter snows hadn't melted. In fact, in 1978 I had hiked about to the middle of them and then lost the trail completely. This was about the middle of July on a terrible snowy year.

The trail now draws closer to the summit a couple of hundred yards away. I saw the Somas Bar Etna Road. To the right and heading northeast is the little town of Etna, which I was hoping to hitch a ride to. Towards the west and downhill a few miles is Sawyer's Bar.

Sawyer's Bar was the route that the PCT used to travel through and in 1978 it was buzzing with mining activity. There was a gold scare or almost a panic. People all of a sudden felt that paper money was weak because of the gold standard.

Gold went from $250 to $750 an ounce. Everybody that had a claim was working their butts off. They had a bar down there that a retired guy bought. He had lived in the Orange County area of Southern California. The guy thought he would purchase the place, make a few dollars and kick back a little. He found out that he would be incredibly busy as long as gold was priced so high.

Suddenly the trail opens up and I'm on the ridge with a road running through it. First thing I'm thinking about is food. I haven't eaten a thing all day and it's now high noon. I have just about enough water but not really enough to drink or wash up.

Just then a small green truck pulls up and out steps a young dark-haired girl, probably not even 20 years old yet. She gives me a wave and I wave back. She then comes over and asks me if I'm a PCT thru-hiker. I tell her yes and she said that she thought I looked like one. "Yeah, I guess we're pretty straggly and weather-beaten by the time we get this far north, that's for sure."

Her name was Donna and she asked me if I had seen any trail workers. I told her no and asked who's working on the trails. She tells me it's the Job Corps and she had to find them today, but it shouldn't be a problem. They're supposed to be eight miles north of Etna Summit. "Well if you head out now, you could be there by 4:00, just in time for dinner."

Donna asked if I were going down to Etna. I told her that I thought so, although I probably have enough food to get to Seiad Valley, but barely. She said I could eat at the Job Corps and they would give me enough food to get to Seiad Valley. Donna asked where Seiad Valley was. I told her it's about 50 or 60 miles from here on the Klamath River. "Is that near Happy Camp?" "Yeah, right on. Happy Camp is just a few miles west of it." She had heard that Etna has a nice place to stay, Hiker's Heaven. I said I had heard that and that it's pretty nice and reasonable.

Donna said she had to leave and then gave me some water, a half gallon bottle from her truck. "Thanks a ton," I said. "Have a good hike." "Thank you." Off she went heading across the road towards the trailhead on the other side. I yelled out, "Keep a cool stool and live by the rules." I was trying to be funny. She laughed a little but I think she was a little embarrassed.

I sat back down and started to stir my ramen when all of a sudden an old guy and a middle-aged lady came down the trail where I had just walked, and they went over to their horse trailer that had been parked there on the gravel turnoff.

Being a friend to all men on earth, even Northern California ones, I say hello. The lady asked if I were a thru-hiker that started in Mexico. I said yes I was. She then asked me if I needed a ride to Etna. I said I thought I would but what worried me was getting a ride back up here. "I'm going riding tomorrow. I can give you a ride around 9:30 or 10am." "Cool, that would be great, thanks."

A few minutes later I'm coasting down from the summit, some 12 miles to Etna. The guy drove very slowly which was good because of all the weight he was pulling with those two giant horses. They were really nice people. I told them my story. Living in Etna, I knew they had heard all of this before.

It was educational listening to old Doug talk about the death of Etna. It was basically a lumber town and when they started closing down the forest to logging, the town fell apart. "In the old days when I was a kid living here, you really had only two choices when you grew up: joining the military or logging, one or the other. Now most young people leave for the city. The new people who move in are older retired people. The place is just not the same and it probably will never be the same."

That's a drag, man, but I can say the same abut my little town La Habra,

ECSTASY OF MISERY

22 miles south of majestic L.A. In 1957 when I moved there it was a far out little town of 10,000 people. Orange groves, avocado groves, lemons and groovy things like that grew in abundance, and open fields or hills separated towns. The weather was fantastic. The ocean was a short drive on a two-way road and the same for the mountains.

Within ten years it all changed. Mass amounts of people flowed into the city and it tripled in population. It's so crowded that you can hardly recognize it. Cute little La Habra is not so cute.

I went on to tell the old man how it's gotten so costly to live in Orange County, and how my dad's house that cost him $18,000 in 1957, could sell for about $475,000 today. I can't afford to buy a crib there and told Doug he should consider himself lucky that Etna is still quaint and that he lives in beauty and clean air. The guy didn't say too much after that.

They dropped me off just down a ways from the Hiker's Heaven house. I walked into the office of the hostel and talked to a guy who ran the place. He told me there was just enough room for me in the dorm. A young girl showed me to my bunk.

I was surprised that there were so many thru-hikers here. The girl told me that there were at least 10 hikers there. There also was a guy doing a documentary of the PCT. She said that he had been using my bunk until he decided to stay in the suite upstairs. She went on to say after I finished putting my stuff on the bunk that if I wanted, she would wash my clothes for only $3.00. "It's a deal."

The young girl then headed back towards the house. I'm now in a long room with about 10 cots and a double bed. No one else was here right now. I then saw the shower room and took advantage and got a hot shower in.

As soon as I pop out of the steaming bathroom, who appears but Wahoo and Lou. "Hey dudes, how was your 35 mile day?" They told me that they had accomplished their goal, but it had taken a toll on them. In other words, they were wasted.

They had walked from 6am that morning and passed me and continued until 10pm that night. A long hard 15 hours which left them with hot spots on their feet. Probably one reason for the hot spots is that you stretch out your stride an inch or so and that makes your feet hit a little differently which after 15 hours of foot pounding can cause blistering. They had arrived here about 9am this morning compared to my arrival at 1:30. But it looked to me that they were not the best off for it.

Wahoo then started telling me who was here. I was surprised at some of the names. Belcher and Puck, who I thought were behind me, Leprechaun, who I heard had dropped off the trail because of foot problems, Batteries Included, Chance and a guy named Sasquatch, who's filming a documentary.

Wahoo said, "A few people left for Seiad Valley this morning in Sasquatch's van." "That's stupid to skip the Marbles," I said. Wahoo went on to say they wanted to do the pancake challenge in Seiad Valley. "The guy who cooks the pancakes is going on vacation for a week and the restaurant won't be open when they hike through there." "Well the best of luck to them. I've been through Seiad Valley three times now and that guy hasn't been there yet, and it looks like he won't be there again." "He's afraid of you, Wrong Way. He fears you." "That must be it, Wahoo, the guy must know when I'm coming!"

Now with my ego resolved with the help of new buddy, Wahoo, I decided to walk to town and pig out. Breakfast is the only meal that is served. Everyone says it's excellent. For 15 bucks a night one gets a bunk, a shower, and a super breakfast. Not bad at all.

The town of Etna was small, consisting mainly of a dozen streets or less. You had that back into the old west feeling. The drug store had ice cream shakes. It said on the door, "PCT Hikers Welcome". The black cherry chocolate shake was dynamite. I had a beef sandwich to go with it.

Beef is a good thing on the trail. It provides plenty of protein and vitamins. But it also provides creatine for the muscles. Creatine is in the muscle cells. It helps retain water in the muscle cells so the muscle can flush itself out better.

It was a blast walking around this place. I grabbed some cheese and Ben and Jerry's ice cream out of a pretty good little store. Then I headed back through the interesting little town and arrived back at the hostel.

A substantial amount of people were now at the place. There was Batteries Included, who was holding his stomach with one hand and in the other carrying a white box of Seiad Valleys famous two-pound pancake gut bombs! Also, there was Leprechaun and that guy named Chance that I had met very briefly at Belden Town just as I was leaving. There was also a tall guy, probably in his thirties. He had driven a van to the back so I figured he had to be Sasquatch.

I said hi to everybody as I walked to my bunk. "Hey, Wrong Way. I heard you got waterlogged or something," said Puck. I said, "Yeah man, back of Hat Creek Ridge. It started to rain at 1:00 in the morning and I didn't have a tent or tarp." Puck thought that was psycho and wanted to know what I was thinking. "I was thinking it wasn't going to rain, man, and in one more day I would have had my new tarp." "Well, it's going to rain some time." I thought it was just negative luck, but now I'm totally positive once again.

Puck said, "Wrong Way, I don't know how you made it from Mexico to here." "Skateboard, dude, how did you get here?" That quieted the young Puck boy down a bit. "Listen, man, if I weren't here I'd be home in LA removing tree stumps in hot smoggy backyards. A little rainstorm like that was quite refreshing." "Weird," said Puck, as he left the room to get his laundry.

Leprechaun turned on the TV and popped a cold one. I just kicked back on my bunk drinking a cold one and eating chips that Sasquatch had left for everybody to help themselves.

After watching a real corny action movie I took a walk outside and then joined the little party that was going on at the outside patio. Sasquatch spotted me and asked if I were Wrong Way, the guy that might have seen a space ship or something. I said, "Yes that's me" and he went on to say that he was doing a documentary on the Pacific Crest Trail and wanted to hear my story. I said that I'd tell him my story. He told me to wait and then ran upstairs to the private room he was renting and came back down with a giant camcorder that records your rap and all the rest.

So I tell the guy the story and I told it good too. I've had plenty of practice the last couple of weeks. I ended the talk perfectly with an explanation of what really happened or at least what probably happened because if it didn't happen between ELF and the loggers, then it was a visit from space, a real shocker! Maybe I could even tell Connie Chung. Oh no, she's retired now. How about Geraldo!

Back to reality. This guy, Sasquatch, loved my story. After talking to him I went back over to the outdoor deck and sat down and listened to the hiker's adventures. A little bit of politics crept in along with the war in Iraq.

The heaviest story was that of the Sasquatch man. This guy was an entertainer. He supposedly had a daytime local TV show for a while. The guy was supposed to have the only real pictures of Big Foot. He told the story of it and it was pretty amazing.

Some of the hikers spoke about their disbelief in Big Foot, why there aren't any pictures of him, and why there are no bones found when one of these things die. Wouldn't a truck or a car have hit one of these things in the last 50 years? As we talked, the cool guy who owns the place passed around shots of Johnny Walker.

That night I hit the hay, or I should say the bunk, a little late, but better late than never I guess. Breakfast was served at 8 – 9am, and man, was it great: plenty of everything too. The Hiker's Heaven had two shuttles going back to the summit. One left at 9:30am and the other at 1pm. I took the early one, might as well try and get a decent mileage today. I was really getting anxious to get to Oregon. Today is August 13th. Damn, half of August has almost gone by and I'm still in California.

At 9:30 an older lady that works at the place gave me, Chance, and Salvador, a hiker that was heading south, a ride to Etna Summit. It was pretty scary. The lady drove like a nut, butting in the other lane on turns. I got the feeling that she was just trying to get our attention or something.

She reminded me of a lady that had always been on the conservative side or something and now her husband has left her and she's gone freaky, trying to kick out the jams. Chance finally told her to slow down, which she did. I was really glad too. The lady was a goofball, man.

At the summit we all took courtesy pictures of each other. I had Chance take a picture of me with the Marble Mountain sign behind me. The crazy lady wanted a picture with the sign, too, but she was too heavy and unstable to walk the 60 feet of trail to the sign.

ECSTASY OF MISERY

Right after the picture-taking I jammed down the trail leaving the others to clown around. It felt great to be back on the PCT once again. My pack was full of good grunts, maybe a little on the heavy side, but not much. I had plenty of cheeses, candy bars, pastries and Oreo cookies that are great on the trail.

Down the mighty PCT I went, thinking about all the characters in Etna. I hope Batteries Included is feeling better from his gallant try at the pancake place. I guess he just missed eating the most when his head fell on the dish of pancakes. That Sasquatch guy was pretty weird. He doesn't walk much of the trail but drives to different places where PCT hikers meet and gets his stories that way. Time can go by fast sometimes on the trail when you think about characters like the ones I've been meeting lately.

The Marble Mountains are probably considered one of the prettiest mountain ranges in Northern California. They sometimes remind me of the baby Sierras, a lot of glaciated canyons with lakes and creeks.

I was kind of interested in where the new portion of the PCT went through. I've heard it's faster than the old days when the trail wound its way through a lower part of the Marbles, which had more streams and lakes. I remember small waterfalls and pools with green moss, flowers and ferns growing together like an artful gardener manicured them.

Now it looks to me like the new PCT, as it often does, skirts the ridges and stays away from these popular parks, giving the wilderness experience once again to everyone who hikes it.

After a few more miles of scenic ridge walking, I run into a group of horsemen coming around the bend and I try and get off the trail quickly. I usually like to stand above the trail. I feel safer here because one of these huge animals can't fall on you. Sometimes the people on horses want you to stand below the trail so you look smaller and that way it won't spook the stock. The first rider didn't mind me standing where I was standing. That was cool because usually the first guy is the head guy.

I say howdy to the guy and he asked me if I'm a thru-hiker going all the way. I told him yes. He then tells me that they have one of the officials of the PCT right behind them, and that his name is Joe Sabonaskie. "Oh yeah, he's head of the southern section of the PCT." "Yes, we're here having a big meeting tonight at Cub Springs, just down the trail from here." I told the guy that was probably where I heard the sound of the Job Corps workers.

Soon the rest of the pack train passes me by, including Joe Sabonaskie. He starts to come by me on his horse to say hi. He asked me if I'm a thru-hiker and I told him yes and that he may have heard of me from Eric Carpenter of the Orange County Register. "Yeah, I know Eric, hey are you the guy from La Habra that he's doing the story on?" I said, "Yes I am." "Well, congratulations, you're doing great."

I told Joe that I was at least two weeks behind and that I was thinking about flip flopping at Ashland and head to Manning Park by bus and then walk south back to Ashland. He said that he wouldn't do that, and how I might run into the late summer fires they often have in Oregon. He thought that I should go right through and how I will be surprised at the mileage I can make in Oregon, that I'd probably have a lot of 30 mile days and hardly realize it. "Just keep walking, Wrong Way," he said with a smile. He then asked if I wanted to have dinner with them tonight at Cub Springs, that they had a ton of food, steaks and everything. I thought about it for a split second and told him no, I would have to backtrack a couple of miles and besides I had plenty of good food in Etna. "Well, we'll see you later," said Joe, as his pack train headed back down the trail.

Wow, I couldn't believe it. What a small world. There went Joe Sabonaskie, way up here in the Marble Mountains and he tells me like Madame Butterfly told me, to just keep on trucking.

A slight climb out of Etna Summit and I'm now strolling along a great trail that has just been worked on. The Job Corps have been here, all right. I wondered if that young lady caught up with her friends. She said they were about eight miles north of Etna Summit.

A few hours later I arrive at Mule Springs where I stop and get water and eat lunch. I soon hear a noise and there's Chance. He has caught up with me. Having plenty of water, Chance says hello and continues on. A few minutes later, just about the time I was going to leave, a young redheaded kid comes by. He seems to be limping and not in a very good mood. He had a uniform type scene on so I figured he is part of the Job Corps. The young kid passes me by acknowledging my existence to some extent.

After he passes, I start heading on down the trail, with views of Painters Gulch below me. I follow the poor kid until I hear the sound of other voices off in the Douglas firs, about 300 yards off the trail. I think about going over there and checking out the scene, but I've done enough socializing lately; it's time I make tracks. God, I'll be happy to get to Oregon.

Down the trail I headed again. Chance was out in front of me and there were probably eight people in back of me, because by now that second shuttle has dropped them off. The sun is starting to wind its way down now and late afternoon is here again. My legs feel rested from the Etna break and so I'm planning to walk late tonight.

Before long I arrived at Shelly Meadows. I remember Shelly Meadows from 1978. The old trail and the new trail must be the same, at least at this junction of the trail. A little ways up the trail I ran into Chance who was talking to another hiker who had on a small day pack.

I approached and nodded a hello. Chance was asking the guy all kinds of questions about the trail and the trail guidebook. I listened in and started catching the drift that this was Mike Stone, head of the Pacific Crest Trail representatives from the National Forest Service. I remember talking to the guy on the horse about the main guy of the whole trail who was going to be at the conference at Cub Springs,

It was pretty interesting to hear this guy answer questions about the trail guide. I came up with a positive statement about how I felt Section O was really an improvement over the last few times I tried to hike through here. I said there was one rough spot, which was right around Peavine Creek. Otherwise the trail wasn't bad at all.

Mike was happy to hear about that and he told us that they have a horse club out of Redding, California, that came up every year to work on Section O and next year the Peavine Creek area will be the target of this trail maintenance club. We're really lucky to have them.

It was starting to get late, time to think about dinner and a camping spot. So Chance and I said good-bye to Mike Stone and we headed up the trail. It was hard keeping up with Chance. His pace was just a little bit faster than mine. So at the first water source I told him I was going to eat here and then camp a little further up the trail. Chance headed out with his hiking poles, clamoring away at the rocks on the trail.

I found a comfortable rock to cook from. I took out all my stuff and lit the stove. I was hungry and beef stroganoff sounded really good to me. Right after I lit my stove and heated the water I heard a rumbling sound. I looked up and saw a cowboy on a horse towing mules behind him. He was coming down the trail towards me.

What a drag with only an hour of daylight left, I didn't think another pack train would be coming through. So off goes my stove and I drag my stuff out of the way. As for me, there's only one way I can go and that's just below the trail.

"Sorry," says the cowboy who is pulling at least eight to ten mules with no riders. They were huge and muscular as they pounded across where I had just stood. The dude said that he hated to mess up my dinner plans. Then for a second one animal cuts the inside corner of the trail and trips a little. Man, I practically had that stumble predicted. I jump backwards as the animal stumbled. "Sorry," again says the cowboy as he finally disappeared over the hill.

What a scene. Dust was all over the place. A giant road apple lay at the foot of the rock that I was so peacefully resting and cooking from a few minutes before. I went back to making my dinner but stayed away from the rock. I'm sure glad that the whole trail isn't like this. Stock hasn't bothered me as much as I thought it would on this trail so far, basically because there haven't been that many horses or mules.

That evening I walked another couple of hours. I camped in a rather pleasant area just a little past Man Eater Lake. I was wondering if this lake got its name because it looked like an ant trap. You know when ants get caught in them they just keep sliding downward toward the bottom of the hole.

This lake reminds me of that, but only for men that get caught into the lose granite around the steep lake. A careless hiker, like an ant, slides down towards the water, but then tries to hike out. But everything slides out below him. Slowly he slides into the deadly dark blue water and then is swallowed by a tumultuous monster! I doubt that's how the lake got its name. Some ancient dude probably got half eaten by a mountain lion or a bear. You know, something normal like that.

That night I put up my tarp with the 10 foot long part as my two sides. I wanted to try this because in the morning it would be cool to sit up and put my shoes on without the back of my head pressing against the bottom of my tarp. No question that I can sit up in it now. I think I will set it up this way if the weather looks good, but if it looks anything like a storm, I'll set it up the low and long way.

The next morning I got up with the sun, well at least for the most part. I was pretty much on a hill that the rising eastern morning sun cast its rays up on my high flying tarp. By 6:15 I was rolling, hoping to get as close to Seiad Valley as possible.

The PCT was looking like a high-flying airplane as it circled past lakes and canyons below its crest. Campbell Lake, famous Cliff Lake and Summit Lake were just a view of precious jewelry, shining and blue in a golden morning sun. Down the way a little bit I have a late breakfast at Soft Water Springs. After eating I barrel on towards the Marble Valley Guard Station. I don't recognize any of this trail and there was no guard station in 1978.

A few hours later I reached the guard station, but I didn't go in because there was a party of youngsters that occupied the place. They waved and I waved back. I still headed slightly downhill and then I jammed back uphill for a while, until I cleared a small ridge. I then headed down gradually to Paradise Lake, with King Castle nestled in a huge cliff that rose above the lake.

I remember meeting a guy named Rick Grey when I hiked through here way back in 1978. I still can't believe that was 25 years ago. Paradise Lake looks like a popular lake because of the couple of additional trails, the Kelsie Creek Trail, and RYU Patch Trail. I take a couple of pictures here, including King Castle, which is a rock formation embedded in a cliff just above Paradise Lake.

Now I'm heading across Big Ridge. My elevation is a steady 7000 feet. Buckhorn Springs is my next stop, but the springs are a disappointment, very little water running freely. You could get drinkable water here, but it would be a hassle. I move on and discover another couple of springs and I tank up at the second spring.

It was somewhere around here that I had met Brian Jacobsen, who in 1978 hiked all the way from Mexico to here. It took him five months because of all the snow and lousy and poorly marked trails. I keep looking around for what might be the actual place I talked to him but I'm not sure.

Anyway, one thing for sure: I'm really getting close to Seiad Valley. A couple of more miles I pass a couple of dirt roads that I don't remember from back in 1978 but I march on. The trail is marked very well. Soon I disappear into a forest of Douglas fir. Down the trail I go, along Cliff Valley Creek until it joins Grider Creek at a footbridge.

Walking across the bridge I discovered on the other side the skeleton of the man from San Francisco via Hong Kong University via Germany. "Hey man, Carston, isn't it?" He said yes. I told him that I had met him just past Castle Crags, that I was Wrong Way. He said he remembered. "You didn't go down to Etna?" I asked. "I didn't need to." "That place was pretty nice, only 15 a night and a huge breakfast in the morning." I told him about it but he said he probably wouldn't have cared for the breakfast, being a vegetarian. "Oh man, that's too bad, I'm sorry I didn't know."

Carston kind of looked at me rather curiously after that response. He was making some food up for himself. It looked like some ground up green stuff soaked in olive oil. I took one look at that stuff and decided to jam. "See you on down the line." The trail now was basically downhill and it was getting dark. So I tried to keep a lookout for any flat place to camp. The trail that I'm on now takes a 4,000 foot, 13 ½ mile drop to the Klamath River Valley below.

I headed downhill walking along and above Grider Creek. Pounding down the spooky dark trail, I couldn't find one decent place to crash. One side of the trail was an embankment, the other side was a cliff with the water pounding down below. The trail itself was dusty, lumpy, and sometimes rocky. So I sort of had no choice but to forge on. I decided to march on down to Grider Creek Campground. For sure there would be a flat place to sleep. They would probably have picnic tables and water faucets. That sounded like paradise right now. I wonder where Carston was, definitely in back of me, but where did he camp?

Soon I crossed the second footbridge and then an hour later I crossed over the water again on the third and last bridge. I could tell by the position of the last bridge that I was probably four miles at least from the campgrounds.

It was kind of a drag walking down Grider Creek at dark and not really enjoying it. There was the sound of falling water, but not the sight of it, which was a negative. But sometimes long distance thru-hiking had its unpleasant moments. A hiker can't always plan for beautiful clear sunny sights.

Finally around 10pm I saw some lights on the opposite side of the creek. The trail crossed another bridge and I then was at the campground. A guy carrying a lantern strolled up to me and said, "Riding those horses late tonight?" I told him that I couldn't find a place to bed down in the last 10 miles so I decided to bring it all the way to the campground. "Well, there was another fellow that went by a couple of hours ago." "Oh yeah, that would probably be Chance," I said. "He's probably at a campsite down river a bit, being Thursday there are still campsites available."

I said good-bye to the guy and headed down that campground road and found a pretty cool place near the water faucet. I took a giant drink and washed my face. I already had my meal so I just put out my stuff and crashed on top of a sturdy picnic table.

I fell asleep in no time. What a day I had. I probably covered close to 30 miles. Tomorrow would be town day, if you count Seiad Valley as a town. It had the basics: a store, a restaurant, and a post office. It also had one other element that makes it belong to the civilized world and that of course is ice cream!

The next morning came quickly. I really didn't want to get up early. I had only six or seven miles to go before I reached the town center. An intruder in camp rudely awakened me. It was Chance. I couldn't believe it. The guy was sleeping just a few feet away from me and I hadn't even noticed. He thought that was cool because he had purchased his tent because of its inconspicuous color. "Yeah man, I didn't even see you." We laughed and within 20 minutes Chance was gone. I could tell he wasn't worried about breakfast. He was planning on Seiad Valley for his breakfast setting.

Just as I turned the corner to reach the main road out of camp I saw an old guy in front of me clapping his hands together and telling someone to get out of here. I walked up to the old boy and smiled a bit at him. He told me that he was scaring off a bear that was just down the road a piece.

I looked but didn't see any bear. I'm sure that there was one because he was pretty animated and at car campsites like these, are always prone to attract bears. I asked the guy where he was heading and he tells me Seiad Valley, where he was hoping to catch a bus to Eureka and back home to Tacoma, Washington. It seems like Jim here has hiked from Castle Crags to here in seven days. He also had stayed a night at Etna's Hiker's Heaven.

We decided to walk along together to help kill some time. The guy was pretty cool. He was going to section hike the PCT. This year he took one week off. Next year he was going to take two weeks and hike from Seiad Valley to possibly Crater Lake.

I told him about my exploits from back in the 60s until now. We both had good stories to laugh at and one story we had to chuckle about was at Etna's Hiker's Heaven and Sasquatch's story about a bear that circled his campsite all night, freaking the guy out so that he had to head back to Etna's hostel the next day.

I think the guy might have thought that the bear might have been the notorious Big Foot. He definitely was freaked about Big Foot, maybe even a little obsessed about it. The dude was pretty funny, especially after he had a couple of those Johnny Walker stingers.

The conversation went back and forth for a while. Before we knew it we were crossing the bridge that straddled the Klamath. Walking across the bridge we paused and took a few flicks. The Klamath looked great. It looked pretty full and wide. I know that there's been plenty of gold taken out of this baby. Next we walked by the Seiad Valley sign where we both stopped to take pictures. Then a mile further we reached the Seiad Valley store, restaurant, and post office.

The first place I went to was the store where I grabbed some chocolate milk and a couple of jelly doughnuts. Jim went into the post office to find out what time the bus to Eureka arrived. The news wasn't good because the next bus from Happy Camp to Eureka wouldn't arrive until 4pm tomorrow.

It looked like Jim was going to have to hitchhike. He bought some bottled water and stood across the road. I went with him and said good-bye and wished him luck. I then went over to the mid-river RV park where I should receive my supply box. The place didn't upset me; my supply box was safe and sound.

The morning had turned to mid-day now and it was getting hot. I decided right away to spend the rest of the day here. I could use a half day rest from my 30 mile romp the day before. Besides that, the place had pay showers. It only cost $6 a night to stay here. I had to pitch my tarp up behind the shower house. It wasn't too bad.

After setting up my tarp, I walked back to the store and bought some shampoo and an ice cream sundae bar. When I came out of the store I was amazed that Jim was still trying to get a ride. So I went back inside the store and bought a Haagen Dazs ice cream and some Gatorade and took it out to him. He was thankful and tried to give me some money, which I refused. I told him to hang in there and make sure the oncoming cars saw his backpack near his feet. People will pick up backpackers, but old bums like us they drive right by.

I said good luck to Jim for a second time and I walked back to the RV park and to the pay showers. For about $3 I had an excellent shower. When I got out of the shower I looked across the street and Jim was gone. The ole boy had gotten his ride to Eureka. That's great because he was so desperate to catch that 9am Greyhound bus out of Eureka so he would be in Tacoma by 6pm Sunday evening.

The next step for me was the laundry room. I washed damn near all of my clothes except for what I was wearing. Those clothes would be washed a little later by hand.

Right about the time my last garments were washed and thrown in the dryer I noticed a lonely, tall, skinny figure walking into town. Yep, there wasn't any mistake, it was Carston the vegetarian, looking tired and beat but still making pretty good progress. "Hey dude, over here, it's me, Wrong Way, once again."

I told Carston that I was taking a half day off and that it was too damn hot to hike now. Carston looked up towards the sun and said, "Yes it is." "The restaurant isn't open so there's no pancake eating contest going on, but the store has quite a lot of stuff." I went on to tell him that there were pay showers at the RV park and it only cost $6 for the night. "Alright," says Carston as his skinny skeleton type body disappears into the store. I go back to my campsite and kick back, waiting for my clothes to dry. The temperature in this valley is nearly 100 degrees.

Carston emerges from the store and the post office with his supply box. From the store he buys carrots in a little plastic bag and some fruit. Man, I think to myself, this cat probably never gets plugged up, that's for sure. But where he gets his carbs for his engine I just don't know.

The dude comes out eating rabbit food. I sit down with him at my campsite in back of the coin showers and laundry room. He shows me what he eats and how he prepares it. No need for a stove but instead he has a hand grinder in which he grinds up his grains. He uses a lot of olive oil on everything, which adds calories. He eats bread, but it has to be brown bread with no sugar or honey in it. I asked him what in the hell is wrong with sugar; it grows from sugar cane. "It's not good for the system." Then what's wrong with honey, it's totally natural, man. "It's stolen from the bees." Unbelievable, this guy can hardly eat anything.

As I sit there eating those little carrots of his, which by the way were quite good and it's something I should eat more of, but I'm thinking, my god, how drab can a diet get? Having no dairy foods is the most amazing thing. That means no ice cream, no yoghurt, no cheese, no milk, eggs, or butter. I'm astonished that anybody can live like this, especially someone who is burning off thousands of calories per day hiking up and down hills with a pack on his back.

His backpack, by the way, was heavy, not ultra-light at all. For a sleeping bag he couldn't use down, but had to use fiberfill. The poor guy couldn't wear leather and his sandals were made of plastic.

I told Carston that I felt sorry for him and I admire vegetarians that won't eat meat, but the no-dairy thing was way too bizarre for me! "Don't you splurge once in a while and have something good?" I asked. "No, not at all. My favorite food that I have once a day in San Francisco and when I was in Hong Kong is a coconut." "Oh well then, that sounds exciting man."

I'm thinking to myself here's a German dude, raised in Germany, educated in Hong Kong, and now lives at San Francisco University, man, you have to come to the conclusion that somehow this guy has to be half a bubble off.

Then Carston tells me that he does eat chocolate. "All right, dude, you are human after all. Let me guess, since you live in San Francisco, you probably go for Ghirardelli's, being that they are located there." "No, I like Hershey's." "Cool," I said. "Do you like it with almonds or just plain?" "Neither, try this, it's Baker's chocolate." "What the hell is that man, a new flavor to hit the scene?.

Carston explains to me that Baker's chocolate is used for cooking. He then asked if I wanted some. I said that I'm always ready for a chocolate rush. So he cuts a small piece from his large chunk and gives it to me. It smelled great so I popped it in my mouth and started to munch it.

Oh, it was awful, bitter as hell. I spit it out right away. "That's absolutely terrible, man." Carston is now laughing, thinking he's funny. "Carston, you're one of the weirdest f.....ers I have met on this trail or even in the world, man. But to each his own. I mean, whatever blows your dress up."

As for myself, I'm going to the store right now and get something natural like Gatorade Frost to wash the horrid bitterness out of my mouth because it's the only mouth I have and if too much of this hits my only stomach, my whole personality might turn bitter. I took off and jammed to the store while Carston laughed his ass off. "Hey Wrong Way, if it changes your personality, maybe it will be for the better!" "Yeah, that's funny man. I'll be sure to write that down in my memoirs, dude."

By the time I came out of the store, Carston was ready to leave. He was going to try and get in four to five miles before it got dark. I told him good luck, but once he reached the trailhead about a mile or so down the road, there was nothing left but a 5000 foot climb and really not much of a place to crash. I said he might as well stay here and head out in the cool of the morning.

I was about to say that the store opens at 7am and he could get some hot coffee. I stopped myself from mentioning it because I know the guy would just say that he didn't drink coffee. He's just not the type: green tea maybe, but coffee would be too heavy for the guy, he might flip out.

After Carston left I started to walk back to my campsite when I saw some ragged figures walking down the highway heading for the store. When they got closer I could tell that it was Wahoo and Lou and in back of them it looked like Batteries Included, Puck, and Belcher. I gave them a wave and watched them walk up. "Wrong Way, how did you get here before us?" I reminded them I had left before they did on the 9:30 shuttle.

Wahoo said, "So this is Seiad Valley." He didn't think that it was much of a place. I told them that there is a lot of history here. I showed everybody the store and post office and told them I was staying here for $6 a night. No one looked interested. Everyone was incredibly anxious to reach Oregon. I told them Oregon is still a couple of days away and like I told Carston, there's really no other place to camp, and after they reach the trailhead they would have a four or five thousand foot climb and about five miles to do it in.

That didn't matter to them. They all wanted to go on and none of them looked like they were in a good mood. "What the hell do you want to stay here for, Wrong Way? There's nothing here, the restaurant is closed and so is the post office." I said that it has been okay for me, how I had taken a hot shower and did all my laundry, and also have a soft place to camp.

None of them looked interested and headed down Highway 96 towards the trailhead. Oh well, happy camping on a poison oak slope. I went back to my tarp with some chips, beer, and cheese dip, and partied alone. Two hours later at hiker's midnight, 9pm, I was sound asleep, ready to kick some trail mileage butt tomorrow. It's too bad these modern day hikers just don't have respect for the historical hiking past of Seiad Valley.

That night, with the exception of a couple of bouts with small black ants, the cousins of those giant black ants of the forest, I slept like a baby. The next morning I got up about 6am and was hiking down Highway 96. The store was closed and wouldn't open until 7am. No way would I waste a half hour for a java rush, so I march right down the road to the trailhead.

About a mile later I reached the big PCT emblem that denotes the start of PCT out of Seiad Valley, heading north. Now I had a long five mile climb ahead of me. I was pretty psyched up and my legs were rested so I tackled the ascending trail with enthusiasm. The trail begins by switch backing up a pretty steep trail to Fern Springs, where I stopped to swig down some water. My next water source would probably be Kangaroo Springs, six miles further.

It was only about 9am now and already it was 80 degrees. Today was going to be a hot one for sure. I knew as I gained elevation the temperature would drop a little. Most of this section, which is the last section of California Section R, is forested and gives shade to hikers. Other parts are barren due to heavy logging.

In the old days, before 1976, the PCT hikers usually followed Interstate 5 from Castle Crags straight north passing close to Mt Shasta and catching the Oregon Skyline Trail near Mt Ashland. Actually, I believe Pilot Rock was the start. The Oregon Skyline Trail and the Washington Cascade Trail were developed many years before the Pacific Crest Trail. These mountains, the southern Cascades, were high enough to promote excellent views of Shasta and Shastina. They also had water most of the time, year round. So it was a good move to send the trail through this way, although this way did lengthen it.

Right before I got to Kangaroo Springs I met two hikers heading south to Mexico. One guy was an older guy, and I never got his name. The younger called himself "Smiles a Lot". It was a good name because the kid seemed to smile quite a bit as I talked to him. He asked me if I had met many southbound hikers and I told him only one at Etna. He told me there were supposed to be about 10 people going south but most of them quit in Washington after some late season snowstorms.

I told Smiles a Lot that north to south wasn't too bad of a way to go, but you definitely want to get through the Sierras by October because snow starts building up in November. September has flash storms but the snow usually melts, even at high altitudes. The kid was kind of in a hurry because the older guy had marched on, so I said good luck, dude, and off we went in our respective directions.

At Kangaroo Springs I had lunch and filled my water tanks. A couple of local bow hunters came by and asked me how far it was to Highway 96. I told them about six or seven miles. They seemed pleased. I asked if bow season is open now and the guy told me yes, that yesterday was the first day. That's something to worry about, flying arrows, but I do have some respect for bow hunters. At least they're not shooting deer with high-powered rifles and scopes. The sound of a bow is nothing compared to the cracking echoing noise of a gun.

The trail climb is pretty much ended now. Actually at Upper Devils Peak most of the elevation has been gained and now the trail has its regular ups and downs.

It was kind of cool to see a trail that I'm familiar with. In fact, some of this trail, by the time I finish it, I will have traveled it three times. Maybe that will make up for the extremely small parts of the trail that I have missed completely.

A few miles down the trail I caught up to Puck and Belcher. They told me that Wahoo and Lou were just ahead and that Carston and Batteries Included were somewhere up in front. Puck told me he had lost his energy level. Belcher said, "It's nothing to do with energy level, he just gets lazy." This pissed Puck off and he began arguing with Belcher, which from what I understand is nothing new. Avoiding a lovers quarrel, I bolted on heading east again towards Cook and Green Pass.

It was now only 2pm and I was already at Cook and Green Pass. I was amazed that I had reached this place so fast. It's definitely a testament to being in excellent shape and having a light pack. In 1998 it took me all day to get here and it ended up being my camping site for the night!

Shortly after Cook and Green Pass I reached Copper Butte area. I was now cruising at an elevation of nearly 6000 feet. The temperature was a mellow 80 degrees and I know that I'm lucky to be this high because down below at the Klamath it was probably close to 100 degrees.

At Copper Butte I caught Carston sitting in the shade of a lonely pine tree. He looked tired and told me he didn't get much sleep last night. He was going to take a short nap before going on.

I really think that his problem is nutrition. I just don't think he gets enough carbs even though he eats those unsalted peanuts. On the other side of the coin, the guy wouldn't have gotten this far if he didn't know what he was doing. Twenty years of strict vegetarianism is a long time. The guy has also walked portions of the ATP and the Himalayas, as well as the Alps. So I guess I shouldn't worry about him. He's 38 years old. Carston is a big boy, as well as a skinny boy.

At about 3pm I reached Bear Dog Springs where I took a 20 minute break and powered down some power bars. The damn things are good for you,

ECSTASY OF MISERY

I guess. They stick to your ribs, but man they can get real old.

With Carston right in back of me, we both headed on an open ridge, hiking around White Mountain with a fantastic cool breeze blowing from the west. I love this section of the PCT. I really don't know why except that it might be because they were the first mountains I ever walked, when I first started thru-hiking back in 1978. The High Sierras are of course the first mountains I ever backpacked, which are more spectacular, but this little range of mountains are very pleasant indeed.

It was now getting late in the day and it was time to start looking for a place to eat dinner and camp for the night. The problem now was that the next water wasn't for another eight miles or so at Buckhorn Springs. I didn't know if I wanted to go that far, but unless I got off the trail, that was the next water source.

So I marched on with Carston and his plastic sandals and reached Buckhorn Springs about 7:00 that evening. Carston was cool enough to filter some water for me, as well as Wahoo, who we had caught up with. Super Lou was back at the trail, waiting for the water to cook with.

After getting our H2O, Carston and I headed the quarter of a mile back to the ridge to make camp. It's not a bad idea to camp away from water if you can because this is the only water hole in the area and a lot of creatures visit it at night, especially male deer that like to make weird noises probably just to scare you.

Burney Falls

Dave and Brooke at Burney Falls

Seiad Valley on the Klamath River

Ah man, closed again!

Journey Thirteen:
Oregon at Last, So Pee and Be Free!

Back on the PCT again, I hiked about a mile which overlooked a bow hunting party below in a dirt road turn off. Here I made my crash site. Carston stumbled ahead a few hundred yards where he crashed for the night. For me it had been another great and wonderful day on the mighty PCT. I had climbed out of Klamath Valley and hiked a total of 25 miles. Tomorrow would be a great day because I would finally reach the end of the California portion of the PCT and head to Oregon. I should march with my head held high and should keep my feet from wondering too much!

The next morning after a good nights sleep I was hiking before 8am. Carston was nowhere to be found. He must have started early. No problem, I would probably catch the guy before noon. I had hiked about three or four miles when I took my usual late breakfast at Bearground Springs. The springs were really running slowly, but with patience I got all the water I needed.

Long ago, at Mather Pass in the High Sierras, I had lost my wide mouth polyester bottle which was great for gathering water and making my morning shake. I had kept this bottle for about 30 years. It was orange from all the iodine I had added to sterilize the water. It was like an old friend.

I did find out that a quart bottle of Gatorade worked just as well. It could be crushed up when empty and it stayed crushed up if you put the cap on before it gathered air and expanded again. This would also cut down on space.

From Bearground Springs I hiked down the trail, walking on a pleasant ridge. I arrive at infamous Wards Fork. I call it infamous because this is where I got lost back in 1978. The trail was terrible then. I just lost confidence in it. I remember that I felt like going home at that point because that was the second time I lost the trail since I had started in Ashland, Oregon, only 40 miles away!

Wards Fork had some five dirt roads that converged on the spot. It looked the same as it did in 1978. The trail wasn't much better. Weeds seemed to be the problem here in this open area. Now I know where the trail went and I found it quite quickly. Just like 1978, there still wasn't any trail emblem or white diamond. One reason for this was because people steal them. There's an array of dirt roads that people can take to get to this spot so I'm pretty sure that this is the reason, but it's just my theory.

Now after leaving the conglomeration of dirt roads I was starting to get excited because Donomore Meadows was just a short mile away. Just a short distance further was the Oregon border. Before I knew it I was at Donomore Creek and there was Carston. He was trying to filter water out of the creek. I stopped and talked to him for a bit. I said, "Come on, man, let's hit Oregon together." But Carston said he was going to take a nap. I guess he didn't have a good night of sleep.

So I headed on walking across the side of the huge meadow. I realized that the trail did not go through the middle of the meadow as it used to but now was located on the side of it. This was probably done to keep the meadow from being damaged by foot and horse traffic.

I remember in 1978 on my Oregon state walk I saw a beautiful cinnamon bear here. He cut across the trail, not seeing me. When I looked for him he was beside a creek bed. Then I couldn't see him anymore, but I heard him tossing large rocks out of the creek. He was probably digging for grub worms or something along that line.

A half mile further the trail left the meadow and began climbing a bit. It then turned and leveled off a trifle and by god there it was, the Border Tree, USA. The tree has two signs on it. One side of the tree reads "California" and the other side of the tree reads "Oregon". Holy wandering soul, I made it to Oregon. California has finally been conquered, all 1720 miles of it. Yeah, time to celebrate and write in the register. Finally, finally, I was out of California!

I took my camera out and lo and behold, I didn't have any pictures left. Oh well, that's the breaks. Just then I heard some people talking. It was Puck and Belcher coming up the trail. "Hello dudes. This is it! You're at the Border Tree."

Puck and Belcher were really happy, of course. Then they did their ritual thing they have done ever since they walked the Appalachian Trail. Every time they get to a new state they take a leak. I couldn't believe it. They both imme-diately did a "number one" right on the trail. I turned my head, a little embar-rassed, especially when Belcher squatted down. Kind of gross, but to each his own, I guess.

I began looking at the register. Most of the usual people had recorded their little stories. There was White Stag and his make believe dog. Shizz, Long Haul, and Choo Choo, T-Bone, Free Radical, and Batteries Included had been by this morning. Batteries Included was the last one to sign in.   Billy Goat was now just 10 days in front of me. There was Prune Picker, Apple Pie, The One, Dave and Brooke: they were three days ahead of me.

Also signed in the register was Huff and Puff with his usual cartoon. Northerner was here. Rob and Bandana, Mercury and Just Paul, Luna, Special Agent, Tea Tree and Chance were only one day in front of me.

The first two people for this years trek were the couple from Japan that had started in early April. I didn't see Cruising Carson or Zeb Zebonaskie, who was supposed to have finished the trail in a ridiculous 72 days! And finally up in the right hand corner was Lugnut and a guy named Tripping Ant. I guess this dude has a problem with ants. He seems to stumble over them. You should learn to pick up your feet a bit and walk like a man, my son.

Reading these registers about the people in front of me always makes me wonder who is in back of me. I don't think there are too many. Maybe five or six, but it's hard to say. I just have a feeling that most people that are in front of me are folks I haven't met in person and probably never will.

You know, I just might write a book about this trip and maybe a few will read it and see their names and maybe they will say, "Thanks, Wrong Way, for mentioning me in the Class of 2003."

I guess I spent about a half hour at the California and Oregon border. Then I headed out once more on my quest for the Canadian border. Into my mind came the thoughts of what kind of a great adventure Oregon would give me. California sure did. Now Oregon would probably do the same. Oregon, however, like Washington, is just over 500 miles. They're less that one third of the length of California.

As I headed out from the border I felt refreshed and with a great sense of accomplishment. The miles flew by as I withdrew inside of myself. I have a great talent for daydreaming. It can help to pass the time, but it also can be a little dangerous. I have walked right by major trail junctions doing this. I would find myself wondering where the PCT had strayed!

Soon I was on the ridge looking down on Kettle Lake and Creek as I rounded the Observation Gap. The trail there almost joins a dirt road. It then passes by Jackson Gap and comes to one of my favorite springs in all of Southern Oregon, Sheep Camp Springs.

Sheep Camp Springs is out in the open. The cover of hemlocks and firs are gone. It's kind of hot. Just below the trail and right above the dirt road is a rushing spring that powers itself through a man-made pipe and falls three or four feet to the ground. The water is cold and sweet!

The first thing I did when I got to the springs was to put my head right into the water. What a rush; the water was really cold. I grabbed my cooking pot and filled it up then walked a good 50 feet from the water. I soaped my head and face with biodegradable soap and then thoroughly rinsed off the soap. Oh yeah! The good ole head shampoo! After that I dumped out my old water and filled up my water bottles with the Sheep Camp Springs water.

Then with one major drink of the fabulous stuff I hit the trail again, feeling totally refreshed. This is one place that I've been lucky enough to have visited all three times that I've walked this trail. I also have regained a total of 15 years of my life. Instead of being 56 years old I'm really only 41. The reason is because Sheep Camp Springs is a fountain of youth. No one knows this but me and I think I'll keep it that way!

Down the trail I now felt like a champ. A few hours later I passed Wrangle Gap and a small paved road that actually leads to Ashland. The trail guide has it numbered Road 20, which later turns into Road 22. After rounding Red Mountain it was time to start looking for a place to crash for the night. After passing Siskiyou Gap I made my crash site at Long John Saddle, which has an assortment of flat areas to sleep on.

What a day! It has been 24 miles and a new state. California was great, but it was nice to finally be out of it. Now, however, I have to make a decision. Am I going to flip flop at Ashland or go on? I was leaning toward going on, but I still think heading to Manning Park and then back to Ashland would definitely have its benefits.

Washington can get nasty as September creeps by. October can be a real mess and may even close out. Yes, last year a hiker could walk until November, but this isn't last year. I'll have to make a decision when I get to Ashland. Trail Perfect may have some information by then about the transportation element of all this, what it costs and how long it will take, etc. I'll just have to wait and find out. But right now I'm going to fall asleep looking at the multitude of stars that decorate this big beautiful Oregon sky.

The following morning I got a real good start. I slept in an area in which the morning sun hit me early as it warmed up the earth around it. It was 6:15 when I started hiking. This was town day, USA! My goal for this day was to be in Ashland, Oregon. This was my next package pick-up. It probably was the largest parcel pick-up on the trail. My backpack was very light. Most of my day hike would be down hill. Up and around Siskiyou Peak I strolled at close to a three mile per hour pace. At Grouse Gap many PCT hikers take refuge at the Grouse Gap Shelter which lies about a quarter of a mile off the road.

I looked down from the trail to see if I could spot anybody. I don't see any thru-hikers but I did see a couple of bow hunters in front of the shelter. I was sort of looking for Batteries Included who I knew was only a few hours ahead of me. Chance, wherever he was I couldn't say. That lad was definitely making tracks. Brooke and Dave were probably the next people in front of me. But I'm sure they were probably already at Hyatt Lake by now.

An hour later I was under Mt Ashland at Mt Ashland Campground where I was able to capture some cold H2O. From now to Interstate 5 and Callahan's Restaurant was basically a downhill climb. The problem is that the trail is not the best. It would be a lot faster if one walks Road 20, but that's not the trail.

It's always best to walk the trail while you can because there will be times when the thru-hiker on the PCT really can't or it would be a struggle to do so. Things can always happen: sickness, injury, fire, storms, no food, and other problems. So in order to do the most miles on the trail, don't take short cuts unless it is really necessary. I don't believe anybody walks 100% of the trail. If you can walk at least 98% you have done a great job!

ECSTASY OF MISERY

Down and down I hauled looking for civilization. Once while hauling downhill I felt a mean sting on the top of my foot. It hurt like hell. I pulled off the trail and took off my shoe and sock. I found nothing but a red mark, probably a bite from a red ant. Those little dudes, unlike the big black forest ants, will sting like hell. Shake it off, baby. It's almost Miller time.

So away I sped until I finally came to a new building that I saw under construction back in 1998. It was a bed and breakfast. Out in front of the place there was a picnic table and a PCT drinking fountain. I say this because there is a sign that says, "Welcome PCT hikers, please rest here. Help yourself to the water, but please no camping."

Fair enough. I thought the owners probably have tons of money wrapped up into the place and they really don't need their paying guests to look out the window and see a bunch of rugged, ragged hikers sleeping on and around the water faucet or picnic tables! Even though we can be wonderful people, guests probably would think we're bums.

I stopped there and had my usual brunch. This time I had a strawberry shake with a chocolate power bar and some trail mix for dessert. I had some of those strange candies that Trail Perfect's dad, Charlie Robison, likes to toss in my supply boxes. My oh my, what a sharp cherry flavor it had.

After 15 minutes or so I was back on the trail weaving my way down when I heard the sound of Interstate 5. The shifting gears of those 18-weelers can be heard for miles before you have a visual. I now had my first sign of the long snake-like highway that runs through the western United States.

An hour later I arrived at the service road that runs beside the highway for a while. Heading due north down the highway I then head under the Interstate and around the little road that leads to Callahan's parking lot. There's the door and oh yeah, they're open. My big fear was that they would be closed for the day since it was Monday. Many times it seems like restaurants are closed on Mondays.

It was now 12:30pm, Monday, August 18th, 2003, and clear the way – it's time to eat. I've never had dinner here at Callahan's but this makes the second time that I have had lunch here. Callahan's has always been hiker friendly, as I've heard. They had a place in the back where hikers have stayed for free. It's probably not easy to put up with hikers all the time. But thru-hiking through here is seasonal. July, and especially August, is when most hikers travel through here.

I ordered lasagna with a Bud. While having lunch I started a conversation with the waitress about the usual stuff. She probably knew that I was a thru-hiker. I'm sure she's talked to hundreds of us.

I asked the waitress what was the best way and time to hitchhike out of here. I was a bit concerned because the on-ramp out in front looked very slow. In fact, I hadn't noticed a single car that went up that on-ramp while I walked down the service road on the way to Callahan's.

I also hear that it was illegal to hitchhike on the Interstate in the state of Oregon. The waitress told me that she would talk to a guy named Steve who works there and gets off at 2pm. He's a student at the University of Southern Oregon and lives in Ashland. A few minutes later she told me that Steve wouldn't mind giving me a ride to Ashland.

I waited in the lobby for a while. During that time I wrote in the PCT register that was on a desk by the receptionist. I read about everybody that had stopped in that year. It really helped to kill time.

Right around 2:00 Steve came out and we went outside and got in his truck and took off to Ashland. He asked me about my trip. I told him a few highlights but didn't go into things too deep because I'm sure I wasn't the first guy that he had given a ride. I didn't want to bore the kid. Besides, he was talkative and it was interesting to hear him talk about college life in Ashland.

As we went through the town Steve told me about the town and pointed out things of interest. He dropped me off near the Columbia Hotel, right in the middle of town. It was very hot, about 95 degrees. Every time I've ever been to Ashland, it's been hot.

I read in the town guide that the Columbia Hotel was one of the most economical places to stay in Ashland. Economical in Ashland is expensive compared to other places because it's a tourist town due to the Shakespeare Festival they have there. I knew there was a youth hostel in town, but I really wanted a room of my own. I felt that it would be easier to seal my tarp. I knew that they had an excellent camping store. There I could buy some seam sealer which I need for my tarp.

I found the hotel pretty easily thanks to the PCT Town Guide that every thru-hiker should have. A long set of stairs got you above the main street pretty quickly and there was the reception desk. The guy who checked me in was a backpacker himself and had just hiked from Castle Crags to Seiad Valley.

The man said to me, "I've got a room for you at the trail hiker's price." "Oh thanks, I sure could use some rest." "Have you been pounding the trail pretty hard?" asked the guy behind the desk. I said yes, and that it was also pretty hot. "Well, the room's $65 per night." Reluctantly I said ok. It was about 20 bucks more that I thought it would be but I was tired and it was hot. So I paid the price and I wasn't thrilled about it.

Then the first negative news was the bathrooms were at the end of the hallway. I thought that for 65 bucks I would at least have my own bathroom! The dude showed me my room and I opened the door and walked in. It was rather small and hot inside.

I look for the air conditioner, but guess what? There wasn't one, only a fan on a windowsill. There was a view of an alley below. I open the window and whip on the fan. It helps a little but not much. There was a sink on one side of the room and it had running water. So I guess I should be thankful for that. On further inspection I found that there was absolutely no television, no radio, and no telephone. This place was a rip off. This is the PCT hiker's special? Sixty-five bucks for this?!

I was bummed a little, but hell, it would be for just one night, so I hastily prepared to go to the community showers, which at least were clean. I felt a good shower would make me feel better and I was right.

After getting back to my room, I just wanted to flop down on the bed and take a snooze, but I couldn't. I had to get to the post office as quickly as possible. It was now 3pm and the post office closes at 4pm. Thanks to the PCT Town Guide, I found the place pretty easily and to my relief, my package was there. After getting my package I head back to the Columbia Hotel. While walking, I check out the town and notice it is definitely a tourist town. There were all kinds of interesting restaurants, candy stores, ice cream places, gift shops, and a few taverns. With the Shakespearian plays going on every night I now can see why the room is so high in price.

I returned to my room and put my package on the bed. I still can't rest, not if I'm going to leave tomorrow. I now have to go to that fancy camping store and see if I can buy some fuel for my stove and some plastic-based seam sealer for my tarp. This trip takes me in another direction down Main Street and left on another street. I can't find the place at first but a young person tells me where it is.

The store is excellent for me. I'm able to buy a canister of butane and they have the kind of seam sealer I need. Thanks to Dave of Dave and Brooke, I get the right kind for my impregnated nylon tarp. I even pick up a flex band for my glasses. My glasses have been bugging me by constantly slipping down to the end of my nose. This elastic sports band should keep them from doing that.

Now it's time to return to my room and apply the sealer. I want to give it as much time to dry as possible. I get back to the musty Columbia Hotel and apply the sealer and it doesn't take long, but what a smell! I better open that window a little and turn that fan up a bit.

It was time to wash clothes and I believe I'll do this right in the sink. In my new supply box I have the usual supply of laundry detergent. Trail Perfect puts it in a plastic zip lock bag. I get a fresh amount in every supply box. It's a hassle buying it sometimes and if you have some and a sink, you can always do your laundry, regardless of a laundromat or grocery store.

While the laundry was drying, hanging from anywhere I could hang something including a makeshift clothesline, I start loading my pack with the new food supplies. The old food I didn't eat, usually Top Ramen, I put aside. If there isn't a hiker's box, I leave if for the maids.

Now by god it's time to party on. I go heading for the local tavern first to get a feel of the local city dwellers. I know bars aren't the best places to go. I don't recommend them to all thru-hikers, but you would be surprised sometimes on what you can learn from the locals. To me it can be quite interesting.

This time at the local tavern called Gabby's, I really didn't learn too much, except that liberals suck and Hollywood movie stars should shut up about Iraq. I guess war must be good, but I don't believe there were any 9-11 terrorists from Iraq, but what do I know. I'm just a kid myself. One beer is enough for me on this empty stomach and now it's time to pig out at the local greasy spoon.

After a giant cheeseburger and a pineapple malt, along with a chef's salad to keep it organic, I head over to Chubby Bill's Ice Cream Parlor where I nearly got sick on a chocolate sundae. That was enough. It's time to retire to the sanctuary of my stale room with no TV.

Down the hall from my room was a pay telephone. I've been planning to call Trail Perfect from this phone. My cell phone is in my drift box that is probably at my next stop, Hyatt Lake. So I head down the hallway towards the phone but it's too late, there's a woman using it. No problem with that, it's still early and I have all evening to talk to Linda. I go back to my room and listen to my miniature transistor radio. It's pretty boring because there is nothing on that draws my attention.

About a half hour later I go back down the hall, but the young lady is still on the phone. Still not a problem. I'll just go back to my room and listen to my little radio that picks up five stations and nothing interesting.

I waited about a half hour before going again to the pay phone. Lo and behold, the same person is still on the phone. This is getting ridiculous! But being a patient gentleman, I go back to my room and listen to some country music coming from the tiny speaker on my dinky radio.

I lie down on my bed and then fall asleep only to be awakened 40 minutes later. Oh my, I better get to that phone. It's now 10:30 in the evening and I don't want to call Trail Perfect too late.

I head back down to the phone and once again, to my utter amazement, the damn girl is still gabbing on the phone. I'm pissed off now. The chick has been on the phone for three hours. It's time to stand up for your rights, so I do what I have to do and stand out in front of the phone booth. It gets her attention. Finally she hangs up and then walks by me and says, "A person can't even sit around and take a short phone call any more." I didn't say anything because I'm a gentleman; besides, she was as big as I was.

I finally get through and Trail Perfect answers the phone. We talk a bit and then she tells me what I have to do to get to Manning Park, which included a $150 bus ticket. I learned that I would have to go to Vancouver first before heading to Manning Park. I probably would lose three days doing that.

The other way was to hitchhike or take the bus to the border, then head down the highway to Manning Park by hitchhiking. You know what I told her. "I'm going straight through. I'm taking the advice of Joe Sabonaskie and the young girl, Madame Butterfly."

I may run into horrible weather, but it was the chance I was going to take. Linda said that she would call my parents and let them know my decision. I told Trail Perfect that she was doing a great job in making up my meals.

After the call I walked back to my room, but couldn't sleep. So I went to Gabby's Bar and had a couple cold ones. I then came back and finally fell asleep in my TV-less air conditioner-less and bathroom-less room.

The next day I slept in and enjoyed a restful morning. I might as well, since I don't have to be out of the room until noon. At 9:30 I headed down the street to a greasy spoon breakfast place, which was great. Coming out of the restaurant I notice two raggedy guys heading towards me. It was Puck and Batteries Included. I talked to them a bit and learned that Belcher was at the youth hostel where they all were staying. Wahoo and Lou were also there; they got in a few hours ago.

Batteries Included was desperately looking for new running shoes, but was appalled at the prices. "This is Ashland; it's expensive here." "I've heard that there's a bus that will take you to Roseburg for only $2 and the prices in that town are much cheaper than in this tourist town." Batteries Included said that he might just do that. The cheapest pair of shoes that he had seen was 80 bucks.

They told me that the Ashland Youth Hostel was quite good. They actually had a large room with bunk beds reserved for PCT hikers. "Thanks for the info. I wish I would have stayed there. It's too late now, I'm heading back to Callahan's in about a half hour." I bid good-bye to my young know-it-all buddies and grabbed my stuff out of my room at the famous Columbia Hotel. Then down the road I headed, back into the great wide open. But first I must walk through the town until I reach the on-ramp of Interstate 5.

Towards the southern end of town, I decided to walk into a convenience market and buy a Gatorade. The temperature is close to 100 degrees. Even though my feet are pretty tough, they're not use to the flat, hot pavement. Blisters on the bottom of the feet are the last thing I want.

Standing outside of the store, a young guy comes by and asks me if I'm walking the PCT. I tell him yes, and that I'm just trying to get a ride back to Callahan's now. "Well, you're in luck, I'm heading to Eureka to see my grandmother. I'll be glad to give you a lift." "Oh man, that would be great." So off I went with Tim, who was also a college student taking environmental studies.

It was interesting listening to this kid and learning about the glaciers that are receding at both the north and south poles. It's due to global warming, which could also cause violent storms and floods as well as a continual rising in the earth's temperature a little each year. It was nice to meet a young person who seemed to care about the world around him. Back in Southern California it seems like a lot of young men just cared about how much horsepower their cars have or how big of wheels they can put on their oversized trucks.

Tim gave me a ride just past Callahan's. He even let me out on the service street. I thanked him and he yelled at me, "Happy Trails, man." I crossed the road and headed out of the area. I know from my 1998 hike that for the next three hours I have a hot ascending trail to deal with. The next well-known landmark would be Pilot Rock, a hot five miles away.

This section in the trail guidebook is probably the least scenic area in the whole state. It's a section with many logging roads. Except for the Pilot Rock area, there was very little scenic beauty. This area was controlled by the Bureau of Land Management.

Many hikers skip this portion of the hike in order to spend more time in more scenic areas of Oregon. There are also areas of the trail that travel near public land and peoples cabins. The way I feel about it is, so what! It's part of the PCT and it's a fast part, one can make good time on it. At least there were trees that shade a hiker on this trail. That's better than some of that Southern California desert stuff. Although I have to admit that the southern deserts are more scenic and beautiful.

I hike at a continual pace up towards Pilot Rock. It's hot and I'm not in a hurry. Finally I reach the rock at about 4pm. If a hiker wants he can climb Pilot

Rock and grab some views, especially of my old friend Mt Shasta, which now lies to the southwest. The thing about Shasta is that it's getting kind of old.

I've been getting a view of it for the last three weeks or more, not that it isn't beautiful. But it makes you wonder when you're going to finally vacate the vicinity. It was time now to start looking for a crash site. I think crash site is a better word than campsite. Campsite is more of a longer stay, with a little fishing perhaps. For a thru-hiker, it's more of a crash site. Sometimes when the weather is good a tarp or a tent isn't even put up. One just crashes on his ground tarp and insulation pad. Then he cooks while lying down, washes his cooking pot and only has to roll over to do so.

I have now just an hour of light left and that's one thing that has really started in the last few weeks: the sun going down earlier than it used to. Instead of walking until 9pm, it's now getting dark at 8pm. This makes early starts even more imperative: an early start lengthens a short day.

I remember from my 1998 hike that there was a nice spring ahead. I also remember walking Oregon how I was one tired dude when I got here. It was 10:30pm and I had walked two hours in the dark to reach the spring because I was completely out of water. I actually fell first and then heard the trickle of water. It was quite dramatic. I was sure glad to have water. Without water it gets scary, whether you're in Southern Oregon or Southern California.

A few minutes later I reached the springs. The old shack that used to be here had fallen, back in 1997. In 1998 I saw its remains. I don't know who built it or when. You might have to ask Brice Hammick, a trail builder and hiker extraordinaire, to find the answer to that one.

Here at the springs I gather my water and head on. I don't like to camp too close to water because of animals and insects. The last time I was here, a rat ran across my chest as I tried to sleep on the fresh green carpet of tall grass near the water. That's not cool. This time it's not too dark to hike another mile or two. A short time later I found a nice place just west of Soda Mountain. That evening I just ate some cheese, trail mix, and junk food, then I slept under the stars. I didn't bother to put up my tarp.

The next morning I got a pretty early start. My goal for the day was to reach Hyatt Lake, which would be another package pickup. The trail now was lighting fast. With a light pack, it was reasonably easy to keep a three mile per hour pace. The hiking is quite bland here, with virtually no views. Logging roads crisscross the place every so often. A few times the trail goes within 50 yards of peoples cabins. It's always hot here, but it's not ugly and it's shaded.

At Green Spring Summit I crossed a highway that led basically west to Ashland once again. As I hike past Pilot Rock, I really felt like I was heading to Canada once again. This was a refreshing feeling. After hiking around the Mt Shasta loop, the PCT now was a straight shot right through the heart of Oregon.

At the intersection of Highway 66 a hiker can get water by hiking east about a half mile to Keene Creek. My water reserve is down to a quart. I decide to hike on for Hyatt Lake is now within range.

A few miles further, on a level walk, I reach Little Hyatt Reservoir. The dam has a water flow coming off of it. It looks like a huge waterfall. If you take a picture of it you can't tell that's a man-made reservoir flow. I have had people see my pictures of this and say, "Wow, nice, where is this place?" To be here, however, is not very spectacular at all.

After leaving Little Hyatt Reservoir, I climb for a short distance and then the PCT becomes as flat as a pancake as I head towards Hyatt Lake Road. The road to Hyatt Lake Campground veers to the left. Looking directly across the road, I see the PCT emblem on a fir tree. I walk across the street and sure enough, there's a trail. I don't remember this trail from two years ago. At that time you had to follow the road to Hyatt Lake Resort. I decided to take this little edition of the PCT and it paid off. Before I knew it, I arrived at Hyatt Lake Recreation Area.

The trail opened up to a meadow, a small beach and a lake. As I walked across the top of a small dam I can see that the snack shack is still located in the same place. Around the outside of the shack there are six or seven shabby looking thru-hikers or just hikers at the picnic tables. Their faces I do not know.

I walk on down there and sort of introduce myself. I say sort of because you don't get too formal. You let others kind of ask you, "Who in the hell are you?" Then you let them know that I'm trying to pull off the same stunt that they are. So this is what I did but I sort of had to do it quickly because they were leaving. I found out that their names were Rob and Bandana, Special

Agent and Tea Tree. There was a guy walking with them. He called himself "The One".

I tried to bribe them with free beer to stay a bit but they were adamant about leaving. They told me that they had spent two and a half days in Ashland. They had managed to watch a Shakespeare play. The girl with the red bandana who called herself Bandana said, "You'll be seeing us down the trail for sure." Suddenly I was alone again. It was 4pm now so I decided to stay for the night. PCT hikers could stay for free if the camping site was open.

I got my supply box and a couple of Buds. The trail hike is getting more interesting all the time. I'm catching up a little on the Class of 2003. Then suddenly there was a noise behind me and Carston came floating down the trail. "What a trip, Carston. Que paso amigo?" "You know where I have been," Carston spoke out, "Walking, what else?"

You could tell that this dude was a little tired. He said that he just wanted to get his box and leave. I was going to tell Carston that there were all kinds of goods in the snack shack, but I remember that the poor guy couldn't eat any of it.

I told Carston that the snack shack had just closed, that it opens early in the morning for the fishermen who go out in the boats. Carston however was upset and determined to get his box so he could leave. Whatever, man, I said to myself. Only one other hiker in this whole damn place and it has to be Carston, a real barrel of laughs.

I took my junk food, beer, and backpack to the campsite and set up my usual sleeping quarters, right on the ole picnic table. I then went down to the bathroom which had a coin pay shower. I felt great as I dried off. I thought I should tell Carston about the showers. So I walked pretty close to nature boy's campsite and yelled out at him, "There's a shower here, y'know." "There is?" he said. I told him that's one reason why I'm staying here, plus the great little restaurant down the road. I also said they have a great breakfast and I was going to have steak and eggs tomorrow.

I went back to my campsite just in time to shoo off a squirrel that was about to invade my pack. I cooked myself some mac and cheese. I washed my dishes really well, because places like these can often draw a bear's attention.

ECSTASY OF MISERY

The guy at the shack told me they hadn't seen a bear in a long time.

The next morning I awoke about 6am but went back to sleep until 7am. I woke up just in time to see Carston head off. He gave me a wave and off he went. At 8am I started down the road to the Sky View Restaurant and Resort. I was happy to find the place open.

There were only a few characters in there. I sat down at the nearest table. When I was here in 1998 an older woman and man ran the place temporarily for their son and his wife while they were on vacation. The food was excellent and plenty of it too.

When the waitress came over, I ordered steak and eggs with a short stack of buttermilk pancakes, hash browns, orange juice, and coffee. The food came reasonably soon and it was awesome!

While I was eating I started rapping with the cook who I found out was the owner. I told him that I was here in 1998 when I was just walking the state of Oregon and how great the food was. He told me that the two people I saw here then were his mom, who died in 2002 and his dad, who died soon after his mom.

I told him I was sorry to hear that. I asked him how business was and he said terrible ever since they made the area a wildlife habitat. Only about one third of the amount of people come by there or stay any more. That's why the restaurant at Hyatt Lake Resort is closed. He went on to say that it's hard to pay a cook and a waitress for full time when the visitor traffic is so slow. I told the guy good luck and I hope things change in the future.

It was now 9am and time to boogie out. Everybody had left. Back at camp I adjusted my pack and put on one shirt that I had washed out the night before. Down to the lake I went. Making a right turn, I went by the snack shack. No need to even think about food now. I was stuffed with a major power breakfast. This should hold me over till dinner and I was planning on hiking until dark, If possible.

I was soon back to the trailhead at Hyatt Lake Road. Here the trail travels above the road for a couple of miles until it turns off to the east at Wildcat Glades. Good views were abundant on this trail segment of Hyatt Lake, with its flooded trees still standing surrounded by water.

After climbing over a small ridge of mountains, I soon came to Howard Prairie Lake which is another flood lake. There's a resort on the opposite side of the lake. Klum Landing Campground looked huge as I strolled by it. It looks like a pretty good place to camp, but it was only 2pm. I still had too many miles to conquer today.

It was another warm day, over 90 degrees. I decide to get water out of Grizzle Creek when I get to it. But that was a mistake. The whole area smelled putrid. The water that slowly drains out of Howard Prairie Lake travels down what looks like a man-made canal about 10 feet wide. Oh boy, you would have to be pretty bad off to get water from here, and if you drank it without treating it you'd be even worse off.

Walking at a faster pace now, I left the Prairie Lake and was soon above it heading north. I was now a little concerned about water. The next source was about four miles away at a place called Griffin Pass Big Springs. I just hope that the water is still running. It's not uncommon that during this time of the year Oregon Springs can dry up. The trail was flat and fast.

Soon I arrived at the springs. A sign pointed H2O, 100 yards up the trail. The water source was running slow, but still coming out of the ground good enough. After a little patience I filled my tanks up and off I went. It was now about 4pm, still enough time to make another seven or eight miles.

A mile past the spring I circle around Old Baldy Mountain, 6340 feet. The trail now gradually descended to Dead Indian Road, which I believe runs into Ashland some 26 miles away.

It's now starting to get late so I sat down on a funky old log. I'd rather sit on a rock because one time I sat on an old log and a damn scorpion came bobbing out.

All right, about four miles further on is Butte Creek, a water source and a potentially flat landscape with the possibility of a good crash spot.

So off I go. The trail as usual is in excellent shape. The day's heat was dropping quickly. Finally arrived at the south branch of the creek that had no water at all. I was concerned about the situation but on the map it was the next fork of the creek that had the most blue in it.

ECSTASY OF MISERY

About a half mile further I reached the main fork and was glad to see that the water was flowing a little bit. I found a real nice flat spot between the PCT and the dirt road below. Tomorrow would be a day when I would climb out of this Bureau of Land Management country and enter another Oregon wilderness. That will be Sky Lakes Wilderness.

Tonight I had to cook in the dark, chicken alfredo. I still have an onion but it's starting to turn brown and soft. I'll toss some of it in the pot. Those barbecue potato chips are crunched up so might as well toss them into the pot as well.

That breakfast at Sky Lake Resort sure did its job. I haven't had anything to eat since then, not even a power bar. That night I listen to my super small transistor radio I carry now and then. It can become a good source of entertainment, weather, time, and news. For only adding four ounces on your back, it wasn't a bad deal.

The next morning I was up at 6:30 and walking by 7am. Today should be a pretty good day, the last of Bureau of Land Management beautiful Sky Lakes Wilderness. At Highway 140 I can hike in to Fish Lake Resort and have lunch. It sounded good but for now I'll just have to play it by ear. Fish Lake lies about a mile off the trail; round trip it's a good two miles. It's something to think about.

After digging a hole I headed out towards the highway by rounding Brown Mountain, 7311 feet in elevation. After walking a short mile, I saw the sign that read, "Brown's Shelter, 75 yards".

This is a cool place to stop. Brown's Shelter is a rather new shelter, built some time around 1996 or 1997, I believe. It has a great water source, a cool pump that sweet cold water comes out of. Inside there are wooden platforms around the perimeter of the place. You can sit there or sleep there. There's also a PCT Register. I head down the trail and arrive at the shelter where I go right for that water pump.

The cabin looks good but a little more weathered than in 1998 when I did my Oregon hike. It would be – that was five years ago. I decide to make breakfast here, why not, it's a perfect place. Just as I was mixing my morning shake (today would be cappuccino flavor), who walks up but the strange dude himself, Professor Carston of the University of San Francisco. "Carston, dude, how did you get in back of me?" "I don't know, you probably passed me last night."

We sat there fixing our fixings, me with a super shake and a couple of granola bars, and Carston with his ground up grain coated with olive oil. Then Carston exclaimed, "I'm getting sick of my food." "Dude, I don't know how you've gone this far, you're diet is pure insane." "It's okay if you're back in the city where you have an assortment of stuff you can buy." I told him that out here you're burning off 6000 calories a day and how he could find himself in the hospital if he didn't start eating right. "I have to eat what I have to eat, man." This was the first time I ever heard the guy say man as an exclamation mark! It sounded funny. This guy was starting to use my lingo.

After lunch we both felt raindrops, so we ducked into a shelter to resume our lunches. I checked out the Register to look for names. There was Billy Goat, who was 10 days ahead of me. There were most of the usuals. I didn't see Zeb, never do, or Cruising Carson, but there was Chance. Wow, he stayed here last night. I wrote a few funny things. I thought I would write a note to Wookie and Island Mama. So I did. It went something like this, "Wookie, Island Mama, surf's up, get back to the trail, don't malinger, winter is coming on," and signed it Wrong Way. They'll probably never see it but if they do, it will surprise them.

Well it's time for me to leave. I don't know if I'm going to stop at Fish Lake, maybe I will. "If it's raining I'm going to stop for sure," said Carston. That kind of surprised me. I didn't think the guy ever stopped.

So down the trail I jammed, heading for the Valley of Pines below. As I got lower I began to see bicycle tracks along the trail. That usually is a sign for a trailhead and a vehicle campsite, but here it was, kids staying at Fish Creek Resort.

A little further and I came to the sign that read, "Fish Creek Resort, Food, Cold Drinks, and Lodging." I had to make a decision and it came pretty easily. I decided to skip the place. It wasn't that long ago that I had that power breakfast and by going to the resort I would lose some three hours or more. In 1998 I stopped in on a weekend. It was crowded but it was a nice place.

ECSTASY OF MISERY

Fish Lake, which I believe is a natural lake, has a deep blue color.

Moving on now I soon arrived at Highway 140. I think if you take it west you will come to Medford, Oregon, the next major city after Ashland. If a hiker goes east, he will soon arrive at Lake of the Woods, which used to be the old PCT route through the Oregon Sky Lakes Wilderness.

The trail now stays up high on a slope, high above most of the lakes. That's too bad in a way because many beautiful lakes are missed going this way. The new route doesn't have very many aerial views of these lakes either. They seem to stay hidden for the most part. One good thing about the new route is that you bypass many mosquitoes, especially in June or July. There are fewer in August but there are still a ton of them.

I'm traveling in a new section of Oregon's Trail Guide following the Cascade Canal for just a short distance. It then breaks off into a viewless forest route, towards more adventure. Now and then a few mosquitoes fly in to bug me, but not bad enough to smear myself with Deet.

About an hour later I run into a family with two boys and a cute little girl about eight years old. The boys were around 12 and 14. They had just come down from Mt Laughlin, having bagged the peak. The husband and wife were very nice. They wanted to learn about the mighty PCT so I told them quite a bit about it.

The husband actually sounded like he wanted to try it with his sons some day. I told him it wasn't easy, but if you're prepared mentally and physically and have decent lightweight gear, you can do it. It's 80% mental and probably 20% physical, and luck is also a factor.

I also told the family that girls do really well on the trail in fact. One young lady back in 1994, named Jenny Jardine, walked the trail with her husband in only 94 days. She still holds the record today? The little girl and her mom smiled at that one.

Then they asked me about how long it was going to take me. I told them at least 150 days or more. But it's so much nicer to sort of take your time because you experience so much more. You're able to stop and rest at nice places like Ashland and Sierra City. They gave me some Ocean Spray cranberry and raspberry juice, along with a couple of out-of-sight apples. I said good-bye and congratulated them on their Mt Laughlin ascent and then they were gone.

I chugged down that juice in a minute. It was great. As I walked along the trail I started munching on those awesome apples. I came around a bend and there was the Mt Laughlin trail junction. A sign read, "Mt Laughlin, 4 miles." If I weren't behind schedule, that would be a nice little side trip. Mt Laughlin is about 9495 feet, just about the same as Mt Baden Powell is back home. But here it's a major peak. In Southern California , I believe Baden Powell is the forth highest peak, behind San Gorgonio and Mt San Jacinto.

It's now 1pm and it's time to push it a little. The trail is in good shape and although it was warm, about 90 degrees, large trees shade me, and the juice and the apple the family had given me gave me a real boost of energy.

The trail now was uphill for the most part, but very gradual. I kept a good pace for about an hour until my natural fruit energy wore off. At 2pm I took a quick lunch and headed back on the trail climbing slowly, higher and higher towards Devils Pass. At 7pm that evening I turned off the trail at Squaw Lake trail junction and headed down to Squaw Lake to crash for the night. It looked to be a quarter of a mile, not too bad, but much better than camping here in the rocks.

That night after dinner I thought I would put my tarp up just because there were two perfect trees to tie my rope to. The sun had set now leaving the place a golden color for a few minutes. Across the lake there looked to be a couple of campers, but besides that I was the only other person. Down below the lake you would probably find quite a few campers because that lake was huge. It was called Four Mile Lake.

I tried to get a radio station, but no luck. I gave the cell phone a try, but no luck. I guess I was in the wilderness alright. Not a bad day at all for me. I figured I did about 25 miles. I'm glad I didn't stop at Fish Lake. It worked out for the better and I got to meet a cool family who scaled Mt Laughlin. I had one apple left that I ate, and somewhere around hikers midnight, I was asleep.

The next day brought on rain. I was surprised a bit, but really glad that I had put up my tarp. It kept me from hustling in a bit of a panic during the dark hours of early morning. This way I just went back to sleep.

The rain was soft and subsided about 15 or 20 minutes later. When I awoke a few hours later I couldn't believe it was 8:30am. At 9am I was walking. Not a good start at all, but it was a nature deal. I think I really needed the rest. By the time I got back to the trail it was 9:20am, so I picked up the pace a little and headed on towards Devils Peak.

The trail resumes in a viewless forest and soon travels near the east side of Imagination Peak. Toward the west there's a very flat part of a mountain peak. It was almost like a mesa. A small long lake with no name lies on the mesa's west side.

Near the Deer Lakes Cluster I sit down and I'm amazed at the topo strip map that now shows where I am. Up in front of me and just to the east are hundreds of lakes. The Dwarf Lakes area has tons of small lakes spread out like blue polka dots, unbelievable. All these lakes are far below the ridge where the PCT traverses probably about 250 to 350 feet below the Rogue River Ridge.

Powering along at a 2.8 miles per hour, I notice that the sky is fast becoming darker and darker. Now way off in the distance I can see dark clouds with a sort of dark fog below them. That means those babies are dropping mass quantities of H2O and by god, they're heading right towards me!

Wow, I look up a second time and those distant clouds are not so distant. Yellow alert, yellow alert. Off comes my pack. Where's that poncho? Oh yeah, it's in my clothes bag! I carry my clothes in an acrylic net bag that weighs only two ounces. I put my poncho in the pocket of my nylon running pants, easy to get to in a hurry. My tarp is at the top of my pack. Also easy to get to, but a very slim chance that I will need the tarp, unless the rain comes down in torrents.

Off in the distance is a giant rainbow, unbelievable. But what's that? Oh man, it's the sound of rain drops. No, it's the sound of hail. Oh hell, hats off to the Gods! I head to the nearest tree which breaks the fall of those hard little nodules. Here's where I could use an umbrella. For a few minutes it was okay until I heard the sound of a closer than should be bolt of lightning. What am I doing under this fir tree, which is about the tallest tree around here, with lightning bolts flipping around!

It's time to leave, I believe, and off I jammed into the great "white" open. Almost as soon as I did the hail subsided and then it started to rain. The thunder kept on popping. I just kept walking with my cheap poncho that was doing a good job. What a time to head to Devils Peak!

The sky was almost black now. The rain came down in sheets, like waves of rain. The thunder and lightning had moved on. I took refuge under a small white pine which at least broke the impact of the rain. I stayed under that little tree for about 10 minutes that felt like an hour.

The rain slowed down now to a regular type of precipitation and I made my way down the sloppy wet trail. At first I tried to avoid all the puddles but then I didn't care since my New Balances were soaked anyway.

Soon I was on top of the Devils Peak area. Even in the rain the cliffs of Devils Peak looked beautiful. Definitely a colorful quantity of sheer steep rocks. Just past the summit I ran into a section hiker who was about my age. I talked to him for a while. His name was Bill and he was a retired firefighter from Portland. He was walking the PCT by only doing day hikes, usually once a week. I was amazed. It takes a partner to drive to all of the locations. It also takes a lot of topo maps to find out where Bill could be dropped off. I forgot to ask him where he had started but I'm sure his destination for that day would be Highway 140 at Fish Lake Resort area.

Bill felt that he could make the entire trail this way, except for the High Sierra portion. His wife was his car transportation. She had a Jeep Cherokee. Now and then they needed it but most of the time he would enter the PCT at a paved highway. He might have a couple of miles to walk before he rejoined the PCT or when he left the PCT. He said it wasn't too bad. I said, "Amazing, you should write a book about it." "Yeah, I probably should," he said.

The rain had momentarily slowed down. It started to perk up again so we decided to head our separate ways. One thing I asked Bill as we headed out was how are you going to hike the mighty Sierras? He was about 50 feet from me by then and yelled out, "By then my grandson will be old enough that we can hike it together." Wow, that's nice, I said to myself as I walked down the hill into the pounding rain.

That dude is too much. One advantage he has is that he only has to take a daypack. No need for a sleeping bag, tent or cooking stuff, including food. He probably walks with a super light pack which helps to do a lot of miles during the day. Far out!

One of the problems with that is logistics and having a dedicated wife to drop him off and pick him up. The further he gets away from Portland, the more expensive the endeavor becomes because of all the travel time. Like what's he supposed to do when he gets to Southern California? That is a long way from Portland, Oregon, and that's a lot of motel rooms, unless maybe she just sleeps at car camping spots and sleeps in the jeep, or maybe she has a nice tent.

While the thoughts of Bill and the day hiking run through my mind, I'm constantly pounding downhill in the soft rain now, making excellent time. I soon arrive at the creek that dumps water into Gross Lake. But the water is a peculiar orange color. I don't know if that's from the rain or that's the way it usually is. I sit down and have some breakfast. Instead of using this water I used the water I got out of Squaw Lake this morning.

After breakfast I'm heading down the wet muddy trail and notice the damage it has taken and is taking right now. The water has poured onto the trail and the trail has turned into a little creek in many places.

It makes me take in more appreciation for the trail workers and the amount of labor it takes from volunteers and the forest service for keeping this trail up. I can now see how those small logs along the trail, which become steps to the hiker, definitely help to divert water off the trail. They work great!

You can be a hiker that's walked the trail many times and still not realize the fragile aspect of this curling snake. If two or three years go by without the usual trail maintenance, there wouldn't be a trail at all, in most places anyway. Hats off to the mighty trail gorillas. They deserve almost all the recognition. Thank you Pacific Crest Trail Association, you're awesome.

The rain started up once again, although it didn't feel quite as cold, probably because I was at a lower elevation. Soon I splashed up to a double trail junction. Seven Mile Trail ran out to the east and the Rogue River Basin Trail which led west down to the very beginning of the Rogue River of Oregon. Amazing, just like the Sierras, I was up in the heavens where major rivers start.

After a Snickers break I headed down the trail. Although it's only 6:30, it's dark because of the clouds in the sky. It would be nice if the rain would stop at least long enough to set up my tarp for the night. So just past Mikie Mountain and Ethel Mountain, I made my camp for the night.

It's funny to set up your camp in the rain. Everything is soaked and you have to sleep on the wet ground. The rain has finally started to slow down for good. I can see the parting of the clouds now and a slightly blue sky is emerging.

The first thing to do is set the tarp up. There were trees all over and I had a real nice flat place to sleep. I then put down the ground mat that helps to keep you off the muddy ground. After the ground mat is in place, then it's time to move in. You're sheltered now. You can usually relax a little. Just about the time I put up my tarp, the rain stopped. The tarp blocks the drops of rain that blow off the high pine trees.

The drainage is good, a slight sloped terrain. What you don't want is to stand where it might start flowing in from either of the two openings. I go ahead and prepare my meal of chicken tetrazzini. I tried to pick up a local radio station. I finally got to Art Bell. He is the head guy who is the president of the UFO Club of America. That's all I need is to have another visitor from outer space man. The one near Sierra City was enough for this trip.

The next morning I awoke to a fog infested forest. My god it's starting to look like Washington. I just hope that this isn't the sign of an early winter. Now I'm thinking that maybe I should have flip flopped, but there's nothing I can do about it now.

I was off hiking at 6:30am. This was town day. My goal was to reach Mazama Campground today, that would be cool. I could spend a night there and head out Sunday for the famous fantastic Crater Lake. Today was Saturday, August 23rd. I was closing in on Crater Lake. Like most hikers, my mileage was improving. I was averaging 25 miles per day.

I keep walking down the trail on a funky morning. After a couple of miles I had to head through some tall grass and weeds which, of course, soaked my pants and shoes that were just starting to dry out.

That problem was eliminated when I arrived at the Oregon desert. The desert was a spot of flat land about a mile long and a short mile wide that had very little vegetation. The trees were small and there were very few weeds or bushes. Just as I reached this strange place the sun came out and the fog immediately lifted. It was summer again. What a feeling! The rain had officially ended and the air was extra fresh and clean. There was a little mud here and there, but at least there wasn't any dust.

I was heading down the trail at a good pace when I came to a sign which read, "Stewart Falls, 2 miles". Oh no, I don't remember any Stewart Falls from 1998, before Mazama Campground.

Definitely pissed off at myself, I got the trail guide out to figure what I did wrong. I had simply taken the Stewart Falls Trail that branches off the PCT. This is not the first time that I have done this without knowing how. So, for me, it wasn't too much of a shock.

The Stewart Falls Trail rejoined the PCT five miles after the mysterious trail junction that I had just missed. It was too late to go back, for I had already walked a mile out of the way. To go back I would lose two miles, but if I go on, I don't think I'll lose more than a mile and I'll get to see Stewart Falls. The guidebook recommends this alternative route if you're thirsty. Good deal. Ill have breakfast there. So off I went again, not feeling too bad about what happened.

An hour later I started coming across water in the form of a spring and a creek. Soon I hear the sound of crashing water. I turn off the main trail and then go through a small campsite, right up to some fine looking falls, probably 35 to 40 feet high.

I think I'll take a breakfast break. After eating, I head back to the main trail and head north again, slanting all the time in an eastern direction, until I finally reach the regular route of the PCT. Wow, what a trip that was! I have water now. It's hot and by god, that's the last water until Mazama Campground, some 10 miles away.

So with a bounce in my step I head down a fast, easy, wide trail towards Mazama Campground and Crater Lake. After walking a fast mile the trail brings back memories of the Nike Girls. The Nike Girls were a group of five girls that were sponsored by Nike, I guess to hike the PCT.

Back in 1998, when I was section hiking, walking the state of Oregon, I met these young ladies heading south down the trail, going north to south. I believe that they had flip flopped like almost all the hikers that year did due to the heavy snows in the High Sierras. I don't know to this day if they even made it back to Kennedy Meadows which is where they probably flip flopped. About 90% of the hikers grab a bus and head up Highway 395.

Was it this area where I talked to the girls, or this area? It's hard to say and totally not important. It is important, however, to reach the Mazama store by 4pm because that's when the post office closes. If I don't get my box then I'll have to wait until Monday since the post office is closed on Sunday.

I'm now in Crater Lake National Park. Sky Lakes Wilderness is history. But like a lot of other beautiful places, the PCT skirts this wilderness with an aerial view of the place. The amount of lakes in this area is incredible. The trail now is becoming wider and the terrain is almost flat. I utilize the flat area to haul butt. I'm keeping a three mile per hour pace and soon I hit Highway 62. To the west 65 miles is Medford, Oregon, but only one mile east to Mazama Campground.

I leave the trail here where it crosses the road and keep heading north towards Crater Lake. It's 3pm now. I have one hour to get my supply box. I keep a good pace until I reached the Mazama Campground store and post office. There's a sign telling hikers to leave their backpacks outside. I hate doing this, even if it's only for a few minutes. I do take my hiker's wallet, which is a zip lock baggy with money, ID and credit cards. I keep it on my person at all times when I'm in town or crowded campgrounds.

First I go right over to get my supply box. I tell the guy my name and he tells me to wait a minute. After he checks out a customer with a small bag of groceries he goes into a back room to retrieve my box. A minute later he comes out and asks, "What was your name, Rainey?" "No, Raley, Robert," I said. He then goes back and doesn't come back for a while. Now I'm worried. He should have found it by now. A couple of seconds later he reappears. "I can't find any box with the name Raley on it."

Oh my God, Houston, we do have a problem. I tell the guy it's been sent some seven or eight days ago from the LA area. It should be here by now. My heart sank. I was tired and bummed out.

I go outside and try to call Trail Perfect by cell phone. "Can you hear me now?" "Hell no." Just like usual, Verizon sucks. A guy walking by tells me there isn't any cell phone reception here. So now I have to use the pay phone and of course there's always someone using it when you need it most.

Finally I talked to Linda. "Hey Linda, I'm at Mazama Campground. I just got here and guess what?" I hear her quickly say oh no. "Yeah, no package." "I sent it last Monday, six days ago." I asked her if she had sent it by priority mail and she said yes and that she sent it to Crater Lake post office. "I'm at Mazama Campground, you should have mailed it here." Linda said the town guide said Mazama Campground doesn't accept PCT packages any more and to send them to the post office at Crater Lake, which she did. I told her that they do accept packages.

Then I got kind of pissed and told her I just lost a day, how I busted my ass to get here and now I can't leave until Monday. She asked if I couldn't get to the Crater Lake post office. I said, "Nope, it closes at 4pm and it's 4pm now." "I'm sorry, Bob, but the trail guide says no packages." I told her that I was devastated . When Trail Perfect hung up, I could tell she was a little upset. Nothing to do now but go and get a campsite. It looks like Ill be here for a couple of nights.

I then venture up to the ticket chalet and ask for a campsite. The lady shows me on a map where my campsite is located and it would cost $16 for the night. "Wow, that's pretty high. I'm walking the PCT. I don't even have a car." The older guy in there told her to give me the senior citizen discount. "From now on you're 62 years old." "Ok, yeah, I appreciate that." I gladly gave the lady eight bucks and then headed to my site.

I hate leaving my stuff alone but it looks like a safe place. So with my money and ID I head back to the store area and go right for the public showers! It cost $3 and it was definitely worth it. Leaving the showers, I run into Wahoo and Lou. They have their stuff all laid out and it looked like they have enough food to last both of them for a week. "Hey dudes, what's happening?" "Wrong Way, you're here," says Super Lou, who is Wahoo's wife. "Yep, I arrived about an hour ago."

They wondered if I had gone to Stewart Falls by mistake. I said yes, that I never did see the sign and asked if they saw it. They didn't either. "We wanted to get here earlier so we could hitchhike to Crater Lake Lodge for their famous buffet they're supposed to have, but damn it, by the time we put our stuff up, it will be too late." I told them they could stay with me for free. They wanted to pay me but I said don't worry, that I paid the senior citizen discount and only paid $8 instead of $16. I told them that this place has all the amenities plus Crater Lake is a big time tourist attraction.

So Wahoo and Lou stayed with me and they bought me a six-pack of Corona beer, some chips, and cheese dip. I go back with them and show them my campsite. But then I head back to the store to buy some batteries for my light that straps around my head and a couple of packaged burritos, the kind you heat up in the microwave.

While I was there, Puck and Belcher arrived and I rap to them for a while. It seems like there's some heavy-duty animosity between the two. I keep out of it. Then out of nowhere, Rob and Bandana appear. They take a quick shower and march on. They're going to thumb it to Crater Lake for that buffet. I tell them it's kind of late, damn near dark, but they take off because somebody's dad is there with a vehicle and a campsite for them.

From what they told me, Chance, Leprechaun, and Batteries Included are also there. As they march out to the highway, I told them that I'd be here tomorrow night too, so if anyone wanted a cheap campsite, look for number B-23. "Ok, we will but I don't think anybody wants to come back here, Wrong Way."

Man, that's cold. There they go, off to party without me. Wrong Way is stuck here with a store, showers, and all the other amenities for eight bucks a night. I brought my stuff out of the store and headed back to my campsite. I told Wahoo and Lou about everybody I had seen. They also thought those guys were pushing it but if someone's dad is there to chauffeur them around, then maybe it would be worth going there. For another half hour Wahoo and I sat around drinking those Coronas and powering down those chips with the cheese dip.

I hit the hay about 10:30. The tranquility of the wilderness is gone now because I now have motorized car campers all around me and many of them talk and play music late into the night, up to 11pm.

The next morning I sleep in. Wahoo and Lou arise earlier and are anxious to get to Crater Lake. They now plan to spend the day there and catch the buffet at 5pm and then hike out of there until it gets dark. Then they would camp somewhere around the lake. I say good-bye to them and kick back in the sack for another couple of hours, giving my legs some rest. There's not a whole lot to do today so I might as well take it slow.

After a microwave breakfast I decide to call Trail Perfect and let her know that I'm sorry about the phone call the day before. I was pretty damn tired and was pushing it. I lost a day by staying here, but it's always good to rest. What I'll do is hitchhike up to Crater Lake and have my ride drop me off about a half mile below the lake's rim where the post office is located. From there I'll just walk the road to the rim.

The road to the rim I've hiked before. It's a pretty good climb. Most PCT hikers get a ride. It's a road walk that most hikers don't want. The true way of getting to the rim is to follow the PCT past Highway 62 to Light Spring Trail and then head to the rim approaching it from the west. If the PCT were strictly adhered to, there wouldn't be any sight of the lake at all. One would simply walk by it on the west side and head directly to Red Cone Springs, tank up on a lot of water and then walk to Mt Thielsen, some 22 miles away, where the next water is available.

In the last few years, however, with so many people wanting to see the lake that the PCT travels around, half of the lake departs on its northward journey to Mt Thielsen area. Most hikers, I bet 90% of them, walk the rim drive road instead of the trail. It's twice as fast and half as hard and you still see tons of scenic views of Crater Lake.

Finally, there is one other alternative route. That route breaks off just past Red Cone Springs, then heads directly north like an arrow to Diamond Lake. From Diamond Lake it heads east to catch the PCT after it travels by Mt Thielsen.

After lunch I finally get a chance to use the washing machines. They really need a bigger place for the laundromat. It was very difficult to get a washer or a dryer.

The rest of the day I just kick back and take it easy, getting plenty of carbohydrates and sugar from the company store. For a while I try to experiment with my cell phone by climbing up a few trees trying to get reception, but to no avail. Towards the end of the day I pay for another night at the campground for only eight bucks because after all, they believe I'm 62. After looking at the bathroom mirror, I can see why they might think I'm that old. My beard is damn near all white. Hey, that's what all of those mosquitoes can do to a guy!

About 5pm I decide to go to the store and buy some canned beef stew that I can cook on my stove for dinner, when who shows up but Carston. The guy crosses my path once again. Wahoo and Lou told him that I was at this campsite so he thumbed a ride down here from the lodge. Then from here he can catch a bus tomorrow to San Francisco.

It's not too much of a surprise to me that he's made it this far because the guy doesn't make the pit stops that I do. For instance, at Etna and Ashland he just remained on the trail. I can understand that, for the guy has just 20 days to hike and he wanted to do as much of the PCT as possible. It's cool to have him here. We talked about the trail and other stuff.

That night, at his suggestion, we go to a forest service campfire show, like the one I went to at Tuolumne Meadows. It was fun. This show actually had a stage and we learned quite a bit about Crater Lake.

For instance, the fact that it was caused by an implosion, not an explosion like most volcanoes. This seismic event happened some six million years ago. The effect was felt all over the world. A whole mountain just sank below the ground; it blew rocks and volcanic material around its sides and cast debris all through the atmosphere. At the end of the show they had a group of Girl Scouts getting their merit badges for cleaning up the forest. It wasn't one of the most exciting outings I ever had but I was glad that I went.

After the show we headed back to the campsite. It was about 10pm now and I offered Carston a cold Corona as a toast to his trip and our acquaintance over the past 20 days. But of course he couldn't have a beer because he can't drink beer. So I just headed to my tarp and turned in.

The next morning I got up about 7am and started packing my stuff to leave when Carston asks me if I could watch his gear while he went and took a shower. So being a nice guy, I do, and I'll be damned if the guy was gone for an hour or more!

Carston finally comes back to the campsite and is surprised that I'm still here. This was the same damn thing that Mario pulled on me back at Lake Marina. "You're still here," he says. "Yeah, man, you asked me to watch your stuff! I'm not going to walk off and leave your things setting there to be possibly stolen." "Oh," he says and so I grabbed my pack and fling it on my back and I just leave. Carston said good-bye. I say nothing, but to myself I'm thinking why don't you go suck on a turnip.

A few minutes later I start hitchhiking towards the lake. I wasted almost an hour and a half watching Carston's stuff. Maybe someone ought to force feed that skinny dude a steak before he dries up and blows away. I do have to give him credit for the 20 days he hiked the trail. However, he made it because he's experienced at being a vegan and he knew what he was doing. If he didn't I think he could have really harmed himself. I'm not talking about a vegetarian who doesn't eat meat, but a person far more eccentric.

About a mile after leaving the campground I finally got a ride by two young men who were going to Crater Lake to purchase tickets for the boat ride. Only one boat is allowed on the lake. This is to protect its purity and tranquility.

Crater Lake and Wizzard Peak

Journey Fourteen: Make No Mistake, it's the One and Only Crater Lake

Finally I had arrived at the post office. I was expecting two packages: one package with food and the other with my new running shoes. I walked in the post office and asked the guy for my two packages. He went back to the storage room and came back with one package. He then, of course, asked me for my ID. I reached for my wallet and started digging in it, but to my shock and dismay, there was no driver's license!

I freaked out. I began to nervously go through my wallet once more. But again couldn't find my license. What in the hell have I done with it? The guy asked me if I had a credit card and I showed him my Visa card. He said that'd do it. I got my two packages and went outside.

I then started putting my new supplies in my backpack and threw out some of my trash in the bin at the side of the post office. I was still flipping out when I went back inside the post office to ask the clerk if he could call the Mazama Campground store to see if they had my driver's license. He said he would, that he has the number written down somewhere.

The clerk finally got through on the phone and talked to somebody at the store. "Say, Emma, did you find a California driver's license? This fellow here feels that he might have left it on the check-out counter when he purchased some items in the store."

A few minutes passed and then the reply to Charley at the post office there wasn't anything there. My heart sank. I thanked Emma and Charley hung up the phone. I was really bummed out now. How would I deal with not having an ID? I definitely needed one to get out of Canada and possibly to get into Canada as well. I could call my parents and ask if they could send my birth certificate. I felt like a real jerk. The only place I could have left it was when I purchased food in the store because I used my credit card almost every time and they always wanted to see my ID.

ECSTASY OF MISERY

I started to walk out of the post office totally dejected when the phone rang. Charley answered it. "Oh yeah, I'll tell him. I think you might have brightened his day." Charley tells me that the lady at the store had just found out that a California driver's license was given to dispatch earlier this morning.

I said that was great, but where was dispatch. The clerk said that I was in luck again: it's just down the road about 100 yards. I was told to ask for Phyllis, that she was the secretary there. "Thanks, man, for your help. I'll head right down there." On my way out I put my old New Balance trail running shoes in the trash bin. They had done me right but were pretty shot now, having crunched the trail from Echo Lake Resort near South Lake Tahoe all the way to Crater, Oregon.

I then headed down the road to dispatch near park headquarters. There was a large maintenance yard and I asked a forest service worker where was dispatch. They pointed to the log cabin office. I walked in and asked for Phyllis and the lady at the desk was Phyllis. I told her that they might have my driver's license. She asked me my name and I told her, then she hands over my license. Man, what a relief!

About a half hour later I reached the rim and went over to take a few pictures. The lake is actually gorgeous, a deep blue with incredibly pure water. Crater Lake is one of the deepest lakes in the world and the deepest in the United States.

It relies on the snow melt every winter to refill it. There are no creeks or rivers that flow into it or flow out of it. Just to the side of the middle of the lake is Wizard Island. It looks like a little mountain peak that rises out of the deep blue.

It's weird to think that this was once a mountain peak, some 12,000 feet or more that actually fell into the earth. The ashes from the implosion were actually seen in China! It was considered a major earth-shaking event that had ecological effects on many portions of the earth. It happened some six million years ago, a bit before Wrong Way's time.

After a cool view of the lake on a beautiful day, I headed over to the snack shack, dodging other tourists as I went. For a tourist stop this wasn't a bad place and the prices are pretty decent. I ended up ordering a medium pizza with pepperoni, olives, mushrooms, and Canadian bacon. I had a cherry coke to drink. It definitely wasn't the best pizza I've ever had but it sure wasn't the worst either. For dessert I had some Dreyer's ice cream.

When I finished shoveling down at least 4000 calories I headed up toward the lodge. Some hikers had told me that if you stand in a certain area you can get a cell phone connection. The reason I wanted to use the cell phone was because the rates are cheaper than the pay phone. I came up to the lodge and then went east towards a field and tried my luck, but to no avail. I did get a good view of the mountains from the south, including Mt Laughlin and Mt Shasta. Shasta looked like it was a million miles away. A lady saw me trying to phone and said she couldn't get any reception either, but locals who had a local carrier could often get a connection.

So back down the road I went heading north, back to the snack shack and the gift store. Suddenly in front of me I spotted Chance heading out on his way north. "Hey buddy, what's happening?" "Wrong Way, did you just arrive?" I told Chance my story about how I had to spend an extra night at Mazama Campground. He told me how he had been living it up the last few days at the lodge. Bandana, Rob, Puck, Belcher, Wahoo and Lou with Batteries Included really pigged out at the lodge's famous buffet.

Chance asked me, knowing that I'd walked Oregon once before, if the trail around the lake was a sure thing. I told him yes, but there were a lot of unnecessary ups and downs. Most people walk the highway. The trail does promote some great views of the lake however. "Thanks for the tip, Wrong Way. I think I'll walk the road. I've seen the views of the lake the last two days."

Chance told me that his brother had visited him and a bunch of them pitched in and bought some bottles of water and drove north to Highway 138 where they put out water caches. "Did you put much out?" "Yeah, about eight gallons yesterday," Chance said. I told him that should help because the last water from the lake's north side is just north of Mt Thielsen, and that's over 20 miles away.

I thanked Chance for the tip and said I'll be looking for the caches. "Later, dude." Chance said, "See you on down the line for some more thrills and how about some High Crimes and Misdemeanors." "Oh yeah, that too."

ECSTASY OF MISERY

Chance then jammed at his fast pace with those 16" guns of his, powering himself forward with his hiker walking poles. Well, that's great, a water cache between here and Thielsen. That helps.

I followed at a slower pace back to the snack shack and the public telephones where I called Trail Perfect and talked to her. I told her about my driver's license fiasco and that I would be leaving Crater Lake in a few minutes. I told her to please call my parents and let them know that I'm a third done with Oregon.

Right after talking to my home base associate and loving buddy for many years, I decide to call Chuck Hinkel and the dude answers, which was a surprise that I didn't have to leave a message. What I hear from Chuck, however, is disturbing. He has a medical problem. The left side of his face has a bulge in it and the doctor believes he might have cancer of the pituitary gland. He had been dizzy the last couple of weeks and was having recurring headaches. Tomorrow he's going to the University of Southern California Medical Center to find out more about the situation. Then Chuck told me to make it to Canada.

I couldn't believe it. I was shocked. I told Chuck he'd be okay. I felt like hell. That was a downer. I was going to get a salad from the snack shack but instead headed out in bewilderment. There's nothing I can do except call Chuck back in a couple of days to find out what U.S.C. had to say. I began heading towards the trail. It was only 12:30 but already it had been quite a weird day, with Chuck's problem and my driver's license. I had a couple take my picture with Crater Lake in the background. They said smile and say cheese, but instead I said shit to myself. I didn't want to bum them out, especially since they just got married.

The rest of the day I plodded along, watching out for the traffic on Crater Lake Rim Road. I went by the Watchman Overlook and then Hillman Peak. Finally four or five miles further on I broke away from the lake heading straight north were I crossed the trail coming out of Red Cone Springs. Now I was on the real PCT again, heading down a treeless mesa paralleling the road.

I pounded away at the trail hiking north on an almost perfectly flat terrain. I felt like a high plains drifter, racing the sun, hoping to get to Highway 138 and the water cache where I would crash for the night. I finally arrived at the road which bordered Crater Lake National Peak, and Mt Thielsen and Cascade Crest area. I crossed the road and began looking for the cache that Chance told me about. I couldn't find it. I looked for a good half hour before I gave up.

Around 10pm I made camp at a trail junction where the PCT was joined by a trail that leads down to Diamond Lake which used to be the main route on the PCT before this Mt Thielsen route was built some time in the past. I had just enough water for dinner and a drink. Tomorrow I would look again for Chance's cache and if I don't find it I will make the decision to go on or head down to Diamond Lake for water. For now, however, I needed to sleep, for it's been one hell of a day for sure. I lay awake for a bit, thinking about Chuck and his problems, my girlfriend and home. I guess I was homesick. What a long strange trip it's been!

The next morning I got up and noticed my right little toe was in pain. I'm afraid these new sneakers are a bit tight. I immediately put Vaseline on the little toe. This would help the abrasive effect on the toe. I found a stick and I was lucky to find this, it was the perfect size. I put the stick in my right shoe and pressed it next to the area of my small toe. I added as much pressure as I could trying not to break the stick, about nine or ten times. The idea here is to try and stretch the side of the toe area of the shoe if possible. The little stick was so perfect for this task that I put it in my backpack to work on the shoes throughout the day when I take my breaks.

It was now time to decide if I should go to Mt Thielsen or head to Diamond Lake for water. By looking at the topo strip map I figured that the mileage to Thielsen was nine or ten miles, pretty much all uphill. Diamond Lake was seven or eight miles, mostly downhill and flat. There's a store and restaurant down there but because I have eaten so many calories the last few days at Mazama Campground and Crater Lake snack shack it didn't appeal to me.

I was a bit thirsty but I will forge on to Thielsen. First, however, I would give the mystic water cache one more shot. So I laid my pack down just off the trail and headed back to the highway. I thought that Chance had told me that the H2O was north of the highway. To be safe, I crossed to the other side and retraced my steps for the last time.

ECSTASY OF MISERY

Almost immediately I found the water cache. It was not the half gallon water jugs I'm use to seeing but quart size bottles that were sort of hidden behind a log. Oh yeah, I was a happy dude. I would be styling now all the way to Thielsen Creek.

Upon grabbing the bottles, however, I found that they were empty. Oh no. One by one I picked them up and then the next to the last quart bottle was full. Hallelujah, Hollywood, at least I have a quart of water. I immediately drank half of it, getting the water into my system. I then headed back across the highway and picked up my pack and headed once again northward.

The PCT now heads through a nice forest towards Mt Thielsen. Most of the hike is now climbing without too many views. Three hours later at about 10am I reached Mt Thielsen Summit Trail. At this point I got a pretty good view of Diamond Lake below. A few minutes later I heard somebody coming up the trail. It was two ladies. I rapped to them for a bit. They were mother and daughter heading for the Mt Thielsen Pinnacle which lay at the very summit of 9182 foot Mt Thielsen. They climb it every year about this time and there were gorgeous views from the Pinnacle.

The ladies headed up the trail. I thought about going but the nagging and taxing goal of Canada was too strong. Today is August 26th. In five days it would be September. I remember when I did Washington back in 2000. I was so concerned and nervous about getting to Monument 78. It was scary then because August passed and September arrived and the weather got darker and darker. Now here it was August 26th and I was only one third done with Oregon. Oh man, when will the big dump hit?

So down the mighty PCT I went, heading for the Mt Thielsen run-off water. In about one mile I arrived at the Thielsen Creek, a beautiful creek, freshly made by the melting snow that was only a half mile away. Here I stopped to drink and fill up my tanks but I wasn't the only one there. Upstream just a little ways from me was a fellow with the same idea.

A few minutes later the old boy came up to me and asked if I was walking the PCT. I told him yes and he said so was he, but he was not in a hurry about it. Right away I could see this guy walked to the beat of a different drum. He was going to walk the whole PCT but was going to take years to finish.

His name was Bloody Stick because of the wooden staff he was walking with would often become bloody from his thin skin. The guy was just getting over a severely sprained ankle from when he got lost at Section O in California. "The goddamn trail was so bad, I got lost and then stepped on a log that rolled under me, and that happened somewhere down Bear Creek. I was laid up for damn near a week".

I asked the guy how he was doing now and he said, "Okay, but I'm about to run out of coffee and cigarettes. My Social Security check hasn't arrived yet. "How do you know that it hasn't, being out in the boonies, man?" I ask. He said that he has a pager and the lady at the post office down here will page him if it comes in.

Then the guy invited me to his camp that's just off the trail. "I just did my laundry and it's drying by that smoldering fire. They should be dry in a few hours and I'll probably head on." "Then you're heading to Canada?" He said that he's been heading to Canada for five years, a little here and a little there. "I'm achieving my life's goal," I said. He asked what that was and I said, "A permanent trail bum of the Pacific Crest Trail." Bloody Stick said it sounded like a noble endeavor.

I then noticed on his right arm a tattoo with an eagle and the American flag, just below it read "101 First Airborne, Vietnam." He had spent two years at the Hanoi Hilton. "Wow, man, that's something, it's something no one can imagine, man." "Yep, it's hard to forget alright, but such is life." "I was lucky to get out of that one, but I had to spend two and a half years in India to pull it off," I said. "I understand that place can be bad on the bowel movements." I told Bloody Stick that he was the man and said, "Thanks for going, you did what you thought was right. You did show that Americans were willing to go to the other side of the world to make a stand on communism."

I told Bloody Stick that I thought I had some coffee in my bag. In fact, I had been carrying it for the last 200 miles. I don't even seem to have time to drink it except at night and that's not conducive to falling asleep. "What about when you get up?" he asked.

"No, the harsh reality of just getting out of my sack is a rude enough. I gave the instant coffee to Bloody Stick and you could tell he was happy.

ECSTASY OF MISERY

"Thanks, buddy."

I told the guy I had to punt. I wanted to get to Echo Lake tomorrow. "What's your hurry?" he said. "I'm running late and I'm afraid of the big dump."

"The big dump, what's that? You mean you need a toilet to take a big dump? You must be really stoved up." I explained that it's a big snow storm that could keep me from reaching Canada this year. "Oh hell, just pick up where you left off next year," he said.

"I wish I could but I'm not a free man like you are. I may never come this way again." With that I left Bloody Stick at his camp with his smoking laundry and headed once more into the mystic.

It's good-bye to the lightning rod of the Cascades, which is often the nickname for Mt Thielsen. From what I've heard, it should be a required road trip. Hikers beware because it's a short hike but terribly steep. The trail was now quite fast, and I ambled toward 8031 feet Tipso Peak. I trudged along past mountain hemlocks and lodge pole pines heading for my destination for the day, Tolo Springs.

I remember back in 1998 I met Jason Lakey from Montana, he was a forest service worker there. This guy, trail name "Keep On Keeping On", he actually hiked from Crater Lake Lodge to Tolo Springs in one day. He was the first one that had started in Mexico to get to Canada. Most people that year flip flopped at Kennedy Meadows. This guy, however, went straight through the Sierras during a year that had a ton of snow.

The second guy through was Jonathan Bream, trail name "The Ghost", right behind Keep On Keeping On. I was glad I met both of these guys. I believe both of them walked the PCT in just over four months in a hard year, and in my opinion, they actually walked the trail. What I mean is, in my book, they had at least walked 98% of the trail or more. There's been a lot of great hikers on this trail but believe me, there have been a whole lot of not so great ones too.

I took a late lunch on a ridge just above Maidu Lake, which left me almost completely out of water. Now I would have to reach Tolo Camp Springs today. That's the next place for water. After a good lunch and the last of my pepper jack cheese I head down the trail with thoughts of Bloody Stick on my mind. I just can't imagine two years in a Vietnamese prison camp. Man, what a drag. It's got to do something to one's head, and I doubt that it's a good thing either.

The PCT, which is kept beautifully here in Oregon so far, winds around Mule Peak and about a mile later I arrive at Tolo Camp Springs. As soon as I got to the flat areas on the ridge, which is actually the campground, I noticed two tents and a couple of guys talking. On closer examination I realize that one of the guys is Chance. "Hey, buddy, what's happening?" "Wrong Way, we meet again." "Yeah, I can't believe I caught up with you."

Chance asked if I got the last bottle of water at Highway 138. Yes, I sure did, but it wasn't easy. I got there at dark and didn't find it until 7:00 the next morning. There was only one bottle left. "I know. I left it for you." I was surprised.

I hiked down to Diamond Lake Store." I told Chance that he shouldn't have done that, that I would have survived until I got to Mt Thielsen Creek. "I promised you there would be water, Wrong Way. I didn't want you to find nothing but empty bottles." "Man, that's damn white of you buddy. I appreciate it." I then asked Chance how he liked Diamond Lake. I told him that it used to be the old official route. "It's hurting pretty bad. There isn't any trout any more."

They had introduced fish that was supposed to eat the algae that was collecting on the lake but these fish also ate a lot of the trout's prey. The result is horrible fishing. Next year they're going to re-stock the lake, but this year the place is like a ghost town. "The restaurant is closed, only the store is open." "Bummer, I hope the place picks up in the future," I said.

A few more minutes of rapping and an introduction to Rick, a section hiker, then Chance and I headed down to the Springs which lay two or three hundred feet below the campsite. It was a hassle getting water from the springs. They were quite funky, with a lot of smelly mud around them. I didn't have to get water in 1998 down here because of a group of section hikers who gave me some filtered stuff. They were the same ones who gave water to Keep On Keeping On when he came jogging in at 9:30pm that night after starting 41 miles away at Crater Lake Lodge that morning! Back at camp we all talked and had some great laughs before we fell asleep around 9pm, or "campers midnight".

The next morning I was the first to get up. Chance was still asleep in his tent and so was Rick. I left at 6am almost in the dark. The days were really starting to get shorter now. Fall was on its way and I was still in Southern Oregon. I broke camp pretty quickly, probably in 10 or 15 minutes, due to the fact that I hadn't put up my tarp. So down the trail I went. My goal for the day was to get as close to Shelter Cove as possible so I could get there the following day and perhaps rest for a good half-day.

The early morning now was getting quite nippy. I kept my hands in the pockets of my nylon running pants. About a good half-mile after leaving camp I came to a trail junction with Tenas Peak Trail. I stopped there to check the map and to make sure I was on the right trail. Sure enough, the Tenas Peak Summit Trail broke off from the PCT and headed in a southerly direction.

So off I went, heading down towards Windigo Pass. About an hour and a half later I stopped at a creek to have breakfast. I probably spent 20 minutes there eating away when I began to be concerned that something was wrong. Where was Chance? Chance has a quick pace and usually gets pretty early starts. Why hasn't he caught up to me while I was eating breakfast?

After breakfast I headed back down the trail for another mile or so, walking slower and looking for foot prints. The trail was a good one, comparable to the PCT, but I hadn't seen the PCT emblem or the white diamond for some time. Now I began to worry. I should be at Windigo Pass now. This didn't seem right.

Suddenly I started to hear the noise of vehicles and I knew something was wrong. I checked out the topo strip map. Next to the page border it said Highway 138, 7 miles! I somehow got off the wrong trail and I was off the boundary of the topo map because the noise of the automobiles couldn't have been more than a mile away.

I've blown it somehow. Some way I had missed the PCT and had taken another damn trail. It was probably a trail that went from Highway 138 to Tenas Peak and probably had a trailhead at Highway 138. I could do one of two things. I could hike down to the highway and try to walk or hitchhike to Shelter Cove or go back to Tolo Springs Camp and find out how in the hell I went wrong.

I decided to head back and solve the mystery. God I am pissed off. How could I have done this? I'm infuriated with myself. Even though it was uphill almost all the way, I pushed nearly a four mile per hour pace.

About two hours later I was very close to Tolo Springs Camp when I rounded a corner and saw the flash of two huge animals standing up trail. They bolted off almost before I could get a good look at them. They were huge and looked like they could be moose. Wait a second. Are there moose in Oregon? I don't think so, but I swear I saw two of them.

A few minutes later I reached the trail junction with the Tenas Peak Summit Trail. I actually sat down to examine the map to make sure I was heading in the right direction. It looked from the map that I was. The portion of the summit trail is on the map but this map heading down to the highway isn't! Maybe it's a new trail. Where is the PCT? There is only one way to find out. I'll just have to head back to the Tolo Springs campsite and retrace my steps.

In just a few minutes I found out the problem. Right ahead of me was the PCT emblem, high on a Douglas fir tree. I had simply turned down this trail instead of heading straight. It was early in the morning and I had made this stupid turn to nowhere. I guess so early in the morning I don't think correctly. All I had to do was look up. I would have easily seen the emblems. There was nothing wrong with the trail markings. I bet only one fool out of a hundred has ever made this mistake. This is one morning that perhaps a cup of coffee would have been very appropriate and might have kept me from making this ridiculous mistake.

I headed down the PCT, happy to be back on it as well as relieved, but absolutely crushed. I had just walked some 10 to 12 miles out of the way. Yep, six miles down and six miles back up. Man, what a drag. I felt like hitting myself. I thought I was an ace. The time now was 12 noon. I had wasted damn near a half day. Down the trail I headed to Windigo Pass and finally at 2pm I reached Road 60 bordering Windigo Pass.

At the trailhead I noticed a yellow note. Reading it I found out that Meadow Ed had written it. The note said that he was walking different parts of the trail and that he was walking this section from Mt Thielsen to Windigo Pass.

You have to give the guy some credit for hiking. He's a big-boned guy with the build of a football lineman and he's 59 years old. One mile for him is equal to five miles for some of those young marathon type bodies like Frog, for instance.

From the pass and after eating lunch it's now 1:30. I headed once again to my destination, Shelter Cove over a distance of three miles. I slowly climb and head past Cowhorn Mountain. The trail descended a little and then levels out a bit as I entered the heart of Diamond Peak Wilderness. It was now 4pm, time to sit and have a break. Where will I crash tonight? It looks like Summit Lake will probably have to do. Trudging along I pass some hikers, a guy and a girl. Then three hours later I finally arrive at Summit Lake.

The trail skirts around the western edge of the lake along a dirt road. There are a number of campers there. Many of them have already started to light their campfires. Even though it's dark and I'm pretty wasted, I decide to walk towards the northern end of the lake in order to get a good start to Shelter Cove tomorrow.

After getting water out of the big blue lake I made some beef stroganoff for dinner from one of those Lipton dinners and some cheese with a flour tortilla.

What a day. I walked at least 26 miles today, but only 16 miles the right way. Way to go, Sherlock. By 1am I'm ready to crash for the night. I lay my mosquito-netted head down on my makeshift pillow. I check out a few million stars and fall asleep.

The next morning I arise early, about 6am, pretty much in the dark. To-day is resort day and my goal is Shelter Cove, Oregon. Right away I note that the ole legs are stiffer than usual. I think this is due to the angry fast pace that I made back to Tolo Springs Camp after I found out I was lost. Yep, lost in space. I just tortured myself with an ultra fast pace.

By 6:15 I was hiking and passing a ton of small lakes both to the left and right of the trail. Even though it's late in the season, there are a number of mosquitoes that cause me a bit of a problem. Out comes the Deet. It's the first time I've used the crap since Sky Lakes Wilderness.

It's good to have a beard because one can apply Deet to the hair instead of to the skin. Since it's not a real crowded sky of the little bloodsucking bitch-es, I use a 45% solution. It works well, giving me relief for about an hour, and within an hour I should be out of this lake zone.

I know that this area is relatively a new route for the PCT. The old route, which I have traveled, sits lower and lies to the east, I believe the old Oregon Skyline route. That area is more accessible to huge campgrounds that are located at the Crescent Lake area. This means more car-camping and horseback riding. The trail was obviously moved here to make the PCT more of a wilderness experience.

Soon I arrived at Mountain Creek. To the left of me is Diamond Mountain at an elevation of 8744 feet. Here at Mountain Creek I take a late breakfast of Carnation Instant Breakfast with extra thick milk. I also had a couple of fruit bars followed by some trail mix. That's about all I have left for food, except for a power bar and instant mashed potatoes. My pack is now at its lightest.

The temperature is a perfect 70 degrees as I head out north once again, anxious to reach Odell Lake and Shelter Cove, which are probably 10 or 11 miles away. It's now 1pm. Arrival time should be about 4:00 or 5:00 pm.

An hour and a half later I come to a half-decent lake with no name. I gather some water there and then apply potable water. I'm hoping I won't have to drink the stuff, but just in case, I carry a half quart.

At Midnight Lake I dump this water out in favor of the cleaner, deeper-looking lake water. As I head back down the trail I'm treated to the view of what I think is a reddish-looking little fox that scampers up a short ridge and disappears like Houdini. A few backpackers go by me. They look like teenagers, a group of five guys and six girls. That's a good balance. Man, it must be nice to be young!

Trudging along I see a number of backpackers heading towards me looking fresh as daisies and excited about the trip into the Diamond Peak Wilderness. Very soon I reach the trail sign that reads, "O'Dell Lake and Shelter Cove, one mile".

Twenty minutes later I crossed some railroad tracks and entered the Shelter Cove Campground. I immediately walked up to the log cabin store. This store also serves as a post office and the owners will hold packages here. Before I ask for my package I grab some Gatorade and chug it down. I like Gatorade and Powerade too, for besides hydrating you and supplying electrolytes, the sugar hits the old blood stream and really gives you a lift, at least for 20 minutes or so.

I asked for my box, no problem, it's here. That's always a good feeling to be greeted with. The lady collects the $2 fee, which I think is quite fair. She tells me that there are some picnic tables outside where I can sit and work on my pack. I asked the lady for a campsite for the PCT hikers and see that there's a special campground for us, free of charge. "All right, thanks a lot."

I then walked over to the picnic tables with my pack and ice cream sandwich. At the table I started working on my pack, dumping my trash out at the nearby trash bin and putting my new supplies in my pack. There's a letter from Trail Perfect and $30. I always like her letters. It helps to raise my spirits. Her choice of food is excellent, with a lot of variety. Oh yeah, there's some of that tangy chewy candy her dad, Charlie, always tosses in.

Just as I finish loading my pack, I hear, "Wrong Way, you finally made it." I look up and there is Rick, the guy I met with Chance at Tolo Springs Camp. "I got here an hour ago. What took you so long to get here?" "Dude, I got lost, went the wrong way and damn near ended up at the Old Cascade Highway!" "Wow, how did you do that?" "I don't know, man, tripping out, looking for a new attitude. It's my nature, that's how I got my trail name."

So Rick and I headed to the store and bought plenty of junk food and a couple of beers too. I don't consider beer junk food because the hops and herbs in there are plum good for you. Rick showed me the free PCT campground. All it was were some flat places to crash. There was only one picnic table but a section hiker and his wife occupied it. I popped my tarp up between two trees. Then Rick and I headed for the pay showers and laundromat.

After all these chores it was back to the store which had fresh grilled chicken they sell. While walking out of the store I noticed a strung out looking hiker who looked a bit familiar. "Hey dude, don't I know you?" "Yeah, I met you at the Saufleys, you're Wrong Way." "Wow, it's you, Frog, unbelievable, you finally caught up with me."

I gave Frog a Budweiser or two and started telling Rick about the Frogman, how he took two weeks off at Tuolumne Meadows, that he wasn't getting enough exercise so he spent a week in Yosemite Valley rock climbing. The second week he spent camping with his ex-girlfriend and now, here he is. Rick asked Frog how many miles a day he travels. "I don't know, probably 35 in this type of terrain." "You mean every day?" "Every day that I walk," Frog said. I said, "Yeah, he likes to party a lot. That's why he's not up in Washington some-where." Frog laughed a little bit. He thought the party thing was kind of funny. Frog said he'd been pounding the turf pretty hard the last 11 days without any rest and planned to take a layover day tomorrow.

I asked Frog if he heard about Zeb supposedly finishing the trail in 72 days. Frog said that he didn't know how he could have walked that fast, looking incredulously about the matter. Rick said he must be really fast. "Not really," said Frog. "I walked all the way with him from the Saufleys to Mt Whitney with Choo Choo, and both Choo Choo and I have a little faster pace. But I'll say one thing about him, he hardly ever stops except maybe to pull out a candy bar or something." "Yeah, but 72 days, that's too fast." "I heard of at least five layo-ver days, two of them were with the Saufleys'" I said. "Yeah, that's right," said Frog, "and who knows how many other layover days?" I said, "At that rate he probably will have nine or ten, that means on the days he walks he will have to hike nearly 45 miles per day and that's just too much. The guy has to eat and pick up packages; he's bound to do some negative miles like I did yesterday."

I told Rick and Frog that I get so tired of people bullshitting about what great hikers they are. "What in the hell can you see in 72 days? What experi-ences can you have compared to someone who takes 125 to 150 days? You're going to have to walk at night. Sounds pretty miserable."

One more thing I had to say was that I haven't seen the guys signature on any of the registers, including this one at Shelter Cove. Frog acknowledged what I was saying, but I could see that he didn't really want to comment on it any more. He was Zeb's friend for quite a few miles and nobody wants to not believe in another guy's story. Zeb was a nice kid; everybody liked him. Now he was the new record holder for the Class of 2003.

That night I probably fell asleep around 10pm. I had one of the best sleeps that I ever had on the trail because I didn't get out of the sack until 9am the next morning.

I was soon on my way down to the store where I met Rick sitting out on the table that rests on the wooden deck that overlooks beautiful Odell Lake. "Hey Wrong Way, try the blueberry muffins, they're outstanding." So I popped into that store and bought two muffins, one blueberry and the other a cinnamon spice with raisins. To get me started for the day I bought a large coffee. I was in heaven, man, what a way to get up. The coffee and the muffins were fantastic.

I went and sat with Rick and talked to him for a while. Then Frog and those two other section hikers came by. They were an older couple. The guy had an outstanding white beard. He liked his beard because little kids thought he was Santa Claus. We all sat there for about 20 minutes listening to trail hiking stories.

Then the subject of the fire came up. According to Jim, the guy who looked like Santa Claus, the trail was closed from Elk Lake area all the way to Olallie Lake. "You mean the Three Sisters Wilderness is closed?" I asked. "Yeah I believe so. You will have to get a ride around it." Frog was bummed out because he had heard that the Three Sisters and the Jefferson Wilderness were about the finest part of the PCT in Oregon. I told him what he heard was true.

I mentioned that my girlfriend, Linda, had told me when I called her the night before that the trail was only closed from McKenzie Pass to Olallie Lake and there was a shuttle of volunteers that will take you to Olallie Lake.

Rick came up with the idea of calling the forest service and I thought about calling the PCT Association. I had their number handy so I decided to call them using Rick's awesome calling card. I called and got a recorded message about the trail. It did mention the fire and according to the tape, the PCT was closed from McKenzie Pass to Olallie Lake, just like Trail Perfect had said.

After that call I called the PCT store to get a human voice, which I did. The lady at the store told me the same thing the tape had said. She added that there weren't anymore volunteer shuttles because of problems with day hikers and section hikers jumping on board. Now you were on your own.

There was a way to hitchhike by taking two different highways and then going east at Detroit, Oregon. Or you could hitch a ride down to the town of Three Sisters and grab a bus that would take you north all the way to Timberline Lodge. The problem with that was you would miss the trail section between

Olallie Lake and Timberline Lodge.

It was now 10am and I walked back to the campsite to pack up and get going. Rick wanted to come along, too. He was a cool young kid, 22 years old. He was a Biochemistry major at the University of Washington. Rick has lived in Bellingham, Washington, all of his life. He was all right and had some good stories of his life in Washington. Rick also knew about the famous pizza place along Highway 58 just west of Willamette Pass. I was planning to pig out there before heading north again into the great wide open.

By 11am we were heading up the trail leaving Cascade Summit, and Shelter Cove about an hour later. We arrived at Highway 58 and then headed east a short mile to a huge skiing lodge. It was quite a place. We walked up a flight of stairs and entered the lobby and soon found the dining area where they sold the pizza. We ordered a huge ultra large pepperoni pizza and a pitcher of the local dark beer that Rick recognized. Then we sat down in front of a big screen TV. It was great. The pizza was delicious, as was the beer.

We must have sat there for two hours feeding our faces. In fact, we ate all the extra large pizza and ordered a medium pizza with pineapple and ham. To go with the two pizzas we drank two pitchers of beer. I ate so much I thought I was going to burst. Rick was amazed. He did quite well himself, having at least six slices and a couple of glasses of beer. For me, it was definitely carbohydrate loading. But too much of everything is good for nothing!

Finally at about 3pm I came waddling out of there and we headed back down the highway to the trailhead. At Willamette Pass the trail starts to steadily climb. We passed Princess Creek about a mile further on the PCT, which is also where the Old Oregon Skyline Trail reaches Lower Rosary Lake. This is a pretty good size lake with a lot of campsites. You can see why, being so easily accessible from Highway 58 and only about two miles from the highway.

After Lower Rosary Lake we came to Middle and North Rosary Lakes which are much smaller. My stomach at this time feels a little better but I still feel stuffed and it has slowed my pace down, which is a good thing for Rick who has only been hiking for five or six days. For the rest of the day we rapped about our lives. I tell about my past three hiking experiences and he tells me about living in Washington state. It was nice having somebody to talk to. The time goes so fast.

It was now starting to get dark. The days are really starting to get shorter, as well they should be, for it's now August 29th and a in a couple of days it will be September. And here I am, only halfway done with Oregon.

Rick gave me some hope, however, when he told me to just keep walking, that I might run into some snowstorms, but it will most likely stop before too much snow falls on the ground. At the worst I might have to hold over a day or two until the snow melts. Last year Rick told me that a person could hike all the way up to November if he had to. He said that the winter snowstorms seem to come later as the years go by. Rain, however, was a different story. Rick said that I will definitely get some rain.

Eight o'clock rolls around. It is pitch dark when we get to Bobby Lake Trail. I told Rick let's take it to the lake because I've heard there are excellent camping spots there. So off we went with our lights strapped around our heads, trudging our way to Bobby Lake.

I told Rick about the 1998 hike when I missed this trail and took Trail 3663 down to the highway that went close to the huge Waldo Lake. "It was a bummer, man. Instead of just heading back, I walked the road for a while and slept in a real funky scary place. The next day I walked a couple more miles until I took Twin Peak Trail back to the PCT." So I thought it would be cool to hike this little section past Bobby Lake in order to patch up the gap in the mighty, sometimes illusive, PCT.

A few minutes later we arrived at Bobby Lake. It was too late really to look around for the awesome campsites that I've heard about. So we just found the first big flat spot we came to and set up Rick's tent and my tarp. Rick had the courtesy to let me know that he snored like a constipated bear so I moved a good 40 feet away from the guy. I have already learned my lesson with Snickers in the High Sierras. A loud snoring backpacker can mess up your night all right.

That night something special happened. Rick noticed it first, a celestial event for certain, Red Saturn. I have heard that Saturn's orbit would put the planet as close to Earth as it ever gets and that the planet would glow red. Wow, here at Bobby Lake I could finally see it. The last few nights I never noticed it because of all the trees that blocked the view. It was very impressive. We both took pictures of it even though I doubt that it will come out, especially with my little single use camera.

For dinner that night I only had some cheese and a flour tortilla. I wasn't hungry enough to cook because of the huge amount of pizza bubbling around in my gut. By not cooking I was saving fuel.

The next morning, August 30th, I got up early and was ready to leave. Rick was obviously awake because his snoring had stopped. I went to dig a hole and then came back and talked to Rick through the tent. "Hey buddy, I'm going to head out. I'll wait for you if you want me to but I plan to get at least 25 miles in today." "No, that's all right Wrong Way, I'm going for 15. Twenty five is too many for me; I'm not in that kind of shape." "All right, man, it was great hiking and pigging out with you. Best of luck in school." Then Rick said, "Thanks, just remember to keep on trucking. Don't stop until you get to Canada." "Alright man, keep a cool stool and live by the rules."

I left Bobby Lake pretty early, getting a good start. The words from Rick about the weather in Washington were a relief, but tomorrow is the last day of August; the summer is nearly gone. The days are shorter and I'm still in the middle of Oregon. My legs are feeling pretty good and my left knee has really never given me a problem since I left Mexico nearly four months ago.

My only problem now is my constant Morton Toe Syndrome. Now and then I will stub it on a rock. Wow, it can be painful. Another problem I have is my right little toe due to my new shoes that I received at Crater Lake, but it was already starting to work itself out. Chronic shin splints bother me once in a while, but so far, so good. I'm lucky so far to have walked this far, lucky that my loved ones at home are okay and just plain lucky to be here.

Late in the morning I reach Charlton Lake, a rather large lake with a nice blue color. A group of people were busy carrying a canoe down to the lake. In fact, as I now look out across the water, I can see many people at their campsites, eating, laughing, and having fun. It reminds me of the Rolling Stones song, "Smiling faces I can see, but not for me, I sit and watch as years go by."

I'm 56 years old now and I don't have a pot to piss in, but I've seen and felt so many things from my two and a half years in India with the Peace Corps, hitchhiking to New York and some 6000 miles on the trail of the Pacific Mountains. I've been around the world and I'm thankful for that. I'm lucky, that's for sure, lucky to still be here walking the earth. Well, I guess that's my Sunday sermon to myself. Now it's time to dislodge myself from this rock and head north on the greatest trail devised by mankind, the Pacific Crest Trail of the United States of America.

Shortly after leaving Charlton Lake I hear the sounds of walking feet behind me. I look behind me and there's Mr Speed himself, the young Frogman of Canada. No use in speeding up, might as well let the Frogman pass. "Wrong Way, I thought you would be further along than this." "I would have but I spent some three hours devouring pizza and beer." "That's no excuse," he says. "Let's see what you got then, man." "I think the only reason that you caught up with me is because you've been yellow blazing it all the way from Mexico." That pissed the Froggy Boy off and he tore out in his spandex shorts at a five mile an hour clip.

I started hauling butt myself, trying to catch up with him and for a while, I did. The terrain was flat and fast, with a few turns here and there. In fact, Frog was leaning into his turns like a roller derby player! I finally felt tightness in my hamstrings so it was time to slow down. There's no sense in pulling a muscle. At 56 years old, the flexibility is gone. A hiker at this age has got to know his limits or he may not be able to walk very well the following day.

Pretty soon I headed around Taylor Lake and Irish Lake, which were very pretty and located right next to each other. To the east of me were an incredible number of lakes, according to the trail guide. I was now in the Three Sisters Wilderness. I rounded a bend and who do I see but the Frogman, coming out of the bushes where he must have dug a hole. "Had to dig a hole, buddy?" "Yeah," he says, and then flies by me once again as I chuckled to myself. Down the trail I went on another perfect day. About an hour later I reached a small lake called Storm Lake and once again found Frog, but this time he was eating lunch.

So I sat down and prepared lunch for myself. I started rapping to Frog. He wasn't angry any more and he started telling me about his life of adventure. He had walked the Appalachian Trail last year and was always doing cool things.

After he walks the PCT he's going back to Calgary where he lives, and then ride his bike to Provo, Utah. Wow, some guys have all the luck.

By the time I had prepared my chicken and noodles Frog was done with his lunch and got up to leave. Before he did he turned around and gave me a compliment. "You know, Wrong Way, I have to admit that you're a good example for an old fart that keeps in shape. I don't think there are too many guys your age that can do what you're doing!" "Well thanks a lot, young stud, I appreciate that." Then Frog was off again, heading north at an insurmountable rate of speed.

One thing Frog told me was that Elk Lake would accept packages. In the town guide I read that they didn't, but once again being a computer illiterate has not helped me on this trip.

A few minutes later I was off again walking by a host of small lakes. This was a land of thousands of lakes, more than Sky Lakes Wilderness, south of here. That evening I reached Cliff Lake, one of the large lakes in the area, and a place that I had camped before.

In 1998 I had spent a night here. The place had a shelter, but it was condemned at the time. I was surprised that the place was still standing. There's a sign posted not to enter, but the place should be torn down just in case someone enters it because it looks like it could fall at any time.

Cliff Lake looks like its descriptive name. Rocky cliffs surround the lake, a little bit like a lake a hiker sees in the Sierras. The last time I was here I met a couple that was heading south back to Kennedy Meadows. They were in love and had met on the PCT somewhere down south. She was from New Jersey and he was from Eugene, Oregon. I wonder if they made it; I wonder if they stayed together. They sure were infatuated with each other, that night anyway.

Tonight I camped in the same spot that I camped back in 1998, but this night I had a much sounder sleep. The trail back to the PCT is about a quarter of a mile and at that trail junction a hiker has to be careful that he or she doesn't hike west toward Porky Lake. This is a land of a zillion lakes and I'll tell you one thing, I wouldn't want to be around here during the mosquito season. Speaking of seasons, today is the last day of August. I can't believe that tomorrow is September.

ECSTASY OF MISERY

Down the trail I jam. Today I can get a hot meal at Elk Lake Lodge. I was at this place back in 1998. At that time I had a supply package pick-up at the lodge. The lodge also had somewhat of an infamous character named Leroy who owned the place.

Hikers would tell of his harsh treatment of them and all his crazy signs he had hanging on the walls. For instance, "Don't read the books, this isn't a library." Another read, "Do not put trash in this can, it's not your personal garbage disposal." Don't do that, don't do this, no, nope, not even that. I actually felt that it was quite humorous. Hikers who stayed the night had to stay in one designated area.

There was one positive thing about the place. Leroy did serve some good food. His cheeseburgers were excellent as were his breakfasts, and he had Dreyer's Ice Cream. I believe the guy didn't like hikers because he made little money off them and probably because thru-hikers, especially, have a bit of a smell to them. He thought I was okay, probably because I spent a few dollars there. I was older than the usual hiker and I gave him a compliment on his food.

During my short stay there I was fortunate to meet a great trail hiker named Brice Hammick. I first saw him when he came walking out of a nasty rainstorm, a storm that even the locals were a bit shocked by. The rain came down in sheets and torrents. I was glad that I was in the lodge. However, my gear was outside under a picnic table with my tarp draped over it.

When the rain stopped an hour later Brice and I walked over to the designated sleeping area. I was delighted to find that my stuff had stayed dry in what I think was just about the largest rainfall I have ever seen. I have seen some mean ones in Oklahoma where I went to school for a year, and in India where I went through the monsoon season. The drainage at the thru-hiker's hill was elevated so all the water rolled away from the hiker. If someone happened to camp below the hill, their stuff would have washed straight into the lake!

Brice set up his tent a few feet away from me. We began talking. "Dude," I said. "What in the hell are you doing out here? Man, you're not the youngest guy I've seen on the trail." "No, I'm not, but I still do all right. I did 18 miles today." "How old are you, buddy?" "I'm 78 years young, son." "Wow, dude." He told me to call him Brice and I then asked what did his wife think about all of this and the old man said, "She's happy that I'm doing what I love."

Brice then tells me about himself and I was amazed. He lives in Oregon and is a retired trail builder; he still donates his time working on the mighty PCT. He had walked all three major trails in the United States: the Appalachian Trail, the PCT, and the Continental Divide Trail, all after he was 60 years old. "Holy smoke, dude, I mean Brice, that's outrageous. I thought I was old at 56, just trying to walk the trail through Oregon." "You're doing fine, just keep on walking, you most likely have a number of years left."

I remember it just like it was yesterday. Here it is 2003, and I'm still free on the PCT. Soon I notice that the multitude of lakes is dissipating. I can see by the trail guide that I'm drawing close to the Elk Lake Trail Junction. Suddenly I'm walking through a fire rampage area.

I had heard about this fire a year or so ago. For a while the Elk Lake Lodge was in danger. Frog thought it had survived. Heading out at a pretty fast pace, I notice that there are a couple of senior citizens on horseback. They tell me that the cut off trail is only about a half mile ahead.

Two miles later I reach the turn off where I have to make a decision. Should I go or should I stay. Hey, wasn't there a rock and roll song like that? "Should I stay or should I go now?" No, I better not start to mutter it or it will stick in my head and I'll think about it over and over until it drives me crazy. Just like that damn Locomotion. It took me a week to get over that one.

Finally the hunger pains for a greasy gut bomb flow across my mind. Down the trail I go heading for Elk Lake Lodge. About a half hour later I arrive at the place and it hasn't changed a bit. At least until I get to the lodge itself. I notice that the multitude of "Don't do that or this" signs are gone!

Inside the place looked the same. I ordered a cheeseburger and fries with a chocolate shake. The waitress looked like she was half here and half somewhere else. Finally after 25 minutes she brings me a dried up, funky cheeseburger. Instead of fries, I get one of those little bags of Lays Potato Chips. It's not a complete disaster, however, because the chocolate shake is excellent. I guess at least that's one thing that was a carryover from Leroy's ownership.

ECSTASY OF MISERY

After eating I check out the PCT camping hill. The lake just doesn't look as blue as it did before. I remember that there is cell phone reception here and I make a call to Trail Perfect who gives me the current news on the fire ahead. Then I phone Chuck Hinkle, who I've been worried about. I know that by now he has been checked out at the University of Southern California Medical Center.

So I call Chuck, but he wasn't home. His friend Wilma was and tells me that he is doing better and the tumor is benign. That's great news. Then she tells me that he had a blood clot that has to shrink before they can work on the tumor. I tell Wilma to let Chuck know that I had called. I say good-bye, greatly relieved about the news.

I've been at this place for about an hour and a half. The place seems dead, so I take my pack up the trail with my belly filled and feeling relief. I head north once again, in search of the Three Sisters.

The PCT now climbs slightly and then heads over to the western slope of Koosah Mountain, with a moderate elevation of 6520 feet. Near the eastern slope of this mountain I enjoy a fine view of Elk Lake, Hosmer Lake, Bachelor Butte, and finally the South Sister, at an elevation of 10,358 feet.

From there I head down northwest, still thinking about the funky hamburger at Elk Lake Lodge. I soon arrive at Camelot Lake. The lake looks pretty shallow to me. I take out a bit of water and then march right on heading for the South Sister.

Almost immediately after leaving I notice the presence of smog, but this is not smog like I'm used to in the LA and Orange County area of Southern California. This is smoke. I'm now definitely getting closer to the humongous fire that I've heard about since I arrived at the Crater Lake area.

A half mile further I enter a part of the trail that I always seem to remember, Wickiup Plain. This is a large bizarre flat area in which the South Sister lays almost beside it. This is high plain drifting at its best. I love it. The trail is easy and you can see it for at least a mile or more in front of you.

I can now smell the smoke. The area also looks dryer and not nearly as green as it was back in 1998. It could be because it's later in the season, but I've also heard that this part of Oregon had a lot less rainfall in the last few years.

Down the trail I can see two figures heading towards me. I soon can tell that they are two girls. A few minutes later, we approached each other. They were Jill and Janis who were hiking from McKenzie Pass to the Horse Lake Trail that will take them to Cascade Lakes Highway where one of their cars is parked. From there they will drive back to the pass area where they would pick up their other car and head back home to the small town of Sisters, Oregon.

These two girls were really funny as they tell me stories of their small town. Janis had lived in Reseda, just a short distance from LA in the San Fernando Valley. She got into too much trouble there so her family sent her to Sisters where she has lived for two years now. Her friend, Jill, was born in Bend, Oregon, but now lives in Sisters. I said good-bye and they said good luck on my trip and then they were gone.

About a half hour later I arrived at Mesa Creek with a few springs running down into it. I'm hungry now and with fresh clean water I decide to make dinner. Mac and cheese with a couple of flour tortillas do me right. For dessert I had a Three Musketeers candy bar and some raisins.

It's starting to get late now. I have perhaps an hour or so of light left, so I might as well try and get a few more miles under my belt for the day. By 7:30 it's already pretty dark. I think the slow increasing smoke causes most of the darkness from the fire. Just past Separation Creek I crash on a barren gravel and sandy type of beach but without a lake or ocean. It's pretty flat and actually kind of soft too.

The sunset in the west is quite a sight as it dips into the horizon underneath all the brown smoke. This is a lonely place but there are no insects and it's a soft landing for the night. There's absolutely no place to tie up my tarp. I hope it doesn't rain. My little transistor radio picks up a country western station from Bend, Oregon. They don't mention any rain so I fall asleep feeling pretty confident.

The next morning it was relatively easy to get up due to the fact that I was completely out in the open and the sun hit me rather early. It was a beautiful morning. The smoke had at least temporarily left the area. Just to the east of me was the Middle Sister lit up in gold from the morning sun. I broke camp in about 10 minutes and was hiking by 6:30am.

ECSTASY OF MISERY

The walking was very flat and fast from here. I would walk around the North Sister and then head somewhat of an eastern direction circling the North Sister and then north a bit to the highway below. It was a good 20 miles or more. That would be my goal for the day to reach McKenzie Pass at Highway 242. Here I would be restricted to go further north on the PCT because of that damn fire that's been burning now for almost three weeks, or I would have to hitchhike west to US Route 2, then north to Detroit, Oregon, where I would again have to hitch a ride to Olallie Lake.

Here it is, I'm dodging a fire that I was told I wouldn't have to if I didn't flip flop. It really doesn't matter. This isn't a race. Fires hit every year or so near or along the PCT. A thru-hiker is lucky these days if he is able to hike the whole PCT. Southbound hikers are especially vulnerable to Southern California fires that pop up from September to November. They're usually caused by the Santa Ana winds and maybe sometimes with so many people with four-wheel drives who want to try it out, the hazard of a fire becomes greater every year, especially in the drought years.

Hikers that are faced to take alternate routes, even if they have to get a ride, are credited for the area they missed. For me, I'm lucky because I have covered this part of the trail from McKenzie Pass to Olallie Lake and it's a beautiful one too. The Santiam Pass area, with Three Finger Jack, is awesome. The Jefferson Wilderness is definitely a jewel in itself.

I decided to have breakfast at Sister Springs and Obsidian Falls. Usually there are many people around this area of the Sisters because it's beautiful and easily accessible. But this fire and this smoke make it a deterrent. In fact, as I look at my watch and press the date button, "Oh my, it's September the first today. Isn't this Labor Day weekend or something?"

Obsidian Falls are really quite nice. The water cascades down a cliff about 35 feet or so and the water is good and sweet. I don't cure it with my iodine pills. I haven't used my pills in quite a while. I really can't stand them.

After breakfast I head back to the trail which is only 150 feet away. I make a left hand turn and I'm back on the trail. At this point I have circled the North Sister and the trail enters a heavily volcanic area. Minnie Scott Spring is a delightful place to visit. Water here comes right out of the rocky sandy ground below. This is great water and one of my favorite springs along the whole trail.

The trail now climbs up Cinder Field, nothing but volcanic rocks; something like moon lands in the Sierras but the rocks are a dark brown color. Some of the little hills here are almost sandy and when one takes a step, a hiker's foot slips back making the going a little tough, but no big deal. The fantastic PCT then heads right by Yapoah Crater. Oh man, what a scene, what a great day to be alive. I then notice more and more smoke rolling in.

A couple of hours later the trail crosses Scott Pass and for the first time since I saw the two girls, Janis and Jill, I find a guy and his dog sitting on a volcanic rock. The guy doesn't look too happy. His dog jumps off the rock and comes over to me and gives me a sniff. "How's it going, man," I say to the guy.

The guy tells me not too well and begins complaining about the fire. He goes on and on about it. "I can't believe that they can't put the damn thing out. They could have, but no, they have to go out of their way to protect Camp Sherman. While they're doing this the fires go completely out of control." I said that's the way it is usually done, to protect any structures. "No, the only reason they protected the dump is because his highness, President Bush, was going to stop there for a visit. In fact, the fire started just a couple of days before he got there. I think it was started so he could push his 'thinning the forest out' program."

This guy went on to say a guy from Bend, Oregon, said that the people in the area say it started in two different areas just three miles apart and there weren't any lightning strikes that night. "Sounds like arson alright," I said. "Yep, and it was also started on President Clinton's birthday too." "Pretty suspicious," he said. "I drive all the way from New Mexico to walk this section of the trail and what do I get but a damn fire."

The guy was definitely upset; I thought it was kind of cool because I'm a bit of a complainer myself. That's how I run, that's how I motivate myself, too. Now I get to listen to this guy who completely carried the conversation. He just knew that Bush's people or the lumberjacks started the fires. I told him that I heard on my radio Bush making that comment how the forests needed to be thinned out, and he said it was on national TV too. "Do you know all the money behind this for the lumber companies and forest workers and such?" "Quite a bit, I've seen a lot of it in the last 2000 miles, sometimes it looks like they're doing a pretty good job and sometimes it looks horrible, like just south of Sierra City."

I started to tell him the story of the 'space man' but he didn't really want to hear it. Instead he rambled on about Oregon and how he hated the place. Meanwhile, his dog was having a great time running around in the thin forest and the rocks. "Muffy, get over here." Muffy looks up and then reluctantly returns to the guy on the rock.

Finally the dude calms down a little and I introduce myself as Wrong Way from LA. "Wrong Way," he says. "Why would you call yourself Wrong Way, for god's sake?" "It's a long story, dating back to high school football and my 1978 hike of California." "Okay, well my name is Bernard and my trail name now I guess is "No Gear". A guy I met named Smiles A Lot called me that when we crossed the trail near Crater Lake." "Hey, I met Smiles A Lot, he was walking the whole trail north to south," I said. "Yeah, that sounds like the guy." We both agreed that it's a small world.

I then tell No Gear that I'm going to have to hitch a ride west to Highway 2 and enter back through the highway that goes east from Detroit, Oregon, to Olallie Lake. I told him that I'm probably going to camp at a campground near McKenzie Pass. "You know, Wrong Way, if you need a ride to Olallie Lake, I can at least give you a ride to Highway 2." "That's great, but I don't want you to go out of your way."

No Gear said that it wouldn't be a problem and that he could take me all the way to Olallie Lake, but that he had both his van and motor home parked down the highway. "Well, I have a California driver's license and I'm insured with AAA." "Oh yeah?" he starts to perk up. He asks why would I want to go to Olallie Lake. "I'm tired of this smoke and I can do the section from Olallie Lake to Timberline Lodge."

No Gear said to me, "If you can drive all the way to the next gas station and then to Olallie Lake, I can then spend some time there and drive up to Government Camp. Then I would hike back to the lake, pick up my trailer home and return to Government Camp." "That sounds cool, man," but in my mind I'm wondering how does this guy shuffle two vehicles around. He can't unless his dog Muffy can drive!

Okay, it's a done deal. So Bernard Goldscream and I head down the trail towards the highway and McKenzie Pass. Along the way I'm hearing No Gear talk about his exploits of the PCT, which were kind of impressive, for he had hiked every bit of the PCT to this point. It's taken him eight years, but somehow he's done it.

What I didn't understand was how he shuffled two vehicles around, so I asked him. "Well I park one at one location, then I usually hike south to another location and then hike back to the one in the previous northern position." "I see, but what do you do to the previous one you parked when you started?" "I simply drive that one to a new northern location and walk south, back to the one in the southern location." "Okay, man, I get it." But something is wrong here, I'm saying to myself. Somewhere along the line it's not going to work out. I'll let the reader figure it out. Right now I'm just too damn tired to crunch the numbers. This guy is so far out, I feel like I'm back in the 60s on a tab of "Sandous Orange."

Down the trail we both walk with Muffy jumping around and splashing herself in a couple of small lakelets on the way. After reaching the highway we walk east a little towards a parking lot. We then climb into the van but Muffy is reluctant. No Gear has to pick her up and put her in the van. "She doesn't like this van too much because it bounces around. She prefers the motor home," No Gear says.

So now we head down to the McKenzie Highway for a mile or two. We then turn off at an open area along the road. Around the bend, low and behold, we pull up to No Gear's motor home. It wasn't very big, but quite nice from the outside, probably 20 to 25 feet in length.

This area was actually a parking lot for a trailhead that went south back into Three Sisters Wilderness. The smoke here was pretty bad, but as evening came, it seemed to lift. I made my crash site at the far end of the parking lot where there was a large pit of gravel. I spread some of the gravel out and crashed there. It was very comfortable. That night I fixed No Gear and myself dinner, since I had plenty of extra food.

ECSTASY OF MISERY

No Gear started telling me about himself. First he lived in Georgia, where he bought a house but was run out of the neighborhood by drug dealers. I asked him why he would buy in a neighborhood like that and he told me it was actually a nice place when he first looked at it. "Hey, Wrong Way, drug dealers often live in nice neighborhoods, they can afford it." I asked why he moved. He said, "Because of the constant traffic and a couple of shootings." "Yeah, that would do it for me," I said.

After that No Gear moved to New Mexico where he lived on an Indian reservation. "I almost got in a wreck with the chief's son and they told me on no certain terms that I better leave! Then I got interested in hiking the PCT and I've been at it quite a few years now." "Well, that's a fun life. How do you support yourself? That stuff takes money." "Well I won a lawsuit and came into a few dollars." "Oh yeah, why did you sue?" No Gear thought for a second. "I'd rather not talk about it." "Okay, man, that's cool. I think I'll crash now. It's been a long day," I said.

So No Gear headed back to his motor home with Muffy. "Hey, I'll see you around 9am," he said. "That late?" "Yeah I don't get up too early." I told him okay, bro, and I'll see him then. I lay down on my sleeping bag for a while trying to figure out this guy's trip in life. Man, he was a peculiar dude.

The next morning I stayed in the sack longer than usual due to No Gear telling me about getting up late. It was nice to sleep in, but by 8:30 I had to get up and go dig a hole. After that I spent some time making a small breakfast and reading my Oregon road map. 9:30 rolled around but no No Gear.

Finally at 9:45 I decided to knock on the guy's motor home door. Right before I did that, however, I heard the dude starting to stir around inside. Then the guy starts making these loud yawning noises, I mean loud ones.

So I go back to my campsite and sit down on the gravel and start killing time by throwing pieces of gravel at a tin can. It's now after 10am. By now I would have been on the trail and already have walked eight miles. The loud yawns keep going on now intermittently. Finally the door opens up and Muffy jumps out and takes a pee.

It's now time to get No Gear into action because it's after ten and I'm bored as hell out here. I knock on the side of the damn camper. No Gear pops his head out of the window. "What?" he says. "Hey, man, it's 10:30, we're burning daylight out here. I thought you got up a 9:00." "Oh sorry, I'll be ready to go in just a few minutes." About 10 minutes later No Gear comes out of his box, raises his hands in the air and makes one of those yawning noises. "Sorry I slept so long. I had a long day yesterday." He asked how long I've been up and I told him about two and a half hours. I thought I slept in!

A few minutes later he gave me the keys to the van and we were off, heading east down Highway 242 to Highway 2, and then north about 35 or 40 miles to Detroit, Oregon. It felt really weird to be driving again. It had been a while since I had driven a car. The highway was very narrow at times, consequently the going was slow, but finally we reached Highway 2 and made a right turn and headed north.

Everything was going along pretty good when No Gear suddenly pulls his RV off the road and comes over to me and says he needs gas. "I believe Detroit is only 30 miles or less. I'm sure they will have gas." "Okay," he says. "I hope we can make it." "Well I hope so too. There isn't any gas around here so let's head north," I said. Man, what's next with this guy. It's now after 11am. By now I would have walked 10 miles for the day.

About 15 minutes later we naturally run into road construction and now we're waiting in a line of vehicles. It's now stop and go. After twenty minutes of this we reached the makeshift stop sign. We are in front of the pack.

A Mexican guy is holding up the stop sign. No Gear looks pissed and he's trying to communicate with the guy, but to no avail. Five minutes later after a large dump truck goes by, the Mexican guy gives us the go ahead.

We're off again. It's now 11:30 and we're probably 20 miles from Detroit. Along the way we pass a road junction that reads "Santiam Pass – Three Fingered Jack 25 miles". Wow, I would know just where I am if I were on the trail, but on this small highway, I'm almost lost.

Finally we reach the outskirts of Detroit and on the other side of the highway is a gas station-grocery store. The problem is the middle of the road is torn up and you can't cross it. I follow behind No Gear for about a quarter of a mile, when he suddenly decides to make a U-turn. It's a bad place to do this because there's a curve in the road not too far ahead.

ECSTASY OF MISERY

After waiting for a few vehicles, No Gear makes his turn. It's slow but at least no cars appear to be coming around that curve. No Gear makes it, and now it's my turn. I start the turn. It looks good. I'm about halfway completed when a clown in an orange muscle car comes hauling around the corner. I've finished my turn, thank god, but I can't gain speed fast enough so I pull off the highway just far enough to let him go by. The guy in the orange muscle car then yells out, "You stupid asshole." I can't blame him really, but if the stupid shit wasn't driving so fast, there wouldn't have been much of a problem.

Now I'm pissed off at No Gear. "How in the hell did you ever get this far from New Jersey? No wonder the Indians ran you out of New Mexico." Up ahead, No Gear tries to pull into the gas station, but a chick in a Saturn beats him to the pump. No Gear pops out of his box and starts giving her a hard time. The chick flips No Gear off and No Gear stomps back into his camper all upset and I'm laughing "good for you lady". I'd like to flip him off right now, but it would serve no positive function.

After getting gas, we head out from Marion Junction and head north again on Highway 22 to Detroit, Oregon. About 20 minutes later we finally arrive at Detroit.

No Gear for once did something smart and pulled into a gas station that had a small grocery store. He soon became upset that they didn't have propane for his piss tuber. They did have some good eats. They had homemade burritos and some other delicacies. I bought the food and gave No Gear a couple of burritos and a soda. I had already given him $20 for gasoline at Marion Junction.

Everything was going pretty smoothly now, but I guess I spoke too soon because No Gear got into an argument with the lady that owned the store. We had asked the lady where the nearest Forest Service headquarters was. She tells him it's just up the street.

Then No Gear also brings up his theory about the Bush people or at least lumber company people who purposely started the fire so the President could go up in the helicopter. Then he could push his selective cutting program to thin out the forest.

The lady then gets upset and tells No Gear that it was environmentalists that started the fire! That in turn gets No Gear upset and he says why in the hell would environmentalists start the forest on fire and that it was ridiculous because they supposedly hate Bush.

On and on they went. There was a giant redneck guy in there buying a supply of Miller beer who started to overhear the situation and was getting concerned about it. I jump in and said both theories are absurd. It was probably just a nut or two that started it.

I then shuffle No Gear out of the store and told him, "Co-exist, dude, this isn't your turf. This isn't Hoboken, New Jersey, man. When in Rome, do as the Romans do, don't yell fire in a crowded store. Now let's get the hell out of here before they raise the parking rates."

So off we went heading north when we should have been heading east towards Olallie Lake, because No Gear now had to visit the National Forest Service office. We drive about a mile outside of town. No Gear pulls into the parking lot with me following in his van.

No Gear goes into the place and asks about the latest news on the fire. The lady tells him this and that and he questions this and that. He then starts to tell her how the fire should have been fought.

Trying to ease things a bit, I start making cool little jokes, trying to put humor into the situation, until finally the lady tells him, "Well I've told you all the news I have. We're really sorry about the fire. If we only knew that you were coming all the way out here from the east coast, perhaps we would have tried harder to stop it. It's not like we like to see the whole forest go up in smoke around here. It's the facts, Mr Goldscream, we just didn't know you were coming." And then she walked off, leaving No Gear Goldscream ready to scream!

No Gear was befuddled, festered to the max. He couldn't do anything about it, but asked me why I was so happy. I told the dude that anytime I'm near the Pacific Crest Trail I'm happy, and if we ever get to Olallie Lake, I will be even happier. I asked him if he knew that it's already 1pm and we've only gone 60 miles today and still have 40 miles to go directly east, and some of that may be a gravel road. "So let's go man, the trail is waiting for us, dude!"

Finally, a few minutes later, we headed out back to Detroit and across the bridge with Detroit Lake below us. We made a left turn and headed east. I followed behind No Gear's motor home, trying to get some decent music on the radio, without much luck.

The drive seemed to take forever, like it would never end. Soon we arrived at another intersection that had a sign that said "Olallie Lake, 3 miles". That was good news. The bad news was that the road was pretty bad. No Gear drove at a five to six mile per hour pace. I stayed behind in the van, eating dust all the way to Olallie Lake.

We entered Olallie Lake parking lot and there was the lake. It's usually a beautiful lake with a super view of Mt Jefferson behind it. But now it looked like Baden Powell in August looking across the San Gabriel Valley, back at home. In fact, it was worse. We parked and entered the store. The place hadn't changed a bit. I asked for my supply box. I received it pretty quickly.

We walked around the store and I bought us a cold drink and ice cream. No Gear began asking the kid who ran the store about the fire, how far could a hiker walk south from here.

While No Gear was being a bit of a nuisance as usual, I began reading the PCT register. There was Lug Nut, Huff and Puff, Free Radical, Long Haul, and Choo Choo. Dave and Brooke had come through the day before. Then there was Prune Picker, Northerner, Yogi and Luna, but no Cruising Carson or Zeb boy.

Some of these people were well out in front but there were a group of hikers that were not far ahead, like Just Paul, Mercury, Prune Picker and Apple Pie, who I think were a couple. What really surprised me was the fact that the group of people that were supposed to be in front of me were not in the register! Did they take the bus out of Bend, Oregon, or the Sisters, all the way to Government Camp? It could be because they sure were not in the book.

The last guy registered was the insurmountable Frog. I read his entry. In it he says he got here from McKenzie Pass in three quick rides. He had left today, 9/2/03. Man, that's what I should have done instead of riding with this crazy man, No Gear, which took a while: eight hours just to go north 40 miles, ridiculous to say the least.

I had to interrupt the incessant New Jersey accented No Gear to ask about a shower. The guy told me it was five dollars for five minutes. "Wow, that's quite a bit, man." The guy just raised his shoulders and said, "I don't set the prices around here." Then No Gear said I could use his shower in his mobile home. Sure, why not save five bucks.

From the store we went down the road towards Brittenbush Lake where No Gear almost got his RV stuck. After that we went back to the store area and found a campground, about a half mile south of Olallie Lake. That night I made dinner for No Gear since I had extra food.

After dinner I took a shower in No Gear's RV. What a nightmare that was! It was a mess and smelled of B.O. and dog hair. His shower didn't have a floor. I had to stand on each side of an open hole. "Don't stay too long," he said. "I don't have much butane left to heat the water." That wasn't going to be a problem. I took one of the quickest showers I've ever taken.

On the way out, while trying to negotiate the obstacles that lay every-where, I tore my black nylon running pants. Unbelievable. I hike all the way from the Mexican border through all kinds of terrain, all kinds of bushes, like Manzanita and stuff, without any tears. But in five minutes in No Gear's RV, I rip a funky hole in the right leg.

Now outside and relieved, I sat my sleeping stuff on a flat area. I then cleaned up the picnic table and put things away. This is something No Gear doesn't have to do. Being in an RV, you're shielded from nature, bears, chip-munks, squirrels, and those mountain Blue Jays are no problem, although god only knows what crawling creatures No Gear probably has in there. I say good-bye to the guy, but not goodnight, because tomorrow I will be long gone by the time he gets up.

By 9pm, I'm sleeping. It's been a long day, not physically hiking all day, but a mentally straining day. Dealing with No Gear was very taxing. I haven't learned to set the alarm on my watch but I figure that I usually wake up pretty early anyway, and snooze a little. This time I won't snooze. I'll just go.

The next morning was more like late night. I awoke at 4:30am and was off stumbling in the dark at 5:00. My headlight strapped around my head was really helping me because I had bought new batteries. I headed down the road to the store, which was closed. There were some fishermen heading out on their boats, going for the early morning catch. I headed right for the trailhead which I knew well from my 1998 trip. I then bolted north, toward Canada.

The hiking was easy. In fact, I should be able to get quite a few miles in today with the early start and my rested legs. By 6am I probably had gone some three miles or so when it started to get light. I can't believe how the time is starting to change; it doesn't get light until around 6am now and by 7pm it's dark. The PCT now seems to go around the main local landmark in the area, Olallie Butte. The trail is basically flat and fast. There are no views and no water, especially after Toad Lake.

I remember this area well from my last visit. It's an area that is probably the easiest hiking on the whole trail. Today I have set a goal to hike the most miles that I have ever hiked in my life in one day. It will be a new record to put in the annals of history.

The morning is finally starting to warm up and I have seen quite a few animals scurrying about for their breakfast. That included at least 20 deer and one bear cub who ran off with the speed of a greyhound.

At Trooper Springs I decided to eat breakfast. The water there looked pretty good. Fifteen minutes later I was hiking again, on my quest to do the most miles in one day for me, ever!

Now the trail climbs a little to South Pinhead Butte which really isn't much of anything. I believe I'm now in the Warm Springs Indian Reservation, but I'm not sure. I can see a pretty good view of the fabulous Mt Hood. Just below Mt Hood are Government Camp and Timberline Lodge. At the lodge I will receive my next package. The trail is smooth and incredibly fast and I think I'm doing a four mile per hour pace.

At Warm Springs River I have lunch consisting of cheddar cheese and Ronny's favorite, a honey bun that has been flattened out like a pancake, but it was still great. I made some lemonade, choked down a power bar followed by a Snickers candy bar. After a 20 minute rest, I'm off again. I remember in 1998, I met a young guy here who was rather large and he and his dog were going to Olallie Lake. They were going to hike there in two days and here I was, at 1:00, having already been there this morning.

From this point until Timothy Lake I just got into myself. I thought about home now, because in a couple of days it will make four months that I've been on this trail. I was hoping to hike it in four and a half months but it looks like it may be over five months, if I make it at all. Washington is a tough state. Mile per mile, it's probably the hardest state, especially when you throw in the wet weather factor. My mind goes over the people I've met along the way, especially the trail hikers, how many are on the trail and who's in back of me. I pretty much know who is in front of me.

Red Wolf Pass proves to be nothing at all and Buckskin Butte is a minor joke. Clackamas Lake is tiny but Oak Grove Fork is nice. I reach Timothy Lake at 5pm and it's huge! I don't know where I will crash for the night but it won't be for a while because I'm excited about the mileage I have done so far today and I'm hoping to arrive at Timberline Lodge some time tomorrow.

For starters I will definitely walk around this lake. There are a number of campsites around. But now it's only 6pm and I have at least an hour more of light. There are several people here enjoying themselves. If I weren't in such a hurry I would befriend someone and perhaps receive a cheeseburger for my effort. But perhaps I'm just dreaming. One thing for sure, man I'm hungry.

It's now 7pm and I have just passed Timothy Lake. I'm beyond tired now, more like numb. I want to proceed further. For now a power bar and some trail mix will do. Oh yeah, where's that Butterfinger, baby. It's sugar rush time. It's now pitch dark and I strap my light around my head. A half moon also helps for light. I'm tired. I'm kind of surprised that I haven't caught up with or crossed paths with any other hikers. There have been several people on the trails, but no hikers.

It's now 9:00 at night and I'm really seriously thinking of stopping but I could use some more water. I would like to cook up some beef stroganoff tonight. I will be cooking in the dark. That's why the lights that strap around your head, these headlights, are so valuable. You can see what you're doing and your hands are free to do things like cook.

At 9:30 I hear the noise of vehicles. There's a highway up in front of me. It has to be Highway 26. A quarter of a mile further I reach the place and it's Highway 26 all right. If I can hike another two and a half to three miles I can get to the Salmon River, which is really more like a creek. Here I can get water and enjoy a hot meal.

About three horrible boring miles later at 10pm I arrive at Salmon River Creek where I find a flat place to camp. I prepare my meal, even though I'm not hungry any more. It's funny how you can have hunger pains almost all day and then your body, according to diet freaks, goes into starvation mode.

I guess the body signals the mind through a maze of dendrites and axons that hey, the hunger pain signals are being postponed for now and brain boy, if you don't know you're supposed to eat by now, you either have food or you're totally stupid. Some dude told me that the reason for this is that it gives the body full concentration to either gather food or hunt for food.

Just before I hit the turf to sleep I check the map and I do believe I've broken a personal record. Today I have marched about 40 miles and over my ability, especially at this age. Tomorrow I will definitely cut back and go for 18 or 20 miles.

The next morning I got up at 8:00. I slept like a baby and cried all night. No, just kidding. By 8:15 I was heading up the trail to Timberline Lodge. My legs were very stiff and took about a quarter of a mile to get them loose. My feet ached a little too, especially the right toe. My left toe has finally adapted to my new Nikes that I received from Trail Perfect at Crater Lake. My shoulder was also bothering me some, like it has pretty much done on the whole trip.

It was time for my favorite drug. Ever since I've been in my fifties, it's Motrin, baby. A Motrin 600 will do just fine, but I better have breakfast first. I stopped early and prepared my power shake and downed a couple of fruit bars and then popped down my 600. I'm off again, still stiff, but after about a half hour, 90% of those nagging little pains are gone and I'm a new man!

The trail I'm walking on now is completely new for me because like a fool, in 1998, I got off the highway and walked into a huge RV campground late in the evening. The next morning I hiked the six mile road straight up to Timberline Lodge. What a drag it was. I thought I would never get there, cars whizzing past me.

I was constantly going up hill on pavement. Pavement can give hikers blisters, even if the hikers have walked billions of miles. The foot rubs differently on pavement. If the pavement is hot, watch out. One should make sure he or she has clean socks and a hiker should stop every once in a while and cool the feet off with water or even a cold rock can help.

The trail now is a contour trail and although it's a bit of a climb to the lodge, it's pretty mellow and there's shade.

It's now 10am and I can hear the familiar sound of motorized vehicles. A few minutes later I arrive at Barlow Pass. This time I stay on the good ole PCT and head up the trail to Timberline Lodge. About four or five miles later I reach the amazing and totally beautiful Timberline Lodge.

This lodge is pretty famous. It sits on the southern side of Mt Hood. I believe it's around 60 years old. There's an actual movie that is run once a day that describes how the lodge was built. Skiers can actually ski all year around due to some of the shaded slopes and probably snow machines. The last time I was here, a movie star, I think Brad Pitt, was there. There were several guys around with cameras asking him questions. This is a very popular supply pick-up because of it's proximity to the PCT.

That's where I was heading to get my box first and then eat at the cafeteria that was just below the lodge. I first went to the desk in the lobby of the hotel. I was told that the package pick-up was now at the sporting goods store near the cafeteria so I headed down there and found instead a skiing and camping store. My package was waiting for me. I always feel relieved when my packages are there, although this time there's only enough food for two and a half days because that's what it will take to reach Cascade Locks on the mighty Columbia River.

After receiving my box, the fellow working there tells me that there's a PCT register back at the end of the counter. I walked over and signed it with a couple of what I think are cool one-liners.

I start reading who has been here. There are a few of the regulars but not as many hikers as usual. I'm looking at the last of the list to see who was the most current hiker to go through here. Right above the last name was Shutter Bug, Steady, Sunburn, and Cliff Hanger.

Wow, when did they go through here, oh man, yesterday? I must have missed them on the trail, probably when I was walking last night. I might have gone right by them, maybe somewhere around Timothy Lake. That's a bummer in the summer.

I sure would have liked to have seen them again, that would have been really cool. They may still be here but I doubt it. This place is quite expensive. With Steady's husband they might have gotten a ride to Government Camp. I'm sure there are cheaper rooms down there. It's a drag that I missed them, especially the ancient one, Cliff Hanger.

From the fancy camping store I went to the cafeteria where I had an excellent chef's salad and a cheeseburger. The prices were reasonable for a resort restaurant. I recommend it.

After eating I headed back to the lodge where I was going to make some phone calls, one to Trail Perfect and one to my parents. I had called Chuck a week earlier and he was doing much better, so I decided I'd call when I got to Cascade Locks.

In the lobby, on a wooden table, was a newspaper and on the front page it read, "Fire Ravages Cascade Locks, Oregon". I couldn't believe it. I just played dodge ball with one fire and now of all places there was a fire in Cascade Locks, my next stop, for God's sake.

After calling home, I finally located the forest service person and asked her about the fire. She said she had heard something about it yesterday but hasn't heard anything since. Then she gave me a phone number to the local forest ranger station that was in charge of that area. I called them and talked to the forest ranger. He told me that they were still dealing with it but it didn't look serious and by the time I get there, which I thought would be in about 3 days, the fire would most likely be put out. This was a relief to say the least. I was pretty much burned out dealing with fires.

The trail here travels around the western side of Mt Hood. Rushing creeks that come down from the continuous snow melt of Mt Hood is one of the obstacles that hikers have to deal with. It's now almost 3:00. I have at least four hours of light left. I should try and make the most of it, even though my legs are still weak from my 40 miles I did yesterday.

After just going a few hundred yards, a hiker already starts to leave the heavy tourist impacted area. Salt Creek is the first creek one has to navigate. It's pretty easy. Big and little rocks are usually lined up by trail workers, which make crossing rather easy. But don't get complacent. Little Zigzag Canyon is the next enclave and creek to be part of the PCT experience. There are a lot of rocks and creeks, with numerous waterfalls.

A few miles later I reach Scout Camp and Rushing Water Creek. There are some pretty nice campsites around here and backpackers occupy some of them. As for me, I still have a couple of hours left so I must move on. Following the Sand River for a couple of miles I met four guys camping in some choice campsites that are really illegal because they are so close to the water.

I remember these campsites in 1998. I was actually here about this time of day. I rap to these guys for a while. They were pretty cool. They ask me to stay if I want to but I feel it would be a little cramped here so I move on and cross Muddy Fork Creek.

This creek is large and it's rushing hard. I have to be very careful here. I'm relieved when I get to the other side. This is one of those creeks that are easiest to cross in the morning. The day is finished now. I decide to crash just above Muddy Creek on a sandy area. I even decide to set up my tarp, hanging it between two green bushes. It's been quite a day, only about 17 miles, but a successful package pick-up at Timberline Lodge. Oregon is starting to come to an end. If I can get to Cascade Locks, which is on the border, I will have walked Oregon in about 20 days. In 1998 it took me 30 days. I realize my ride around the fires pushed it to twenty one and a half days if you add that on. It's still an amazing difference. Maybe I will make it after all.

The next morning I awoke at about my usual time. I had a hard time getting out of the sack. Consequently I didn't leave camp until 7:30am, later than I like. The sound of Muddy Fork Creek really helped me sleep last night. The water in this creek is not really muddy, but it's milky in color due to a mineral that washed off the rocks. That's what I was told by one guy.

There's a creek in the Jefferson Wilderness that is actually called Milky Creek because it looks like milk rushing down from its source. Now, however, I'm in the Mt Hood Wilderness and I will be for at least a day, until I reach the Columbia Wilderness and then of course the Columbia River itself.

So, down the trail I go and soon arrive at the Ramona Falls Loop. I missed these falls back in 1998. I think I'll bypass them once again. I don't really want to go out of my way to see the falls, unless they are spectacular, because of the time element. Today is September 4th and I have been hiking now for exactly four months. My original plan was to finish the trail in four months and three weeks, but that's not going to happen. I have to keep moving before the big dump hits!

The PCT now starts to ascend as I work my way out of a valley and then over a ridge where I start to descend Lolo Pass. On the way down I met a middle-aged woman who is riding a horse on the Pacific Crest Trail by doing sections of it. She has already done all of Washington and is now working on Oregon. What makes her different is that she has two horses, a mother horse and a daughter horse, three girls walking alone. I talk to her for a few minutes and then head down the trail to Lolo Pass.

On reaching this pass I can remember well for there are three or four merging roads that crisscross the area. In 1998 I met two older guys that gave me a quart bottle of Powerade, red in color. I chugged it all down at once and man, I was on some kind of a sugar rush that powered me up the trail for about 30 minutes. It then left me totally depleted of energy.

This time I got water out of a small creek just past the road junction and then began a long ridge walk that would lead me closer and closer to Cascade Locks. A few hours later I had lunch at Salvation Springs. There was as cool little frog sitting on a small rock. He didn't seem scared of me so I tried not to bother him as I prepared lunch.

After lunch I continued to head uphill, switchbacking to Devils Pulpit-Preachers Peak. The trail is now lined with huckleberry bushes, hemlock, and fir trees. The vegetation is thick and green, almost like a rain forest. From the ridge I can now look down and see Lost Lake, some 800 feet below.

A few miles further on one can get excellent views of Blue Lake as well. On the west side of the trail there are continuous yellow signs which read, "No camping, violators will be prosecuted". This, the so-called Bull Run watershed, and the signs, are most annoying to say the least. I've heard this is where Portland gets its drinking water.

The PCT then slides slightly to the east as it starts to descend to Indian Springs. The view up here is really nice and like many parts of Oregon, flowers of multiple colors line the trail, even in September.   Down below and towards the north I can see the mountains of Washington, specifically Mt Adams and Mt St Helens.

Down below and not too far away lies the Columbia Gorge, which is the natural border of Oregon and Washington. I soon reach Indian Springs. This is where I spent the night in 1998. I slept on a picnic table. I see a table that could be the same one, a bit older and more rustic, with an assortment of carvings on it. The water here is great. It's a natural spring but to insure its purity the water is directed through a pipe.   I'm sure many hikers visit this campground.

In 1998 I got here in the dark of night and even though I left a campsite that was near the same vicinity as the '98 campsite, I arrive here some three hours earlier. Even though I'm five years older now, it's a testament to lightweight backpacking and incredible hiking shape that I'm in now. It is now just after 4pm. I'm hungry so I decide to make dinner here, with the convenience of the water and the table. It only makes sense. I cook up a Lipton dinner of chicken fettuccini mixed with mashed potatoes. I also have some cheese and crackers. It's now 5:15 and I have about two hours of light left, so I decide to hike down to Wahtum Lake, about three miles away.

The trail from here is basically downhill to Wahtum Lake and it travels near a dirt road for a while before it cuts off and drops into Wahtum Lake campsites. At about 9pm I arrive at the lake and a minute later I find the trail that heads for Eagle Creek and Tunnel Falls. I want to be sure that I'm on the right trail now because Wahtum Lake has been known to screw people up and send them off on bogus trails to nowhere.

It did this to me back in 1998. I took this high trail that comes out of the small parking lot above the lake when I should have taken the lower trail that goes around the lake. I thought that the lower trail was just the local trail that guides fishermen and hikers around the lake to different campsites. I was wrong and I paid a hell of a price for it too. I turned a 15 mile day hike into a 35 mile day of hiking, and it was miserable.

In 1998, after walking three or four miles on a ridge when I should have been a mile down below, I sort of figured out where I was. I was heading for the Columbia Gorge all right, for the sign at the parking lot read, "Columbia Gorge, 12 miles". I knew that I had to find the PCT or who knows how far I would be when I eventually came out from the abandoned jeep road. I found a trail heading downhill so I took it and hiked a good half mile. I wasn't really too concerned about getting lost because I figured that all roads and trails from here pretty much led down to the gorge.

In a short while I met up with a burley guy with a large weed hoe. I told him my problem. He looked a little agitated that I actually got lost. "The trails are damn near perfect here," he said. "I can't understand how anyone gets lost." I said, "It isn't the trails, they're in good shape. It is the signs that are ambiguous." The guy asked, kind of annoyed, what I meant by that. I told him the sign at Wahtum Lake points into a direction that both trails are heading, the high trail and the low trail. I also told him how I took the high trail because a couple of locals in the area encouraged me to take it. "I ended up on that ridge up there."

The guy looked perplexed and told me that the PCT is down a little further and that I was heading right for it. He then asked me where I was heading and I told him to Cascade Locks. "I'm finishing Oregon. I started at Seiad Valley, California, 29 days ago." "Well," he says, clasping his chin to think, "Go down there, you can't miss it, and make a left, that will take you on in to Cascade Locks." He went on to say that he was going to Wahtum Lake that evening and he'd look at that sign.

Before I left I asked, "Sir, please put a white diamond or emblem down from the intersection a bit, designating the PCT. I think that would eliminate any problems in the future." The guy said that he didn't have any diamonds or emblems, but that he would look at that sign. I said, okay, and then left, heading down to the PCT, thinking to myself how all trail workers should have the PCT emblem. It only weighs a few ounces, for God's sake! It always sounds like a big deal to put up an emblem!

I soon reached the PCT and I made a left, which right away seemed to be a little weird. I then headed up a small incline and off I went once again. About two miles further I started to wonder why I was slightly uphill rather than a steep downhill into the gorge. I knew the Columbia River was only 100 feet or more above sea level. In fact, I believe it's actually the lowest point of elevation on the whole PCT. As I continued to hike downhill I became perplexed, and then I saw why. Down below is a large body of water and it wasn't the Columbia River either. Oh my God, it was Wahtum Lake once again. I had hiked around in a giant circle and come right back where I started that morning. I was shocked and very irritated to say the least. I had spent the whole day from 8am to 2pm walking in a circle on the day which was supposed to be my last day in Oregon.

I was so upset. I went down to the lake and had a late lunch, stuffing my face with food because I knew I was in for a very long day. After eating I headed out again. I wasn't going to give up, no way. It would probably be smarter to spend a second night at the lake but I was too damn mad and I was determined to reach Cascade Locks today and finish Oregon in 29 days.

I finished lunch and headed back down the trail, but this time on the right trail. I soon passed the area that I had first joined the PCT after the guy gave me the wrong direction to walk. To this day I don't know if the guy purposely gave me the wrong directions or he thought I was hiking Oregon north to south. The rest of the late afternoon I hiked at a fast pace, still angry with myself and the two people that I think may have given me the wrong direction. I was very relieved when I saw my first trail emblem, the white diamond, as I started to drop into the gorge. Views of the Columbia Gorge were nice but didn't last, as the trail dropped dramatically. Twice I slipped and fell on my butt as the sand on the steep trail slid from underneath me.

An hour and a half later I came down to what I thought should have been Cascade Locks, but it was a youth work camp instead. I had missed the trail that splits off from the PCT and slides northwest, leading a hiker right to Cascade Locks. I was three or four miles east of the place and didn't know it. In fact, I thought I was just west of it, so I headed east down the service area road until truck lights lit up a highway sign and I knew I was heading in the wrong direction. Immediately I headed back one more time into the darkness heading for what I hoped to god would be Cascade Locks. I walked into the night until I passed the area for freight cars and came to a residential area. There was a guy on his porch. I asked him if Cascade Locks was up the road a bit and he said yes. I was really relieved. Was this Twilight Zone experience coming to an end?

ECSTASY OF MISERY

As I hiked along I asked a couple of other people if I was heading into the right direction, just to make sure. I really didn't trust anybody any more. Finally I reached the outskirts of town and stopped into a liquor store to buy some junk food because I was starving. In fact, the last water I'd had a few miles back gave me the dry heaves. I didn't throw up because I just didn't have anything left in my stomach.

Shortly after the liquor store I saw an Econo Inn where I got a room and fell across the bed totally exhausted. It was 10:30 at night. I had been hiking since 7:30 that morning. I figured I walked somewhere between 33 and 36 miles that day, with a pack that was much heavier than the one I'm wearing now. I'll never forget that day, my last day in Oregon in 1998.

So now, in 2003, I lay me down to sleep under my tarp beside the PCT. But this time I will take the old PCT route, the route that heads down Eagle Creek and a host of waterfalls, including the famous Tunnel Falls. That would be tomorrow, September 3, 2003.

Cascade Locks, as I remember it from both 1998 when I finished Oregon and again in 2000 when I started out hiking the state of Washington, is one comfortable place to be if you're a hiker. It's convenience for food, both restaurants and stores, is unbeatable. There's a great pizza place, a couple of excellent hamburger places, a fancy luxury hotel, and a comfortable Econo Inn. There's an excellent laundromat where many hikers have always washed their sleeping bags. The post office is convenient; there's even a park where PCT hikers can camp for free if they are on a tight budget.

The beautiful Columbia River flows by Cascade Locks and a highway that will take you right to Portland, if you need anything major. Then when you leave the place to head into Washington, you have the Bridge of the Gods to carry you over the big bad Columbia River. Cascade Locks is also very reasonable, prices are somewhat lower than a lot of the resort towns like Mammoth or Ashland.

So with this in mind to motivate me, I headed gleefully down the trail. About an hour later the trail began to curve around and join famous Eagle Creek.

At Mile Camp Falls I decide to have breakfast. This area was green and lush to say the least. After a quick breakfast I headed down the trail past Look-out Falls, which were very nice. With each mile, Eagle Creek began to grow. Tributaries were everywhere. Soon, I was walking on a fantastic trail that was carved straight into a cliff with Eagle Creek a hundred or more feet below. Huge deep pools of glassy pure water are below me, as waterfalls like Metlake Falls and Punchbowl Falls added to the beautiful scene.

Then comes the famous Tunnel Falls, falling at least 150 feet down into Eagle Creek. The amazing trail then went directly into a tunnel with the falls crashing down just on the other side. I was surprised at this because I always thought that the trail was open in there and one could see the water from the back side of the falls, but that's not true. It's simply a tunnel about 50 or 60 feet through the edge of the cliff. I took a few pictures, but it was still rather dark from the overcast sky and I didn't have a flash on this single use camera, so I really wasn't expecting a very good picture. For me the best deal on famous objects of nature like these falls is just to buy a postcard.

From Tunnel Falls the trail became a little wider and I began seeing other hikers. The more I headed down the more hikers I encountered. Then there were turn-offs on the trail where people could take pictures. Older people and children appeared as a certain indication that I had only a short distance before reaching the bottom of the Columbia River Gorge.

A half hour later the trail reached Eagle Creek Forest Camp with bathrooms, picnic tables, and running water. It was now noon, so I decided to take lunch; no sense in rushing into Cascade Locks totally famished. After lunch I went into the bathroom and cleaned up a bit. I could hardly believe that the image in the steel mirror was mine.

With lunch completed and a clean face and arms, I began to walk the trail east towards Cascade Locks. I still had a good four miles to go. The trail ran right above the highway, it traveled in and out of gullies, making the hike a little more rigorous than I thought it would be. At one point it crossed the old highway that is now a biking road where I met an old boy that played in a band. He was going to Dallas, a city in Oregon, to play in a tavern. He was cool and I marched on.

The trail from here began more like a roller coaster. I wished I had taken the old highway route instead of this, but then again, this is the old PCT, and I might as well walk it while I can. Finally at 1:30, on September 5th, I entered Cascade Locks and my journey of Oregon on the PCT was completed.

This part of the trail ends near the beautiful Bridge of the Gods over the Columbia River. The town of Cascade Locks sits on the road that's less than a half mile long. Near the Bridge of the Gods on the west side of town is the Best Western Motel. It looks really nice. They have their own bakery below the motel. It has some real gooey good stuff.

On down the road I head past the cool pizza place with its wooden carvings inside. A little farther down is the grocery store with just about anything you need. Across the street are the post office and a coffee shop that also sells Tillamook ice cream. The Cascade Locks Café is really good, especially breakfast where you can get the best chicken fried steak with brown gravy and bits of bacon I have ever had. Back of the café is the Econo Inn with rooms around $40 a night, which was the first place I'm heading. There's also a hardware store and a large park where PCT hikers can camp for free near the river.

I head into the Econo Inn's office. The same Asian people that I rented a room from last time came out and gave me a room for two nights for $80, about what it costs for one night at the Best Western. I went to my room. It's nothing fancy but it has just about everything you want, color TV, a good shower, a small refrigerator, a microwave, and a telephone! Right now I would love to take a shower, but according to the town guide, the post office closes in 45 minutes and if I fail to get my supply box I will have to wait until 9am Monday morning, since tomorrow is Sunday. I dump my stuff in the room and go over to the post office. My package is there, which is a relief. I ask the post office clerk about the fire that I had read about at Timberline Lodge. He told me that only one structure was lost and that the fire was put out before it even crossed the highway.

I thanked him for the information and started to head out of the post office, when lo and behold, there was Rob of Rob and Bandana. "Wrong Way, you made it." "Yeah, I just got in an hour ago." Rob told me that they had arrived there that morning. He said, "There's a party at Bandana's parent's house in Portland tonight and then tomorrow a whole bunch of us are going to the Dead concert." "Wait a second, man, there isn't any Grateful Dead, Jerry Garcia died, man." He said the band had a couple of new guys and they call themselves The Dead. "That's news to me," I said.

I told Rob to have fun, that I'm here to rest my aged body; a rock concert was not my recipe for the weekend. "If this was the 60s, I might be interested. These days I'm only interested in Dylan, the Stones, or John Mayhal. Tom Petty gets a little of my attention sometimes." "You're old school," said Rob. "I know, man, do I know it."

Outside was Bandana in her usual red bandana tied around her hair with those blue fluorescent eyes peaking through. I said hello and she said, "Wrong Way, it looks like you're going to make it." "I don't know. Washington's next, and in that state the way the mountains are laid out and with its wet weather, it can send a hiker home quickly. It makes Oregon look like a cake walk." She agreed because living in Portland she had walked portions of it. She asked if I had good rain gear and a good tent. "Rain gear yes, but I only carry a tarp." "Oh boy," she says. I tell the couple to have fun at the party and concert. "I'll be leaving Monday morning; I have to get my rest."

With that I head back to the Econo Inn. They never really invited me to the party, but that's okay. I didn't want to go. There is a big generation gap. They think they're watching the Dead, but little do they know that 25 years ago I saw the real deal, the Grateful Dead!

I headed back to the motel and took a long hot shower, something I haven't had in damn near two weeks. The shower I had in No Gear's RV doesn't count. My second act is to hit the bed for a snooze as I watched the UCLA team play. I never did find out who won because I crashed out for two hours. Man, I needed it, for I had been pushing it forever since I left Olallie Lake. That day and a half wasn't a restful period either.

When I got up the news was on. Things don't look too good for Iraq. What a mess. About 6pm I really started to get hungry so I headed over to the Cascade Locks Café and had a steak and chef's salad. From there I headed to the store and bought some Ben and Jerry's Cherry Garcia ice cream for tonight and a Heath Bar Crunch for tomorrow. I also bought some beer and cheese dip. Eat all you can is my motto. I have to because when I looked in the mirror before I jumped in the shower, I saw just a stick of a man. I must weigh less than

ECSTASY OF MISERY

170 pounds. That makes about 50 pounds that I've lost so far. There was music going on down at the pizza place but I just wanted to relax in front of the TV, eat my junk food, and make a few phone calls to home.

That evening I ended up watching TV and washing all my clothes in the sink and hanging them out all over the room to dry. There was some work involved but that nap really brought me back to life. Trail Perfect had put some detergent in my supply box like she does with every supply box. This time she added some Woolite to the box. This would enable me to finally wash my sleeping bag. That would be a job for tomorrow morning, if the laundromat with the commercial washing machines is still in business. That night I ended up not only washing all my clothes but also my cooking pot and utensils. At 11pm I hit the soft bed and fell asleep with the TV on.

The following morning I awoke, realized where I was and went back to sleep again. At 9:00 I got up and went down to that excellent greasy spoon and got myself chicken fried steak with plenty of bacon and mushroom gravy on it. I also ate a side order of fried eggs sunny side up with a short stack and blueberry syrup.

After breakfast I walked back to the room, grabbed my sleeping bag and headed to the laundromat. It was still in business and open. I popped my bag in the commercial washer and added my Woolite, not too much because my bag is not a big thick one, and then headed back to watch some Sunday professional football.

The pre-game show had of all things, Rush Limbaugh. I couldn't believe it. Rush Limbaugh, the liberal hater, the same guy that believed Clinton held America hostage. Wow, now he's on TV talking about why there aren't black coaches in the NFL. Watch out Mr Limbaugh or you may not be on the pre-game show for too long.

In between commercials I head back to the laundromat to make sure everything was going okay. You can't be too casual when you're washing the most important article you have in your backpack. The bag was through washing so I popped it in the dryer with my tennis shoe which helps the bag dry. The shoe smacks against it and works the down free of lumps. A half hour later my bag is done. Wow, what a loft it has now. It sure looks good. Mission accomplished.

For the rest of the day it's time to just kick back and relax. There's football and more football. What a wonderful world. Lunchtime rolls around and I decided to walk at an extra slow pace and go down to the Best Western Hotel where they have a bakery. But as soon as I got there the lights go out, just when I was going to buy some Rocky Road chocolate fudge.

I couldn't believe it. They couldn't sell me any fudge without weighing it. "Hey, ma'am, can't you sell me a bit that looks like a pound? I don't mind if I get short changed and that way the store won't get burned." "No, we can't do that," she answers in the most serious manner. "Not until the electricity is back on."

I wait a while and start to get bored. The gift shop even gets old, I'm old, the lady is old, and the Rocky Road chocolate fudge is probably old! So before I get too much older I leave empty-handed.

I head back to the room but make a quick detour to the hamburger stand and got a chili burger, onion rings, and a butterscotch shake. You know, it's hard to get butterscotch any more. Everything is caramel instead. Is caramel really supposed to replace butterscotch, for God's sake? That's even worse than Sierra Mist trying to replace good ole Seven-Up, it's even worse than that, man.

I stumble into my room with my calorie-saturated food, hoping to build up my carbs for tomorrow. I ate and fell asleep, waiting for dinner. Trail Perfect calls me about two hours later. She reminds me to charge my phone before leaving and tells me stuff about home; it seems like the same old thing but a different smell. I guess I shouldn't say things like that because it's not cool. I do miss home.

It was 7pm now so I went to have dinner at the pizza place. I kept looking for possible thru-hikers that may have been walking about, but I didn't see any. The pizza parlor was really nice. They had wooden figures of river captains and other outdoor men around the place. I ordered a salmon and shrimp pizza with a few extra toppings and a pitcher of brown beer.

On the big screen TV they had on a football game. To my surprise, Los Alamitos, a large local high school team at home is playing an Oregon high school team. I tried not to cheer at all for Los Alamitos because all of the locals were rooting for the Oregon team. While in Rome, do as the Romans do, and besides, the score was already 25 to zip in the second quarter. In fact, when it was half time, they switched channels to a pro game.

After dinner I walked back to my room and started to get some of my stuff together because tomorrow I would be heading out. I fell asleep around 11pm, just after hearing the local weather report. It didn't sound good. There will be an overcast sky tomorrow and a chance of a few thundershowers. Oh well, what do you expect? I'll be in Washington. What else is new?

The next morning I was up at 7:30 and was at the greasy spoon by 8:00. As I walked in the restaurant, there at a table were Frog, Batteries Included, and Belcher, but no Puck. "Hey dudes, what's happening?" I said. "Oh we're just loading up and trying to sober up too," said Batteries Included. "Yeah, I heard there was quite a party and concert." Belcher said they just went to the party and not the concert and that the others will probably be leaving tomorrow.

I asked where Puck was. "He's with his mother today, so we won't be leaving until tomorrow, I guess." Batteries Included said that he and the Frog-man were heading out together this afternoon, after they washed some stuff and have lunch. I told them that I was leaving in about an hour but I have some reservations about the weather. "Yeah we heard," Belcher said as she engulfed another pancake. "Welcome to Washington," I said as I sucked down some hot java. The three of them really didn't look too spunky. I think they did a little too much partying at Bandana's house.

After breakfast I headed back to my room, gathered up my stuff, and headed out. I walked down Main Street, past the Best Western, where I thought about getting a gooey pastry, but I do believe I've had enough with carbing out.

A few minutes later I reached the southern end of the Bridge of the Gods, walked past the pay booth because pedestrians don't have to pay, only vehicles, and reached the northern shore. The Columbia River looked gray, like the overcast sky. A large barge passed beneath me. When I reached the center of the bridge I knew I was in Washington and when I reached the other side I walked under the large blue "Welcome to Washington" sign. I was here in

Washington, the hardest state as far as mile per mile, and also by far the wettest.

Echo Lake Resort. The guy in the red is Frog.

Obsidian Mountain in Oregon (Glass Mountain)

"you can't always get what you want"

an alternative root must be found.

Welcome to Washington from the Bridge of the Gods

Journey Fifteen: Welcome to Washington!

The next section of the Pacific Crest Trail through Washington is the lowest part of the trail, just a mile past Bridge of the Gods where the trail reaches an all time low of 140 feet above sea level. One wouldn't think this would be the lowest point; you would think it would be somewhere in the Southern California desert. This section of Washington is also the longest section between supply points of Cascade Locks and White Pass.

The sky is now overcast and drab looking to say the least, as the trail passes a stagnant pond. It then starts to curve into a more northern direction. Gillette Lake is the first lake I reach and it will be the last lake I will see for some time. I begin to climb steadily in the sub-alpine forest, working my way out of the Columbia Gorge area. The forest is lush, with fern and other low-lying bushes covering the forest floor.

Just a few hundred feet past Gillette Lake, two beautiful racer snakes cross in front of me and head up the trail. I pick up speed a little to catch the colorful reptiles, but they leave me in the dust. Man, can they haul ass. I'm glad they're not poisonous. What if they were and they were aggressive and came towards you! Oh my god, you would be cooked. Nature could be a lot meaner than it is. We should feel lucky.

A few hours later after a steady viewless climb, I manage to reach the outer edge of Table Mountain, all 2700 feet of it; big deal, only 2700 feet or so. It just feels that I'm a lot higher than this. I keep trying to find some kind of view of the Columbia River, but the forest is so thick it blocks any views. A small spring that just drips water from a moss covered rock gives me a chance to drink and fill up a water tank since I won't see any other water source for quite a number of miles.

For the rest of the day I walk through this rather boring and viewless stretch of the PCT. It would probably look a lot better if the sky wasn't so damn cloudy. It seems that it's getting darker all the time. My legs are quite rested from the two and a half days I spent at fabulous Cascade Locks, which is good because my pack is on the heavy side from all the food I need for the four or five days until I reach White Pass.

The trail now starts to drop as I work my way down to Rock Creek. Please don't drop so much, I say to my lonesome self. Don't drop too much just to get to this creek and lose my big elevation gains for the last half of the day. But this is Washington, a state that's like a roller coaster, a state in which everything is a pass. There must be 20 passes or more that a thru-hiker must conquer before he reaches Monument 78 on the Canadian border. Then one has to climb another pass to get to blessed Manning Park!

Thinking about this can cause a thru-hiker depression. It's best just to take one thing at a time. After all, none of these passes are like the passes of the fantastic Sierras. Now those are passes, so lighten up, man.

Down I go until I reach Rock Creek, with some great looking campsites. This would be a nice place to crash for the night but I still have a couple of hours that I can walk. There's one thing I can do and that's prepare dinner here and put in another hour or so before I crash somewhere near or even on the trail, if worse comes to worst. I pick out my food that weighs the most to lighten up my pack as quickly as possible.

As I was heating up the stove for my chili mac, I suddenly hear a clap of thunder. A few seconds later, another sound of thunder, but this time it was louder. This was not good news. It was time to set up my tarp since I was in a good flat area with trees spaced not too far apart. I tied my rope and got my tarp and stakes out. I then finished cooking my dinner as the sound of thunder became louder and now there were flashes of lightning.

I tried to eat my dinner, I was plenty hungry, as I sat on a comfortable log that had been sawed off to make a perfect seat. The immediate joy of dinner didn't last long, however, for the rain began to come down in buckets. I was scurrying around like a chicken with his head cut off, trying to put my tarp up. It was a bit of a hassle because with the rain came the wind.

Within 10 minutes I had put my tarp up and dragged my pack and dinner inside with me. While the rain came down I had to work inside, spreading out the ground cover and then the mat. The next thing was the sleeping bag and then I was all set. I felt really lucky to be here at Rock Creek remote campsite. It was much better than being stuck on the trail with just plain lousy places to set up the tarp. The rain came down hard for about 15 minutes and then slowed down to a little sprinkle followed by intermittent hard and light rainfall. The thunder and lightning had gradually moved out now. Even the wind had let up a bit. I had lost a good hour and a half that I could have walked this evening, but camping here was definitely the smartest thing to do.

That night I lay in my freshly washed sleeping bag and wondered what the state of Washington would bring. I had walked the state in 2000, but I had finished a month earlier than this. Here it is September 7th, my first day in Washington, and it pours down rain on me. Like Rick and Madame Butterfly told me, just keep walking, don't give up. I think one thing for sure, I'd better get use to being wet and miserable. It's just a part of Washington one has to put up with, especially at the end of the season.

The next morning I was up early. I had survived the rain quite well. I even slept well. I was glad that Trail Perfect had put my three-layer Gore-Tex rain jacket with a hood in my supply box. She also put in the pants I wear when it rains. They are not Gore-Tex or really breathable material, but they are waterproof. The throw-away poncho had worked great, except it was flimsy and could easily be torn on the heavily shrubbery-lined trails of Washington.

I was now off and hiking on a wet foggy overcast morning. Within 10 minutes of hiking the trail my legs and feet were completely soaked from the lush shrubs. I had debated whether to put my rain pants on, but it just wasn't that cold. As for the running shoes and socks, they would probably be soaked all day. If one keeps walking, then the feet stay reasonably warm.

The fog was now quite thick and I could only see about 50 feet in front of me. Some drizzle was coming out of the dark gray sky as well as drops of water from the trees. It was now time to put on my rain jacket before my shirt and wool flannel got too wet. I clamp down the hood of my rain jacket to the bill of my hat with a clothespin. It works well, but freedom to see left or right is a bit hampered.

Another thing to be careful of are the maps and paper items because they can soak up water pretty fast. A lot of stuff is no big deal if it gets wet such as the cooking pot or knife. But hide those cigarette lighters. If the end of those get wet, they won't work until they dry! A hiker should carry something I don't have with me at present but have on occasion: waterproof matches.

I now reach Sedum Ridge. The fog lifts a little, but the rain picks up as I start to head down to Wind River Road. About two hours later, I reach Road 4306 and follow it for a short mile, until I can see a turn off to a structure, which is Wind River Ranger Station and Trout Creek picnic grounds. I doubt if there are many campers at this time of the year. School is back in session now and this depressing weather would send anybody back home. In fact, it's making me very home sick for sunny Southern California and I've only been in this for a night and half of a day.

From this area the trail heads around Bunker Hill with its lookout tower. It then crosses Wind River and Highway 60 about a mile further on. The hiking here is totally flat, until the trail reaches Panther Creek Campground.

In 2000, I got here late at night. There were quite a few campers at that time. Because I arrived late and left early, the night here was free. I would have put some money in a slot like they have in some campgrounds in California, but I couldn't find one.

The time now was 2pm and I was starving for lunch. There was absolutely no one here now, at least so I thought. I decided to make lunch. I broke open the tuna package and brought out some flour tortillas and started eating while there was a break in the rain.

Just as I started eating I heard a voice, "Hey, do you remember me?" Looking up I noticed that it was "The One" who I had met at Hyatt Lake, Oregon. "Hey dude, what's happening?" I said. "I'm just getting water. Bandana, Rob, and Bandana's sister are on the other side of the campground. Bandana's sister is just walking with us for 50 miles. We went to the concert last night and saw The Dead," said The One. "Cool, man," I said. "I'm just having lunch and then I'm going to hike a few more hours towards Big Huckleberry," I said. "But after I eat, I'll come over and visit you guys." "Okay," said The One as he pumped water out of the ground with a large steel jack pump. After he got his water, The One gave me a short wave and headed out across the campground.

The only way they have caught me here is that they would have had to walk the preferred alternate route out of Cascade Locks. It saves nearly a day of hiking but consists of road walking through a town called Stevenson and then another little place. That's cool. In fact, that's smart. If it's an alternate route then it's a legal part of the PCT.

After The One left, I began powering down my food once again, when a small white truck pulled up and a guy with a straw cowboy hat popped out, looking all concerned. "I suppose you're just having lunch too and moving on?" "Yes, man, I guess you'd be right about that," I said.

The guy looked really uptight, like he was constipated or something. "See that you do leave soon. This campsite is $25 a night and it may be occupied at any time," the constipated redneck said. "Wow, dude, there aren't any vehicles in the whole drenched campground." "That doesn't matter," the irritated clown barked, all frustrated and bothered.

So I just gave him my ole Davy Crockett smile, the one that he killed a bear with when he was only three. I remember seeing that at Disneyland back in the 50s. Now the guy was really pissed off and told me he'd be back in an hour with the police from Stevenson Town and how I would have to deal with them. "Sounds like fun, buddy, why don't you head on down there and bring them back." "I don't have to do that, I have a cell phone in my truck." "Okay, go ahead and call them, Mr Hero."

The uptight dude walks back to his truck and makes a call. I'm done with lunch and was just about ready to leave anyway. I get up, yawn a little bit and start out to the road, still amused at this poor sick bastard. "Hey, where do you think you're going?" "Eventually Canada, but if the police want me for some unknown reason, I'll be up on top of Big Huckleberry and they can come up there in this rain," which was coming down like gangbusters. "They can talk to me there, it's only a 3000 foot climb. Later, buddy, have a nice day!"

Off I walked into the fog and rain across Panther Creek and up a steep switchbacking climb that I doubt any policeman would even think of climbing, especially on a day like this. It's also funny that people will often copy my lingo, like I'll say "man" as a word of expression. Or I will say "dude" to add a little color and they will copy me, I guess to try to irritate me. But I always just say to myself, "monkey see, monkey do!"

ECSTASY OF MISERY

The trail leaving Panther Creek Campground was of course wet and muddy, but getting a foot grip wasn't too bad. The rain finally slowed down a bit. The going was still tough and the trail was quite steep. For a good hour and a half I sloshed my way uphill, heading for flatter land where I could set up my tarp. It's starting to get late with the days continuing to get shorter and the dark overcast sky. I was very interested in finding some place relatively flat, with two trees not more than 25 feet apart, in order to string up my tarp.

Finally I reached the summit of Big Huckleberry, 4202 feet in elevation, just a small hill in Sierra terms. It's all in the difficulty of getting here that makes it feel like you just climbed Mt San Jacinto or something like it.

About two miles further and at a small slow running spring I found my spot for the night. It was raining lightly at the moment. It didn't really matter too much since my pack was soaked anyway. You can only get so wet. At least I was kind of warm and within 10 minutes my tarp and ground cover were in place and it was time to crawl in. After a couple of minor adjustments, I was comfortable.

Five minutes later I had taken my wet pants and shoes off and was in my clean sleeping bag. Cooking isn't much of a problem under a tarp because it has such great ventilation. These are the benefits of a tarp. But the negative part is mosquitoes and other bugs and ground spiders can come inside the tarp. But guess what? There were no bugs or mosquitoes ever since the rain started. I haven't seen any flying demons or crawlies in two days. Those big black ants seemed to have disappeared too. You know, though, I think I would be willing to trade the rain in for the bugs, because this is a miserable scene.

When it isn't raining it's foggier than hell. The fog alone can soak you every morning as soon as you walk through bush, tree branches, and the slushy portion of the trail. My feet right now are wrinkled up like if one takes a two hour bath. At least there aren't any blisters, just sort of an ingrown toenail that is basically just annoying. After a super hot dinner and some hot chocolate, I fell asleep. Tomorrow I guess would be another miserable day.

The next day I awoke to the sound of rain pounding against my tarp. Getting up in the rain is an incredible bummer. Everything is altered compared to a dry morning. Everything that can be done inside the tarp or tent must be done, like putting on all your clothes, including your sopping wet running shoes, or even worse, heavy wet boots. Sleeping bags must be put into the waterproof stuff bag. The wet dirty ground cover must be folded up. The last thing to do is get out of the tarp and bring it down, fold it up and put it away. If you are lucky enough to have dry socks, well they will be soaked as soon as you stand up in your drenched running shoes or boots.

Finally the hiker is ready to leave and starts taking his first slushy steps. It's actually a relief to do so. For now, you're hiking and at least moving. You're usually more comfortable walking than preparing to go in a confining tent or tarp. You definitely don't need coffee to wake you up. Your cold footwear as well as other articles wake you up quite rapidly enough.

Just as I reach the trail I see two figures come bolting down the trail. It's Batteries Included and Frog. "Top of the morning to you, Wrong Way," they laugh as they cut in front of me and head down the trail. "Yeah, top of the morning to you weirdoes too," I say in disgust. "Lighten up, Wrong Way, get a grip on it. It's all in the mind. Just pretend it's another sunny day in LA." "That's right old timer, it's all in your mind." I keep up with the guys for a while but their pace is a little too fast for me.

Soon after they leave the rain stopped for a while, but there isn't any sun. If the sun does come out I must quickly lay out my sleeping bag because the great loft I had in it at Cascade Locks is already gone. In fact, it feels a little damp sometimes. The problem with continuing rain is that after a while every-thing starts to get wet. If there isn't any sun, then it's just about impossible to dry out.

While winding a corner I was surprised to see a guy hiking in front of me with an umbrella. A few moments later I catch up to the guy. The dude is quite old. He looks behind him, kind of shaken a bit by my presence.

I say howdy to the guy and he says hello. "Not quite a beautiful day, is it?" "Not quite," he says. I ask if he was heading out of here, figuring that the old guy is heading home on the first dirt road. "No, I'm going all the way to Canada," he said. "What, really, I mean you don't look like a thru-hiker." "Yeah, because I'm old," he says. "Well, I didn't mean anything by it. Hell, I'm 56." "I'm 62 years old," he says. I asked the guy where he started and he said

Mexico. "I touched the big brown fence." "Oh my god, you must be Billy Goat." "Yes, I'm Billy Goat 2." "What, there are two Billy Goats?" "Billy Goat 1 is about 10 days ahead of us." "Yeah, I thought he was. You know, he is also 62 years old." "Yes," says Billy Goat 2.

Damn it, I say to myself. That makes at least two guys that are older than me and both are 62 years old. "You know, man, I thought something was weird because people along the trail would tell me about a Billy Goat. Sometimes they said he was about two weeks in front of me and other times they would say a couple or three days ahead of me."

This is starting to make sense now, I'm thinking, but it's kind of a bummer. I've been demoted to the third oldest guy from the second oldest guy! "Hey Billy Goat, have you seen or heard of a guy called Cruising Carson? He's also 62 years young." "Nope, can't say that I have."

I asked the old guy when he had left the border and he told me April 12th, which was quite early. "Congratulations, buddy. I wondered why people along the trail always mentioned a Billy Goat. I didn't know how Billy Goat could have met so many people! But now I know, by god, there are two of you."

After talking to Billy Goat I headed down the trail. I did ask the old dude, who was from Washington, about the weather. He didn't help much because he said this rain could last a couple of more days, but it could also last a couple of more weeks. The thought of a couple more weeks really bothered me considerably. Two more weeks of this would be hard to bear.

The rain for the rest of the day was on and off. Hiking after Big Huckleberry was quite flat which is a rare thing for Washington. In fact, this was just about the easiest hiking in the whole state.

I crashed that night at Blue Lake after covering some 27 miles in a continuing light rain. I had caught up with Batteries Included and Frog, who had arrived at Blue Lake a good hour ahead of me.

I had to set up my tarp in a cold rain. I thought I wouldn't make it when my fingers felt frozen while I tied my rope between two trees. My gloves were soaked. I was glad to get my gear all set up and crawl into that bag. I put my frozen fingers between my legs in order to keep them from freezing.

It rained all night. Man, was I homesick. There is nothing like miserable weather to make me homesick. Southern California sounded great right now. A warm house with maybe a fire and a color TV set. I'm a fair weather hiker, that's for sure. But I'm too close to the finish to quit now, though it's still 440 miles to Manning Park. Doubts of my success ran through my mind that night. God, I hate Washington. Who in the hell can live in this miserable place!

The next morning was another rainy soaked affair; another day of hiking through rain and fog. A real bright spot, however, was the efficiency of my 13 ounce tarp. The simple thing really kept the rain out. It provided me with plenty of ventilation. I could cook inside of it, roll over at night to the extreme side, and lift up the side of the tarp and pee instead of getting up and wading outside in the rain. With a 56 year old bladder and not the bladder of a 25 year old stud, this worked out well. It was a real plus!

This morning I awoke to Frog prodding his hiking buddy, Batteries Included, to get up. Frog has those mocking war yelps designed to irritate his hiking associates and now Batteries Included was getting the direct abuse of these peculiar guttural noises. I almost got up to reprimand him of this sick habit he has. But it's really not my business.

About a half hour later I was on the soggy trail once again, with Batteries Included just in front of me. Batteries Included doesn't seem to be in a very good mood as he jammed ahead, trying to catch the fleet-footed Frogman.

The Pacific Crest Trail now entered Indian Heaven Wilderness.   Now on a ridge elevated to promote a view of the north, I finally get a cool view of Mt St Helen and Mt Adams that lie almost directly in front of me. The view only lasts a few short moments before the fog and rain once again obscure the view of what a beautiful hike this could be if it weren't for the weather.

A few hours later I notice by the trail guide map book of Oregon and Washington that I'm now circling around Mt Adams. I can only tell by the map, however, because the fog, clouds, and rainfall hide the beautiful mountain. I remember my Washington hike in 2000 and this was one of my favorite areas in Washington. The weather is everything, however, and now all views are closed out.

What I need now is just an hour of sun to dry out my pathetic sleeping bag, for nearly three days of rain have dampened it severely and its ability to keep me warm has diminished.   With just an hour of sun I could dry it out considerably, but the sun has been absent ever since I left Cascade Locks, Oregon.

Halfway around the mountain I met up with about a dozen horses and riders. I follow them for a while, as I watch the cumbersome beasts trip over rocks with their lazy riders getting off only intermittently to help them climb out of countless gullies, mostly dry but some with water.

Towards the northern side of Mt Adams the group of horse riders pulls off the trail and makes camp at one of their large prescribed campsites. I march on with the rain increasing and snowflakes start coming down from the dark gray sky. For about a half hour it snows, until I fall a little in altitude and the snow subsides and the rain returns.

Up in front of me I see a lone figure walking towards me. The guy soon arrives and we start rapping. "Nice weather," I say. The dude says, "It's not my cup of tea, mate." Right away I knew he wasn't from this side of the planet. His name was Marvin and he was from Down Under.

"Wow, man, this cold weather must be tough on you, being from a hot country and all." The guy kind of looks at me a little weird but it doesn't bother me because foreigners are a little weird at times, but are usually pretty cool. Marvin tells me that he has just come down from Goat Rocks and the place is basically a full-on foreboding blizzard!

"I couldn't see more than 10 meters in front of me, mate. I thought I was in trouble but the trail was pretty good, and when I started to drop in elevation the wind was not as bad, and the snow turned to rain. If you got the will to go up there, you better have a warm bag and a good tent."

"Well Marvin, buddy, I don't have either but maybe things will lighten up a bit." "No, buddy," he says. "The weather is supposed to be like this for another couple of days." Wow, this was not good news for me. "It will be worse news if you go up there, mate, believe me," said Marvin. "I believe you, chief, but I don't know what choice I have," I said. He said, "Down about a mile is a bi-way." "You mean highway?" "Yeah, mate, a highway. Take it out of here and come back later. You probably can bag a ride."

I told Marvin that I'd think about it and to take it easy and that the weather around Mt Adams isn't a cup of tea either. We then parted, the guy from Australia heading south and me heading north in what looks like a blizzard above 5000 feet.

The fact that my old thin sleeping bag was damp after three days of rain bothered me. The one positive note was that the Aussie guy told me there was a campground at Love Springs that has a campfire going on. I should be able to dry my bag out. Down the trail I head at about a three mile per hour pace because it's starting to get late and with the night brings a much meaner cold. My compass thermometer now reads 38 degrees.

After about an hour I reach Love Springs Camp. I don't see any campfire right away but on further inspection I find two bow hunters at a camp with a small smoldering fire beside it. I start talking to the guys and they seem nice, but not as outgoing as I thought they might be. I told them my story and the concern I had about my bag. They told me I could use their fire but I would have to gather wood across the stream under a large fir tree that was still dry underneath.

The bow hunters told me they were a little suspicious of people now since they were ripped off a day ago while they were out hunting. They said that was the first time that they had ever had anything stolen. I told them that things are not like they used to be, that there's very little honor in the world now. They agreed and took off. I started gathering wood from under that fir tree.

It took a while before I got the fire going and by the time I got my bag up to dry it out the fire would almost go out again. I would build it up and try to dry it out but once again the progress was slow. I finally got a half decent flame going and hung the end of the bag just over the flame.

Then all of a sudden there was a flash like a strobe light going off. On further examination I saw goose down on top of my little fire! Holy smoke. My bag had just burst into a flash flame and the end of my bag was gone! "Oh shit," I yelled out, but no one was there to hear me. The down had actually smothered my little fire and I was fed up with this attempt to dry out. Since sleeping bags are stuffed in sections, only the section where my feet go was torched. The nylon had simply melted into a flash flame and the down had fallen out.

I cleaned up the down. I didn't want the bow hunters to know that I had torched my bag. I was totally embarrassed. Here I was Joe thru-hiker, starting from Mexico to here and I torch my bag. Totally un-cool!

After cleaning up the down as best I could, I hauled out of there, once again into a steady rain. The hiking here was almost flat and even though my bag weighed a little heavy because it was drenched, I was able to keep a three mile per hour pace all the way down to Road 5306. This is the road that Marvin, the Aussie, told me to hitchhike out on and though it was a nicely paved road, there was absolutely no traffic.

I waited in the rain for at least 15 minutes, but not one vehicle came by heading in any direction. Fed up and bored, I headed out north again. The trail here was once a dirt road because the clearing between the trees was so wide.

It's funny how things change, especially the weather. I remember hiking here with Tony DeBellis in the year 2000. It was hot. I was actually hiking without a shirt just to catch a little Washington sun. It was rather invigorating too. Now it's 45 degrees colder and raining. In fact, snowflakes would fall for a bit and then rain would reappear again. That was five weeks earlier in the season than this. Oh man, am I too late? Is this the big dump? Had winter come early this year?

Nothing I could do but hike on since it was already 5:00. I should start looking for a place to crash. To hike on would mean that I would be gaining altitude as I head up into Goat Rocks Wilderness. With higher elevation come lower temperatures. Consequently, one needs to camp as low as possible.

The trail crossed a dirt road and rounded a corner and I saw two bow hunters coming towards me in the rain. When I came up to them they said hello and we started talking. They asked me how I was doing and I told them the truth, not too well. I told them about the steady rain that I had been walking in the last three and a half days and that my bag was pretty damp. I also told them that I had burned the bottom of my sleeping bag in a fire that two other bow hunters had let me use.

"That's the sleeping bag you're using to hike the Pacific Crest Trail?" asked the younger one. "Yeah, that's it," I said as I flopped on the ground under a thick pine tree area that was sort of dry. "Buddy, you can't hike Washington with something like that. What's the rating?" he asked. "About 35 degrees when it was new and dry," I said.

Then the surprised younger guy with his silent older buddy said, "If you go into Goat Rocks Wilderness with that you will probably get hypothermia and most likely die! I don't care what kind of tent you have." "No tent, only a tarp," I said.

"What? Oh buddy, you're crazy. Please don't go up there, come to our camp, we have a fire and a huge tent and our truck has a heater in it." I thought for a second and then said yes, I better do that.

So we hiked back up to the trail, made a left and walked a dirt road for a bit until we reached the bow hunters camp. The two hunters had a large dome tent with a large canvas tarp tied between trees and an old but nice-looking truck was parked nearby. A large fold-out table was under the tarp, as was dry firewood.

Although it was slightly raining, they managed to start the fire by the previous hot coals underneath. I began warming myself because I was starting to shiver a little. "Look at you, you're starting to get the first stages of hypothermia," said the younger guy. They asked me what my name is and I said Wrong Way. That cracked them up. "That's a perfect name, guy, Wrong Way, and you said you started somewhere in Mexico?" The older guy finally spoke. "Yep, May 4th, right on the border.

"So you're telling me that you haven't had any rain or cold weather problems." "Yeah, once in the San Diego area and once in the southern Sierras. But at that time I had a down jacket and a bivy bag." "That's what you need now if you're not going to get a new bag, but really, Wrong Way, you should buy a new sleeping bag."

The younger guy, Jim, suggested that I accept a ride with him to Packwood, which is just off White Pass and the PCT. I told him that was really nice but I couldn't ask him to do that, it was too far. But he told me that he and Steve need some supplies and that was the closest town around with a good market.

I told him, "Man, I don't know, I hate to miss Goat Rocks and that fantastic view of Mt Rainier. I was lucky enough to hike it in 2000 and the weather was great. I took a bunch of pictures up there with a hiker named Tony."

Jim said, "Hey listen Wrong Way, by the way, what's your real name?" "Bob Raley," I said. "Well, Bob, I don't know if you've heard the latest weather report, but it's supposed to storm for another couple of days. You might face a whiteout tomorrow." He started telling me how he almost ate it a couple of years ago when he and a friend of his were hunting. "We shot a deer then dragged it down to our camp and we got soaked. We started shivering all over the place, and then we couldn't find the keys to the truck. Thank god I had wired a back-up set under the truck frame. We were able to start the truck and put on the heater."

Jim went on to say how they drove right to Packwood, got a motel room and took hot showers as soon as possible "because hypothermia is no way to go." "Okay, man, let's go to Packwood, you convinced me. I'd like to give you $20 for gas." "Outstanding, let's have some hot coffee, then we'll go." His brother-in-law, Steve, said that he'd stay and watch their stuff.

So about 15 minutes later after having coffee and checking out Steve's incredible $1000 hunting bow, Jim and I headed out in his truck. It was about 5:30pm now and with the black clouds in the sky, we already needed to put the headlights on. The drive was a long one; we seemed to head west for quite a while before we started heading north.

Jim was an interesting guy. He pretty much told me the biography of himself and his eight sisters and brothers. He lived in Washington all his life. It was interesting how the state had changed in the last 30 years. I told him about my life and especially my hike from Mexico to here. The time went much faster because we were pretty good conversationalists.

There was nothing to see because everything was so dark and rainy. We finally arrived at Highway 12 and then we turned north towards Packwood. In another half hour we arrived in the town of Packwood, Washington. We probably drove 70 miles to go only 25 miles north of our previous position.

Driving down the highway, which also served as the main drag of Packwood, we cruised by some restaurants, shops, stores, and a good-sized motel. I told Jim to let me off here to see if they had a vacancy. I went inside the office and asked the lady who was watching a small color TV, and she said, "Yes, we have vacancies." I told her I'd like a room downstairs with a king size bed. She said for one person it would be $50 per night.

I walked outside and told Jim I had a room for $50. He thought that was a bit high. I told him it looked like a pretty cool place. I gave Jim twenty bucks and told him I would like to buy him dinner at the place across the street, but he was in a hurry to get his supplies and get back to his brother-in-law at camp.

I shook the guys hand and thanked him again. I might be in a world of pain if I hadn't met him. I was lucky. Jim drove off down the street and headed into a small grocery store. I headed to my room happy, and even jubilant, that I had a place like this because the rain was still coming down pretty hard and back on the trail it was probably worse because of the altitude factor.

My room had a large big bed, nice bathroom, color TV, and a fine looking shower. It also had a microwave and refrigerator and a telephone. For fifty bucks, it was quite a deal. Hell, it could have been another Columbia Hotel deal like I had in Ashland, Oregon.

The first thing I did was something I wanted to do for about four days, and that was to air out my stuff. With continual rain and never a spot of sun, one's gear becomes wetter and wetter. If I only had an hour of sun I could have had a bag that I could have survived in. But at the same time, from now on I will always have a bag warmer than a 35 degree rating, that's for sure.

I spread out my smelly wet stuff and put them near the heater. I then took a shower. After the shower I headed over to the Packwood Café and pigged out on a pretty good country fried chicken dinner. That night I fell asleep totally exhausted. The TV was on all night. I didn't even know it. I don't even know what I had been watching when I did fall asleep.

The following morning I got up around 9am and then casually walked over to the local greasy spoon. I had three eggs, hash browns, orange juice, coffee and four pancakes. Feeling mucho contento, I walked out of the restaurant and headed back across the pavement to the motel, flopped in bed and slept another couple of hours. Man, this is the life! Later that morning, I washed my clothes at the motel laundromat.

Last night I actually thought I was going to hitch a ride 20 miles west to

ECSTASY OF MISERY

White Pass. But why? White Pass has nothing compared to Packwood. So I smartly decided to spend my needed layover day here in Packwood.

After lunch I finished my laundry by putting my sleeping bag into the dryer. My bag was a little shorter now. I didn't have that extra down around my feet like I did before. So now it was time to beef up in the warmth department. It was time to visit the sporting goods store. But before I did, I decided to send my cell phone and charger ahead to Snoqualmie. This would lighten my load a bit. So far, I haven't been able to get any reception in Washington, so I might as well send it on ahead.

I'm sure glad I did, because in doing so, I was able to talk to the postal clerk about my wet cold experience and how I was going to have to buy some wool socks and other warm stuff at the sporting goods store. She told me that I should at least try the Methodist Thrift store down the road, that the sporting goods store can be quite expensive. "Thanks for the tip," I said. I headed down the street to the thrift store. About a quarter of a mile I found this place and on the outside of the place a sign read, "Garments half off on Thursdays".

I entered the store looking for wool, and man, did I enter the right place. I found an Italian made sweater, 90% wool, god-awful colors, but so what. The price was $2.50, but half off on Thursday, so $1.25! I found a wool cap, thicker and warmer than mine, that cost .75 cents, again, a god-awful color of bright orange. Hey, if I get caught in the big dump and have to be rescued, the helicopter will definitely see me.

I then bought two pairs of wool socks for only .50 cents a pair and fake leather gloves for only .75 cents. This will do it. This will keep me warm under that pathetic sleeping bag of mine, when used in conjunction with my old stuff. The total price for this was only about five bucks. I couldn't believe it.

I left the thrift store very happy. I stopped by to thank the postal clerk for giving me the tip. From there I headed back to the room, but not before stopping to buy some Ben and Jerry's Chubby Hubby. The rest of the day I cleaned up my stuff, including my ground mat, which was really filthy. I called Trail Perfect around 4pm, gave her my phone number and she would then give the phone number to my parents so they could call me.

This was definitely a necessary rest day. Everything was so dirty and wet, but now I had cleaned all my gear up and even my backpack was almost dry. I put it in the bathroom near the electric heater and it really did a quick drying job on it. I loved this green pack; it was a real friend to me compared to my other go-lite pack. It weighed only 18 ounces with a material that dries quickly. For the cost of $79, it was a steal of a deal. I soon fell asleep watching the news of the Iraq debacle and slept for a couple of hours.

I was awakened by a call from Eric Carpenter of the Orange County Register who was following my trip and writing articles every three weeks or so for the family section of the paper.

My parents called after that. It was great to hear from them. My dad, however, let me know that he was tired of mowing the yard. I told them both that it wouldn't be too much longer now and that so far Washington has been incredibly miserable. Each day I think of home as I hike the muddy trail in wet running shoes. My mom said that every night she watches the weather station and it continually shows rain for Washington. I told her if it's not rain, then it's fog, and sometimes snow.

After a few minutes I say good-bye and hang up. Sometimes it gives me a heavy heart but I still feel happy that I'm still on the trail. The weather has got to clear up some time. The local weather report comes on the TV and for the first time, some positive news comes on about the weather. It will be clear of rain for the next couple of days, but then another storm front is moving in! Oh man. Oh well, I'm hungry now. It's time to get some pizza. I head out of the motel room. The pavement is almost dry. There's actually some blue in the sky. The clouds over the mountains, however, are still menacingly dark.

The pizza place is a typical pizza joint with big wooden tables made to look rustic. There are pictures of the local bowling, baseball, and other teams on the walls. I was about to dive into a pepperoni pizza with five other toppings and brown beer to wash it all down when I notice a familiar figure enter the place and walk towards me.

Shoot me down, it was The One. "Hey buddy, what's happening?" "When did you get here, Wrong Way?" "Last night about 7pm. I was rescued by a cool local bow hunter!" "Yeah," The One replies, "We got blown out too. Bandana's mom drove up from Portland and brought us here." I said that I never expected to see anyone in Packwood.

The One went on to say they had got soaked and Bandana's sister who was hiking this section with them is pregnant. "Pregnant, that's psycho, man, should she be walking this trail? Was she actually going to hike over Goat Rocks?" "Yeah, I guess so, she's only a couple of months." "Oh," I said, a little relieved.

The One asked me why don't I head over to the Rainbow Tavern across the street. "Rob and Bandana are there now and we're playing oldies but goodies." "You don't mean the Beatles and the Stones, do you, bud?" "No that's too modern; you know, the 50s and early 60s stuff." I said that I'd be over after I down my righteous pizza. After eating the last piece of crust, I head across the street to the tavern.

Inside I found three thru-hikers sitting and eating pizza while listening to the "Sea of the Heart Break", you know, lost love, loneliness, and all that stuff. "Try the BBQ chicken pizza, Wrong Way, it's delicious," yelled Bandana over the loud music. So I stayed there at least an hour, stuffing my already stuffed belly with BBQ chicken pizza and Moosehead beer.

Bandana put a couple of tunes on and sang along with them. "LA seemed too tough for the man and now he's going back to Georgia." Or something like that. Bandana's voice was kind of funky but the locals in the bar seemed to like it, so I guess that's cool. About an hour past hikers midnight, around 10pm, we all got up and left. "See you down the trail, dudes," I said. "Yeah, Wrong Way," as they mumbled off into the dark heading for their rooms. Those kids are too much. But I still don't think they know my story. They haven't even got to the first chapter of my book.

That night I hit the hay and finally fell asleep around 1am, a victim of too many daytime naps and bizarre dreams.

The next morning I was up at 8am, and headed for breakfast at the Packwood Café. An hour later I was all packed up to go. I only had one stop to make and that was at the local sporting goods store where I bought some aluminum tarp stakes. An hour later I managed to finally hitch a ride to White Pass and once again to the fantastic illusive Pacific Crest Trail.

White Pass is a tiny place with one motel and a small store that serves as a post office. I remember in 2000 that I shared a room here with the amazing 62 year old hiker, Tony DeBellis, alias Kokopelli. It was here that I met John and Millie, all of us senior citizen hikers. I was the youngest at 54.

The weather was sunny and bright. Now it's dark and cloudy. The date then was August 5th. The date now is September 12th. Very late in the season and the weather was showing it. But like Rick and Madame Butterfly told me, just keep on keeping on. That's all I can do.

I walked into the café-store area and asked for my supply package. It was there. Sitting down at one of the tables with a large cup of coffee to give me an energy burst, lo and behold, Frog walked in. "Wow, Frog, when did you get in?" "This morning, half frozen," said Frog.

Frog went on to tell me that he had a real bad night out there. "I got so desperate that I asked a couple if I could get into their tent. They said no, but the guy loaned me his coat or I might not be here now." He had spent most of the night eating candy and power bars and doing push-ups and sit-ups until dawn. "It was the longest night of my life."

I asked Frog where Batteries Included was. "He's still out there, but I believe he's okay. He had warmer stuff than I had." I said that I hoped he was okay. Frog said, "Yeah, if he doesn't show up today, I'm thinking of calling the Forest Service. I rented a room for the both of us and he's got to pay his half of it." He laughed a little but you could see he was a bit concerned. "He'll be okay," I said.

I told Frog my story and how I lucked out with the bow hunters, as well as how I had flamed my sleeping bag. Frog thought that was funny. "Wrong Way, you're too much. You should get a warmer bag before you freeze to death." Then I told him about Packwood and the Methodist Church thrift store. He was interested and said he might just head down to Packwood tomorrow. For now, he was into total rest and thawing out.

I was about to work on my pack by stuffing my food inside when Wahoo and Lou popped into the store. "Hey, dudes." "Wrong Way, long time, no see." "Yeah, I believe the last time I saw you was at Crater Lake." They said they had visited a friend in Bend, Oregon, and she gave them a ride to Timberline Lodge. "We missed some of the trail but we'll make it up some day." "Did you have a good time?" "Yeah, it was a blast." "Well, that's all that really counts."

I asked them when they got to White Pass and they said two days ago. "We were going to leave yesterday, but the weather was horrible," Super Lou said. "So we're heading out now because it looks like it's clearing up a bit." I told them I heard that there might be a day or two before the next storm.

"Well, Wrong Way, we're off," said Wahoo. "Yeah, I'll see you down the line." They both headed out of the store and down the way a piece where the PCT trailhead is.

I started putting food in my bag again. It's going to be about 100 miles before my next stop, which is Snoqualmie Pass. That should take about four and a half days and I have at least five days worth of food on me now. While I was sitting there working on my pack, two dudes that I haven't seen before walked in. I started rapping to them and found out that they were Mercury and Just Paul! "Wow, dudes, I've been reading your entries all the way from near Mexico to here. I'm Wrong Way, from LA." "How did you survive that storm?" asked Mercury. "I was rescued by a bow hunter from Washington. I'm fortunate because my sleeping bag is pretty much shot. In fact, I burned the bottom of it in a fire trying to dry it." "Oh boy, you should head to some major city and pick up a new one, something with a 20 degree rating at least," said the dark-haired dude called Just Paul.

I told them about the thrift store in Packwood where I picked up some wool. I showed both of them my prize possessions. They cracked up at the wild orange color of my wool cap with a little orange ball sewed on top. My green, red, and pink Italian sweater was a big hit too. "Yeah, I got these plus a thick pair of wool socks and some skiing gloves, all for $5.25." "Wow, Wrong Way, that's a steal of a deal." "The main thing is that they're wool, wool can give you warmth even when it's wet."

We sat there for a while talking. I learned that Mercury was actually walking the trail for the second year in a row! "Wow dude, you must be psycho to do this." "I just love it, and I had the time, so I decided to do it a second time." "Man I never heard of somebody doing that in consecutive years." "Well, in our group, the Class of 2003, there are actually three of us." "What?" I said. "Meadow Ed believes it's a first to have three people in one season to re-hike the trail." I asked who else was pulling this off. "Billy Goat, Yogi, and my-self." "That's too much," I said. "Yeah, it's kind of cool, you hardly need to look at a map and you really surprise trail angels and other people you met the year before."

Just then another guy came through the door. Mercury said, "This is Northerner, he's a total purest, to the max." "Oh yeah, right. I've missed some of the trail too," he said. Northerner was sort of a small guy; I always thought he'd be some big dude with a red beard. For the next hour I sat around the place eating freshly grilled chicken and drinking coffee like a beatnik or some-thing.

Soon I met two other people traveling as a couple; they were Apple Pie and Prune Picker. Apple Pie was from Copenhagen and Prune Picker was from Orange, California, close to where I live. It was so cool to finally meet these people.

Just Paul was surprising too. I always thought that Just Paul was the guy that I met near Wrightwood and the same guy that left his hiking poles at Agua Dulce which I brought to the Saufley's place. Not so. This guy was a different guy, a guy that didn't really want a trail name. He asked people to just call him Paul. He became "Just Paul". It's kind of a heartwarming story.

Finally it was time to depart. It was 2:00 now and I figured I could do nine or ten miles for the day. So with a fine caffeine high, I left my new friends and headed up the highway and joined the PCT once again. With a clearing blue sky I headed up the trail on my seemingly never-ending quest for Canada.

Soon after leaving the highway the trail passes Leech Lake and White Pass campground. The weather now has cleared up and the sun actually peeks through the clouds now and then and lights the freshly cleared forest a golden color. I can already tell, however, that with the clearing clouds, the night will be a cold one. But at least I'm prepared for it.

Deer Lake shows up on my left side and there are a couple of tents and some guys fishing on the other side. On my right there's only a half mile further to Sand Lake. This lake looks too shallow to catch fish, but who knows.

My legs feel really good from the rest that I had at Packwood. My pace is quite good, even with a slightly heavy pack and a mild ascending trail. As the sun sets behind spotty dark clouds, the day starts to come to an end. An hour later I decide to call it a day and make camp at Snow Lake in the William O. Douglas Wilderness.

Even though it looks like a clear rainless night, I make sure to set up my tarp. For dinner, I decide not to cook but to have cheese, bread, and trail mix. I'm not really hungry because of the food I have eaten all day long at both Packwood and White Pass. The temperature starts dropping and my trusty compass thermometer reads 38 degrees. I know it's going to be near freezing tonight but at least there isn't any wind.

I climbed into my fire-shortened sack, I put on my long sleeve Patagonia shirt covered by my heavy flannel, then my windbreaker and finally my Italian wool sweater and two pairs of pants. On my feet I wore fresh nylon hiking socks and my new extra thick wool socks. On my hands are my thrift store bought ski gloves that look warm but are really useless. On my head, of course, I have my new bright orange wool cap that I can pull down all the way to just above my eyes. By hikers midnight I'm out. Tomorrow will be a long day, hopefully in the sun, but this is Washington, and it's getting towards the middle of September, so anything can happen.

The next morning I'm up at 6:15 and hiking by 6:30. Disappointing, however, is that fog covers the trail and visibility is poor. Soon my pants are soaked and shortly after that my shoes are soaked. So goes the dream of a warm clear day.

Sometime after the initial shock of being soaked from the waist down once again, I was about to pull off the trail and put on my waterproof pants, when I saw a small figure coming down the trail alone. It's a small dark-haired girl hiking alone.

As she came up to me she said hello and asked if I was a thru-hiker walking from Mexico. "Yeah, I am, I'm just trying to get to Snoqualmie right now." She said that is where she started her trip and that she was doing the PCT by sections. "I've done all the way from Manning Park to here so far. I'm trying to make it to Cascade Locks and that will be it for this year." "That's cool," I said. "You're doing it in the sensible way, but it's too bad you couldn't have done Washington earlier in the season, like in August." "Yeah, that's for sure. In fact, if the weather gets bad again, I might just pull out at White Pass and go home. I really don't enjoy hiking in this stuff." "I said, "Me neither. I'm a fair weather dude from Southern California." "Oh you must be missing home right now." "Yes, I have to admit it, I do miss home."

Before she left she told me that she's Lady Bug and I told her my trail name is Wrong Way. I said that maybe I'd see her down the line some time. "Okay," she says, and off she marched. I yelled out to her before she rounded the corner not to take any unnecessary chances, especially at Goat Rocks. "Okay," she said and then disappeared around the bend.

Oh man, you know being a guy and walking the trail is one thing, but being a young girl like that is another thing. The thru-hiking girls of 2003 have teamed up with a guy or at least a group. That's the right thing to do. Girls are excellent hikers but walking alone on the trail, I don't know. Well, hey, it just might be safer than in a suburb or crowded city, I guess.

Now the trail starts to climb a little more sharply as it rounds three fine looking lakes. Fish Lake, Buck Lake, and Crag Lake, fall to the wayside as the trail climbs to some 5500 feet. For the next five miles the trail really doesn't cross a creek or go by any lakes until Anderson Lake, which is more like a large pond. Here I have lunch, pigging out on flour tortillas and jack cheese, followed by a store-bought lemon pie,. The pie was great except that it was totally crushed. The trail after this is pretty easy hiking all the way to huge Dewey Lake.

Dewey Lake is a sign that I'm getting close to Chinook Pass and Highway 410. Many campers are at this lake, as well as day hikers, because of the easy access to Highway 410. I remember this lake well when I was hiking with John and Millie and the insurmountable Tony DeBellis. The weather was warm and sunny then but I can't complain now because the sun has just come out and although it's slightly chilly, I'll gladly take this.

The trail goes by Dewey Lake and the small flood lake near its side. I know now that I have a short climb out of the lake area up to a ridge and about a two mile drop to Highway 410 below. Up on the ridge I get a great view of Goat Rocks, 30 miles or more south of me. They are covered in snow. I still believe it's temporary. I think most of the snow on these peaks will probably melt before the big dump hits?   West of me I get a cool view of Mt Rainier. God, this is a beautiful mountain.   Like Shasta and Mt Hood, it's shaped like a volcano jetting up to the heavens.

Soon I'm heading down the ridge, switchbacking away as I go.   Several day hikers and some overnighters pass me by.   I don't bother to talk to them, they're in a hurry heading for the Dewey Lake area and I'm heading for Chinook Pass. About halfway down I come across a Gatorade cache.   There were eight or nine bottles there.   I grabbed a couple of the blue and a green.

There was a note beside the bottles.   John and Jan had put the bottles there.   The note read, "For thru-hikers only".   I guess most people read the note or there wouldn't have been any Gatorade there, unless they had just put them there a short time ago.

From there I headed downhill once again, until I reached the highway below.   There were quite a few cars traveling though because it was Sunday. Over the highway was a small bridge, the archway to Mount Rainier Park, which was written on the side of it.   I crossed the highway to the other side and headed east to a small parking lot that had a bathroom and a trash can.   Thru-hikers should always take advantage of trash cans.   Emptying your trash cuts down on the smells and lightens your pack a little.

While dumping my trash I met a middle-aged couple that was on a Sunday drive.   They lived in Tacoma, Washington, about 60 miles to the west.   I told them my story and they were interested in hearing it. Then I joked that I wished this place had a cheeseburger stand.   They thought that was funny and actually offered me a ride east to a small town where they had seen a fast food place.   I declined, telling them that I needed to climb out of here and find a place to sleep before it got dark.   They offered me some bottled water and I took it.   Then they left heading for home.   Gee, you know you do meet a lot of nice people on this trail.

From Chinook Pass the trail gradually climbs a long one mile grade that is above Highway 410.   Then the PCT swerves away from the highway which is probably 1000 feet below and drifts in a more northern direction until it gets to Sheep Lake.   Sheep Lake is where I was thinking of crashing for the night, but there were just too many people, including some big frisky dogs that damn near knocked me into the lake.

I gathered some water for cooking only. The bottled water I had would be for drinking and cleaning only. The reason I use the lake water for cooking is because shallow Sheep Lake looks like it might not be a reliable source of good water, with all the visitors it gets.

I leave the scene quickly and hike about a fourth of a mile on the trail to where it levels out nicely. It's a little lumpy from the bunch grass but still nice and soft. One minor problem, however, is that there are no places to tie up my tarp. My two friends who gave me the bottled water in the parking lot said it was supposed to clear up for a while, but another storm might be coming in a few days. So just in case of an emergency, I find a lumpy funky place a little ways away where I can pop up my tarp.

I start up my stove and I notice that my fuel is getting a little low but I should have enough for three more nights. That should get me to Snoqualmie. There's a pretty good store in Snoqualmie and also a hikers box. I should be okay. That night I cooked some beef stroganoff, another Lipton dinner, which are pretty good and only half the price, as I mentioned before, compared to the backpackers dinners you can buy out of a sporting goods store.

Right about when my meal is ready I hear a bunch of kids coming up the trail, accompanied by one adult. They're talking about a mountain goat they saw up on the cliffs and they pass by me not realizing that I'm there.

"Come on, come on," they're saying. We can still get a picture of them." Soon they disappear around the bend and I start eating my dinner.

A little later when I'm cleaning my cooking pot that I also eat out of, they come hustling back down the trail and this time they see my headlight, which I have on red because it's a softer color that I like to use around my immediate vicinity.

"Hey, what's that? A kid yells out. The adult says, "It's a camper, what do you think?" The kid exclaims, "I thought it was the tail light of a motorcycle or something." The other kids laugh a little and I hear, "Oh Jeremy, that's crazy, there are no motorcycles up here." The adult man yells out to me "Hello" and asks if I'm hiking the PCT. I told him that I was and he asks, "Where did you start?" I said Mexico and the kids all go "Wow!" and I feel like a newborn champ. The man and I talked just a bit because the kids sounded like they wanted to get back to camp where there was a lantern and food.

The man tells me his name is Chuck and I told him that I'm Wrong Way. He tells me he is going up to Stehekin in a few weeks. I said maybe we'd meet again, though it was quite dark and we couldn't really see each other. So I put on my headlight and shined it on my face, lighting up my nearly white beard, and soon he does the same.

Chuck wished me luck and said, "See you later" and off he goes with a bunch of kids back to Sheep Lake. I hear one kid say, "Doesn't he get scared out here alone in the dark?" "He's use to it," Chuck says in a low continuing muffled voice that subsides as the distance grows.

The next morning was a cold one. My thermometer read 38 degrees at 6am. I stayed pretty warm, except for my feet. I missed the extra down that used to be part of my bag before I torched it. By 6:15am I was off. Not having to deal with a tarp saved me a lot of time. The morning looked pretty good, but soon clouds started to appear once again.

The trail from my crash site climbs right away, still working its way out of Chinook Pass area. The trail switchbacks it's way up to Sourdough Gap. From this strangely named place the trail begins as a ridge walk with great views of South Washington to the south. Mt Adams especially looks cool and like Goat Rocks, it still has some snow on it.

There is absolutely no water for the next few miles. I'm really glad that I have that bottle of Gatorade left in my pack. The stuff quenches the thirst and gives me energy too. Soon I pass Bear Gap and Pickhandle Point and finally Blue Bell Pass Crown Point. At this point the trail actually turns and nearly back tracks itself for about 75 yards before it heads in a straight northern direction.

Heading almost exactly north, I begin to get excellent views of Mt Rainier, as I look over Pickhandle Basin way down below. Last night before I fell asleep I checked out the map like I should do every night, but most of the time I don't. Following the trail I roughly make out the 24 or 25 miles I should walk. I notice that Urich Cabin Shelter is about this distance away. So this is my goal for the day.

Urich Cabin is a place I remember well, for in 2000, a family and friends of about seven people from Washington occupied the cabin with their horses stabled in back. The cabin is supposed to be for backpackers and not horsemen. People on horses are supposed to camp in the southern part of Government Meadows.

My hiking partner of the time was Tony DeBellis, alias Kokopelli, and he was fit to be tied over the matter. The dude gave the grandfather a hard time, then he camped out in the meadow, pissed off.

When I got there with John and Millie, the grandfather was trying to make friends and gave us some excellent apple pie. A younger guy gave me candy and other good stuff. But the vibes were so bad that I left and hiked another couple of miles that day and camped damn near an underground bee hive where I promptly got stung. The next day John and Millie caught up with me. I didn't see the angry Kokopelli for another day or so. Horsemen may be at the cabin or maybe not, whatever, this was my mission for the day.

Once on top of the ridge the hiking was pretty mellow. There were views towards the west and east. As I headed north I passed Bullion Pass Prospect, Cement Basin, and Scout Pass. At Big Crow Basin it began to rain again, not hard, just enough to be annoying.

At Hayden Pass I met three local bow hunters and one guy with a rifle. They seemed to be nice, but the older guy was a bit hostile, especially after asking me if this was the most beautiful country I had ever seen. I simply told him that it was awesome, but the High Sierras of California, especially between Forester Pass and Selden Pass, were my favorites. The guy seemed to take exception to that and started complaining about people from California moving up to Washington to retire and how they drive up the prices of houses and land, then the locals can hardly live there any more. It's the same old thing that I've heard before on other hikes in Oregon and Washington.

I got pissed and let the damn redneck know that California was great in the 50s and 60s before half the world moved there. "Listen dude, my dad bought his house for $18,000 in the late 1950s, now they're selling it for around $450,000. So don't cry to me about people moving in. We get thousands of illegals pouring across our border every year. I've seen my area of Southern California go from heaven to hell, buddy, so don't cry to me about this rain soaked swamp you call Washington!"

The younger guy thought this was funny, but the old man didn't and kept mumbling obscenities through his flea-infested beard, Since they had weapons, I jammed, leaving them there and their quest for shooting deer. This is not the smartest thing to do while walking on someone else's turf. But damn it, I couldn't help it.

From Hayden Pass I hiked at a faster pace, still angry at the world. I should have told the guy that a whole lot of those people that are supposedly moving to Washington had moved to California to make their fortunes by working at high paying jobs. Then they sell their homes at quadruple the original price and move back to their birth state of Washington with a pocketful of gold. I had said enough, however, and I better cool down. Remember I'll be getting to Urich Shelter later today and who knows who could be occupying the place.

The PCT after Hayden Pass began to go from a scenic ridge walk to a rather dense forest walk. At Morgan Springs I was able to get some water, so I decide to take lunch. The place had some decent camping spots spreading out around the trees.

After lunch I followed a footpath for just a short distance, sort of exploring a bit, and I ran into two huge llamas sitting at an empty campsite. I figured it was a campsite for bow hunters or hikers so I left the animals undisturbed. Llamas are continually being used on the trails instead of horses and mules. They do really well on mountain trails and are super sure-footed.

I leave Morgan Springs and head out walking through a viewless forest. I soon pass torn down Urich Rock Shelter, which is supposed to have a spring nearby. From this area I soon pass Rods Gap and the trail opens up into a flat meadow-like area. The elevation here is somewhere around 4500 feet. About a half mile further I arrive at Government Meadow. Then to the right there's a horse trail with a sign that reads Government Meadow Horse Camp. This is where horseback riders should camp, not at Urich Cabin.

I know now that I'm really close to Urich Cabin Campgrounds. That's really good because the weather is continually getting worse. Fog has spilled in all around me. The trees are starting to drip like it's raining. A half mile later, I see Urich Cabin standing in the fog, but looking pretty good.

From a distance the place didn't seem occupied. At least there weren't any horses parked around it. After all, it was late in the year, and for the last nine days or so, except for one, it had been raining continually. As I approached however, I could see smoke coming out of the chimney. When I got to the front porch I could hear voices as I walked up the steps.

I heard "hello" and looked inside and saw a rather big fellow. It looked like Meadow Ed. "Hey you look like Meadow Ed." He said he was Meadow Ed's twin brother. "Wow man, I didn't know Meadow Ed had a twin brother!" I walked in the front door and it was definitely Meadow Ed. It's impossible for anybody else in this world to look like Meadow Ed other than Meadow Ed.

"Wrong Way, you actually made it here." "Yeah, buddy, it's been quite a stroll, walking hard during the day and partying triumphantly all night long." Meadow Ed didn't laugh, he hardly smiled. "You've lost a lot of weight, Wrong Way, you're looking pretty puny." "Thanks man, but do I have to buy a ticket to this joint or is it for all mankind?"

"Did somebody say that they had a joint?" a voice came out of the dark. With further inspection I could see that it was The One. "Hey dude, the last time I saw you, you were sucking down brewskies in Packwood."

The clowning went on for a bit until the Meadow man introduced Gibbon, a guy thru-hiking Washington. He was an old guy from England who looked too old to describe.

Urich Cabin is probably 20 feet by 30 feet with a loft you have to climb a ladder to get to. At the end of the cabin stood a big black stove that had a fire going in it. This stove kept the whole place warm. About a half hour later Wahoo and Lou appeared at the front door. I was very surprised to see them because I thought they were still in front of me. Because of the loft the place could easily handle all of us.

The rest of the evening was spent on conversations about the trail. I introduced one of the conversations when I mentioned Scott Williamson's name as the greatest trail hiker. When I met the guy in 2000, he was 29 years old and had already hiked about 29,000 miles! Now in 2003, who knows how many miles he has hiked. His continual quest to yo-yo the PCT has got his trail name Yo-yo Man. I firmly believe he will be the first man to yo-yo the PCT, that is, to hike from Mexico and Canada and then back to Mexico all in the same season.

Meadow Ed doesn't like the guy because he pulled off the trail in 2000 and didn't tell anybody. This caused a panic and everybody thought he had died in a snowstorm some place between Lake Edison and Forest Pass. People were ready to put their lives on the line, as Meadow Ed did, to find the guy. Just in time, however, he reported or someone else reported that he was up near Seattle some place. So the guy made a mistake. I'm sure he didn't mean to freak everyone out. Since then he has been kind of put down by some PCT officials.

Another subject of interest was the old English guy's heavy-duty gear. He should have been hiking Alaska, not Washington. The old boy's boots must have weighed at least four pounds each. Nothing wrong with this for a guy that's only going to hike 10 miles per day. It must be nice to crawl into a six pound tent every night.

By 10pm everybody found their spots on the floor. Wahoo and Lou were taking the loft. Meadow Ed spoke out loud, "Hey, no fooling around up there."

It was a pretty cool evening with pretty cool people. Outside it was foggy and wet which made inside even better and more desirable.

The next morning I was the first one to leave and was hiking by 6:20am. I said good-bye and thanks to Meadow Ed and then peeled out down the foggy wet trail.

Snoqualmie was now 45 miles away, an easy two day walk. The trail starts out by crossing Road 942 and winding its way around an ugly clear-cut area. For just a short distance the trail becomes a logging road and then breaks off to circumnavigate around Pyramid Peak to Windy Gap.

In 2000 I stayed here for the night and was promptly stung by a bee. The bee actually came out of the ground, the last place that I would look for bees. Right after that, three young hikers came by; one was called Mule, another was Thin Fin. I don't remember the third guy's name. They were all college students who were taking the fall semester off at the University of California Los Angeles.

I talked to them for just a bit and told them that they would be welcome to stay but they were in a hurry even though it was almost dark. They wanted to go on and were taking the road to avoid falling timber that had blown down during a windstorm a couple of years ago. This blow-down was actually due to a fire that took place some five years before. So off those animals went, hauling ass down the road. Man, it must be nice to be young. Later I found out that these guys thought that they were going to catch Scott Williamson. Little did they know that Williamson was only 30 miles away at Snoqualmie. Only one problemo though: Scott was heading south. He had already reached Monument 78, the northern terminus of the PCT and was already halfway done with Washington on his southbound trip to Mexico.

So much for 2000, I'm living in the present and I sure hope those trees laying over the PCT are cleared away by now. Round the bend and a quarter of a mile later, I was relieved to know that they were. The signs of the fire were still there. So was the devastation, but small trees and fireweed were growing all about. Mother Nature was slowly healing her wounds.

An hour later I arrive at Green Pass where I used the last of my water for breakfast and to clean up. By 11am I was heading around Blowout Mountain at an elevation of 5000 feet and the trail starts to descend gradually towards Tacoma Pass.

The trail is pretty fast and I'm feeling my cheerios and holding a three mile per hour pace. My reward for all this is, what else, the rain starting again. Ever since the first day I arrived it's been raining; there's been only a day and a half of decent weather!

At Tacoma Pass I had to make a short detour a half mile down the road to get H2O, where I filled up a tank of what looked like pretty good water. I haven't treated my water now for over 200 miles. I can't stand that orange stuff. The next sure water source looks like 10 miles away at Stirrup Creek.

From Tacoma Pass I head up towards Bearpaw Butte. I love this kind of area. The trees are all small from either a fire or clear-cutting that had taken place. A hiker can get nice views from these areas and it's like walking through a forest of cool little Christmas trees.

The rain has stopped again and that's nice. Up in front is a big comfortable rock to sit on. I sat down and took a break in fresh smelling fragrant air. As I sat there I notice a pick-up truck way down below heading due west. There's a lot of Aspen country here and that gave me an idea. Why not try a cell phone call.

I tried Chuck Hinkle first and got a connection. Chuck wasn't home so I left a message. Next I called Trail Perfect and again got a connection. She had just gotten home from Vons supermarket where she was buying stuff for my next package pick-up after Snoqualmie, which was Skykomish at Stevens Pass. I talked to her for a while. It was over 90 degrees in LA. Linda told me that they still hadn't put out that fire in Oregon. Man, I can't believe that. That damn fire has been burning for a month!

Now for some negative news. Trail Perfect tells me there's another fire in Northern Washington near the Canadian border. I just hope it's not anywhere near the PCT. I said good-bye to Trail Perfect. She said that she would call my parents and let them know that I would call them soon from Snoqualmie.

So off I went, trying to get as many miles as I can in order to get to Snoqualmie as early as possible. The weather has cleared up a little but intermittent black clouds cross the sky at a rapid rate. I wander along the trail and begin to see blueberries growing all along.

I made the mistake and pick the first one. Oh is it good, especially to a hungry and somewhat thirsty hiker. They really hit the spot. I'm picking them like a crazy man. I can't believe there are so many along here. It seems that somebody or some bear should have eaten them by now. The problem now is that I am addicted to them. They're so rich and have almost the texture of a soft avocado. You get the feel of their richness. Finally I force myself to stop. I'm wasting time. I want to get to Stirrup Creek where I've planned to camp.

Ten minutes of wasted time munching blueberries and I'm off. I've wasted 10 minutes of daylight. My headlight needs batteries. For the next three hours I push my pace and at 7pm I reach Stirrup Creek area. The place does not have any open campgrounds as far as I can see because now it's pitch dark and kind of spooky. I have water now, so I've got to crash. It's been a long day. I find a relatively flat area with two trees that I can tie my tarp to. I crush down some weeds before I lay out my ground cover. It feels like I'm in a dense forest area. I miss the Tacoma Pass area with its openness.

Tonight I make some chicken a la king. I only wish that it was fit for a king. At 9:30 I'm massaging my dogs. Oh, that feels good. These poor little bastards have carried me for many miles in my life. Landscape maintenance, backpacking, thru-hiking, football, baseball, and five years of distance running. It's a wonder they still work. Taking those wet Nikes off and giving them a massage sure feels good. Today, September 15th, has been a productive one. I believe I've covered 26 or 27 miles today! It looks like Snoqualmie is about 16 or 17 miles away.

The following morning it starts to pour down rain! Not again. My tarp is still set up well. I've learned to trust it, so I fall back to sleep for a couple of more precious hours.

About 7am I start to get up, but it's tough. I'm comfortable and it's raining out there. Some mornings are just a drag to get going, but I know I must and I realize that this is town day.

When it's raining, one tries to do all he can inside the tarp. It's uncomfortable, however, and here is when I wish I was younger and more flexible!

Finally out of the tarp, I have to take the thing down and stuff it in my bag along with the rope and stakes. I'm finally done. I head down the trail with all my rain gear in tow. I have my nylon pants on under my waterproof running pants in order to keep me warm. I put my three layer Gore-Tex jacket on with my wool Pendleton and Patagonia shirt underneath. I feel much better now that I'm on the trail. To me, getting ready is a real drag. With my hood over my head I barrel out of Stirrup Creek area which is sort of like a miniature canyon, and head towards Twilight Lake and Yakima Pass.

The rain at this time is light and more of a nuisance than anything else. But as I get closer to Yakima Pass the rain slowly becomes heavier and heavier. Suddenly my legs feel terribly cold. They must be getting wet.

I stop under a tree and pull down my waterproof pants and my nylon pants are soaked. It doesn't take long to figure out why. Like a dumb ass I had tucked my Gore-Tex jacket into my black nylon waterproof pants. The rain water simply poured down my jacket and underneath my waterproof pants, soaking everything to the max.

What a stupid ass. I can't believe I did such a stupid thing. I just wasn't thinking. To make matters worse, I had my hands in my pockets which pulled my pants away from my waist a little and that helped cause more rain water to enter. What a drag. I had a major problem now. My legs were getting colder and colder as well as feeling heavier and heavier.

I walk on for a quarter of a mile and finally come to the conclusion that I was going to have to make a pit stop under a dripping pine tree. I quickly took off my shoes and both pairs of pants. I pulled off my wet nylon pants and quickly put my waterproof black pants on. I squeezed out the excess water and put them into my pack. With numb fingers I put my shoes back on and headed back down the trail.

My legs were now lighter and not quite as cold but my body as a whole was even worse off. My gloves were saturated and my fingers were numb. It was scary. There was nothing to do but haul butt. Hiking hard was what really kept me warm. My upper body was reasonably warm. But my legs, feet, and hands were freezing. I actually enjoyed it when the trail presented sudden short upgrades because by pushing up these hills I felt a little warmer.

Most of the time I was slowly heading downhill towards Mirror Lake. Then suddenly the rain was gone and snowflakes began to fall out of the sky. It was actually a bit of a welcome from the heavy drenching rain. I couldn't believe, however, how fast and thick the snow came down. It only lasted maybe 10 minutes. Then the snow fell more casually, thank God, for I was afraid that the trail would be covered.

The snow had another positive effect. The high weeds that grew beside the trail, the same weeds that rubbed against me soaking my clothes as I walked through them, were now flattened out on the ground by the influx of the heavy snow. I was as cold as ever and I wondered as I rambled downhill, what if I sprained or broke an ankle? I would definitely be in bad shape. Stopping could kill me.

As I drew closer to Mirror Lake, the snow kept up. For the second time on this trip I was scared. The first time was the grizzly that growled at 9:30 at night near Big Bear, California. That ended up funny and didn't last too long. Now I was afraid of freezing. I had a feeling that this would not be so funny.

I soon reached Mirror Lake. I knew that I had only about eight miles before I reached Snoqualmie but I also knew from experience that it was a long monotonous eight miles that just never seemed to end. I remember tripping a couple of times in 2000. Now, however, the snow had squashed the weeds and I could see the bottom of the trail more clearly than before.

My feet were now numb. The only thing I could do about it was to keep on keeping on. Finally, great day in the morning, the snow stopped and turned into a light rain. Then the light rain turned into a misty fog and finally all precipitation halted and the snow hadn't covered the trail. The temperature seemed to rise and spots of sunlight popped through some dark clouds. Hallelujah, Hollywood. It was over. I was going to survive.

Mt. Hood in Oregon

Left to right: Scott Williamson, John and Milley. 34 miles south of Snoqualmie, Washington

Journey Sixteen:
Snoqualmie Pass and I'm Out of Gas!

The storm had ended and I was dropping in altitude to boot. Two hours later I finally limped into Snoqualmie, with numb feet and hands. Just before I entered the motel I looked behind me to where I'd been three hours before and I was amazed - the mountains above Snoqualmie Pass were shining in a flow of pure white!

Snoqualmie Pass is different from the town of Snoqualmie. The Pass has only a large modern motel, a store that also serves as a post office, and a gas station with a small store. As small as it is, it serves the hiker pretty much of what he needs. But they don't have a camping store.

A camping store is definitely what I need. I could use another ground cover because mine has had it. I also need warm gloves. The fifty cent skiing gloves that I bought at the Packwood Methodist Thrift Shop weren't worth a damn. I'm also thinking of getting a poncho, the type that I've seen backpackers from Washington wear, the kind that covers the pack as well as the whole body, down to below the knees.

These are some of the things I'm thinking about as I walk to my motel room. All that is secondary right now. My main object right now is to jump in a hot shower and warm my half-frozen body. My right fingers are numb and a couple of toes have no feeling.

The Best Western Motel is a good one. Each room has two double beds, a color TV, and all the amenities, including a laundry and a hot tub. The rate is $75. Kind of steep for a lot of hikers but most thru-hikers team up and split the cost of a room with their buddies. I left a note with the check-in girl at the motel office that if a lone hiker comes in and wants to split a room, I'm interested.

The hot shower was great. I let the hot water power itself against my numb fingers and toes. It helped a lot because I started to feel tingling sensations in these areas. It was now after 2:00 and I was starving. So I was just about to head for the restaurant when I got a phone call from the front desk. A dude named Giddeon, I guess he was named after some fairy tale or Gulliver's Travels or something like that, wanted to share a room. I met the guy at Urich's Cabin and he was cool. I said, "Sure, send the dude to my room."

I waited a few minutes after hanging up the phone, when there was a knock on my door. I opened the door for the strange little guy. "Hey, man, nice weather, buddy." "God," he said. "I couldn't believe all that snow. I was afraid it was going to cover up the trail!" "Yeah, man, being from LA I was freaking out myself. I tucked my rain jacket into my pants and the rain soaked both pair of pants. I really had a bad start that day. Well, dude, I'm heading to pig out. Help yourself to the shower, it will help you thaw out."

Leaving the room I headed down to the restaurant. Man, I was starving. I ended up ordering the fried chicken dinner with a salad and a couple of beers. As I was eating, I happened to look across Highway 90 and I saw Frog barreling towards the motel looking for sanctuary from the storm. The poor guy looked like a drowned rat!

"Hey, Frog, what's happening, man?" Frog looked up and said, "Oh no, it's you Wrong Way. How did you get here?' "I swam and skied, how else?" I said. Frog went over to the desk and checked in.

About then Wahoo and Lou came in looking pretty wasted. Their timing was good because all three water-soaked comrades shared a room. I sometimes don't know why people aren't thrilled to see me. I'm a little outspoken and I love a good argument, but on the other hand, I'm a really swell guy?

I love the word "swell" now because that's a cool word from the past, like the 1920s and 1930s, even the 1940s. I've been watching old movies when I get a chance. Everything is "swell" this and "swell" that. "Gee that's a swell backpack!" "You're a swell guy," Hedy Lamar said to Clark Gable. "I'm going back to my room and have a swell nap!"

Back in my room I started watching the tube and the weather came on. It seems like most of Washington's mountains received snow. It was one of the earliest snowfalls in the last 20 years. More rain for sure was on the way. But they didn't know about any more snow.

It was September 16th – was this the big dump? Were Madame Butterfly and Rick wrong in saying I could probably hike to the end of October, that there might be snow but it would melt? The people on the news were excited. They were hoping for an early skiing season. I guess I couldn't blame them because for the last few years Washington hasn't had many productive skiing seasons.

That evening I called home to my parents first. They had heard about the weather and told me to stay put until the weather cleared up. Trail Perfect heard about the weather too. I told her I might be home a little earlier than I thought and there was a possibility that I won't make it. That's why I told her that I should have flip flopped. I would be in Oregon by now heading south, away from this mess. But no, I listened to the so-called experts and here's the fix I'm in!

My defeatist attitude came out as I expressed my anger at this state. I've been in Washington for 11 days and it has rained for 9 of those days. It's getting ridiculous. That night I took a Jacuzzi and ate like a pig. Tomorrow I would do all my chores, like laundry and re-packing. I had plenty of time since I might be here for a few days. The weather person said there should be clearing on Thursday and this was Monday evening.

I slept in the next morning until 8:00. I had an excellent breakfast and then did my laundry. I was happy that Giddeon was going to spend another night. I got along with him quite well and it helped to split the rent. Later I went over to the store and picked up my supply package and signed the register stating that I was sick of Washington and was thinking of going home. It mostly rained that day, but the good news was that it didn't snow.

That day brought Batteries Included and Billy Goat 2 to the motel. I think everyone was worn out and a bit depressed over the weather. In the late afternoon, I was surprised to look out my window and see Meadow Ed and The One getting out of a small car. The One was limping pretty badly. He must have changed his mind about hiking to Snoqualmie, probably because of the funky weather. Guess I can't blame the guy there.

It had been a good rest day for me. I needed it. It was also a good day to duck out of the rain. The one negative thing was that Giddeon was planning to leave the next day, September 17th, rain or shine, and it was supposed to be raining. I tried to talk him into one more night, telling him that the weather was supposed to clear up on Thursday. But he was adamant about going. My last night, unless I found a roommate, would cost me $75.

The next morning, September 17th, I said good-bye to Giddeon and walked over to the Greyhound bus station. Since I got all my chores done yesterday, I figured I could head down to this place called North Bend and get a few things I needed. I had heard that they had a lot of stores there. So I bought a ticket for $18 and got on board at around 11am.

The bus was going to Seattle, but it made quite a few stops on the way. The first stop was North Bend, only 20 miles away. The bus soon arrives in North Bend. I'm glad I decided to sit up close to the driver because I asked him when the next bus comes in to North Bend headed east. The guy then tells me about 12:45. I was shocked because I was told 2:45. "No, 12:45, believe me," said the driver.

I told the driver my situation and he says that he will drop me off at the mall on the way out of town. "That will help." I said. "How far is it to the bus station from the mall?" "About a half mile or so," he says.

After dropping off the other passengers at the station, he starts to head back to the freeway and out of town. I watch carefully because I want to know how to get back to the station from the mall.

Just as he said he would, he drops me off at the mall and I thank him for helping me out. At TG&Y I found a great pair of wool gloves. At another store that sells coats I found a poncho, but it's not the kind that has enough material to cover my pack. The price is only 14 bucks so I bought it anyway. One problem is that there isn't any authentic outdoor shop here. I probably should have gone to Isaquah, where there is a GI Joes.

I'm now off back to the bus station, when I saw an Ace Hardware store. In this store I purchase a regular seven by five foot blue tarp, not exactly ultra light material but light enough, especially when I cut it lengthwise and make it a seven by three foot piece. Having only 20 minutes left, I notice a bakery in town. I stroll in there and power down a cream puff and take a chocolate éclair to go.

The bus pulls up right on time and I head back to Snoqualmie Pass, having pretty much accomplished what I wanted, except perhaps not getting the poncho I wanted. I'll have to try it out with my pack on and see how it works.

About an hour later I'm back at Snoqualmie Pass, ready for a late lunch at 2:30. The rest of the day I just kicked back in my room and took a nap. Man, that shopping can sure wear a man out.

That evening after dinner, Wahoo, of Wahoo and Lou, told me that there was kind of a party in the lounge and bar area. So I headed there and found a slew of thru-hikers. They included Frog, Batteries Included, Rob and Bandana, the Northerner, The One, Meadow Ed, and myself. Rob, Bandana, and Batteries Included arrived in Snoqualmie today when I was in North Bend.

For about an hour or so everybody sat around drinking beer, and some played pool. Meadow Ed had some kind of mixed drink going on. It was a pretty good time. Towards the end, however, as Meadow Ed was about to turn in, I told the dude that he was a pretty nice guy, but I believe he had a bit of a personality problem. The Meadow man didn't like that too much and turned abruptly and walked off.

I wish that I hadn't said that. But I was just trying to clue the guy in on how he could be a little mellower, sort of like myself. He sure didn't want to hear that. I felt kind of bad as I left for my room. I figured I could make amends to the guy the next day before I left.

That night I prepared my pack. Tomorrow I would leave this place. The weather was supposed to clear up. Today it had rained lightly on and off.

The next morning I woke at about 7am and headed down to the restaurant for a power breakfast. From the door I could see Meadow Ed sitting and talking to Wahoo and Lou. Quickly I went back to my room and got my ancient Pacific Crest Trail patch. I had bought two patches at Lone Pine, California, in 1977 and had sewn them on my pack that I had for my 1978, 1998, and 2000 hikes. The other I had sewn on a baseball cap that I wore walking California in 1998.

It was a cool patch, brown and white, showing a mountain and a sunset. Written on it was Pacific Crest Trail Canada to Mexico. This patch was long before the Pacific Crest Trail Association patch you can buy out of their store now. It was pretty unique and I doubt that there are very many of them around. I gave one to Tony DeBellis and the other to Meadow Ed. He looked a little surprised but not too excited.

A half hour later I walked out of the motel. It was September 18th and there was a bit of sun out, but clouds were abundant and they started to gather as I hiked to the trailhead down Highway 90. The surface road branches off into a small trailhead parking lot and by god, as soon as I put my foot on the trail, it starts to rain. Unbelievable. There is nothing to do but hike. I have a lot of climbing to do to get out of the Snoqualmie Pass area.

The trail switchbacks above Highway 90 and the sound of the cars slowly starts to fade as the trail gains altitude on well-graded switchbacks. After a few miles I notice that I don't have the pick-up that I usually do after a two day rest. A few minutes later, a lady going for a day hike passes me. Even though she didn't have a pack and was in good shape, she shouldn't have passed me like that.

Then about a mile further, I feel a pain in my stomach and then sudden cramps. I have to leave the trail and do a number two. To my displeasure, I have the runs. I figure that it's probably for all the rich junk food and beer I had yesterday. A couple of miles further on, the same thing happens once more. I still believe I'm okay and I head off into the rain, still climbing.

At Ridge Lake, I meet the lady heading back down to Snoqualmie Pass. I talked to her for a few seconds and mentioned my problem with partying a little too much. She pretty much tells me to work it out and I'll be all right. We joke a little bit about getting older and not being able to handle the rich food like we once could. She then heads out and I have to leave the trail once again.

Down the trail I meet a couple heading for Gravel Lake. They're hiking to Stevens Pass and are bummed out that it's raining. I tell them I'm a bit surprised because I heard that it was supposed to clear up today.

"Well, maybe tomorrow, but that's what I've been saying for the last two weeks." The two young people head off down the trail and I head off into the late afternoon rain.

Soon the trail heads around Joe Lake, a real nice looking lake, even under a gray sky. Huckleberry Saddle is next, but here I have to trot behind the tree once more. This is beginning to look like more than just the rich food syndrome.

Right after the Saddle the PCT crosses Chickamen Ridge. This ridge means that I have pretty much climbed out of Snoqualmie Valley, altitude has been accomplished, but I know I have at least two or three more miles to go before I can crash for the night. It's only 5pm but I feel weak and it seems that every half hour or so, I have to go.

Rounding a curve on the super rocky trail, I'm taken aback by four mountain goats, about 60 yards in front of me. There's a male goat and a baby, and I think the other two are females. They're unbelievably beautiful. They're snowy white and the father goat is really muscular-looking with a great goatee hanging from his outstanding mug. They really don't seem to be afraid of me, so I put down my pack and pull out my camera. I take a couple of flicks, then the awesome animals slowly move straight up the rocky terrain that's almost like a cliff.

I head out again. The rain is now starting to come down harder. My new poncho, which is stupid-looking, seems to be doing a decent job. The mountain goats were a source of relief for me, taking my mind off my current health situation.

In 2000, I remember climbing Chickamen Ridge when an Air Force jet came hauling ass right towards this cliff. It was scary. I thought for just an instant that it was going to crash right square into the cliff. If it did, I would be in trouble from flying debris, and maybe a rockslide. At the last minute it kicked up in altitude and just cleared the cliff probably by only a couple of hundred feet!

The jet was totally silent at first. I was actually lucky to spot it. Immediately after clearing the cliff, an unbelievable roar came and it was deafening. The noise had arrived just behind the jet. It was really incredible. The jet was obviously flying faster than the speed of sound. The pilot may have been a young hotshot getting his kicks. I guess he's lucky nobody could get his aircraft number; he might have been in a heap of trouble. Back to reality. I was more than halfway done with the ridge walk. The weather got worse, fog came in with the rain, and visibility was only about 100 feet or so. Finally, the rocky PCT reached Chickamen Pass and now it began to switchback sharply downhill.

ECSTASY OF MISERY

It was now 6:30 and was getting dark earlier than usual due to the putrid weather. I was desperately looking for a place to crash. The trail leveled off and to my left was a small lake about 200 yards off the trail. I found a rather flat spot between trees. In fact, there were trees on each side of me. I tied my rope up and laid the tarp over it. While pushing the stakes into the ground I had to take a break and you know what, what else, my seventh attack.

A few minutes later I was under the tarp taking off my wet things and putting on dry clothes. Finally I lay on my back and rested, but not for long. Nature called again, and it was worse. This wasn't repercussions of too much partying, but I believe I had Giardia.

For the next four hours I had what I would call uncontrollable diarrhea. I didn't have dinner because I didn't have an appetite. Later that evening I started taking Flagyl along with Immodium D. I had a horrible night. I practically had to try and sleep with my butt out of the bag and it was a cold night too.

The rain came down steadily, sometimes in buckets, but I had my tarp up in a good area. I was lucky again to have a tarp because it worked well with all the emergencies I was having. A tent would have been a bummer. I would have had to exit countless times. I knew that I wouldn't be going anywhere tomorrow. It would be a day of just lying on my back, taking my medicine and sleeping.

Some time during the wee hours of the morning, I fell asleep for a while, but as soon as daylight hit, I was back at it. The rest of the day I made sure I took my Flagyl every four hours. As the day went on I began to get better. Immodium was stopping me up. I tried to eat during the course of the day even though I still didn't have much of an appetite.

At around 1:00, during a slowdown of constant rain, I got out from under the tarp and tied the sides of my tarp with extra rope and hooked the rope to the trees which pulled the sides of my tarp out giving me all kinds of room inside.

A few times during the day I heard voices as people walked by on the trail above me. I wondered if it could have been some of my thru-hiking buddies, but there was no way to tell. Towards the end of the day, I was happy about the way I felt. The emergency movements were now gone and so were the stomach pains, but I still felt weak. The rain started to slow down too; there were only intermittent showers that weren't too heavy.

It was a very boring day for sure, no radio, nothing to read or no one to talk to, but I did do a lot of sleeping. That night I cooked a meal of beef stroganoff and I ate quite a bit of mild cheddar cheese. I wasn't too hungry but I knew I had to eat. That night the rain seemed to have stopped; the wind had picked up a bit.

Tomorrow would be a day of reckoning. I was sick of the rain. It's been raining for over two weeks now and if I feel bad tomorrow, I might just head on down to Snoqualmie and go home! If I'm not having any fun, then what the hell am I doing out here anyway? How could I do this? I only have a little bit over 200 miles to go. What am I going to do? Man, am I feeling depressed. Oh well, tomorrow is another day. Things might look better tomorrow.

Around 10pm that night, I popped another Flagyl and fell asleep. During the night I awoke a few times. It worked out okay because I was able to take my medicines. I noticed the rain had stopped. It was a good 15 degrees colder than last night. At about 3am I fell asleep and didn't wake up until 7am the next morning.

The next morning was September 19th. I could hardly believe it. The sun was shining on my green tarp. I lay there a few minutes, letting the place warm up. I got up at about 8:00 and immediately dragged my poor sleeping bag out into the sun, spreading it out over some small bushes. I did the same with my tarp. Almost everything was wet.

I forced down some power bars and cheese and then took my medicine. I was feeling okay, but a trifle lightheaded. I still had my doubts on what I was going to do. The sunshine was a blessing. My stuff dried out within a half hour. That's really all you need. But in Washington, at this time of year, that can be a rare deal.

By 10am I was ready to go and began hiking up the dirt path back to the PCT. When I get to the trail I have to make the big decision: do I turn right and head back to Snoqualmie, or do I turn left and head towards Canada. It wasn't that hard of a decision to make; the sun helped me a bit to make up my mind. I turned left and headed north.

ECSTASY OF MISERY

My head felt light and I was a little spaced out, but in general I felt pretty good considering all the stuff I've been through. My legs were definitely rested since I've hiked hardly any miles. The trail now switchbacked down to awesome Spectacle Lake and crossed the energetic Delate Creek.

Here the trail now switchbacked down steeply, losing altitude that I know I would have to gain later. I passed a number of hikers that were hiking from Stevens Pass to Snoqualmie. They were tired of the rain and a few of them mentioned that it was finally a great day and of course, it's the day they were leaving.

This section is labeled J4, in the Oregon and Washington Trail Guide of the PCT. It is considered one of the most beautiful and one of the most rugged parts of Washington too. Although it's a tough one, I don't think it's the hardest section, probably because it's only 74 miles long. Still heading downhill now, but a lot more gradually, the trail passes Lemak Creek and several other small creeks.

It's now 1pm; the day goes by fast when one starts late like I have. That's perfectly cool because today I feel that I'm lucky to be hiking so well after yesterday. Today would be a light day. If I can get 15 miles today, I will be completely satisfied.

The trail starts to climb once again and then switchbacks downhill to Waptus Lake. This is a tough downhill march. It's steep and rocky and I remember three years ago falling twice here as I walked late into the day trying to catch my buddies Tony, John, and Millie. The view from the top of the ridge is terrific. Mt Rainier is incredible, more snow had fallen on it since I saw it last, Goat Rocks is awesome. I could even see Mt Adams, a faint volcanic pyramid far to the south.

It's hard to explain how beautiful Washington looked now. It was crystal clear and clean, with mountain peaks, most of them covered in snow at the highest parts. To the north, I believe, I could see Glacier Peak and maybe Mt Baker, but I'm not sure. The air is crisp, the sun is warm and totally dynamic.

Down the trail I bail, if I don't make it, I will fail. The walk down to Waptus Lake is an annoying one. The weeds are high and seem to always eat up the trail. To make matters worse, there are loose rocks at ones' feet. Finally after two hours, the PCT and I arrive at Chief Creek. I gather my water here and fill up a couple of tanks. It's now almost 7:00 and it's starting to get dark. Right after I cross Spade Creek, I found some excellent camping spots. I chose one that has two trees about 20 feet apart, perfect for tying up the rope for my tarp.

It's been a rare sunny day, the sky is clear, but I don't trust Washington. Things can change quickly and without my transistor radio, I can't get a weather report. That night I make some chili mac. I should be hungrier than I am, but Flagyl has a way of killing one's appetite. I notice right away, due to the clear starlit sky, that tonight will be a cold one. I'm ready with my wool attack and new mittens factor. I conquer the cold and have a good night's sleep.

The following morning is Sunday, September 20th, and I'm hiking around big Waptus Lake in a golden sunrise. I traverse quite a few creeks. Some of them have bridges and the rest have fallen logs that serve as bridges. Toward the end of the lake I head in a more northern direction and follow Spinola Creek all the way to beautiful Deep Lake.

Just how many Deep Lakes are there? There's probably more Deep Lakes than there are Tamarack Lakes, I'm sure, but there's probably even more lakes named Blue Lake than either of those. At Deep Lake I make my usual power shake breakfast, with fruit bars, and then I'm off again.

The trail starts to climb steeply at about 7000 feet to Cathedral Pass, and Cathedral this and Cathedral that, but this pass deserves the name because there's some really nice rock formations above Deep Lake, which the trail goes reasonably close to. From this new elevation the trail stays rather flat for a while and this is most appreciated right now.

Soon the trail starts to descend about 300 feet, switchbacking its way to a flat open area below. Down here I find two horsemen and a backpacker looking up at Cathedral Rock. Wondering what the attraction is, I ask and find out that they're looking at a mountain goat high on top of Cathedral Rock.

The older guy with the straw cowboy hat has binoculars and he's quite excited about his visual find. I can only see a white speck as does the backpacker. The other guy on a horse doesn't seem to be interested.

"Wow," says the guy with the binoculars. "You don't see that too much.

ECSTASY OF MISERY

Those wild goats are extremely rare."

I really didn't want to rain on the guy's parade, but I went and told him about the four goats I saw 60 yards away on Chickamen Ridge in the rain three days ago.

"What?" says the guy. "You can't get within a half mile of those animals, they're just too aware of their surroundings!" "Well these guys didn't even look like they were too concerned with me. They sure were beautiful." "I think you may have mistaken them for another animal," the guy said.

Being not in the argumentative mood I said the guy may be right and that it had been raining pretty hard. He then offered me a Gatorade that was still rather cool. The other guy also gave one to the backpacker.

"Speaking about the rain," said the older horseman. "The weatherman says that it looks clear and sunny for the next four or five days." I started jumping up with joy. "That's the best news I've heard in damn near three weeks."

"How long have you been hiking out here, buddy?" "About four and a half months," I said. "Where did you start?" "Mexico," I said. He asked where I was heading and I told him to Canada.

"Good grief, no wonder you thought you saw mountain goats 60 yards away. You're probably delusional right now." "Yeah I guess you could be right. Well, thanks for the Gatorade and especially the news on the weather. I'm a Southern California boy and 16 days of steady rain is about all I can handle." The cowboy dudes laughed and I headed north once again.

The hiking was a little easier, at least for a while. The trail seems to head along a bit of a ridge, with views of Alpine Lakes Wilderness to the east. Hugs Lake lies to the east as did Tuck Lake and Ruben Lake. The PCT now climbs a little and reaches Deception Pass. About a half mile after this I had a late lunch at Reception Creek.

From here I made pretty good time, crossing several creeks that basically flow to the east. The forest here in the last few miles consists of mountain hemlock, sub-alpine fir, red cedar, Douglas fir, and elder: quite an array of different trees.

I know earlier in the year this place can be covered in wild flowers. But now the flowers are gone, though bushes like huckleberry and blueberry are turning beautiful with fall colors of yellow, orange, and red.

The trail now bounds along with some ups and downs, with Deception Creek Valley area far below me to the west. That evening at about 6:30 I arrive at Deception Lakes. It's starting to get dark now so I decide to crash here for the night. I find a nice flat spot between the two bodies of water.

The sky is clear. I decide to take a chance and not put up my tarp for the night. According to the cowboy dude it's not supposed to rain for four or five days. A few minutes later I was about finished with my standard Lipton meal of chicken with rice when I heard noises and then saw two lights coming down the trail.

When the travelers got closer they yelled across the stretch of water that lay between the trail and my crash site. "Hello there," said one of them. The voice sounded familiar. "Howdy," I yelled back. Then I heard, "Wrong Way, is that you?" I told them it was I. They started talking between themselves and then I recognized the voice. "Frog and Batteries, is that you?" They said it was .

I told them to come across, that there was some real cool sandy flat area to crash. "No, Wrong Way, we can't. We want to get down to Glacier Lake so we can get to Stevens Pass by late morning." "Yeah, we want to finish the trail by September 28th," Batteries Included said.

"All right, dudes, maybe I'll see you down the line. I'd be in Skykomish now if it weren't for a bout of Giardia." I told them how I spent a whole day on my butt two days ago with uncontrollable diarrhea.

"That sounds bad. How are you doing now?" asked Frog. "Excellent." I said. "That's good," they both said. "Perhaps we'll see you later, Wrong Way."

Then they were gone. I never saw anything but their headlamps. I thought about the statement that they were in a giant hurry, and with the hiking abilities of the 20 year olds, I pretty much knew that I wouldn't see them again. It's time to realize that the end was near, relationships for the last four or five months would come to an end. Finally a social, and even sort of cultural, shock would soon face all of us.

ECSTASY OF MISERY

After scarfing down my food I put on my wool clothing, including my ugly orange hat with that crazy ridiculous wool ball hanging from the end. Looking up to the stars, I couldn't believe the multitudes. It's been many days since I've seen stars.

I'm so thankful to have good weather. What a burden it takes off my shoulders. It makes hiking so much more pleasant. Tomorrow will be town day. I'm only 17 miles from Stevens Pass. From there it's a 17 mile hitchhike to Skykomish. It should basically be downhill, but it still won't be easy.

Just about the time I fell asleep I heard a weird little noise. I rolled over to get up. I then heard a squeak and a rustle of tiny feet flee the area. I got my headlamp just in case the intruder came back.

Sure enough, a few minutes later I heard that same little patter of tiny feet. This time I put my light on and saw a couple of little varmints dash off back to a rocky area about 15 feet away. This time I noticed what they were going after and that was some crumb of Top Ramen that had fallen out of the bag. I picked up just about every crumb and covered the rest under the dirt. That should do it. I then lay back down, checking out the stars once more.

Everything was going quite well. I was just about to crash out when I felt my orange wool hat being pulled off my head! Freaking out, I quickly sat up. I heard a loud squeak and off ran the varmint once more. Damn it, the tiny mouse must have thought that the decorative orange ball on my wool hat was a piece of fruit or something. It was actually trying to rip it off! I grabbed some rocks and headed over to the mouse's campsite and pelted the area with stones. I knew I couldn't hurt the little fart, but I might scare him from bugging me any more.

After that I got back into my sack. With my food locked up in my pack and at my feet covered by my new rubber poncho, I got deep into my bag, ducking my head almost all the way in. Some time after that I must have fallen asleep because the next time I awoke, it was daybreak. That little rascal never bothered me again.

I popped out of the sack at 6am, an early start and a bit dark too. The temperature was 35 degrees. Within 15 minutes I was heading out. The trail stayed pretty much level for about a mile, but then the trail headed downhill at

Piper Pass, switchbacking down steeply to Glacier Lake below. The trail then curves a bit and goes about a quarter of a mile from Surprise Lake. At Trap Pass, the PCT climbs steeply up to Troop Lake and then levels out a little all the way to Hope Lake where I stop and have a late breakfast. It's about 10am and I'm really happy about the progress I have made so far today.

Just after Troop Lake, I would guess about a mile, I notice a black ball of fur moving around in the weeds and low hanging bushes. I keep walking. Right away I can tell it's a black bear out munching something in the late morning sun. The young bear doesn't notice me. I get within 20 yards of the youngster and I figure I might as well take a picture, but when I take off my pack, the bear sees me. He takes off like a scalded dog, jumping across a creek at an in-credible speed! Young bears can run like jackrabbits when they're frightened.

By 12:30 I reach Hope Lake. There's a bigger lake ahead, so I head for Mig Lake, a quarter of a mile further on. Mig Lake, however, is a stagnant body of water. Since I'm just getting over Giardia I didn't want to get sick again.

The trail from here gradually heads downhill towards Lucky Susan Jane Lake. When I reach the lake I can see power lines and the last crest before the trail drops into Stevens Pass. I decide to hold off on drinking water right now. This lake looks too accessible to the general public to drink from. The fact that a couple of guys across the lake are throwing sticks in the lake for their dogs to swim out to retrieve them reinforces the idea to hold out on drinking, even though I'm rather thirsty.

Now the trail drops into what I think is Stevens Pass. But to my surprise the trail starts switchbacking up a ridge. I'm bummed out. What the hell am I doing climbing again? But that's the PCT, full of surprises. Soon I travel under ski lifts and then the trail starts to descend once again. The sound of trucks soon becomes apparent. I'm really getting down now. A few minutes later I cross a small dirt road with a cluster of trees and a parking lot with RVs in it. Just past this dirt road and gravel parking lot is Highway 2 at Stevens Pass.

Me and Billy Goat probably the oldest guy to walk the trail in 2003.

North of Snoqualmie pass

Journey Seventeen:
Skykomish and Stevens Pass

I've made it to Stevens Pass and I'm standing beside an RV that I think belongs to the new trail angel guy who makes pancake breakfasts for PCT hikers. Meadow Ed told us about this guy. I knock on the door but no one answers. There's an aluminum table and some chairs. Beside the door in a bucket of ice is some bottled water. I figure this is for PCT hikers and I grab one.

Drinking it down, I then head to the other side of the highway and start hitching west to Skykomish, which lies about 17 miles away. The last time I was here I had a hell of a time getting a ride. Tony, John, and Millie all got rides first. I felt like they must have known I was from LA or something.

This time I took off my wide-brimmed sloppy looking prospectors hat and put on that ugly looking bright orange wool hat. I kind of look like I have a traffic cone on my head. Nearly 20 minutes of hitchhiking with my sloppy blue hat, nothing. Within two minutes after putting on my orange cone I get a ride. Mice aren't the only animals attracted to this hat!

A guy coming back from a fishing trip picks me up and takes me all the way to Skykomish. I thank him profusely. I ask him if he wants a bite to eat at the local restaurant, on me. He's not interested. He's got to get to Bellingham tonight, so off he goes. I cross the road and walk over to the motel where I stayed the last time. It is 70 bucks a night and I can't get the guy to come down either, but I take it anyway. I'm tired, dirty, and hungry, and Monday night football comes on in about an hour.

Skykomish is a quaint little place. Everything you need is in walking range. It's sort of like Cascade Locks, except there aren't as many places to pig out. It's a pretty historical lumber town, with a railroad running through it. Far to the east is Wenatchee and to the west lies Everett, Washington. Highway 2 seems to be a pretty busy highway. Stevens Pass, where the PCT goes through, is a big ski resort in the winter. The Skykomish River also runs through it.

419

ECSTASY OF MISERY

The next morning I was up at 8am and back over to the restaurant having a huge breakfast of three eggs, six buckwheat pancakes, bacon, toast, coffee and orange juice. My appetite had come back since I had quit taking my medicine yesterday. That stuff can really take one's appetite away.

That morning I called a trail angel named Bob Norton. Before I left Snoqualmie I had given Meadow Ed my radio and cell phone and rain jacket. Meadow Ed said he would leave them at Bob Norton's house. Bob answered the phone and gave me his address.

I headed on down Main Street looking for the guy's crib. I couldn't find it but then I heard somebody yell and looking down the street, I saw Meadow Ed walking towards me.

"Hey dude," I said. "Here you go, Wrong Way. How have you been?" "Sick," I said. "Sicker than hell. I spent one full day lying under my tarp with Giardia." Meadow Ed didn't want to hear it. He had already heard about my last Giardia attack at Richard Skaggs house. He doesn't seem to like to hear negative stuff.

Meadow Ed told me that Mercury and Just Paul were at the Skykomish Inn. He asked if I had seen them yet. "No, man, I'm staying at the Sky River Motel." "Tell me you aren't staying there." "Yes I am, and I'm still there." "Well get out of there," he said. "This place is only $30 night, $20 if you sleep in the main room. That guy at the motel really doesn't like hikers much!"

"Yeah," I said. "He seemed a little put off with me, probably because I look and smell like a trail bum. Hey, I am a trail bum, now that I think of it!" No matter how I try I can't crack a smile on the Meadow Man's face.

I went inside the Skykomish Inn and found Just Paul and Mercury who are hiking partners now. It was a solemn scene. Mercury has to go home; his sister has died of cancer. She has been sick for quite a while and she finally passed away a few days ago. Just Paul didn't look too happy about it either. I think these two have become good hiking buddies.

I took a look at the place. I decided to rent a room for 30 bucks. The place had a TV room, washer and dryer, and according to the Meadow Man, every thru-hiker stays here, except for weirdoes like myself. I went back to my room, got my stuff together, and checked out. When I got back to the Skykomish Inn, four more thru-hikers had arrived: Bandana, Rob, Wahoo and Lou. Then Huff and Puff, Chance, the Northerner, and The One all came in within about an hour of each other.

I wasted no time getting to the laundry room before it got too crowded. After doing my laundry I went to the cool little post office and picked up my supply package. The rest of the day I kicked back and enjoyed all my hiking buddies. In the afternoon a bunch of us went over to the Whistle Stop, had some drinks, watched TV, and shot some pool. There were a few locals there. They were cool. They were use to thru-hikers coming by this time of year. Later that day Puck came in. He had broken up with Belcher and actually flip flopped from White Pass to Manning Park. He had some surprising things to say about the trail ahead!

Fire! There's another fire, from Rainy Pass, and about 30 miles north of that the forest service has closed the trail! You can get through but you have to take an alternate route. Puck tried to explain how he got past Rainy Pass, but it was hard to understand, especially when he explained that he had gotten lost for a couple of days. I'm thinking, "Man, fire in Oregon, fire at Cascade Lock, and now fire just north of Rainy Pass."

Puck told us that the Canadian government had actually closed the border until the Pacific Crest Trail Association told them that there were many thru-hikers heading to Manning Park coming all the way from Mexico. The Canadian Forest Service said that PCT hikers could come through but they should only camp at Manning Park and not along the trail. "Well, that's a relief," Huff and Puff said, as about five of us stood around and intensely listened to the red-haired Puck.

About 2:00 that day Free Radical and Lugnut came in from Stevens Pass and now there were 10 or 11 of us. That night Chance came in from his car trip from Wenatchee. He was cruising with his brother-in-law, I think. Anyway, they brought a ton of awesome food to the Skykomish Inn. There are three baked chickens, salmon, all kinds of fresh fruit, potato salad, macaroni salad, dried fruit and nuts. What a feast. We all sat around watching South Park on TV, laughing and pigging out. That night was a great night for me, to see all these cool people, especially since it might be the last time I'll see some of them.

ECSTASY OF MISERY

The next morning there were two cars heading for Stevens Pass. Bob Norton and Chance's friend took about eight or nine of us to Stevens Pass. At the pass, sitting outside and having pancakes at the trail angel's RV, were Tea Tree and her hiking partner, Special Agent. They were going to Skykomish next to get their supply boxes, so they wouldn't be heading out with the rest of us.

Just about then the young monkeys came down the trail, Eon, Leprechaun, and Johnson the great complainer. They would be heading out to Stehekin and Section K after they had some pancakes. I walked around taking pictures of everyone. This was probably the biggest conglomeration of thru-hikers since the Saufley's place, way back in Agua Dulce.

As for my breakfast, I had already had three honey buns and a giant cup of coffee at the store back in Skykomish. I just wasn't interested in having any pancakes. I was the first one to take off. I walked across the road and then passed a power substation.

The trail then is basically a maintenance road which gradually becomes a trail. It starts out easy, but I know from experience that this is not representative of Section K. This is, in my opinion, the toughest section of Washington. It's a real wilderness with fantastic Glacier Peak as the big daddy highlight of the area. It is 100 miles of rugged ass-kicking country, and the weather should be good for at least five days.

The trail from here gradually climbs past two lakes. Lake Valhalla looks like a shallow lake used by many hikers due to the availability of being so close to Stevens Pass. The other lake is Janus Lake, a deeper nicer-looking lake.

For now I hike along on a trail that is abundant with aster, bluebells, bleeding heart, columbine, fireweed, lupine, money flower, paintbrush, parsnip, and Sitka valerian, at least that's what the trail guide tells me. These flowers and bushes were probably predominant during the spring and most of the summer. But now, and especially after that snow a week ago, most of these flowers and bushes aren't in bloom. It's now September 24th. Fall is definitely here. Like mentioned before, fall has its own beauty of orange and red leaves that now sparkle in the bright sunshine.

Between Lake Valhalla and Lake Janus I'm caught and passed by Eon and Johnson. The young monkeys, because they are between high school and college, sleep in tree hung hammocks. I rap to these young dudes. Their big goal for this trip is to visit Kennedy Hot Springs. These three or four guys have hit every hot springs from Mexico to here. They probably lie there in the hot springs and smoke their weed, contemplating on what they will do in life now that high school is over.

Eon and Johnson are pretty fast hikers, especially Eon. He's about 5'6" and probably weighs about 125 pounds. The kid can tear up hills, especially when he has his rock and roll, hip-hop and rap electric earmuffs on. Johnson is even cooler. He complains his way up hills and according to other hikers, he complains about everything. That's cool. I can relate with that a little myself.

The trail now heads past Union Gap and levels off a bit, then drops down to a small creek where Eon is drinking water and at the same time trying to keep his long ponytail from flopping in the water. Johnson has been telling about his exploits in South America last year. He really likes Argentina. He would like to be an Argentinean cowboy!

While sitting at the creek, a cavalcade of thru-hikers flows in. Besides me, Eon and Johnson, now there's Huff and Puff, Free Radical, Just Paul, Lugnut, Leprechaun, and the Northerner. Everyone is sitting around clowning and drinking the sweet cascading creek water which makes a little three foot waterfall that everyone can get their drinking vessel under.

Some shots are taken at Eon and Johnson and everybody laughs. I guess it's the old story of one generation knocking another generation. Eon says in response, "Yeah, what happened at the Dead concert, you scared the babes away." "Yeah you were lucky there, man" said Lugnut. "Chicks come up to you guys and flutter off. They come up to me and say 'what's happening'?"

"That's because you look like one of them." A laugh sort of rolls through the older generation group and then the younger group of Johnson, Leprechaun, and the insurmountable little Eon, get up and leave. Comments are made as they disappear around the bend of pines that are glowing in the sun.

For the first time I realize that there's sort of a loose social structure here among these hikers. I feel completely out of it. I think Just Paul, who is 46, feels a little displaced too, especially since Mercury, who is also in his 40s, has had to return home. From this creek it's only a short walk to Lake Janus and then uphill about 500 feet, then up towards Grizzly Peak. Most of the guys hiking are planning to probably stay at Pear Lake for the night. The trail of hikers stretches out now, with me pretty much towards the rear of this convoy.

A couple of hours later I was hiking pretty much alone, when a young guy catches up with me and passes me by. "Heading for Canada?" I say as he picks up speed. "Yeah, I sure am," he says. "Did you start in Mexico?" He said "Yes" and I told him so did I. He sort of looked behind him, kind of surprised. The guy looked familiar, but I couldn't figure out where I saw him last.

That night I stayed at Pear Lake with outstanding cliffs in the back of it. The camping spots are limited, and other hikers take the best spots at the front of the lake. In the middle of the lake area, swinging from trees, are the young monkey dudes, Eon and friends. At the end of the lake I crash with Just Paul, Lugnut, and Free Radical. The evening looks prematurely dark because of the dark clouds blowing over the cliffs at the end of the lake. I'm kind of bummed. Is rain on the way? It's not supposed to be. Like everyone else, I put up my tarp for the night, prepared my meal, and fell asleep with the wind smacking against my tarp.

The next morning, September 26th, I arise early. The only other one stirring is Just Paul. In fact, he's actually ready to go before me. We both head out together, walking to the other side of the lake where we came in. We climb up to the PCT and head north.

"I can't stand sleeping in. It just seems that I have to get up at 6am and go to the bathroom right on cue," he says. "That happens to me sometimes, but I usually have to dig a hole after I walk for a couple of miles. I don't usually eat until I've hiked about four or five miles," I said. He said he does the same thing.

On top of the ridge we look one last time at beautiful Pear Lake. Down below we can see that no one has stirred yet, including the monkey kids. "Do you see those guys in hammocks?" Just Paul said. "Yeah, those guys don't get up until 9am. They wait for the sun to warm up the place. I wish I could do that sometimes, but at my age I need as much time in the day that I can get to make enough miles that I need." Just Paul said that he knew what I meant.

Down the trail we go. I notice that Just Paul hikes just a tad faster than

I do, but then in the morning hours I don't hike quite as fast as I do towards the end of the day. About a half mile further on we see two packs at the side of the trail. They're GoLite Gusts, a red one and a green one. Right away I know that it's Wahoo and Lou.

"Wow, I wonder where they are?" "I guess maybe doing their morning number." I said. Just Paul kind of had a little look of disgust and said, "They're almost like Siamese twins, they even have to go to the bathroom together." "Well you know what they say on the trail about couples: 'couples who dig holes together stay together!'" Just Paul sort of laughed and we moved on.

Somewhere in this area is the border to Henry Jackson Wilderness. It's one hell of a beautiful place. The trail goes up and then down. In this morning environment I have already seen six or seven deer and a dozen elk.

Just Paul is up ahead of me now. Catching me again is that young guy I met for the first time yesterday, though he looks kind of familiar. "Top of the morning to you, buddy." "Thanks," he says. "Hey dude," I say. "What's your name?" He said it was Anthony. "That rings a bell, dude," I say. "I think I saw you at the Mt Laguna store way back in early May." "Yeah that could have been me, I guess." "You had a butch haircut and gaiters on. Remember. It was storming outside. I think you were getting a room like I was." "Yeah, that's right, but I don't remember you."

I told Anthony that the reason that he didn't remember me was that I was 50 pounds heavier then and didn't have a beard. "My name is Wrong Way, by the way. I thought as buff as you look that you would be finished by now." "I would have been but I had to take a couple of weeks off and go back to Georgia for a wedding."

"Well, it looks like you're going to make it. I remember you had walked the ATP last year and you said the PCT would be a lot easier because it's a contour trail. How do you feel now?" Anthony said, "Well, the ATP is steeper, but the PCT is harder in a lot of ways. That Southern California weather was demoralizing, to say the least!"

I rapped to the guy for just a bit. He headed out with me following for a while. The trail then heads over Cady Pass, one of the millions of passes one has to traverse in Washington. A few miles further down the trail I came to a cute little lake called Sally Ann. Here I had lunch with Just Paul, although he was just about finished with his lunch when I started to have mine.

Still in the Henry Jackson Wilderness, the trail headed up and around Kodak Peak. The trail now switchbacks up to Wards Pass on a trail loaded with greenish mica schist. Looking down towards the sides of the trail one can see white quartz, shiny and clean from the recent rains. Soon there are excellent views of Mt Rainier, Chimney Peak, Mt Daniel, along with the Stewart Range. Just a little further on, the fabulous snow-covered Glacier Peak comes into the northern view.

The trail drops down to White Pass where the shrubbery once again looks like it's lit up by neon lights. The colors of red, orange, and yellow are spectacular. At Red Pass I run into Wahoo and Lou who had passed me when I was having lunch. Free Radical is there with them.

I guess they were having lunch or just resting. In fact, breakfast and lunch are non-existent to tell you the truth. Most thru-hikers eat all the time. Dinner is probably the only true meal. But from morning to night, most hikers are sticking something in their faces. With the amount of calories needed to keep up the energy one has to be damn near eating all the time.

I gave my friends at White Pass a wave but head on, for I know it's a long walk on a side of a cliff before I get to Red Pass. Just past White Pass I catch up with Billy Goat 2. I can't believe it. I thought the Goat was well behind me.

I credit his progress to steady persistence. He didn't stop too long at Stevens Pass. He gets up early and puts in long days, he's one in a hundred, a guy who is 62 years old, and can hike the way he does. Billy Goat 2 takes my bragging rights away from me. His same-named, same-generation comrade, Billy Goat 1 is only about a week in front of us now.

Now it's the long trudge up to Red Pass. I pull ahead of the Goat, determined to make good time to the pass. Free Radical passes me. I walk behind him for a short while, forcing him to keep up his quick pace telling him to keep charging or I will pass him and destroy his ego. Not that I could. No way. But it's fun freaking the young dude out. He pulls ahead now and he's very animate. At about 50 feet ahead of me, I cheer him on as he hits beautiful Red

Pass.

Red Pass is one of my favorite passes in all of Washington. It comes to its summit at a 180 degree turn. From there a hiker can get great views to the west. There's Skullcap Peak and just to the north is Black Mountain.

Walking a bit to the east a hiker gets a great view of what lies below, White Chuck Cinder Cone, an unnamed frozen blue lake, and White Chuck Glacier. Further north and lower in elevation is White Chuck River, heading towards the northwest.

At the beginning of Red Pass, Free Radical and I were joined shortly by Just Paul, Eon, and the incredible 62 year old Billy Goat 2. From the past I remember that I had made a cell phone call in 2000 to Jim Rowntree, my mechanic, who owns a repair shop. I thought I'd call him again, but it was already after 5:00 and figured Jim would be gone, so I called my parents.

It was a pretty cool call too. I told my mom where I was and introduced my friends, including Just Paul. "He didn't want a trail name, Mom, so people just started calling him Just Paul. So now his trail name is Just Paul." "How can he have a trail name if he doesn't want one, if everybody calls him Just Paul?" I said, "Because Just Paul is his name, Mom, not Paul, but Just Paul." "Not Paul, but Just Paul, you're talking in circles, honey." "Okay, Mom, Paul really doesn't have a trail name, so for now we call him Just Paul," I tell her. "That's what you should do, honey. You don't want to call anybody a name that he doesn't want to hear and he's probably a nice young man." "Well, he's not that young, Mom. In fact, he's pretty old."

I look up from the phone and I can see everybody cracking up. My mom then asks how old Just Paul is. "About 46." "That's not old, he's just a kid to me," my mom answers. I say to Just Paul, "You're just a kid to her, Just Paul, I mean Paul. People were getting a kick out of this. I wanted my mom to talk to Billy Goat 2 but the cell phone connection faded out before I could even say good-bye.

The sun was starting to fade into the western sky and the temperature started to drop. So like bullets, everybody started darting down the trail, heading for White Chuck River below. Bounding down now the trail hooks around White Chuck Cinder Cone with a small creek to the right side of the trail.

ECSTASY OF MISERY

About another mile down the trail I run into some good-looking camping spots, but one young backpacker is already there. I knew that Wahoo and Lou were close behind me and this might be a good place for them to crash for the night because by the time they get there it will be pretty dark. So I decide to move on. Most of the hikers are just ahead of me, with Billy Goat 2 just behind me.

The next hour I hike on down to White Chuck River, which looks more like a creek from this altitude. I follow the trail that follows the river, with me now intently looking for a flat place to crash.

Nothing looked too great for a while, until finally there was a flat meadow off the trail and near the creek. I noted this in my mind and walked a trifle further down by the creek but in a flat dirt area there were already some backpackers.

I started rapping to them and they told me that the campsites down the river just got worse. "We told that to the other guy who just came by but he headed off anyway." "Okay, thanks," I said and walked back to the grassy place that wasn't really a campsite. I spread out my new plastic ground mat and then the rest of my stuff. There wasn't a place to tie up my tarp. I'm sure I won't need it anyway.

While fixing my dinner I could hear hikers just above me. Right away I could tell it was Eon, John, and Leprechaun. They had a worse place to crash than I did. At least I have soft grass. Then I remember that they hang from trees in hammocks, no need for a soft terrain. All they need are two trees to swing from.

That evening I lay in the sack thinking about this trip. Tomorrow will be September 27th. In my original plans I had 'guesstimated' finishing the trek on the 23rd. That was four days ago. It now looks like I'll probably be on the trail for five months!

The next morning I was up early. I was cold and a bit wet from the fog. I was anxious to start hiking. Getting up in the cold or the rain is a drag, but once you start walking you warm up and start feeling better. In fact, once I put on my running shoes, I get a sense of freedom. You can move now! I hit the trail about 6:15 and the trekking was an easy slow glide downhill, with White

Chuck River to my right and then to my left.

Soon the trail crossed Baekos Creek where I was able to get a decent view of Black Mountain Glacier. Within a half mile after that I met up with Free Radical, Lugnut, and the Northerner, just getting out of their sacks. I rapped with them for a short time and they mentioned that Just Paul had already left. "But we'll catch him," they said.

I took off following Baekos Creek for about 100 yards until it headed north once more. According to the trail guide, I was now in Glacier Peak Wilderness. Walking along the trail I continue to see these almost tame birds, called grouse. I guess these birds aren't hunted around here because you can see them standing absolutely still above the trail sometimes only 15 feet away.

Another animal that I've seen a ton of in Washington is the marmot. Some of them are pretty tame. One can see them this time of year gathering bunches of grass in their mouths and taking the grass into their dens. They use it to insulate the whole place for the upcoming winter. They are cute little buggers. I have never heard of them raiding backpacks for food, but that doesn't mean it hasn't happened. Sometimes when the trail dips into a mountain valley, a watchdog marmot will make a high-pitched scream to warn off everyone that an intruder has entered their domain.

The trail now heads up and crosses Sitkum Creek and like a lot of these creeks, the trail makes a log crossing. This area is a rather flat area with plenty of water. Consequently there are a lot of good-looking campsites. A little further on there's a trail crossing, Trail 643 to Kennedy Hot Springs and Guard Station. That's what Eon was talking about on Red Pass. Those young guys will all go down there to those hot baths for sure. For me, there's no way I would ever take a trail out of my way, unless I make one of my classic mistakes.

I was feeling kind of washed out today. I started to get some weird lower stomach cramps. A short time later, I had to take a sort of emergency stop. I was bummed out; I had the damn runs again. I wasn't sure this time if it was something I ate or if the damn Giardia was back.

I feared the latter, for the simple fact that I hadn't continued on the Flagyl. I was feeling so good after the day of rain out of Snoqualmie that I only finished the second day and a half of the medicine. After a couple of more hours I pretty much knew that it was my stupid decision that caused the Giardia problem to reinstate itself.

About an hour and six pit stops later I start taking the rest of my Flagyl. I was surprised to find out that I only had three pills left. Somehow I have lost some four pills. I really can't do anything but finish the pills I have. I also start taking Imodium D instead of waiting as long as I did last time.

An hour later I reach Pumice Creek where I meet Huff and Puff having his lunch of cereal and milk. I tell him my problem and he sympathizes with me. A few minutes later Free Radical and Lugnut appear. They sit down to rest and eat. We discuss my problem and Lugnut says that he might have some Flagyl being sent to him at Stehekin. In fact, it's been sent a couple of times so far but Lugnut always leaves before it arrives. I tell him I'll be more than glad to purchase it from him.

"Oh, that's cool, Wrong Way, I'll just give you the stuff." "Thanks, man, I appreciate it." I skip lunch because I'm afraid that if I eat I might have to go again. I just have some water and I take a second dose of Imodium D.

The rest of the day I was running at about 60%. I took my time, slowing down my pace but keeping steady on my trek. Just past the Pumice Creek area the PCT really starts to climb, switchbacking all the way up to fantastic Fire Creek Pass. Most everyone was ahead of me, except for Eon and the boys who took a side trail to Kennedy Hot Springs, also Billy Goat 2, Wahoo and Lou.

The top of Fire Creek Pass, like Red Pass, is outstanding. It's probably more spectacular than Red Pass. A hiker can see in many directions. Although Fire Creek Pass is only 6350 feet, it feels like one of the major passes in the High Sierras. To the right and looking far to the north are Kennedy Peak and Glacier Peak, Plummer Mountain and Fortress Mountain. A bit to the west, I believe I see Mt Baker, which is probably the coldest mountain peak in Washington, with the possible exception of Mt Rainier.

On top of Fire Creek Pass I rap with this backpacker named Mike. He's interested in hiking the PCT some day. I tell him as much as I can. I also tell him the address of the Pacific Crest Trail Association so he can apply for membership. Joining the PCTA is a very smart thing to do. You can get all kinds of information and inspiration from this organization.

Sometimes I wish the PCTA would spend a little more time on hikers than they do, but in reality it's the trail builders and the organization keepers who are the real heroes. Having hiked the PCT from Ashland, Oregon, to Mexico in 1978, I found out the hard way how miserable and even dangerous the trail could be without trail builders. I don't believe the Forest Service can do it alone. They have many other things to do. Since the PCTA has been in service, the trail has improved greatly.

From Fire Creek Pass the trail heads down steeply, switchbacking to small but beautiful Mica Lake. This little jewel is an outstanding color of blue. It is so pure that a hiker can look all the way down to the bottom. Past Mica Lake, the trail drops down and switchbacks like crazy, all the way to Milk Creek. Then it drops again, with mass quantities of switchbacks, until it joins Vista Creek. There the trail follows this fast running creek for about a mile or more.

The trail soon crosses the creek, probably 2500 feet below the pass and comes to a small grassy meadow. Here I take a break. My legs feel weak, as does the rest of my body. I think it's this damn medicine for sure. The grass is soft and the sun is out so using my pack as a pillow I decide to take a nap.

Before I nodded out, Tripping Ant comes by. I mention my problem to him. He's sympathetic and tells me to take it slow. Right after that come Huff and Puff and Free Radical who are sympathetic too. But when Wahoo and Lou go by I have that feeling that they didn't really give a damn. Wahoo does look at me for a second, but follows the irritated Lou, who I think wears the pants in that relationship, over the small meadow and into the woods.

I soon crash out and wake about 45 minutes later quite a bit refreshed. It's now almost 5:00 and it's starting to get cold so I head out for the last half or so of the hiking for the day. The trail climbs a little bit then levels off and drops a little to the upper Suiattle River.

After reaching the river, which is basically a rushing creek at this stage in its development, I notice Wahoo and Lou just beside the river on a flat dugout area. Upon further inspection I see that there are several of the carved out flat areas. Thick bushes surround these 25 by 25 foot areas.

It's now after 5:00 and the way I feel, this will be it for me today. Wahoo and Lou, to my surprise, are going on. I tell them that there's a good long climb out of this place before you even see any good camping spots. I remember this place well from my 2000 hike of Washington. The two of them decide to move on, however, and off they go.

I soon make my place at the highest level. As I look down the trail to where I came in on, I can see another couple coming down the trail. A few minutes later they arrive. While rapping to them I found out the guy is Billy Goat's son and his son's wife. I tell them they should be really proud of the Billy Goat Man for hiking the PCT at his age. He's tied as the oldest dude with Billy Goat 1. I tell them I think I'm the next oldest guy who should finish the trail, at 56. They seem to be two really nice people.

I could tell they both had many concerns about the Goat since he left Mexico in the middle of April. "You know what?" I said. "I have some concern for him right now. There's a mother bear and her cub on the trail," I confirm as I look down at the trail we all had just come in on. Billy Goat's son comes up to look at what I'm talking about. He sees the animals too.

"Man, my dad will be coming down the trail any time now." "Oh don't worry, he'll be all right. They'll run off when he comes down." "I don't know, I think I'll go up there and shoo them off, just in case," said Billy's son.

So the guy heads up there, gets within 100 feet of the two bears, and blows his police whistle. Both of the bears stand up on their hind legs and stare down at the guy, not budging an inch. I'm a little concerned. Bears standing on their hind legs are not cool at all. Billy Goat's son moves backwards down the trail, wondering what to do next.

Just then, out of the blue, comes the man himself, Billy Goat 2, pounding down the trail with his white beard and white hair flying behind him. His hiking poles were like shock absorbers for his descent. Mama bear takes one look at this sight and bolts down the trail with her cub. She then hauls butt off the trail to the woods above. I couldn't believe it. What a funny sight. I can understand how the bears must have felt looking at this spectacle, but I also had a sense of relief.

Before long, Billy Goat is in camp and being served hot food that the couple had prepared for him. About an hour later, and almost in total darkness, Bandana and Rob appeared. They ended up crashing in the middle flat area. I talked to them for a short time about the day and the beautiful scenery and then I went off to fix my own meal. After dinner of shepherd's pie, I took my Flagyl and another Imodium D. It was more under control. At least I was able to put in the mileage. That night under the noise of cascading water from the small river, I fell asleep early, probably around 8pm. I slept like a baby and didn't wake up until 7am.

The next morning I was hiking by 7:30, feeling pretty good compared to yesterday, but then again, the day was just starting. From the Suiattle, the trail climbs rather steeply, switchbacking three or four long walks and finally climbing to the top of Middle Ridge.

Just behind me are Billy Goat's son and his wife. Billy Goat himself leaves incredibly early, usually in the dark. This is a key to his success. Being 62 and slower than younger hikers, he relies on a long day, as well as the fact that he started in the middle of April. That's well ahead of 90% of the hikers. What I heard about Billy Goat 1, who is about a week ahead of me, is that he does the same thing.

A few minutes later on top of Middle Ridge, I round a bend and there sitting on a large rock is Billy Goat 2, with a pretty young hiker beside him. I stroll up and the young girl says, smiling, "Wrong Way, it's you."

I look at her and didn't really recognize her at first. The she tell me, "It's Brooke." "Wow, Brooke, I thought you and Dave were way out in front." She said they had taken a few days off when her parents came to Snoqualmie and Dave got sick but that he was okay now. "That's cool, but where is the dude?" "He's digging a hole right now." "I hope his movements are better than mine." She asked if I had diarrhea and I told her yes; then she said that's what Dave had. "Yep, it goes with the territory."

Just then Dave comes barreling out of the bushes. "Wrong Way, you were complaining about how the trail gets old the last time I saw you near Castle Crags." "Hey, life gets old, I'm old, Billy Goat is old, but we don't run home. It's do or die, baby. I've been here before and I just might be here again, son." "Well, at least he recognizes you," Brooke said. "He didn't know me at first." "That's because I have a face only a mother could love," I remarked. That brought a few laughs from the group.

ECSTASY OF MISERY

A few minutes later we were all off down the trail in single file. Youngest first and the oldest last, for we all knew each other's pace. We all knew that we would all be hiking together for only a short time because our paces would spread us apart.

After hiking through the forest on the trail for a mile, the PCT heads down for a bit and then back up to Suiattle Pass and the beginning of the south fork of Agnes Creek. A side trail branches off the PCT and follows the creek. The PCT, however, stays above it for a while and then curls away from it after passing under Sitting Bull Mountain.

While hiking along I notice a figure in front of me. As it draws closer, I can see that it's an older man. When he comes up to me he congratulates me on my hike, already knowing that I'm a thru-hiker. I tell him that the guy he should give a congratulatory pat on the back is Billy Goat 2, who is just behind me. He's 62 years old and he's chugged it all the way from Mexico to here in one season.

The man said that was great about Billy Goat and that he had also done that too, back when he was Billy Goat's age, "I've also walked a couple of other long trails since then." I said, "I met a guy that had done a lot of hiking. I saw him at Elk Lake, Oregon, in 1998. Brice Hammick is the old boy's name." "Yeah, I've been told the guy is quite a hiker," he says. He then leaves heading south. "Good luck, buddy," I say as I take off to the north.

As I walk I start to think, oh my God, could that be Brice Hammick? It looked a little like him, but Brice has to be over 80 years old by now. Maybe it is, man. I better check. So I put my pack down and jogged back down the trail for quite a ways, but the guy is gone. What a mind-blower this is, I guess I'll never know.

That night I finally find a flat area, but only on the trail. It's dark now and it's only 6:00. The days are really getting short. I'm proud of the 18 miles I did today. They were tough hiking miles and it doesn't help when you're half sick either.

It's another beautiful day. The shrubbery along the trail is becoming more colorful all the time. Some of the reds are brilliant in the morning sun. The yellows flow as a soft cool breeze cuts through them. The trail now descends a little bit steeper and soon there's a small trail junction heading uphill to the left. I know by experience that this is not the PCT. A short distance further the mighty PCT has reached the south fork of Agnes Creek. The trail now becomes a wooden bridge.

The other side of the bridge is Hemlock Camp, a large area with quite a few campsites, but no tables or toilets or anything like that. I remember in 2000 I was ahead of Tony DeBellis, John and Millie, and Tough Old Broad, who I had just passed a mile before the bridge. Here at Hemlock Campsite I had gotten lost by taking a trail on the wrong side of the camp. It actually had a sign which read "PCT", with an arrow pointing straight up. I followed the trail beside a creek, called Glacier Creek, for almost two miles. The trail was excellent and I felt I was going in the right direction.

After not seeing any PCT symbols, I checked my compass. It's rare to see symbols of the PCT in Washington because they don't like to put the emblems in the trees, especially in the wilderness areas.

Almost in a panic, I hauled ass back to Hemlock Camp and promptly found the trail on the other side of the campsite. I finally caught up with my compatriots near Spruce Creek Camp. I was pissed and let Tony know it. What the hell was that stupid sign with the arrow. I still don't know to this day!

Back to reality now. I headed through the camp and went basically north, down Agnes River towards High Bridge. High Bridge is my goal for the day. At High Bridge there's a bus that picks up hikers twice a day and takes them to Stehekin. If they want to leave and go home, one can take a boat to Chelan where Highway 190 can take you out of the area. Otherwise there is no road that leads to Stehekin. A person must take a boat, hike, or fly in.

At Spruce Campsite, which is just another small remote camping area, I take my brunch, powering down my power shake, fruit bars, and the last of my cheese. Imodium D has plugged me up pretty good. I had my last Flagyl yesterday morning. Not enough for the cure, but at least everything is under control and the weather is great!

The PCT keeps on heading down beautiful Agnes Creek, which has become more like Agnes River now. It's quite a beautiful hike. The trail is nice and it's fun to watch the action of the water below. Within half an hour the trail reaches Swamp Creek, with another tributary, Swamp Creek joining Agnes Creek. I barrel through the remote campsite and hit about a three mile per hour pace. I was anxious to get to High Bridge because I'm not sure what time the bus arrives. The PCT Town Guide says the bus arrives at 11:00. I believe I can make it by then; if not, I'll have to wait until 4pm.

One hour later the trail glides away from Agnes Creek where it will be about a half mile further to the north fork of Agnes Creek. Just after this point the trail reaches Five Mile Camp and crosses Pass Creek.

Shortly after that, Agnes Creek is twice as large, as it comes back into view and lines itself up with the trail once more. The PCT soon passes Weasel Creek and Trapper Creek simultaneously on the left and right. Agnes Creek is larger than ever as the trail leaves Glacier Peak Wilderness and now enters Lake Chelan National Recreation Area.

Summer is over and the brush is turning orange and red

Journey Eighteen:
Stehekin, That's an Awesome Bakery!

Agnes Creek is now what is called Agnes Creek Gorge. The trail switch-backs some 10 times. It finally reaches High Bridge. Down below, the Agnes Creek joins the Stehekin River and flows westward to Lake Chelan. On the other side of the bridge a wide path becomes a dirt road and leads up to the High Bridge Ranger Station where the bus picks up hikers and fishermen.

Upon crossing the road and walking towards the ranger station, I see a number of hikers sitting around waiting for the bus. A few hikers I recognize immediately, including Lugnut and Free Radical. "Hey Wrong Way, how's the Giardia treating you?" "Well, I'm plugged up, but I feel weak and I'm out of medicine, so I hope your stuff comes in," I said to Lugnut. "I hope so too. I'll be glad to give you the stuff."

Free Radical looks at his watch and said that the bus should be here any time. Just then Bandana and Rob come down the trail. "Hey, we actually made it to catch the 11:00 bus, I guess," said Bandana. Bandana then goes on to tell her story of their trip from Skykomish to here. It was pretty funny. There's one thing about Bandana, she's either talking or eating all the time.

The bus finally drives up at 11:15. The fare is $6. I was surprised because it was only $3 three years ago. I gave the driver the $6, which was the last of my cash. I received $50 in my supply box, but for now, I was totally broke.   We all pile in the bus, including four other backpackers and a couple just out for the day, and we head down the road for Stehekin.

There would have been a few other thru-hikers that would have been on the bus including Huff and Puff and Dave and Brooke, but none of them were stopping at Stehekin. Huff and Puff was going to be picked up by some friend who lives nearby east of the PCT where Dave and Brooke live.

The bus gets about halfway to Stehekin and stops, giving everybody a chance to take a short walk to some rather large waterfall. It was far out. Then the driver drops us off at the Stehekin Bakery. We all jump off and grab some outstanding gooey pastries.

This bakery is famous on the trail. It's for sure a place to stop. It's like Callahan's in Ashland, Oregon, Crater Lake Lodge buffet and perhaps the pizza place near Echo Lake Resort, places to pig out and build up carbs. Rob loans me $5 and I get a giant piece of blueberry pie. Oh man, it's the best. The blueberries are hand-picked in the local area, fresh and sweet.

Fifteen minutes later we were back on the bus heading for Stehekin. The distance between the bakery and the lodge is about two miles, a bit too far unless I rent a bike at the Stehekin bike rental, because today is the last day the bakery will be open for the season.

Unbelievable but true. Tomorrow there will be the traditional outdoor sale on an honor system where you pick out what you want and put the money in a wooden box. I'll have to see how I feel tomorrow, but I doubt that I will be back.

A few minutes later we arrive at the lake with the lodge, boat docks, campground, and store with the post office inside. Just as we drive up, I'm shocked to see at the campground none other than Meadow Ed waving at the bus.

After getting off the bus, I'm amazed at how plain-looking Stehekin is. In 2000 it was bright and beautiful, the lake looked like a blue diamond. But now it was dull-looking due to what looked like smog hovering above the water. The haze was not fog or smog. It's smoke from the fire just north of Rainy Pass. The storekeeper told me that the smoke seems to blow into Lake Chelan in the late afternoon.

The Stehekin Lodge, like everything else, has gone up since 2000. It was $70 then, it's $80 now. I was about to ask around to see if someone wanted to share the room and expenses. In 2000 I shared one with Tony DeBellis and for 35 bucks each, it wasn't too bad of a deal. I heard that the PCT has its own campground and most of the hikers stay there. So I decided to try it out. It's the same place where I saw Meadow Ed when I came in on the bus.

It seems to be an okay place. A pit toilet isn't too far off, and there's plenty of room and trees to set up my tarp. Meadow Ed was also staying there and had his tent set up a short distance away. It was now 5:00 so I headed down to the lodge for dinner. I had fried chicken, bread, applesauce, baked potato, and salsa. It probably wasn't the best of food, but to a half-starved hiker, it was great.

Outside, the late bus had just arrived and it looked like Eon and the young monkeys arrived, and also Wahoo and Lou. Probably tomorrow there will be others, most likely Billy Goat 2 and his son and daughter-in-law will be there. After dinner I took a pay shower that was okay and then went back to the campground. Meadow Ed was there with a few people.

I went up there to join them for a bit. Meadow Ed said, "Yeah, I know you're sick again, Wrong Way. We don't have to hear about it." "Hey, man, I wouldn't think of it, Meadow Ed. I don't want to ruin your night." Anyway, I sat around the fire and listened to stories of modern hikers by Meadow Ed and his feelings about the election in California, with the ousting of Gray Davis. I said to Ed, "Hey, I'm voting for Gary Coleman, he's cool." Meadow Ed definitely didn't like that one either. I helped to build up the fire and then after cracking a few people up with some story of the ancient PCT of 1978, I went back to my crash site. I was promptly run out of there by raiding mice. No problem, I just moved over to the picnic table and crashed on it.

It had been a long day for me. Even though I only hiked about 12 miles, it was rough because of my affliction with the Big G. I plan to stay here tomorrow and take a good rest. Perhaps Lugnut's medicine will arrive. I hope I'll be able to call home on the only phone in town, which is a satellite phone, and do my laundry and pick up my package.

The next morning I will be able to take off on the last leg of my journey, Stehekin to Manning Park. One problem, of course, due to the fire north of Rainy Pass, the trail is closed. All thru-hikers must take an alternate route. Meadow Ed explained it somewhat, but there's a map of it in the visitors center where I can really scope it out. At least the weather is nice; Indian Summer seems to continue. Thank god for modern day miracles.

After breakfast I spent some time reading the PCT register. Most of the hikers I've met were in it. Frog and Batteries Included had signed in a couple of days ago. Billy Goat 1 was only seven days ahead of me, and Choo Choo and Long Haul were 15 days in front of me. It looks like she has a pinched nerve in her back and neck. She may not even continue; she writes that the pain is so intense that she may have to call it quits. She praised Choo Choo for carrying a lot of her weight. This seems to be the body's natural reaction to carrying too heavy of a load. I had mentioned this to her back at the Pink Hotel, but you know young people, they think they know it all and you can't tell them anything!

I wonder where Ronnie from Israel is. I don't see his name, and no Cruising Carson either. And where's Zeb the speedster? I haven't seen his entry in over a thousand miles. Most everybody is here, however. So I write my name in the register too. "Wrong Way, from LA, September 29th", just behind Wahoo and Lou.

The rest of the day I pretty much rested and took my new Flagyl that came in the mail to Lugnut. I gave him $10 for it because he's nearly broke. My new supply package came in from home. In this package there was a little more cash so I had something besides a credit card when I get to Manning Park.

I'll probably go to Vancouver by bus and spend the night there and fly out the next day back to LA. Trail Perfect has sent me all the fares of the different airlines to home, including flights out of Seattle and Portland, just in case I get a ride down there. She also has information for bus and train fares and schedules to home.

After breakfast I march over to the Visitors Center where there's a great looking relief map of Northern Washington that is 10 feet by 10 feet. It's interesting because you can see the Pacific Crest Trail, which is marked out by dotted lines traversing over the mountains, creeks, and passes from Stevens Pass area to the Canada border. It gives a hiker a reflective view of what he or she has been through. The Visitors Center also sells books, maps, and other things for tourists.

I pick up a brochure and map combination of North Cascades National Park, Ross Lake National Recreation Area, and Lake Chelan National Recreation Area. This map shows the alternate route to Canada we have to take due to another never-ending forest fire. This year, 2003, should be listed as the year of the fires on the PCT.

During the middle of the morning I finally got a chance to get on the satellite phone. I called Trail Perfect and let her know that I was in Stehekin and that I received my package. I thanked her for all the schedules of trains, planes, and buses. I told her that I would leave for Manning Park tomorrow morning. She told me that she had heard about the fires and that she would tell my parents that I am in Stehekin.

That was about all I could say to her, for already there was a line-up of people wanting to make phone calls. I always try to be fair on phones like this and not take too much time with my calls. I can't say that about other people, however. They are self-absorbed and seem oblivious to people waiting. Stehekin should install another phone, if possible. That would really be a great thing to do!

After lunch I did my laundry in the sink at the laundromat. There is only one washer and one dryer and they seem to always be in use. Next year at the PCT campgrounds there's going to be a bathroom with a large sink to wash out hikers clothes. That will definitely be an improvement over the pit toilet they now have.

For the rest of the afternoon I sit and lay around at my picnic table, looking over the smoky Stehekin Lake. Wahoo and a friend walk by down below me and on to a boat ramp where they dive into the lake and swim around a while.

The late afternoon bus from High Bridge goes by. I can see Special Agent and Tea Tree, but I don't see anybody else. I thought about renting a bike and heading down to the bakery. They are having the last day of honor system sale. But my appetite isn't what it should be due to the medicine I'm taking and it's best just to let my legs rest. Alcohol is another thing I can't indulge in. I can't even have a beer.

Since there are quite a few PCT thru-hikers around, Meadow Ed is going to have a chicken BBQ tonight at 7pm. But at 5:00 I head down to the lodge for dinner anyway. I'm a bit hungry and I want to eat as much as I can. My weight is really too low. I weighed about 220 pounds at the Mexican border and I bet I'm around 160 pounds now. It's good to be thin and light doing a trail like this but there's a point where one gets too thin and if that occurs, a hiker will lose muscle and strength and his hiking abilities can depreciate.

ECSTASY OF MISERY

While walking down the dirt road I met Billy Goat who must have come in on the morning bus from High Bridge. He looked pretty wasted. He's definitely going to need to take a day off. I had a pretty good dinner and as I was about to leave, Tea Tree and Special Agent arrived to pig out.

I went outside to head back to the camp when I started to fool around a bit. I went up to the window, knocked on it slightly and Tea Tree and Special Agent looked up from having their faces buried in their food, I started to beg for food like a starving bum. They cracked up and yelled at me "Get out of here, you old bum." "Yea, go back to LA, you look like a damn pervert," said Special Agent.

It was really quite cool to get such a reaction from the young hikers. I don't know just how the other people in the restaurant felt, especially the waitress, and Meadow Ed who I believe was looking at me with a disgusted look. For me, however, well I thought it was totally cool, Caribbean cool. I felt like Jack Nicholson with a white beard, an Academy award-winning role that all my friends at home could be proud of.

After heading for the store and buying some wonderful junk food, I went back to camp. At around 7:00, Meadow Ed's party was starting to kick in. I went to gather some wood. Meadow Man had bought plenty of chicken as well as other things, like beans, potatoes, bread, and corn.

Quite a few people wandered by, like Bandana and Rob, Tea Tree and Special Agent, the Northerner, Lugnut, Free Radical, Wahoo and Lou. Just Paul couldn't make it because he had taken off that morning. Billy Goat was probably too tired, or didn't give a damn, for that dude was an entity by himself.

The get-together went well, quite a few laughs. Meadow Ed was telling his entire story about past hikers and stuff. I was feeding the fire now and then. One question came up on why the time it took thru-hikers to finish the PCT was getting shorter and shorter.

Some people felt that the trail was getting better, with more bridges and other things. Some felt the equipment was continually getting lighter and lighter. Meadow Ed felt that global positional units keep hikers from going the wrong way.

I guess all these things are part of it, but for me, I believe it's due to the new technologies in the battery-operated head lamps, especially the new LED burners that provided decent enough light, and a light that won't burn out for many hours. Regular flashlights were brighter but they would burn out in a couple of days. Now a thru-hiker can put a LED burning head lamp on and maybe hold a second one in their hand and have plenty of light to walk far into the night. This can be especially effective in the California desert when it's much cooler at night.

The big problem is however, that you don't see anything but a hazy trail. To me that's not experiencing the Pacific Crest Trail at all, but just working out some skinny guy's ego. "Hey, I did it in 94 days." "Well, I did it in 82 days." "Oh yeah, I walked it in 74 days." But what in the hell did they experience and see, except moonlight, stars, and a hazy trail. How ridiculous is it going to get? I wouldn't be surprised to hear some one say they did it in 48 days, and barefoot too!

If records are kept, there have to be mandatory signatures on many register books because there are just too many ways to cheat. So personally, I'm not that impressed with these new spectacular thru-hiking times. Just suspicious.

The party pretty much ended just after 10pm. I headed back to the picnic table and got ready to crash. The weather report was for clear skies for at least the next four days. That was a totally positive thing in my book.

The next morning I got up at about 7:00. I wasn't sure when the bus left; I thought around 8am. By getting down there early I could have one last major breakfast before leaving. It was now September 30th and tomorrow will be October 1st. Oh man, I never thought I would still be hiking this trail. With the latest weather report, I wasn't concerned any more with the big white dump or even rain. It looks like Washington's Indian Summer would continue for a while.

At 8:40 the bus pulled up with me and Tripping Ant, Billy Goat, and his son piling on it. I was kind of surprised to see Billy Goat. I thought he would take a full day off. But the dude is a tough hombre. Billy Goat's daughter-in-law wasn't going. She had some kind of nagging injury so she was going to take the boat ride to Chelan, then a bus to Manning Park, in order to meet them at the finish. She didn't look too happy about it. Her eyes were red and teary; she definitely wanted to come along. Tripping Ant was a surprise to see because I didn't notice him at all the last day and a half. I believe he took the boat to Chelan where he met with his dad. Pretty soon the bus was off, heading towards High Bridge. We passed the closed bakery and then Rainbow Falls. Twenty minutes later we reached High Bridge Ranger Station where I got off. I was the only one to get off the bus here for the others were going to take what is called a more scenic route and avoid the road walk or hitchhiking thing.

For me, I wanted to at least walk to Rainy Pass, which is the official route, and then walk or hike the 17 miles westward to Ruby Creek where the Devils Dome Loop Trail started. This would be the alternate route to Holman Pass, where once again I would join the mighty PCT. After saying good-bye to my comrades, I walked around the other side of the ranger station and joined the PCT heading north to Rainy Pass.

It was here in 2000 that I started out hiking with four other people, all of us good friends, but something weird happened. We all split up pretty much on our separate ways, at least I did. There was Tough Old Broad, aka TOB, who left early because in her seventies she has her own 10 mile per day pace; John and Millie quit early at Fireweed Campsite and they seemed to be arguing with each other. They pretty much told me to go on, that they would see me in Canada.

Tony B, as usual, was out in front, so I just kept hiking. After a couple of miles, I heard, "Hey, don't you ever look around?" There was Tony, camped above the trail. That night I crashed near his campsite and the next morning at some ungodly early time, we broke camp for Rainy Pass.

In the parking lot was an excellent 5 by 5 map that showed our mistakes. Soon we were on the right trail which was really just as high. Tony got on my case, telling me he doesn't know how I had made it this far and that he wanted me to keep the map out in front of me at all times and how I should buy another compass, on and on, like a besieged man, he raved. Needless to say, I was getting more and more pissed off.

When we got to a side dirt road that looked like it might go to the next trailhead, I mentioned it to him and he freaked out. "Looks don't count, look at your map, damn it," he yelled. "You can see right here that the trail goes along the highway on the right side and then joins to the trailhead." "Ok, whatever, asshole, I'm going up here to check it out." He didn't say a damn thing but headed down the little highway looking for this invisible trail. I walked up the dirt road about 150 feet and could see that there were cars parked about a quarter of a mile away, an obvious trailhead parking lot!

Tony, in the mean time, was a good quarter of a mile down the highway starting to walk back. I gave him a yell and waved, "It's here, man." A few minutes later he arrived. I apologized for calling him an asshole, like a fool I might add, because he was a raving jerk all the way up to the trailhead.

I finally had had enough. When he pulled over to the side of the trail to blow his nose he told me to go on, and go on I did. He never saw me again until a day after I reached Canada. That was only because the bus to Vancouver was an hour late. I had put all my anger into hauling butt out of there and even though he's a super hiker, he never caught me! John and Millie told me later that he had tried.

I don't know why everybody was so irritated when they left Stehekin that morning. There was only 90 miles to go and the weather was good. That's what happened and to tell the truth, that's why I'm glad I'm hiking alone right now!

Back to the current reality. Now the PCT heads by Loon Lake which is probably a well used lake due to it being so close to the road. It's amazing sometimes how you can get deep into thought about something in the past and all of a sudden you have done serious yardage. Before I knew it I was at Bridge Creek Campground, where I had lunch.

Here I examined my pack for it was quite heavy. I rationed out the food for three more days. I had quite a bit more than I needed, so I put my extra food into a bear locker, a gift to whoever camps here. I probably left there three pounds lighter than when I arrived.

From Bridge Creek Campground the trail leaves Stehekin River and High Bridge Creek. Here the trail passes Dolly Varden Campground, Shady Campground, Bridge Creek Campground, and finally North Fork Camp where another creek joins beautiful Bridge Creek. After this, the trail crosses about a quarter of a mile from Bridge Creek and enters North Cascades National Park.

It's about 4pm now and already it's starting to get dark. There are other campsites ahead, like South Fork Camp and Fireweed Camp, where John and Millie stayed, but being rested and getting a later start, I decide to get as close to Rainy Pass as possible and make the most of the dry weather. Even though the weather report is for clear skies in Northern Washington, one can never be too sure.

I start heading past Fireweed Campground and the trail begins to climb a bit more steeply. Just about a mile further I suddenly notice a bear about 100 feet in front of me. On further examination, I notice that there are two cubs playing at her feet. She's a young female bear, for she's not too large, probably weighs in the neighborhood of about 150 pounds. One thing for sure, she's big enough to ruin my day. A bear this size can run like a jack rabbit and climb trees like a squirrel.

After halting my progress for a bit, the bear, although looking at me, shows no intention of moving. She probably wants to head down the trail, like I want to head up the trail. For now it's a stand-off. I decided to take a picture of these three, which is probably a stupid idea, since all I have is a single use camera and objects 50 feet away look like they're 300 feet away in the pictures.

I take a flick anyway and when the flash goes off, the female bear's head gets low and the stare is on. This isn't cool. I know better than this, so I back up a little and wait it out. The cubs are oblivious to all of this and simply play and frolic at mom's feet. Time passes, but no one moves.

I really don't want to head back down the trail and I'm tired of just standing there getting the stare. So I decide to talk to the bear, talk nicely to her. I say things like "Well there, you sure have beautiful cubs. What a lucky girl you are." Stuff like that. I try to say it in a soothing baby voice, trying to use my charm.

I guess, by god, it worked. The young mother bear loosens up a bit. You can see her relax and then she heads down off the trail toward the huckle-berries below! I give her a minute or two, then I slowly walk at a non-threatening speed up the trail and past the area where the bear was. At last the coast is clear. Wow. About a mile after this I find a flat place just off the trail and set up camp.

It's been a good day even though I got a late start due to the bus schedule. I still covered about 20 miles. Tomorrow is October 1st, so I start another month. I should reach Rainy Pass tomorrow quite early and then I'll either walk or hitchhike the 17 miles to the alternate route. All because of another fire.

The next morning I'm up and out of camp by 7am, and man is it cold. The sun comes out soon and the place warms up quickly. Along the trail I see three or four deer munching on grass, scrounging for their breakfast. Soon the trail comes out of the clearing and lo and behold, I have arrived at Highway 20. About a half mile later I'm just across the road from the Bridge Creek Campground.

I know from experience that the trail does not head out of here, but runs alongside the highway for about a mile before it arrives at Rainy Pass. I'm tempted to just go ahead and take the PCT here regardless of the fire warning. But with my luck I would probably get busted, get a fine, or go to jail. I do know by the smoke that the damn fire must still be going.

I decide against it. I'm bummed out as I head down the road for a 17 mile hike to Devils Loop Trail and the alternate route I will have to take. At first I decide to walk it. After all, Meadow Ed said that in this situation it's ok. I was getting bored after about four or five miles. Road walking is a drag, so I start to hitchhike, There are very few cars on this highway at this time, so I hike as I hitchhike just in case I never get a ride.

Probably four or five cars go by, but no luck. Then it dawns on me that I don't have my hitchhiking cap on. Immediately I reach into my bag and pull out that funky bright orange wool cap with the orange ball hanging from it, the mouse attracter. I put the thing on and the very next car that comes by pulls over and stops. In fact, I wasn't even hitchhiking at the time. I was walking and was offered a ride.

I get in the car with two big dudes. It's kind of freaky. It's not like the safest situation, but as we drove, one of the guys starts talking and I can pretty much tell that he's cool. These guys are on a business vacation. They travel all over the southwest, places like Las Vegas, Laughlin, San Diego, and the LA area, refurbishing pool tablecloths, the green carpets on the pool tables. This time each year they visit their customers because most of them need the tables done yearly.

Before I knew it, I see Jackita Ridge Trail Number 738 trailhead parking lot. The two guys pull over and let me out. They get out and made some peanut butter and honey sandwiches. One of the guys offers me a jug of water, which I take, because according to Meadow Ed there isn't any water for quite a long ways. After 15 minutes I bid the dudes farewell and I'm heading for Jackita Ridge Trail.

The trail heads around an ancient log cabin and takes me across a creek to Jackita Ridge Trail which leads me to Devils Pass Trail which ultimately leads me to the PCT at Holman Pass.

The trail starts to switchback after about a quarter of a mile climb and it becomes steeper and steeper. I realize right away that this is not a contour trail. The gallons of water on my back feel like a ton of lead. I can't believe how steep this trail is. It makes me appreciate the contour type trail that the PCT is.

To make matters worse, I'm not at my best due to the Flagyl I've been taking. There's a point that one gets to in losing weight that too much muscle is also lost. I believe I reached that point some time ago. The trail is not only steep, but it's hot too. I figure the more I gain in altitude the cooler it will get.

I've been climbing about 40 minutes now, when I hear a noise. I see a figure coming down the hill. When the figure gets closer, I notice it's pretty small but I can't tell if it's a female or male. A few minutes later we cross paths. I'm not in a very good mood to be friendly but still say hello. The strange person says hello too but I'm still not sure if this is a man or a woman.

I ask the person "Are you heading down to civilization?" "Yes, I've been up on Devils Peak and I came in on the Pacific Crest Trail about a week ago." "From where?" I ask. "Holman Pass," the strange person answers. I went on to say this is a mean ass trail and I miss the PCT right now. "I had to take this route to get around the fire. Only 60 miles left before reaching Canada and I have to go around another fire on a trail like this with very little or no water." "Oh there's water," says the stranger. I asked where and the person tells me several different places, including a creek that I will be passing.

Man, I'm thrilled to hear this. The person of mystery also describes the trail and what to look for along the way to Holman Pass. I thank her and tell her that she made my day. I call this person "she" or "her" right now, but I could be wrong. She then leaves heading downhill toward Highway 20. After she takes off, I notice a large rock on the side of the trail coated in shade by a Western Hemlock. This would be a great place for lunch and even a bit of a celebration.

Sitting on the rock, I pull out my heaviest food: the package of tuna, which has been so great on this trip, cheese, and trail mix, followed by a half melted Snickers bar for dessert. Having way too much water now, I wash my face and hands and drink up a storm. The rest I pour out, except for a quart. On further examination, I see I still have more food than I need. So I start dumping food out of the packages on the side of the trail where no one will notice. I keep the empty packages.

About a half hour later, I'm ready to go. I have four pounds less water and three pounds less food. This makes my pack about seven pounds lighter. That should make a big difference, especially walking up a hill this steep. The bag goes around my shoulders and I buckle down the funky hip belt it has, and it's lighter all right.

Moving up the hill now, I'm putting out the same pain and the same energy, but instead of going one mile per hour, I'm going two miles per hour. A half hour later, I reach the top of this ridge. I've probably climbed nearly 3000 feet. It's also cooler and there's a view too. Things are looking better now as I gaze to the south at distant Mt Rainier. Up here it seems like I'm almost walking on a mesa. It's quite flat and now the going is much easier. To my left side and north is Jack Mountain, 9066 feet high and looking great.

For the next few hours I keep a pretty fast pace. I'm so glad it's a pretty nice trail. After a bit I find water, at what I believe to be Devils Creek. The stranger was right. There is plenty of water. With Jack Mountain and Devils Dome, the water runs off from the two peaks, and it will take care of me for today.

That evening I crash along the side of one of these small creeks. I don't bother putting my tarp up. I always spot an emergency place that I can set up my tarp if I have to. It's been quite a day. Canada is drawing closer and closer.

ECSTASY OF MISERY

I just hope this alternate trail doesn't fizzle out, but according to the small stranger with the big hat, it doesn't. I fall asleep that night looking up at the millions of stars, knowing that this will all be coming to an end quite soon.

The next day I'm up at 6:15 and hiking at about 6:30. I happen to look down at my $6 watch and press the date button. Holy smoke, it's October. Today is October 1st; September is over. I feel like I'm now hiking on borrowed time. In 2000 I finished on September 1st, exactly one month earlier than this. I thought I might finish this trip on or about September 23rd, oh well, just keep hiking. It looks like another beautiful day.

Actually, in this part of Washington, the PCT is surrounded by the Picket Range of mountains along with Mt Shuksan and Mt Baker, which are probably the whitest and most snow loaded mountains in all of Washington, and probably the whole darn PCT. The PCT here actually travels east of the Cascades, which catches most of the precipitation. Kind of good news, I guess, if a storm is blowing in from the west or northwest. But I wouldn't stand around here too long waiting for or daring one to come along. Not in October, that's for sure.

I'm now hiking the Devils Loop Trail. The rest of the day I plow along on this trail, feeling like a high plains drifter until I head into a long green valley.

Here I find some young people camped just on the other side of a slow running creek. I start to gather some water out of this creek when a young girl approaches.

The girl tells me that she and her friends were at Holman Pass two days ago. They are with a youth organization called something like 'future leaders'. They were supposed to hike 40 miles from Harts Pass to Highway 20 at Ruby Creek, then go on a white rafting trip, and then ride mountain bikes from some place to Spokane, all in one month. This is their fifth day. She then tells me they passed two guys walking the trail a couple of days ago. They were kind of tall and skinny. I'm thinking to myself that this could be Lugnut and Just Paul who had left a day earlier than I did from Stehekin.

I told her I was planning to reach Holman Pass tomorrow, but she told me it was too far. Just then I looked down the trail and there was Prune Picker, who usually hikes with Apple Pie. "Hey man, what's happening?" "Nothing much. Same old thing but just a different smell."

I told Prune Picker that the young girl was with a youth organization and she says they were at Holman Pass two days ago. Prune Picker said that he was hoping to be there tomorrow. "The girl said it's too far." Prune Picker looked down. "It's about 30 miles, that's not too far." "How many miles a day do you guys travel?" "About 25 per day," says Prune Picker, kind of bragging to the cute young girl. "Wow, 25 miles per day. We're lucky to do 15." I told her that they would be doing that too if she and her friends had hiked from Mexico with ultra light packs.

Prune Picker told me that Rob and Bandana, as well as Apple Pie, were just in back of him taking a break. I told him that I was going on and probably would be hiking till dark. The young girl listened to us talk and got bored and headed back to her youth group. I told Prune Picker that I would see him up on the trail and perhaps we could all camp together. He headed back down the trail. I popped on my pack and headed up the trail. It was about 3:00 now; I still had at least three to four hours to hike.

The Devils Pass Trail from here heads eastward down to the small valley. As the small creek became stagnant, the trail swerved left and headed north, heading back over the valley and soon climbing out of it. The trail kept climbing right up to Devils Pass and then skirted along the side of a cliff that was lit up in orange and red from the far setting sun out of the west. Soon it was getting dark. I headed down Devils Pass, rock after rock, until grass and trees appeared. A short distance later, I found a flat place near a small creek. I decided I would crash here. It was almost pitch dark now.

I set up my campsite, laying out my stuff. I heated up some chicken and rice, and then I heard voices and the sound of feet pounding down a rocky trail. It was Prune Picker and Apple Pie. I could hear them say over the running water, "Let's stay here." "It's me, Wrong Way, I'm over here. It's pretty nice with soft grass." So they came over and pitched their tent. Just then I heard the unmistakable chatter of Bandana with Rob heading toward us. I chuckle a little. "That girl can sure talk." "All the time, she never stops unless she's eating," Apple Pie replied. "Hey, over here," yelled Prune Picker. A few minutes later, Bandana and Rob were crashing in the flat green area.

For the next few hours we all listened to Bandana talk about Portland, her school days, her golden years, as she explained it. It was kind of interesting calling them her golden years. I think all of us fell asleep to the voice of the like-able, funny, chattering Bandana of Portland.

The next morning I was up first. I think older people just get up earlier naturally out here. Billy Goat left early when it was still dark. Just Paul is an early riser too. Just before I left I gave Bandana some of my food, which I still have too much of. I just didn't have an appetite any more, due to the Flagyl. Bandana thanked me and gave some of the food to Apple Pie who was running a little short. After having dropped at least another pound out of my pack, I headed down the trail, looking forward to rejoining the Pacific Crest Trail once again.

From here the trail slowly heads downhill and back up just a little before it gets to Deception Pass. Here I decided to have breakfast at a small running creek. I was about finished when Bandana came down the trail alone. "Hey, where's Rob?" "Oh, he's on his way, he had to stop and dig a hole."

I was about to leave when Bandana started telling me about her relation-ship with Rob. She told me that Rob was from Buffalo, New York, where he managed a gas station and he really didn't want to go back. "I think Rob has more potential," she said. "Well, take him to Portland, maybe he can find some-thing better," I said. "He is coming to Portland for a week before he has to go home to Buffalo." "Maybe he will head back to Portland after visiting his family and friends," I said to her. She said she has been traveling with him since Cas-tle Crags. That's probably two months. I told her that she has some decisions to make. She said that she had a couple of weeks, and she'll worry about it lat-er.

Bandana went on to say that she and Belcher were going to get a place together. "Belcher? Do you think she is still on the trail?" I said. "Oh yeah, she'll never give up, she'll make it." "Wow, I wonder if Puck and her have crossed paths yet. Puck is heading south, you know." "Yeah, I'm sure they have, but Puck isn't nice to her. So I don't worry about them becoming a couple again." "Well I'm sure everything will work out. I'll see you later on the trail and in Manning Park. You'll like it, it's a nice place, great food too!" That kind of lit up her eyes and I left heading down the trail thinking that there are going to be a lot of broken hearts when these couples all come to the end of their journey.

For about two more hours the trail headed east as it dropped lower, the vegetation became thicker, the trees got bigger. Pretty soon I was going towards a valley, the trail now became level, but undulating, like waves on the sea. Soon the trail became wider and finally there it was, a group of signs in front of me.

Then just about the prettiest sight you can imagine, an antique Pacific Crest Trail emblem, buried in the bark of a large pine tree! Another sign pointed east towards Holman Campground which was about three miles away on the west fork of Pasayten Creek. The trail to the south ran into Okanagan National Forest and the Pasayten Wilderness and of course the trail heading west, the trail I was just on, leads to Devils Dome and Deception Pass.

I sat down to celebrate by having a power bar and my last Snickers bar, when Rob and Bandana came by. They told me that they were going to hike late tonight and camp at Hopkins Lake which is about 11 miles away. I guess they wanted to get to Manning Park by noon, so they could get a room. I told them I would just hike until it got dark. As long as I reach Manning Park Lodge by tomorrow, that would be cool with me.

About five minutes later Prune Picker and Apple Pie strolled in and gave me the same information. Then they left. For me, there wasn't any sense at all in rushing towards the end; it's over. On top of that I was running at about 75% due to the medicine I was taking. I was determined this time to follow through to the last pill and not make the same mistake that I previously made.

Alone once again, I headed north on the mighty PCT. The going was fast. The trail was now a contour trail. I was glad to be on it once again. A sweet tasting spring appeared a couple of miles north of Holman Pass. One of those colorful frogs jumped in the water. I knew that within a month the animals I see now will be surviving in a winter environment. Their lives, like mine, will be different, but they will resume their lives the same way here in the spring and summer next year. For me, it will be in another world, but perhaps, with luck, I can return some day.

A few miles further I started to climb again, actually traveling on a few small switchbacks and leveling out to a place I recognized from three years ago. It was a remote campsite with a small spring that I camped with two other guys and a party of horseback riders. I knew now that I was at the bottom of a climb to Woody Pass.

Camped beside the trail, there was a tent and two guys. I recognized the smaller guy was the Northerner. The other guy was Huff and Puff. The Northerner left as I got closer to the tent. I started talking to the cartoon artist Huff and Puff. "Are you guys making camp already?" I said. "Yes, there's plenty of water here and I'm not in a hurry to finish." "This is a pretty nice place to camp. In fact, I camped here three years ago with several other people. It was in the spring time."

I talked to him for a few minutes. He told me that he had actually come straight up from Rainy Pass, right through the fire zone. He almost got caught too. He had just dusted the ash from the trail off his legs at Heart Pass when a couple of jeeps with firefighters came barreling up.

They asked him what he was doing. He told them he had just come from Holman Pass and was heading south toward Rainy Pass. They told him that there wasn't any way he could get to Rainy Pass on the Pacific Crest Trail because it was closed due to the fires. He tried to look bummed out and said "Well, I guess I'll just head back north again and maybe come out at Manning Park." The fireman replied that he hoped Huff and Puff wasn't one of those crazy people walking the whole PCT. Huff and Puff emphatically said, "Oh, no sir, Im not that crazy."

Then the fireman asked to see Huff and Puff's permit. Huff and Puff nervously went over to their packs to get it when the sound of a radio came on. He couldn't really understand what was said on the radio but the firefighter hauled butt back to their jeep and jammed. They warned him if they see him again that they will give him a ticket. Puff figured they probably were off to fight another hot spot that often pops up after a fire has been contained. "Wow, buddy, saved by the bell, dude," I said. "Yeah, I was lucky. All I had for a permit was the 500 mile permit the Pacific Crest Trail Association gave me."

After talking to Huff and Puff, I decided to head on. I still had a couple of hours to go before darkness would come. I bid them good-bye and told him if I don't see him in Manning Park to have a good life, and I left, once again heading for Canada.

The pass is one of the passes that climbs, but it's a mellow one. Over a distance of a couple of miles, one climbs maybe 500 or 600 feet. The climb now was really nice. The sun was starting to go down and the place was all lit up in that golden light. This golden light would hit the shrubbery that was turning its fall colors. It was almost a surrealistic feeling.

Once on top of the pass, the trail switchbacks a few times down a rock trail before it levels off and heads back up to Woody Pass. While walking along here in 2000, a rock dislodged from its resting place for some reason or another and came bounding down, skipping across the rocks and switchbacks, missing me by just a few feet. The rock in turn dislodged several other rocks, but they were small and didn't come too close to me. This kind of thing happens to almost everyone, but on this 2000 trip, it happened several times. So far on this trip, nothing at all.

It did bring back memories of the huge crashing noise near Fuller Ridge remote campsite and the horrible loud grinding sound in the Russian Wilderness when some huge rock had made a sliding movement. I never saw the rock for it was far above the trail. I did see some dust rising above the small white pines.

These things happen but are rare. Getting hit by a natural sliding rock is probably like the earth getting hit by a meteorite or something like that. However, if you have hikers ahead of you on switchbacks cruising along, then you might stay alert, for the odds, obviously, increase.

From the lowest part of the rocky pass the trail starts to climb again, as it enters a green area of bushes, grass, and small trees. It was starting to get dark. Down below the trail I could see a flat grass area that looked quite cool for crashing.

So, now I headed down there in clumpy bunch grass, watching my step so as not to turn an ankle. That would be crazy, to turn an ankle with less than 20 miles to go! It would be sad, but comical to say the least.

The grassy spot was nice, with a huge cliff just in back of me a couple of hundred feet. Here I laid out my systematic bed roll and prepared dinner. This would be my last dinner in the wilds, for this would most likely be the last cooked dinner on this trip. I pulled out a package of beef stroganoff. This is probably my favorite meal on this journey. The temperature really started to drop so I put all my thrift store wool on, including two pairs of pants.

It had been quite a day, rejoining the PCT and making it to Woody Pass. But tomorrow, well, tomorrow would be a heavy day, especially an emotional one, for tomorrow, October 3rd, in the year of 2003, Wrong Way will have hiked the PCT in one season, south to north.

I was glad I decided not to flip flop. In some ways it cheapens the trip. In other ways, it might be a necessary thing to do, especially in those very snowy years. I hope Shutter Bug, Cliff Hanger, Sunbeam, and Steady make it. I wonder where they are now. Maybe around Burney or Old Station, perhaps Belden. Somewhere in these thoughts I nod off, probably around hikers midnight.

The next morning I awake about 6:30 and the first thing I see is the magnificent cliff in back of me all lit up by the morning sun. It's another beautiful day to hike. It's too bad the first 16 days were so horrible. Look at the beauty I missed. I'm lucky to have hiked Washington before in order to see those things down in South Washington. The PCT should actually be hiked at least a couple of times. It doesn't mean you have to do it in one crazy run, but section hiking is probably the key, because each time I've seen the trail, it looks so different and different events and people materialize too.

From my cool campsite I'm now hiking up the forty feet to rejoin the trail. The morning stiffness is there as usual. Now on the trail, I notice my watch. It's 7am, straight up. Not having to dig a hole yet I head out once again in search of Canada.

A few minutes later I reach Woody Pass and a trail junction which, if taken, leads down to Coney Basin and Castle Creek. Actually Woody Pass is almost anti-climactic compared to the first part of it. The trail now heads down a ridge and this provides easy hiking for the next few miles.

The views are nice with pleasant scenery in most directions. I concentrate on looking north, trying to figure out where Canada starts and the USA ends. The terrain gets a little tougher in here, as I head up what is called Devils Stairway. Man, I'll say one thing, the Devil sure owns a lot of beautiful country. There are countless Devil Passes, Devil Post Pile, Devils Peak, Devils Creek. He sure is a popular dude. I hope I don't ever meet him, especially while hiking the trail!

A few miles after climbing Devils Staircase I round a ridge with a lake far below. Looking at the maps I discover that this is Hopkins Lake, the lake that Bandana, Rob, Apple Pie, and Prune Picker were hoping to get to last night. Wow, they must have had a long day! It looks like quite a ways down there, too. I'm kind of glad I camped where I did. What's the hurry anyway.

The trail winds about halfway around Hopkins Lake and over Hopkins Pass where it levels out and again into a rather smooth flat area. Right now I'm carrying at least a three mile per hour pace. I'm not sure this is because of a lighter pack or the anticipation as the border draws closer.

About an hour and a half later, I reach one of Washington's trillion passes as I coast over Castle Pass without a climb. The trail soon joins Route Creek and then follows it north for a couple of miles until it gradually slides to the west. The trail is now flat and pretty much cruising through a lush valley in Okanogan National Forest. A series of small slow running creeklets soon cross the trail. It's at the second little creek that I run into a small problem.

I'm hiking along knowing that I'm really getting close when I'm challenged by a vicious Grouse standing at least 10 inches high and weighing a whopping 10 pounds or so. The bird comes out of the bushes to the middle of the trail and won't leave.

I stop and look in astonishment as the red face Grouse comes slowly walking up to me. The bird wants to rumble with me. I start rapping to the creature. "What the hell, buddy. Aren't you afraid of me? What's your problem? I've come all the way from Mexico, little buddy, and I can't turn around now."

The bird slows down and looks up at me with a cocked neck, its eyes blinking and its beak starts opening and closing rapidly like it's trying to talk back to me. I can't believe this, but it's happening. The blackish bird with red between its eyes and around its beak doesn't back off but draws closer and closer. The bird then gets within one foot of me, gives me one more look, and then powers into the top of my foot and starts pecking it!

Then the vicious creature follows this up by pecking up my leg, halfway to my knee. It's here that I perform my Magic Johnson spin move, then run up the trail, leaving the nasty little red-faced feathered monster to itself! What a revolting development. Everybody told me to watch out for bears, mountain lions, and rattlesnakes. No one mentioned a wild red-faced grouse.

The famous Stehekin Bakery, 90 miles from Canada

Journey Nineteen: Monument 78, Northern Terminus, and Canada

I was a bit amazed as I continued my journey towards Canada. Should I tell people about this when I get home, or will they even believe it? I already have the strange encounter with whatever it was just south of Sierra City. Man, neither one is going to sound very credible. I better forget this one.

Shaking it off, I went back into about a three mile per hour pace. The trail made a sharp left turn and started switchbacking down. About four moderate switchbacks later, the trail turned north again, and there it was, Monument 78, the Northern Terminus of the Pacific Crest Trail!

Sitting on the ground just a few feet from the wooden monument was the Northerner. I was sure glad to see him because I was worried about not having anyone here to take my picture. I thought I might have to hold the camera and take a picture of myself with the monument behind me. The Northerner was recording what everybody had written in the last trail register with some kind of hand-held device. He took time out to take about three or four pictures of me. One was with a small piece of paper that said "Thanks, Chuck". This was what I did when I left the Mexico and USA border and I thought it would be cool to do it at the Canada border.

The Northerner then went back to recording what people wrote and told me he would be done in a couple of minutes. I told him not to worry, just take his time. A few minutes later, he took a break and I grabbed the book which is stored in the metal cone part of the monument.

On this separate part of the monument which sits out in front of the wooden monument looks like a small steel monolith which comes to a point at the top. It's probably about four feet high and embedded in cement. On the side of the structure there's a small steel plate that reads "78", for, of course, Monument 78. A hiker must pull up on the structure which separates and reveals the last register book inside. There's a printed sign on cardboard which reads "Register Book Inside". That wasn't here the last time I was here.

Inside the book I turn back the pages to where the Class of 2003 starts. There are a few section hikers first including people heading from north to south. One of the names was Smiles A Lot, who I had met near Seiad Valley. One of the first people who came in was Zeb, who ended his trip on July 27th, taking 74 days to complete it.

I won't go into this because you know how I feel about it, so I didn't bring it up to Northerner. It was too joyous of an occasion. But I just had to mention one thing to see the Northerner's reaction. "Wow, Zeb the speedster. I haven't seen an entry from him in some 1100 miles!" No reaction from the man from the north so I just kept reading the log. The Japanese couple who left on April 1st made it towards the end of August. Towards the last week of August more thru-hikers appeared. But the bulk of them came in the middle of September and right up until now.

The first names were of course the people that I have only read about and never saw. There's T-Bone, Tuna and Yogi, who like Mercury and Billy Goat were actually hiking the PCT in consecutive years. There's Choo Choo and Long Haul, who I had met. It looks like they finished about two weeks ago. I stayed even with them.

I don't see Ronnie from Israel, but I'm sure he made it. Then there was Stretch, Hatchet, Free Radical, Frog, Batteries Included, Just Paul, Lugnut, Bandana and Rob, Prune Picker and Apple Pie, Dave and Brooke. Way before these names are the Clean Machine, the Navigator, and Mike A from Seattle who is a fine hiker I met at the Saufley's in Agua Dulce. Names I didn't see that I thought would be in front of me were Grunt, the guy I met in Tuolumne Meadows, and Cruising Carson who I hadn't seen for 1000 miles.

Most of the hikers had actually arrived in the last two weeks and especially in the last few days, like Chance, Wahoo and Lou, Belcher, Tea Tree and Special Agent, and Billy Goat 2.

Then theres the people behind me, many I have met like Greg, who I call Mr Natural; could he have made it? Detour, perhaps. I'll never know and then there are a few others still out there that I will never meet. I doubt there are very many. I guessed that around 300 had started and probably 100 to 125 actually make it. According to most trail angels, this wasn't a big year probably due to late snows in the Sierras and the local Southern California mountains along with a lot of bad weather at the start.

"Well, here you go, buddy," I said, giving the book back to the Northerner, but not before I enter my own two cents. "Robert 'Wrong Way' Raley, October 3rd, 2003, 1pm. I have finally made it at the age of 56. This completes about 6000 miles I have hiked and enjoyed along this fantastic trail. It's in my blood and has been part of my life since 1966. Congratulations to everybody. May your re-entry back to society be a smooth trek."

For one last time I took a long view at the monument, which consists of five large beams coming up out of the ground at different heights. On the back beam, which stands the highest, the Pacific Crest Trail emblem is fastened to its side. This is a tin emblem sitting about seven feet off the ground.

The front beam has letters embedded in it, which reads "Northern Terminus, Pacific Crest National Scenic Trail." On the third highest beam is written "Canada to Mexico, 2627 miles." At the time this monument was constructed, the trail was about that length, but since then the trail has lengthened to 2650 miles. The 2658 miles that is often used for its official use included the eight miles from Monument 78 to Manning Park and that's the eight miles I have left now before the trek completely ends. The monument is located in the middle of the demarcation cut in the forest which is used as a border marker between the two countries. It's about 50 feet wide.

Looking at my watch it reads nearly 2:00. I have been here almost one hour. It was now time to boogey. A major cheesy pizza awaits me. Thinking of food cheers me up and gives me motivation to leave for the monument stay is somewhat emotional.

The exit trail now continues north and soon to Castle Creek where another trail branches off. The exit trail now heads above the creek and slowly starts to climb. There are a few dry creek beds which make the hiking a little more strenuous, as the trail goes down and then up sharply. One can easily tell now that this is not the PCT. The trail is a bit rough in areas, but not at all hard to follow.

Soon the trail goes by a very nice campsite with picnic tables, water, and flat area to crash. If it was any later than what it is now, I would definitely spend the night here. One reason is that a hiker could head in to Manning Park and easily get there by late morning which would be best for securing a room at Manning Park Lodge for the rest of that day and night. Arriving late is a bit risky, especially if it's on a weekend. Manning Park Lodge seems pretty popular.

From here the trail climbs even more steeply and then passes Windy Joe Mountain at 5987 feet in elevation. Now the exit trail starts to descend to Highway 3 and Similkameen River. Although the trail from Monument 78 to Manning Park is only eight miles, it can feel like 15 miles because of the anticipation to end it all, and it's just plain anticlimactic.

The hiking is easier now because it's basically downhill all the way to a white gravel trail that's almost like a sidewalk. One can tell he's getting closer by the sound of the traffic.

Finally there's the highway. Just before the highway there's an actual PCT Camp where one can stay if he or she is on a tight budget. There's also a campground called Cold Springs just a mile down Highway 3 that's supposed to be nice. A hiker can then walk into Manning Park in the morning to catch the bus.

My feet right now are starting to ache because of the quick downhill speed that I have been cruising at. Now leaving the trail, I'm walking down the highway, facing traffic, for almost a mile. There it is, Manning Park Resort. I've made it. The hike is done!

Now for the journey home. It should be a hell of a lot faster.

The Northern Terminus Monument 78 and the Demarcation cut in
the forest. USA left side Canada on the Right side. Non-Ultra light,
Year 2000

Year 2003 switched to ultra light pack

Journey Twenty: The Trip Home
and Back to Reality

Manning Park Lodge is a large place with quite a few rooms. In the winter it becomes a ski resort. The rest of the year it's occupied by hikers, horseback riders, fishermen, and hunters. Outside of the lodge's office are beautiful chainsaw sculptures including a giant bear with a salmon in his mouth. The rate for a room runs about 75 Canadian dollars for the night during this time of year. It can be an excellent deal for vacationing Americans who may benefit from the USA – Canadian exchange rate.

I enter the lounge area and head right to the office. The young lady asks, "Can I help you?" I tell her I want a room. She knew I'm a thru-hiker. It's pretty easy to tell, especially since this is the time of year when tri-state hikers arrive. She tells me that all the single bedrooms were taken and there were only cabins left, which of course, are more expensive.

I ask her if there are any thru-hikers around that have a room with two beds. There is Just Paul and Tripping Ant. They're fellow thru-hikers. "Can you ring them up for me? I think they'll probably want to help me out and save a few bucks."

So the young lady, with the name of Janice on her lapel, calls Just Paul's room. There is no answer. "He must be out," she says. She then asks, "Paul isn't his last name, is it?" "No, Paul is his first name. Just Paul is his trail name." "Oh Paul is his first name. I thought you might have said Justice Paul." "No, but you know it's my last night, give me one of those cabins." I feel incredibly wasted right now. Janice took my credit card and checked me in. I knew that the 85 Canadian dollar cabin would probably be like 70 in American dollars. It still might be possible to find a thru-hiker coming in, maybe Huff and Puff or even Billy Goat, and there were cabins that had three or more beds.

As I was about to leave, Just Paul entered the scene. "Wow, dude, I'm glad to see you. But I wish I would have seen you a little earlier. I heard you had a room with two beds but I had to get a cabin." "Oh, Wrong Way, that's a drag," said Just Paul. Then Janice spoke out, "I can still give you the room. I doubt if the charge has gone through." She cancelled my cabin and gave me a key to Just Paul's room. It probably saved us 35 to 40 dollars each.

I grabbed my pack and was about to leave when it dawned on me that in 2000, I found out the lodge has a great scale, like a doctor's scale, in the back room. I asked Janice if they still have a scale and she said that they did. "Do you want to weigh yourself?" she asked. "Yeah, I sure do." She said that I wasn't the only one that asked about the scale. "No I guess I wouldn't be."

I went to the back room and got on the scale with just my walking clothes on, including my Nike running shoes. I knew I probably would never see my weight this low again, for I wasn't just skinny as hell, but I was also empty and dehydrated. Stepping on the scale, I worked the slide weight and Holy Moly, I checked in at 154 pounds. Down from 220 pounds. This was a loss of 66 pounds or so. Some of that I regret to say was muscle. I know from experience that muscle would pop back within a month. The muscle doesn't really leave; it's just that muscle fiber shrinks.

I thanked Janice for everything and left for my room. I want to say that Manning Park Lodge is very hiker friendly, at least from my two experiences and what I've heard from others. Especially when you figure that they have to put up with our haggard looks and smell. Right now I was going to do something about the smell as I headed right to my room and the shower.

The shower was great. That would be my last super shower for probably a long time. A super shower is a shower that you need to take after at least three or four days of trail dust and sweat. It's different than a shower at home after a day of work; that's nice, but a super shower is super nice.

It was now about 6:00 and before I have dinner I've got to do my laundry, but not all of it, just clean clothes for tomorrow. I can always wash my stuff in Vancouver before I grab a jet home. By washing these things now I can start the drying process while I'm having dinner.

About a half hour later, Just Paul comes in and mentions food and I'm ready for dinner now. I put on my new t-shirt that I had bought a few hours ago at the Manning Park Gift Shop. I bought it so I would have something clean for the evening. It was on sale and with the exchange rate discount it only cost me about 10 bucks. It was pretty cool too, with a bear lurking behind what looks like blueberry bushes! By 7:00, Just Paul and I were in there ordering our meal. I bought Just Paul's dinner to help pay for the room. During our conversation I ask Just Paul how he was going to get back to San Diego. He told me he had a ride with Tripping Ant and his dad, to Bellingham, Washington, where his wife was going to meet him. From there he and his wife were going to visit relatives, then drive home after a few days. I sort of rudely ask if I could possibly get a ride to Bellingham because I could grab a bus from there and go to Seattle where a flight home would be 175 dollars which is less than a flight from Vancouver.

As I ate my dinner, however, I was thinking strongly about taking a train out of Vancouver. It would be a three day trip home, but a beautiful one, and perhaps I could sort of unwind. The negative there is it would mean two nights on the train and unless I get a sleeping coach, which cost a small fortune, I would have to sleep in one of those reclining seats.

About the middle of dinner, Tripping Ant and his dad came in and sat in the booth next to us. Right after that, I popped the question and they said sure, that I would have to share the back seat with Apple Pie who had already asked them the same thing. They told me that they had a truck that would easily hold us and our stuff.

Well, this was good news. A free ride to Seattle and then perhaps a train ride home. I would still have to spend two nights on the train. In a way I'm going to miss going to Vancouver because it's an awesome city, with great sushi, too. But I need to save money. I was going further in debt every day.

After a great dinner, we headed over to the bar and pizza lounge because Free Radical and Lugnut told us there was going to be a blow-out party. Besides me, Tripping Ant, Just Paul, Apple Pie, Free Radical, and Lugnut, there was also Rob and Bandana with Prune Picker and a couple of girls I didn't know. I wasn't hungry, not just because I just finished dinner but due to the fact that I had taken my last damn Flagyl and I really didn't have much of an appetite since Stehekin. I also couldn't have a great Canadian beer either because of the medicine.

ECSTASY OF MISERY

We all sat down at the table and ordered the awesome pizza that they make there and just about everybody but me had a fine beer. There were quite a few people inside the place because it was Friday. While we were munching away and talking about our hikes and other things, one of the girls from Prune Picker's table came over to our table. She started talking to Apple Pie, but it wasn't too friendly. "I don't understand," she said. "Why didn't you pay for your lunch today and your drink last night?" she said in disgust. "Because I didn't have to. Prune Picker pays for me, bitch, whether you like it or not," said the half-smiling Apple Pie.

The girl headed back to her table really pissed off. She then started questioning Prune Picker about something, but no one could hear. I knew right away what was going on and it was substantiated when Apple Pie said to us, "That's one ugly skank. I can't believe that could be his girlfriend. She is so ugly." Just Paul looked at me and said, "Well here we go again." So I figured that this had taken place earlier today or last night.

Things were pretty cool for the next few minutes. The pizza came and so did the drinks. There was a football game on the wide screen TV and I was listening to Tripping Ant's father talking about his bout with cancer and how he was cured now, a great story. I believe that's why Tripping Ant had left the trail for a couple of weeks. Otherwise, at the pace he travels, he would have finished some time ago.

Then all of a sudden another girl marches over to our table. From what I understand, this is Prune Picker's sister. She came up to the table and told Apple Pie that it would be best if she left the bar. Apple Pie said, "Absolutely not, you don't own the place." "My brother has been going with Janet for two years, it's quite serious, and I don't know what his relationship is with you, but I think it would be better if you left right now." "Tell that ugly skank to shove off. I'm not going anywhere."

Prune Picker's sister then went back to her table and you could see that she was telling everybody the news, because they all looked over at our table in a most unwelcoming way. Apple Pie flipped them the bird. Tripping Ant's father spoke up and said, "Hey we're all here to have a nice time, so let's keep it cool." "Yeah," I said. "This isn't the way to end a great accomplishment like you did, Apple Pie. Let him go. You probably have a boyfriend back in San Francisco that's waiting for you."

To my amazement, everyone laughed. Apple Pie looked at me with a crazy look and with a couple of tears in her eyes. "Wrong Way, I'm married!" I couldn't believe it. I looked at Tripping Ant's father, who was about my age at least, and said, "Man, I'm perplexed. I guess I'm old school." Tripping Ant's dad put up his hands with his palms in the air. "I'm with you buddy."

I was having a pretty good time stuffing down pizza and drinking a coke. I was starting to get tired. This had been a hard day for me and most of the thru hikers had gotten here yesterday or earlier that day, giving them a chance to rest up, not to mention that they were half my age.

The next morning I awoke about 7:30 and left about 8am. Just Paul and I went and had breakfast together. We saw Apple Pie, Bandana and Rob there too. I wondered if Billy Goat and his son would come in. I hope they do because I'm one of the few people who can sort of understand how it must feel to complete the trail at 62.

We left at 9:15 with Tripping Ant's dad in his truck. I was actually leaving my beloved Pacific Crest Trail and heading back into the badlands. I guess about 50 miles later we reached the border check. Here we had to show our identifications. The guy was friendly, especially when Tripping Ant's dad told him that he was bringing back Pacific Crest Trail hikers that had started at the Mexican border. A few minutes later we crossed the border and headed south to Bellingham, Washington. While cruising south in the truck, Tripping Ant's dad gave me a Thomas Guide of Georgia, showing me the coastal town they lived near. It looked pretty far out. Water inlets from the Atlantic, plus creeks and rivers, were everywhere.

I also looked up the area where the Appalachian Trail goes through. Tripping Ant told me as he drove, a lot of things about the grandfather of thru-hiking trails. For me, however, I would rather walk the Continental Divide Trail if I ever have the time. But would I ever do the PCT again? Yes, I might. Who knows. I might have a shot at it when I'm in my 60s, though with each year of age, the trail will become more difficult.

At Bellingham, we let Just Paul off at a Best Western Inn. We all said good-bye. It was kind of sad, just like the foggy, gray day. Now it was just weird with just Tripping Ant, his dad, Ralph, Apple Pie and me, we headed south once again. In Everett, Washington, we stopped for gas. I offered Ralph some bucks for gas but he wouldn't take it. There were a few fast food restaurants there. I headed for Taco Bell and the others went to McDonalds and Burger King.

The day was drab and dull without any sun, which is probably normal weather for here. Just before we reached Seattle, Tripping Ant's dad offered us a ride to Portland if we wanted one. Wow, that was cool with me. The closer I get to LA, the cheaper the train fare. I don't know why they now offered me and Apple Pie the ride to Portland when before it was just Seattle. Maybe they liked our company. I think Ralph and I related because we're both about the same age.

Towards the end of the day we finally arrive at the Washington/Oregon border, and of course, just east of this, about 60 miles away, is one of my favorite little places, Cascade Locks. Portland is just 10 to 15 miles away. Tripping Ant knew of this cool youth hostel in downtown Portland. But first we stopped at Trader Joe's where I purchased cheese and some other organic things. Tripping Ant is a vegetarian, sort of a health nut I think, a bit to his dad's annoyance.

After visiting the store we decide to walk down to the hostel which is only a block or so away. Ralph stayed in the truck and tells Tripping Ant to go down with us to see if we get a room. I think that Ralph is concerned about leaving Apple Pie in the middle of this big city unless she has a room.

We got to the hostel and saw some young people coming and going. To our surprise, there were no rooms available. It's Saturday and the place is filled! So we head back to the truck. When I saw Ralph, I yelled, "Hey buddy, we couldn't leave you. We like you too much."

The next thing is to find a place to crash for all of us. Tripping Ant found a phone booth with a phone book and called all kinds of places. No luck, until he found a motel six miles out of town. They'll hold the room for an hour or so, giving us plenty of time to get there. About an hour later we arrive and get a room. It's upstairs and kind of small with a double bed. Ralph and Tripping Ant take the bed and I slept on the floor. But it's cool.

The next morning we all started to stir at around 8:00 and by 9am, we were off, heading for the Portland Airport. Apple Pie wasn't interested in taking the train to San Francisco, she just wanted to get home and so did I. Besides that, if I took the train out of Portland, I would still have to spend a night on it. Apple Pie would arrive in San Francisco, where she and her husband live, at 1am. This way Ralph and Tripping Ant would only have to drop us off at one place. There have to be many flights going to San Francisco to LA throughout the day.

Down the highway we went, heading for the airport. Tripping Ant wanted to hike at Government Camp where he was going to visit for a couple of days. Then he and Ralph would drive back to their home in Georgia. I mentioned to Tripping Ant that it was funny how things turned out. He was the first guy I saw thru-hiking on the trail back at Mt Laguna, and he's the last guy I will see on this trip.

A few minutes later we pulled up to the Portland Airport, which is small compared to LAX. It's even smaller than Ontario, California, airport. We all said our good-byes. Ralph gave me a strong handshake, which was nice.

Apple Pie and I walked into the section of the airport that listed Southwest. I went to a window and she went to another. I told the lady I wanted a flight to Ontario, California. She asked me if I had a reservation and I told her that I don't and I wanted to purchase a ticket. They had a flight leaving for Ontario via Sacramento leaving in 45 minutes. I believe you can make it if you hurry! Well, that's okay. I don't want to rush around. I'll take the next flight which leaves at 2:00 which was on standby.

That didn't sound too good. It was 9am now. I would have to wait four hours for a plane that I might not be able to get on. "There's a flight at 1pm and it's not usually crowded. You should arrive at Ontario around 5pm." I didn't like the way that sounded either so I decided to buy a ticket on the 10:15 flight.

I paid $200, which was about $160 cheaper than flying out of Vancouver. They put my backpack into a large plastic bag and labeled it and then told me to hustle down the way to gate 11, but I'd have to go through security first.

As I neared Sacramento, I thought about the other thru-hikers that would be going through re-entry into society. The change from the trail back to home, work, and things like that. How about the couples that had teamed up. I feel that I have an advantage here because it will be nothing really new for me. The main reason is the Peace Corps in which I was away in India for two and a half years. That re-entry was a bit tough. Physically, India was tougher, but mentally, the USA was more taxing.

The plane is already starting to cut its speed just as I finished my last peanut and sip of coke. We seemed to make a half circle and then we landed. All out for Sacramento, they said. The passengers get up and start to leave. As soon as they are gone I move over to the other side of the plane so I will be able to look out the window and possibly see the mighty Sierras off to the east.

Minutes later, the pilot starts taxiing. Another few minutes later, I was looking towards the Sierras. I knew Sacramento was west of the Donner Pass area. I was hoping to see Yosemite Valley and possibly Bridal Veil Falls, but no luck. It was just a little too hazy. In my 2000 trip back from Washington, I had a great view of the two falls.

Now and then I could see mountain peaks and I believe that I did see Mt Whitney, but I'm not sure. A few minutes later the Sierras were gone and the desert appeared. It looks like Antelope Valley. Looking around inside the plane, I notice that most people, or should I say nobody at all, seemed to give a damn.

Sooner and faster than the Portland to Sacramento section, the plane cut back on its engines. Looking down I could see the beginning of the San Gabriel mountain range, the mountains behind LA, the mountains that John Muir said was the most inaccessible range of mountains.

Now of course there are trails and roads, but in John Muir's day, they were probably real tough and almost impossible to hike. This was due to their steepness and the ground that can tear away from your feet and finally, thick vegetation, especially in winter. People always have to get rescued from them. It's best not to get too far off the trail when hiking this range, which I call the great wall of LA.

The plane now starts to circle around and I spot Cajon Pass, with Highway 15 running out to the desert, with tiny vehicles heading east to Las Vegas, the Colorado River, or maybe Arizona. The plane straightens out a bit and we start to land. Touchdown, baby. I'm home.

The place was sunny and bright. I could see sunshine out the window. Soon I was walking down the ramp and saying good-bye to the flight attendants. Now inside the restricted part of the terminal, I began heading to the baggage claim area which was downstairs.

Following the rest of the people, I headed down the escalator. About halfway down I could see people waiting for their family and friends. Then all of a sudden I saw my mother and then my father, and they pretty much saw me at the same time. I knew I stood out like a sore thumb with my long white beard and my floppy miners hat. I looked like an old skinny prospector for sure. The two of them however recognized me pretty quickly. I reached the bottom floor and gave my mom a good long hug and shook hands with my dad.

The freeways were wide open and before I knew it we were coasting to a stop in my driveway. I got out and grabbed my pack and went inside. There was Emma, our Golden Retriever. I sometimes call her Peaches. She looked a little grayer than when I had seen her last. After she smelled me a bit, she knew it was me and got very animated. From there I went into my room. I closed the door and turned around.

Suddenly, like a bolt of lightning, I was shocked out of my mind. Never before have I been so freaked out in all of my life. I felt like I was burning up. Sweat dripped from my forehead, as I wiped it I screamed out loud!

Then immediately I heard a loud knock on my door. "Are you all right?" my dad's voice blurted out. I was awake. It was me that was lying on that bed! If this was a dream, then it would be the most vivid dream I ever had. But I wouldn't call it a nightmare, for I had a good feeling about it. Sort of an ecstasy of misery type of ordeal that can't be real.

Brice Hammick, famous hiker

and trail builder at Elk Lake, Oregon

The Right Way to Hike the Pacific Crest Trail, by Wrong Way

The truth is, there really isn't any perfectly right way to hike the mighty PCT. It's basically an individual thing, so I will list the things that worked for me. I've hiked the trail in regular backpacking gear, in sections. Then I have hiked the trail in one season, the ultra light way. It's your choice. You can even hike it using both methods. Having been lucky enough to hike the trail both ways, I believe the ultra light method is best, for me anyway.

Equipment:

Tarp or Tent

For shelter, I prefer a tarp over a tent. The tarp is lighter. My tarp was 10 by 8 feet, weighed only 13 ounces. With rope and titanium stakes, it was probably less than one and a half pounds and is very roomy. The tarp has more ventilation and never gets wet inside. It's faster to put up and take down. It doesn't shield you completely from your environment and is less expensive than the tent. Set the tarp low in bad weather and high in good weather.

The negative thing about tarps is it doesn't prevent mosquitoes or other insects such as the pesky black forest ants from crawling in the sack with you. It also doesn't provide as much privacy as a tent. If one is going to go with a tarp, do this: wear running pants and a long sleeve shirt in your sleeping bag. Also wear a flip up mosquito head net, the type that is pushed away from your face as you sleep. Doing this helps avoid insects, mice, and other bugs from crawling on you, at least for the most part.

Another good point about the tarp is that you can cook inside of it if the weather is terrible. Note: as of now there's a tarp tent being sold at the PCT kick-off party which was invented by a trail angel. It's very light and not too expensive. Many give it a 5-star rating. You must carry walking poles, however, to use this item.

ECSTASY OF MISERY

Cooking Stove

The most popular was the alcohol-burning stove. For me it seemed cumbersome and slow. I used the propane/butane powered stove with a titanium pocket rocket burner. It was light and fast. I bought the stove new and I never had to clean it during the five months. For lighting the burner I used BIC cigarette lighters. I had a couple of them in plastic zip lock bags.

Flashlight

I used lead-burning lights that strap around the head, plus a small lead-burning flashlight. The head light, however, is a must. It really helps by freeing the hands to prepare a meal or do anything in the dark. Lead burners last 10 times as long as the old flashlights but don't put out quite as much light.

Knife

I had a Victory Max mini knife with only a blade, can opener, bottle opener, toothpick, and tweezers. It weighed only one and a half ounces. Make sure you keep a bright string or ribbon tied to it so you don't lose it.

Hiking Poles

Hiking poles are excellent, I liked mine a lot, but they hurt my shoulders and my right hand went numb. They seem to help going up and down hills. I recommend them even though I had to send mine back after the first 1000 miles. They're better than nothing in the snow but they don't replace crampons or an ice ax. Many hikers feel that they can help save the knees when going down steep parts of the trail. Hiking poles can also be used as poles for tents or tarps. I used mine a few times to pick up trash that I left on the ground, saving my back. I'd put the trash in my pocket and didn't have to take my backpack off again. I give them the thumbs up, but they're not necessary.

Plastic Bag

This is a fantastic thing to take on the trail. I used a compactor bag to line my pack. This keeps everything inside waterproof. I also carry a heavy-duty regular old plastic bag, either 30 or 33 gallon capacity. It has many uses, including, as I mentioned, for waterproofing. It can be used to put your trash in. It can be used as a poncho type rain coat by just punching a hole for your head and arms at the top of the bag. You can slide it over yourself and it will actually provide more warmth than a breathable raincoat, such as GoreTex. I've washed my clothes in them and it works pretty well. It weighs nothing, costs nothing, and is a wonderful thing to have. Put some in your supply packages now and then; you can't lose.

Ice Ax

It's a lifesaver for sure in snow passes, like the fantastic Sierras. I've never owned one before this trip; in the past I used a two-pronged gardening hoe. I'm the only person I know that's done this. It was a great tool that had many uses. Hiking poles however took the place of the hoe on this trip. There were a few times that my hoe assisted my slide down a snow bank, but it's not nearly as good as an ice ax. You can always send your ice ax home or ahead of yourself when not needed. Get yourself an ice ax. Be safe.

Ground Cover

A sportsman's blanket, I think, is the best. Get the one that has red plastic on one side and aluminum color on the other. It's tough but you might have to have a second one sent to you after you reach Oregon. They take a beating, so I cut mine in half, making it three feet wide instead of five feet wide. This cuts down on some weight and bulk.

Sleeping Pad

I used a closed solid type pad that covered my shoulders to my knees, around 40 inches long or so. It's super light and won't deflate if a sticker penetrates it. I also used a Thermarest, a short type one, but I saved 11 ounces using a solid pad.

Cooking Pot and Utensils

I used a quart container. Make sure it has a lid. I ate out of my pot, no need for a plate. I use a durable plastic spoon and a titanium cook pot.

ECSTASY OF MISERY

Clothing:

<u>Hat</u>

A very important item. I had an old miners type hat. I've used a baseball hat too. But probably the best is made from a material called Solumbra which is 100% UV proof, from a company called Sun Precautions. Their main company is located in the state of Washington. They make all kinds of clothes. The hat has a long bill and has material that covers the side of the face and neck. It's light, comfortable, and white to reflect the sun. It's also easy to wash.

<u>Poncho</u>

The poncho gets a big thumbs up from me. There are actually three basic types. The throw away or emergency poncho gets a special mention because it's terrific. I personally used this type of poncho all through California and Oregon. It's super cheap (only costs a few dollars), it's light (only weighs an ounce or so). It takes up very little space in the backpack, especially when it's in the package it comes in. Rain gear for two dollars and an ounce in weight with no bulk, you can't beat it.

I used two plastic clothespins to anchor the head part of the poncho by pinning it to the bill of my hat. This kept it from blowing off. Purchase three or four of those babies. Even if you use one, have another sent in your supply package. This will keep the poncho in its package neat and tight. Then you can throw the one you used in the trash or possibly a hikers pack.

The second type of poncho is the heavier duty rubber poncho one can buy for $15 - $25. They work a little better perhaps than the throwaway ponchos but are heavier and bulkier.

The third type is the ultimate poncho and I have only seen them in Washington. It's a heavy-duty poncho with extra material made specifically to go over the backpack. I tried to buy one in Snoqualmie but didn't go to the right town to do so. The ultimate poncho provides excellent protection for both you and your pack. This is beneficial because so many pack jackets don't really work very well at all. The negative points about this poncho is it's a little heavy, weighing in at 12 – 16 ounces. It's a bit bulky and probably a little expensive.

If I were going to hike the trail once again I might just go with the emergency poncho for California and Oregon and the ultimate poncho for Washington.

The Breathable Parka

The breathable parka, such as two or three layer GoreTek type of jacket, works great and keeps rain off your arms a little better. It's not too heavy or too bulky, but it's very expensive. They have cheaper breathables that might also work pretty well.

Make sure they have ventilation, with items such as armpit zippers. Be careful because some breathable parkas have very little insulation. Don't substitute them for something warmer thinking they will do the job. They won't.

Rain Pants

Rain pants are not a must because legs seem to stay pretty warm as long as you are moving. I got lucky, however, and bought some running pants that I didn't even know were waterproof. I trained in them. I noticed that they were much better than my other running pants. Only after testing them in the bathroom sink did I find out that they were indeed waterproof. I never used them until I got to Washington, where they were great.

I put my Solumbra khaki pants on first, then my black running rain pants, and that really kept me warm in near freezing rain. They were super light and only cost about $12 in the Reebok Outlet Store in Laughlin, Nevada.

I recommend something like this when you get to Washington later in the season, otherwise my regular running pants worked okay. I don't believe you really need an expensive type breathable pants for the legs.

How About the Feet

The best thing for the feet are running shoes with nylon socks. It sounds crazy but here's why. You're feet and ankles all the way up to your calf muscles are going to get wet. You can't pull a pair of heavy ridiculous rubber boots out of your pack. Leather boots with thick socks get heavier than hell and take forever to dry. Running shoes are just the opposite. The trick is to just keep walking vigorously and your feet will be all right.

ECSTASY OF MISERY

General Clothing

Don't wear cotton. I love cotton, but it gets wet from sweat or anything else and it takes forever to dry. Sun Precautions has a long sleeve shirt that works great. Patagonia has long sleeve shirts that dry in 15 minutes. I always wear long sleeve shirts for they protect me from the sun and insect bites.

In insect country I spray or rub Deet on the long sleeves. Therefore I don't have to apply it directly to my skin. I use the 90-100% pure Deet. It's really the only way to go. The weaker stuff just wears off too quickly.

Underwear – nylon bikini underwear works best for me. They're light-weight and dry fast.

Belt – I don't wear a belt because running pants have a drawstring that works well and is so much lighter.

Pants – I usually have one running type of long pants. I love stovepipes. Make sure they are long enough to go around the top of your shoes. If the pants are too short, rocks and other debris will get into your shoes when you are hiking. Gaiters are used by a lot of hikers, but they're not really necessary if your pants are long enough.

Socks – A hiker should carry at least three or four pairs of nylon socks. They're light and not very bulky. Having three or four pairs ensures the thru-hiker that he has clean socks on almost every day, especially when you first start out on the hike. I didn't do this and I paid the price on the roads leading in and out of Big Bear, California. Nylon socks are easy to wash and dry quickly pretty much overnight. I also carry a pair of thick wool socks to use on cold nights in my sleeping bag. They can also double as mittens. They're light and only slightly bulky.

Jacket – I wear a 90% wool Pendleton. I also have a very pliable wind-breaker. Down jackets are good, but are a drag if they get wet. Fleece is a good way to go too. The trick is to take enough to keep warm but don't overdo it. When you are hiking you are putting out tons of heat. Then at night you're in your sleeping bag. Remember, you can always go with the layer system, put-ting on several warm items, even if they are dirty. If you are getting rocked by the wind and if you don't have a windbreaker, pull out that plastic bag I told you about. It works great as a windbreaker.

THE RIGHT WAY TO HIKE THE PCT BY WRONG WAY

Sandals – like I stated earlier, I only take running shoes. It's the lightest way to go and less bulky. Sandals are cool for crossing streams. You can take off your socks and walk across, then put them back on after crossing. This way of course, you have dry socks and shoes. With sandals, sticks get jammed between the toes. I saw this happen. Your feet are really dirty and the skin has a tendency to crack with wearing sandals too much. Sandals are nice in town when you're taking a rest or layover day. It's up to you. A lot of people like them, but they're not necessary.

Shorts – they suck in my opinion. I don't understand why people wear them. First, your legs get dirtier than hell, mosquitoes, bugs, and ants munch on them. The sun pounds on them. They do nothing to protect you when you are hiking through bushes or Manzanita. Nor are they any protection from poison oak or snake bites. If you do wear shorts, especially in Southern California, you should wear gaiters too so you won't be constantly stopping and digging small stones out of your running shoes or your boots. Shorts are a bit lighter perhaps and a little easier to wash, and less bulky too. But the freedom of knee movement is, I think, a bit exaggerated. Go ahead and wear those half pants, but when you take your first fall or run into a jumping cholo plant, remember what Wrong Way said.

It is important to keep as clean as possible while on the trail and that goes for your clothes too. It's difficult to do sometimes, but remember these are small towns and you are representing the mighty PCT. There will be people following your footsteps. We want people to like us as much as possible. Refrain from lewd acts or boisterous noise. Have respect for everyone.

Other Stuff:

Umbrella

I give the umbrella a mild thumbs up. One big problem with the umbrella is wind. It works pretty well unless there's a wind. Then it becomes cumbersome. If you run into a driving rainstorm with lots of wind, the umbrella can be ripped to pieces. Another problem with the umbrella is the fact that hiking poles and the umbrella don't mix unless you have three arms. The hiker can always put the poles in his pack but they become useless weight. The umbrella really only helps keep rain off the top part of your body. Usually you get wet from the middle of your thighs down. A bigger umbrella will keep you dryer but it will catch more wind, weighs more, and has more of a chance to catch the sides of branches and overhangs on the trail. The umbrella can be bulky to carry.

I also find the umbrella a tedious thing to carry in a rainstorm. One hand has to hold the umbrella at all times. It can be switched to the other hand but it's still a hassle. Umbrellas that are tied to the pack or anything else don't ever work for any length of time. At least I've never seen it.

A couple of positive things about the umbrella: one, it can keep out not only the rain but also the sun off your head and shoulders; two, if you have a tarp, you can put it at one end of the tarp to block out light or just provide some privacy.

Compass

A compass is a must. It helps to be able to read the trail guide. Make sure you read the page that tells you how to use the guide, its symbols and other things. An altimeter, I guess, is fun, but not necessary. A GPS is nice but not necessary. The trail is marked pretty well. If you have a problem, always go back to where you were, and make sure you are on the PCT. Don't forge ahead blindly, like I have done, or you might end up with a trail name like mine, Wrong Way.

First Aid Kit

My first aid kit consisted of painkillers. Aspirin, Motrin, and Tylenol are probably my main staple. Motrin I used quite a bit in the early days of the hike, basically for blisters. It really takes the edge off of a headache. I used it only once in a while but since it's made different than Aspirin and Tylenol, I chose to carry it to cover all the angles, you might say. I used Motrin also early in my walk. I had prescription strength Motrin 600 mg. After I got myself in shape and my feet in shape, I cut way back on using it.

Triple Antibiotic

It is very important to fight off skin infections. One day I was using my hiking stick and was flipping it around as I was walking the trail and it sliced my hand open between my thumb and forefinger. That night I applied the triple antibiotic on it and the next morning it was healing very well.

Ace Bandage

For sprained ankles, severe cuts, or even a tourniquet if need be.

Chap stick

It's a must. I neglected to use it in the Sierras and my lips split right down the middle. Then I accidentally hit it with my thumb and it bled like hell. So use the Chap Stick regularly.

Carry an antifungal ointment for athlete's foot. Try to get a prescription of Flagyl for Giardia. Sunscreen, bandages, biodegradable soap, washcloth, paper towels, duct tape, toilet paper, and handy wipes. Handy wipes can come in handy not only for cleaning your hands, but they can be substituted for toilet paper and used with water if you don't have any. Handy wipes or baby wipes can save the day!

Toothbrush, Toothpaste, and Comb

Eye Glasses

I'm a failure when it comes to eyeglasses. I have ruined three pairs in my last two trips. Be sure to have them in fully crush-proof cases. I carried mine at the first of the trip in crush proof cases that were open at the top. The damn winds from Mt Laguna to Chariot Canyon blew burnt sand and stuff into my cases and ruined my sunglasses and regular eyeglasses. They would have been better off in a sock.

This was one of the biggest bummers of the trip. A $300 loss! Both pairs were scratched to hell. I got my regular glasses replaced with the help of Trail Perfect who had my prescription. My shades, however, I never replaced. The only time I used them was for short periods of snowy white passes.

In 1998, I wrecked two pairs by letting them drift to the bottom of my pack where they got scratched right on the apex of the lens. It's such a drag to have to hike in scratched lenses, going through beautiful country that I may never see again. When sleeping, keep your glasses in cases away from you, maybe in your running shoes, so you won't roll over on them and crush or scratch them.

ECSTASY OF MISERY

For arranging for your thru-hiking eyewear, you should start with getting a warranty for scratch coat lenses for two years. Get this in writing for your records in case you damage the eyewear on the trip and require replacement lenses.

Prescription lenses can be ordered inexpensively in polycarbonate material that is virtually impact proof. These lenses will take a bullet at point blank range and not break.

Memory titanium frames and some scratch coated lenses come with lifetime guarantees. Again, get these warranties in writing before you begin your trip, not after they are damaged.

Excellent over-glass protection is inexpensive with "Cocoons" over RX sunglasses. They are excellent sunglasses that are made to be worn instead of or over prescription eyeglasses. They provide sun and scratch protection.

Mirror

I never thought a mirror was important. But when I hiked into the Berkeley Youth Camp bathroom I changed my mind. I bought a steel one at a drug store. It works great and is unbreakable too.

Cell Phone

In 1998, I was asked by my family and Trail Perfect to carry a cellular phone. I didn't like the idea very much. Hiking was a chance to get away from it all. I went ahead and took one and it really came in handy, also for a few other hikers who needed to call home. I called home once to ask for more warm clothes and bags sent to me. I even reserved a room in advance and it was nice calling my family from a beautiful pass.

In 2003 I took the cell phone one more time and it worked out okay. But there were times it didn't work. The reception doesn't seem to have gotten better. Certain places from Forester Pass to Lake Edison it didn't work. So be prepared.

Sleeping Bag

I made a mistake taking a sleeping bag that was rated at 35 degrees. I recommend a bag that rates down to 20 degrees. This temperature is about right, not too thick, which causes excess bulk and weight. But it is just right for the PCT in the time of year you will be hiking it.

I also recommend a bag that is pretty much new. Not only was my bag too light, but I used it to hike Ebbetts Pass to Tuolumne Meadows in 1997, Oregon in 1998, and Washington state in 2000.

I didn't suffer too much because I walked these areas at the warmest time of the year. Unfortunately, this isn't possible for thru-hikers who walk the trail in one season.

Water Bottle

My water bottle was a wide mouth plastic bottle with a threaded lid. It was great. It held one quart and I have had the thing for 30 years. Then I lost it on a body slide in the snow of Mather Pass.

After that I used a Gatorade bottle and it worked great. My best water carriers were the plastic containers which are very light and pliable. I usually had two half-gallon containers. They don't cost a whole lot of 'dinero' and they work great.

My Most Important Foods

Number one by far, and this stands alone in importance, is instant mashed potatoes. First, they're light, second they're cheap, and third, they're loaded with carbs! You can cook them in a flash. You can add gravy mix to them. If you cook a dehydrated meal and add a little too much water, just add instant mashed potatoes to thicken it up. In fact, there were many times that I purposely put in too much water so I could add the instant mashed potatoes. They're super light, just keep them like the rest of your stuff in a zip lock baggy and you're in.

The Dehydrated Dinner – These dinners are so easy to cook because all you have to do is heat up water, bring it to a boil and it's done, The rest of the cooking is just letting it sit for 10 to 15 minutes. They are of course very light, but they are also quite expensive if you buy the backpacking store brands.

Trail Perfect found some dinners from Lipton, similar to the dehydrated dinners, that were pretty decent at almost half the price. When eating these dinners I would always eat at least two servings. One serving is not enough for any thru-hiker doing 20 or more miles per day. I'm sure there are other companies like Lipton that put out these type of dinners.

Milkman powdered milk – in my opinion is the best powdered milk sold.

Carnation Instant Breakfast mixed with a rich solution of milk and munched with a couple of fruit bars make a fast decent breakfast.

Trail mix is a must. Eat those peanuts, and raisins are especially great.

Cheese – it keeps pretty well and has calcium, vitamin D, and plenty of protein. It also comes in many varieties from mild cheddar to pepper jack.

Tortillas add a little weight to your pack but they are great on the trail. They can take the place of bread. Be sure to buy flour tortillas because they stay fresher than corn tortillas which can dry up quickly and fall apart.

Tuna in aluminum packets works well. The tuna for lunch by Star-Kist has little packets of relish and mayonnaise with crackers if you want to make a little tuna salad. Wash the package with water and spray mosquito repellent to keep the smell down for Mr Black Bear.

Pastries, like honey buns, are great in the morning or any time.

Power bars, fruit bars, candy bars, almost any kind of bar, the more fattening the better.

Candy – Snickers are supposed to have the most calories per ounce. The average thru-hikers needs at least 6000 calories a day.

I like Snickers but I also like some other candy bars, so I ate a variety of them. Probably the most practical candy on the trail is M&Ms. These little dudes are colorful and they don't melt like Snickers. You can use them in trail mix. I like both plain and peanut. Plain is probably better in the trail mix, but peanut M&Ms are better right out of the package. Big Hunk, Abazaba, and Charleston Chews are a good deal because they hang in the mouth longer and are lighter in weight.

Cereal is easy to make. There are all kinds of good ones, including granola, but I always like Grape Nuts. Huff and Puff was a cereal eater and he did well on the trail too.

Minute Rice works okay, although I threw a lot of it out. It was kind of heavy and you'll find rice in so many dehydrated dinners. As long as I had plenty of instant potatoes, I was set.

Top Ramen is a meal that is hard to beat. They're light, easy to find, incredibly cheap, and come in many varieties. Because they weigh so little I usually ate them towards the end of each section and before I reached my supply box or a restaurant.

Beef Jerky – This item is great, but you can get burned out on it. I definitely give it a thumbs up. It works the jaw muscles and gums and has protein to the max.

Jell-O is a pretty nice thing to take along. It's good for the blood and can be eaten right out of the box. A hiker can heat it up and drink it like coffee. Watch out though. I remember one time on my 1978 hike of California that in the last few days of my hike I made that drink just after climbing out of Chariot Canyon and was about to hike along the desert rim. I must have mixed it too strong because I had a sugar rush like you couldn't believe. That stuff hit my empty stomach and I was walking on air. It was intense. I give Jell-O a mild thumbs up.

Instant Pudding – is pretty nice. It's kind of heavy but it can make a nice dessert from time to time. In 2003 at Bear Creek near the Middle Fork of the Feather River, I made lemon pudding. I let it chill in Cold Bear Creek while I ate the main part of my lunch. Oh man, it was good and rich, quite filling, with a lot of much needed calories. That seemed to put me in a lemon trip after that for a while. I bought lemon Kool-Aid, lemon drops, and lemon flavored Country Time, until I finally burned out and my personality became quite sour.

Tobacco – Quite a few times I have carried a cigar or two. They're light but they can get crushed easily. I also brought a corn cob pipe on my hikes of California. They worked out pretty nice. I enjoyed it from time to time. It also helps to keep away gnats and mosquitoes to a small extent.

Weed – Being a lad of the sixties and spending two and a half years in India with the Peace Corps, well, weed has seemed to have always followed me around and been something I have enjoyed. On the trail, however, it doesn't make it. It makes you too lazy. Ten miles seems like 20 miles. The biggest reason is that it makes one too stupid to follow the trail. I get lost enough; weed would just make it worse.

ECSTASY OF MISERY

I guess if one smokes it only at night after a hard day it would be okay, but that takes discipline. It's too easy to get involved with it during the day. It's also against the law. I have to give it a thumbs down for sure. It just doesn't fit into thru-hiking when a vast amount of miles has to be achieved every day.

The last reason is paranoia. I sure can't see getting stoned all alone in some scary place listening to the forest sounds of the night. It's hard enough being completely straight. For me, it doesn't make it, because 90% of the time I crash alone, which is the way I like it.

Seasonings – I usually just take salt, pepper, maybe sugar, and cayenne pepper, and that's about it. I'm not a cook. So I just keep it simple. I try to keep my food as light as possible.

When I reach stores, restaurants and cafes, I pig out to the max, stuffing rich food down my mouth like a pig. I used to get to these places and rush over to the ice cream sections and eat a half gallon in 15 minutes. But that was when I was young. Now I pig out with good food first, including some vegetables and fruits. Make sure you get stuff with a lot of carbohydrates and don't forget your protein. Then I eat the junk food, chasing it down with beer and cheese dip.

Vitamins – Take your vitamins. They're low in weight, not too expensive, and they may do you some good.

That's pretty much it on the food suggestions.

Tips by Wrong Way

Permits:

If you are hiking more than 500 miles, the PCT will give you a permit for that distance. If you are hiking the whole trail, they'll give you a permit for the whole trail! Join the PCTA. Here's their telephone number and address:

Pacific Crest Trail Association
1331 Garden Highway
Sacramento, CA 95843
Www.pcta.org
Telephone number: 916-349-2109

Choose your year:

This is pretty much impossible for most people to do. The reasons are evident. Most hikers have a one time opportunity to take five months or less off. The great abundance of hikers are between college and a steady job. Finally, there are a few older dogs like myself, some are retired. These old dogs walk it at their own pace and try to have more layover days. This group should have more money in their pockets because they are older and more established.

I suggest leaving early. By picking the right year with an average to less than average snow pack, it will give you an easier hike and more time for layover days. Layover days are more important for an older hiker because an older hiker, especially after 50, needs more recovery time than a 25 year old.

The year 2003 was a difficult year, not the worst of years, but not even close to the best of years. This was due to late snowfall in the Sierras, as well as the mountains of Southern California. Late April and May produced lousy weather for the first 250 miles. The first 16 days of Washington, it rained. But it did clear up after that into an Indian Summer.

It's hard to predict a good or bad year. The hiker must pay attention to the trail conditions and that's another reason that joining the Pacific Crest Trail Association is important. They have a telephone number you can call that will give you a weekly report. Getting totally motivated and then calling it off at the last minute to wait for the following year is a tough, almost impossible, thing to do, but it might pay off in a more enjoyable trip.

Training:

Train for at least four months before you leave. If you're older or really out of shape, you should extend this period to a year. Start slow walking without a pack, then with a pack, gradually increasing weight and distance. Do as many hills as possible. If you don't have hills near you, climb steps or bleachers.

The last month before you leave, lightweight training for upper as well as lower body will help, but most of all, just walk your butt off. If you're a runner, just keep running. It's great and has a lot of carry-over value to thru-hiking. But five weeks before you leave, start hiking and slow up on the running.

ECSTASY OF MISERY

Specific Adaptation to the Opposed Demand, SAOD. SAOD is always the best way to go. Do what you're going to be doing and train that way. Lose body fat, getting down to 5 – 10% percent of your body weight.

Water:

I know that I have already mentioned water. Purification in the form of filters or tablets. I would like to mention the use of water on the trail. Water is extremely heavy and sometimes a thru-hiker has to carry many pounds of it. Remember this tip. When it's dragging you down and the straps of your pack are digging into your shoulders, one way to help the situation is to simply drink it.

Rationing water like they do in Hollywood movies is unrealistic. Get that water in you as soon as possible. Rationing water in the heat of the desert while hiking mountains can dehydrate you sooner than if you simply swigged it down.

Make sure you drink all you can before leaving the water source. However, after that, drink profusely when you're just a little bit thirsty. That will get the liquid inside of you where it belongs, as well as take that heavy load off your back and shoulders.

Desert Hiking:

Many people use the siesta system. Get up early utilizing the morning coolness. Find a shady and comfortable place in the heat of the day. Crash for three hours and start hiking again when it cools off a bit. Hike until dark or later to make up for your siesta. This helps to keep the body from busting butt in extremely hot temperatures.

Trail Guide Maps:

Topo strip maps from the trail guide save you tons of money, weight, and bulk, compared to carrying regular topo maps. Tear the book apart, taking just enough maps to get you from supply box A to supply box B. This eliminates even more weight and bulk.

Read these maps before you go to sleep at night with your strap on headlight. Check out the trail where you will be hiking. Notice where water availability is. Check the terrain and elevation and possible campsites. Do your homework and it can pay off the next day when you read it a second time.

I take a map of California, when I get to Oregon, I take a map of Oregon to Washington. This lets you know the big perspective in case you have to bail out for an emergency or something. Cut off all the maps that are not important, again reducing bulk and weight.

Blisters:

Take care of hot spots immediately. Cool the feet with cool water, if possible. Press your feet against a cool rock perhaps. Apply second skin, moleskin, or tough skin. If you have to lance a blister, be sure to apply triple antibiotic. I didn't do this one time and sure enough, I got an infection. Bad blisters and blister infections should be soaked in hot water and Epsom salt, if possible.

Radio Headsets:

I don't like them, especially walking in rattlesnake areas. One may not hear the warning of a rattle and could pay the price for it.

Space Blanket:

One of the smartest things you can do is carry a space blanket which is made of mylar. If everything is wet, a space blanket wrapped around your body or even in your sleeping bag can save your life. It saved my brother's life back in the late 1960s. He was caught in a cold unrelenting rainstorm in the Sierras. The space blanket costs very little, it isn't too bulky, and it's very light in weight.

Forging Rivers:

There have been a number of hikers who have died trying to cross dangerous rivers in the Sierras, as well as in Washington and Oregon. The dangers are a little less now due to bridges. There are a few things, however, that should be mentioned.

It's a good idea to unbuckle your hip belt before trudging across a torrent of water. If you do slip and are swept down current, you will have a better chance of getting your pack off. Better to lose your pack than your life.

Before crossing a major creek or a river, waterproof your goods that can't afford to get wet. That's when that plastic trash bag becomes invaluable.

ECSTASY OF MISERY

A pack jacket just won't work but critical items in a plastic bag tied at the end can save you getting a wet sleeping bag, clothes, or a messed up camera.

Find a friend or another hiker, if possible. You just might help each other out. Try to cross major water barriers in the early morning hours. Creeks and rivers usually run much slower in the early morning hours than late in the day when the snow melt is at its worst.

Finally, if it looks too dangerous, don't do it. Hike up and down the water barrier and you will usually find a solution. Train hard, learn to read your topo strip maps, and prepare for a difficult hike. The PCT is not a cakewalk. Always think water, especially in Southern California. Carry lightweight food, a light backpack, a light shelter, and light footwear.

Walk steady. A steady pace will do it. If you push it too hard trying to catch a faster hiker or trying to keep up with your friends, you may get burned out or injured. Above all, have a great time. You will remember your trip as long as you live!!

Trek On,

Wrong Way

A Short History of the Pacific Crest Trail

Many people think that the Pacific Crest Trail probably had its beginning in California, probably Southern California where the most people live. It's also considered now to be the beginning of the trail from Campo, on the Mexican border, to Canada. This is not the case.

In 1926, it is said that an educator at Western Washington College of Education in Bellingham came up with an idea to have a continual high trail with mile markers and shelter huts all along the trail from Canada to Mexico. In 1920 the Forest Service had already routed and posted a trail from Crater Lake, Oregon, to Mt Hood, Oregon. This was probably the first link on the PCT. This new trail would be called the Oregon Skyline Trail.

Then in 1928, Fred W. Cleaton became Supervisor of Recreation for the Forest Service and he developed the Cascade Crest Trail, a route right down the center of Washington. Later the Oregon Skyline Trail was extended at both the northern and southern ends. Now a trail existed from Canada to California and in 1937 a design was made for the PCT. Trail markers were created and posted from the Canadian border to the California border.

The Forest Service for California did nothing at that time, but left it to a private person to provide a real link to the PCT. Clinton C. Clark took up the chore from Pasadena, California. At the time, he was chairman of the Mountain League of Los Angeles County.

In 1932, Clark had written a paper on the Pacific Crest Trail. This idea proposed a project to construct a continuous wilderness trail across the country from Mexico to Canada. Soon Clark formed the Pacific Crest Trail System Conference, which had representatives from Oregon and Washington. Clark served as its president for 25 years.

In 1935 the group published a guide book for the PCT that described a very sketchy route of the trail. Clark enlisted Boy Scouts to explore the proposed route. It started at the Mexico border in 1935 and ended at the Canada border in 1938.

The exploration was conducted by Warren L. Rogers, who was Secretary of the YMCA. Rogers served as the Executive Secretary of the Pacific Crest Trail Conference from 1932 to 1957. Rogers continued his interest in exploring and trail building on the PCT until his death in 1958.

During the years of World War II, the Pacific Crest Trail was put on the back burner. In the 1960s, however, backpacking became more popular. In 1968 Congress passed the National Trails System Act, establishing a nationwide system of trails. The existing Appalachian Trail and the PCT were designated as the first two National Scenic Trails.

In 1972, the Pacific Crest Trail Advisory Council finally agreed on a route. The Forest Service would often have a map of the proposed route with a Trail Line, but in most places there wasn't even a trail at all.

Publicity about the trail took place about the time a solo hiker hiked north to south, the full length of the PCT. That started a real interest for others hikers who would soon hike the trail.

The hikers of the 1970s were the real pioneers for the trial. They would often have to retrace their steps and walk highways in order to get to trail junctions where proposed trails didn't exist or were wiped out because of weather or poor maintenance.

During the 1980s, the trail gradually improved after the Pacific Crest Trail Association was born, and the trail really began to come into its own. Finally in 1994 the PCT was finished, at least on paper, with only a small portion still on private lands.

"When setting out on a journey, never consult

someone who has never left home."

Rumi (Persian poet), 1207-1273 AD

A book or two to read

Pacific Crest Trail By Schifrin Schaffer, Winnett and Jenkins.

The books are four in number

1) Southern California 2) Northern California

3) Oregon 4) Washington.

It's the bible of the PCT with all the Topo Strip Maps Included.

Yoges PCT Handbook

(Planning Guide) or anything else written by Jackie Mc Donnell, very

Informative!

Journey on the Crest Written by Cindy Ross

Lite Weight Backpacking Written by Ray Jardine

Pacific Crest Trail Association

1331 Garden Highway., Sacramento, CA 95833

Phone: 916-285-1846

Fax: 916-285-1865

www.pcta.org

ECSTASY OF MISERY

Now I would like to thank a few people who have helped a lot.

Chuck Hinkle for his financial support. Without Chuck, I don't think I could have made it.

Eric Carpenter from the Orange County Register, who followed my story throughout the 2658 mile trip.

Bruce McIver who pulled my book out of the trash can.

Terry Blair, computer whiz extraordinaire, who combined all the types of fonts into one.

Jacky Thomas, hiker extraordinaire and naturalist.

Kara Frazier, Typist

Geri Zullo, who was the major typist, organizer and computer expert.

Valerie Stella, Who typed the final draft.

Mark Sanders at University Printing, who helped with design and layout And would never take my money!
Finally, *my Mom and Dad*, for putting up with my hassles and supported me along the way.

Thanks to all,

Wrong Way